KIWAMERO!

極めろ!
英検®準1級合格力
リーディング

松本恵美子

━━ スリーエーネットワーク ━━

Published by 3A Corporation.
Trusty Kojimachi Bldg., 2F, 4, Kojimachi 3-Chome, Chiyoda-ku, Tokyo 102-0083, Japan

ISBN978-4-88319-934-1 C0082

First published 2024
Printed in Japan

はじめに

　長文読解って難しいですよね。ショートメッセージでコミュニケーションが取れるこの世の中、どうして長文なんて読まないといけないのでしょう。

　私がいつも思っているのは「そもそも人の言いたいことを理解するのは難しい」。なぜなら、人によって言葉の分類方法や表現方法、受け取る感覚が少し違うからです。

　私は普段は、相手の言おうとすることを全体の雰囲気で捉えるようにしています。しかし、単語レベルにこだわって、白黒つけないと気が済まない時もあります。

　例えば、自分が体調を崩して仕事を1か月休んでいるとします。お医者さんからの「職場に復帰する意欲がありますか」という質問に対して、普段の私なら、なんとなく、(電車に乗って、大学のある駅で降りて…、コーヒーを買って…。あの環境に戻りたいな) というイメージを浮かべて「はい、意欲、あります」と言うでしょう。しかし、場合によっては「意欲って一体、どういう意味なんですか?」とか「意欲があるかどうかなんて、そんな質問をする先生は、私に意欲がないと思っているのですか? 失礼じゃないですか」と、「意欲」という単語にこだわって言い返したくなることもあるかも知れません。

　自分に余裕がない時、相手の言っている全体像がわからない時、相手にはできるだけ言葉を尽くして欲しいと思ってしまいます。

　上の場面で、お医者さんがもっと言葉を尽くしてくれたら、「意欲」という言葉を悪く取らなかったかもしれません。お医者さんから「私はあなたの体調が回復するのをここまで見てきました。初めはつらかったけれど、自分の症状に向き合って、よくここまで治療してきましたね。お薬もよく続けてきましたね。あなたがこのまま頑張っていかれるのを信じています。お仕事に復帰される意欲はありますか」と言葉を尽くして尋ねられたら、先生が向き合ってくれた姿勢に対して真っすぐに「はい」と答えられるでしょう。つまり、文章が長くなればなるほど、単語や短文レベルでの誤解を与えずに、その人が考えている世界を受け手に伝えやすくなるのだと思います。

　リーディングにおいては、普通、書き手と読み手の距離は離れています。もしかすると、時間的にも遠い、100年前の作品を読むこともあるかもしれません。そうすると、一言では言いたいことは伝わりにくいでしょう。だからこそ、ショートメッセージでは伝わらないような内容については、たくさんの文章を読まないといけません。長い文を読むことで、書き手の持つ世界観、育った環境、身に付けてきた学問などが時代背景と合わさり、具体的なイメージとして思い浮かぶようになるのだと思います。

　準1級に出題される長文を読むことは、この文章を読む基本を身に付ける練習の場となるのです。長い文章が読めるようになると読むことが楽しくなります。あなたも、長い文章をどんどん読んで、リーディングを極めてみましょう。本書がリーディングを極めたい人の学習の入り口になり、皆様が目標に到達できることを祈っています。

2023年　12月　松本恵美子

目次

アイコン一覧

🚩	正解		✏️	和訳
🔍	解説		✒️	語注
🖥	構造解析			
S	主語		( )	節や句や例示などのまとまり
V	動詞		▭	節や句や例示などの始まり
O	目的語		▭	分詞構文や分詞の修飾句の始まり
C	補語		▨	論理の方向性を理解するのに関わる語句、対比や言い換えなどの対応関係を意識して処理したい語句
S'	節や句の中の品詞はダッシュ付き			
S①	同類の品詞が複数ある場合		▭と▨	▭ と ▨ を合わせたもの
▲—▭ }	注や修飾関係		/	要素が長い場合の意味の区切り

※構造解析はすべての要素を書き込むことはせず、各文で重要と思われるものを表示しています。

チャレンジしよう！

問題文を1文ずつ解説し、場面展開や読み取れる意図などを詳細に確認しながら、正誤判断のポイントを押さえます。

練習しよう！

「チャレンジしよう！」で学んだ解き方の定着と実力の底上げを目指して、大量の問題を解きます。

各パートの訳の確認ページに、その問題文の中で比較的複雑な文を取り上げて、構造を解析する図を掲載しています。

アプリを活用する

■ AI 英語教材 abceed

株式会社 Globee が提供するマークシート連動型アプリ
https://www.abceed.com/

アプリ内で「極めろ」で検索してください。
アプリ内のマークシートの選択肢ＡＢＣＤは書籍本文の選択肢１２３４に対応しています。

（アプリのダウンロード、その他のアプリに関する不具合やご質問に関しましては、上記の配信元にお問い合わせください。弊社ではお答えいたしかねますので、ご了承ください。）

英語の読み手になるために

文章をどう読むのか

　本書はリーディングの本です。書き手の表現したいことを理解するのが目的です。では、書き手は自分の表現したいことを100%表現できているのでしょうか。私は、書き手でさえも、表現しきれているかどうかはわからないだろうと思います。その理由の一つには、「言葉」を使っているからというのがあります。自分の中にあるイメージを「言葉」という道具を使って表現しなければいけないので、当然そこには制約があります。「良い表現を思いついた」と思っても、自分のイメージ以上の誇張した意味合いまで含まれてしまったり、読み手が違ったニュアンスで捉えたりすることもあります。そもそも書き手が自分の表現したいことを意識していないことすらあります。ただ思いつくままに書き続けていたら、結論にたどりついた、ということもあり得ます。だから、書き手の言いたいことを完全に受け取ることは難しいのだと思います。

　書き手が英語のネイティブで、読み手が英語の学習者である場合、その隔たりは、なおのこと大きくなるでしょう。

　だからこそ、英語を読むことって面白いのです。

多読のススメ──まずは読み通そう

　私は洋書を読むのが好きで、さまざまなジャンルの本を読みます。自分の好きなジャンルは速く読み進めることができますが、なじみのないジャンルは、頑張っても入り込めず、難解で、歯が立たないと思うことがあります。ある夏休みのことですが、天文学を扱った本を薦められ、丸々1か月かけてやっとその本を読みました。どうやったかというと、①「単語は絶対に調べない」、②「毎日1時間は読む」と決めて、大学の教室やオフィスで一人になって音読するようにしたのです。難しい文章にぶつかると、立って、歩きながらぶつぶつと音読しました。意味がわからなくても2ページほど無理やり音読していると、また黙読で読み進められるようになりました。読めない箇所が出るたびに、立って音読を繰り返します。意味がわからなくても「音読したから、よし。読んだことにしよう」と読み進めました。その過程はつらかったけれども、1週間も読み続けると、少し作者の世界観がわかる気がしてきたのです。それは「わからなくてもその本を自分の中で消化させる」という、読み方の一つのスタイルができた体験でした。

　そして、その洋書を読み終えたとき、日本語訳版のページを開いてみました。皆さんにも経験があるかもしれませんが、英語で読んでわからなかったところは、結局、日本語で読んでもわからなかったのです。そこで思ったのは「どちらの言語でも一生懸命に読み込めば、わかるところは同じ。それならば、やはり、その時に読みたいと思った言語である英語で読んでみて良かった」ということです。どこか遠いところに住む、生きてきた時代も違う作者のもつ世界観にその人自身が紡いだそのままの言葉で直接に触れられたこと、それが一番の成果でした。

何のために読むのか

　「今、目の前にある膨大な英文に読む価値があるのか」とよく悩むことがあります。これも当たり前のことですが、読む価値があるかどうか、自分に必要かどうか、それは読んでみないとわからないのです。それでも、今まで読んできた、どの英文、どの本も読んで後悔したことは1度もありません。何気ない文章を読み重ねるからこそ、変則的な文体を捉えることができます。同じジャンルでも文の展開も違えば、テーマの根幹を担う単語や表現も違うことから、著者の考えの方向性に気がつくことになるのでしょう。

「英検」の長文には——設問がある 正解がある

　「本当は、書き手の言いたいことを100％理解することなんてできない」という前提に立つと、「英検」の問題には正解が必ずあるということがありがたく、問題を解くことが決して大変なことではないと思えてきませんか。

　「英検」や資格試験の文は設問を作るために、ある程度、要旨や問題点や設問にする箇所を明らかにして作成しています。そして設問は「その文章から読み取れること」を基に「間違いである要素を含んだもの」を誤答選択肢として、「間違いだと取られる可能性がないもの」を正解としているわけです。作成された4択の問題に正解したからと言って、書き手が本当に言いたいことを理解できたとは限りません。でも、書き手の言いたいことを理解できなくても、問題を解くことができれば「英検」に合格することはできます。「英検」はゲームみたいに簡単で面白いもののように思えませんか。

　だから、本書で学ばれる皆さんには、「英検」の問題を解けるようになるだけではなくて、もっと文章の背景に意識を向けて知識を広めるつもりで取り組んでほしいと思います。そのような姿勢で読んでいけば、「英検」の準1級に合格するまでに、英語の読み手としての基本がしっかりと身に付いているはずです。

各パートの形式と解き方

短文空所補充問題　18問（解答時間の目安10分）

語彙の意味を問う問題がほとんどで、知っているかどうかの問題です。わからない単語があっても、思い出すために時間を長々と費やすことはせず次の問題に進みましょう。

単語力をつけよう！

日頃から単語集を使って語彙力の強化を図り、長文を読む際には英英辞典を使って単語同士の関係の中から意味を理解する訓練をしておきましょう。単語を音声で覚えるのも重要です。コロケーションで迷ったときに、聞きなじみがあることで判断がしやすくなることもあります。

長文空所補充問題　6問（解答時間の目安20分）

長文ではありますが、それぞれの選択肢は比較的短く、解きやすいとも言えます。前後の文や空所が含まれている箇所をヒントにして解答を導きます。

長文内容一致問題　7問（解答時間の目安25分）

2級に比べると、1文1文が長く、内容も複雑で、選択肢も長めです。設問を先に見てから、問題英文を読むと、問われている内容を知っている状態でポイントとなる部分を取り上げることができます。

読解力をつけよう！

単語と文法の知識で一つ一つの文を正確に把握することはもちろんのこと、その英文がどのようにつながっているのか、段落の役割がどのようなものなのかを考えるための集中力も必要になります。毎日、時間を決めて、ある程度の英文を読むトレーニングをしましょう。普段からオンラインニュースや洋書を読むことも有効です。丁寧な読みができれば、読解速度は自ずと上がるものですが、時間を計りながら解答時間の目安と照らして理想の速度を体感で確認しておきましょう。また、復習の際には自分が誤答した中に文の長さの違いによる傾向が出ていないか（文が長くなるにつれて段落間の関係への意識が薄れていないか、解答直前に見た文の内容につられていないか、後半の問題ばかり間違えていないか、など）も確認しておきましょう。

※上の解答時間の目安はライティング問題に30分、見直しに5分の時間を残せるように計算しています。

筆記 1

短文空所補充問題

Unit 1 …… チャレンジしよう！

Unit 2 …… 練習しよう！

アイコン一覧

正解　　解説　　和訳　　語注　　構造解析

(1) A: Have you concluded whether this painting is original?

B: I'm sorry to say it is a fake. When I (　　) this lower corner, you can clearly see differences in the colors used.

1 replicate		**2** oversee	
3 magnify		**4** uphold	

(2) The deadline to apply for the job opening at the embassy is next Friday. Only those who pass the (　　) screening process will be invited to participate in an interview.

1 initial		**2** invasive	
3 inaudible		**4** inherent	

(3) As a manager, Tara tried to be a good role model for her staff and always showed (　　) when handling difficult customers.

1 affirmation		**2** blaze	
3 empathy		**4** fright	

(4) The teacher led the schoolchildren through the park while keeping a careful eye on Rudy, who had (　　) from the group and become lost on their last trip.

1 strolled		**2** strayed	
3 pinched		**4** relocated	

(5) We provide (　　) training for all of our part-time employees to ensure they are well-prepared for even the most difficult situations.

   1 hesitant   **2** hollow

   3 premature   **4** comprehensive

(6) By the age of 18, Peter had gained international recognition for his jazz music. He was (　　) the most successful musician his university had ever seen.

   1 unwittingly   **2** doubtfully

   3 viciously   **4** arguably

(7) Researchers recently discovered ruins deep in a jungle, so they brought back several (　　) to analyze how old the site is.

   1 artifacts   **2** deficits

   3 nostrils   **4** calamities

(8) A: Grant's proposal sounds like our best solution to this crisis. Shall we take a vote?

   B: It may be wise to (　　) until the president returns from his meeting.

   1 hold off   **2** set in

   3 get ahead   **4** pass out

問題文

(1)　A: Have you concluded whether this painting is original?

B: I'm sorry to say it is a fake. When I (　　) this lower corner, you can clearly see differences in the colors used.

1　replicate　　2　oversee

3　magnify　　4　uphold

この設問は筆記1の短文問題の中では数問しか出ないパターンで、人物Aと人物Bの会話が行われるかたちになっています。正答と誤答選択肢の単語に特別な専門用語が含まれていることは少なく、それほど難易度は高くありませんが、だからこそ、なんとなく意味がわかったつもりになって、人物Aの発言に出てくる painting などの単語から、誤答選択肢の単語を何となく当てはめて、誤答してしまう可能性があります。

A: Have <u>you</u> concluded whether <u>this painting</u> is original?
　　V~　S　~V　　　　　S'　V'　C'

人物Aが「この絵がオリジナルかどうか、結論は出ているのですか」と聞いています。単純に Is this painting original?「この絵はオリジナルですか」と聞くよりも、whether this painting is original の名詞節が Have you concluded の目的語となっていることで複雑に見えますね。

B: I'm sorry to say it is a fake.
　　S V

そして、人物Bが「残念ながら偽物です」と言っており、この後に続く When 以下の文で理由や情報が追加されると考えられます。

When I (　　) this lower corner,
　　S'　V'

誤答選択肢はどれも意味がわかりやすいので、かえってトリッキーかもしれません。A の発言に出てくる「絵画」というのは「複製する」可能性も「持ち上げる」可能性もありますし、絵を描くことを「監督する」こともできますし、人物のどちらかがどちらかを「監督する」可能性もあるので、ぼんやりとしたイメージからなんとなく解答するのではなく、人物Aと人物Bの会話の焦点にあるものを理解して解答しましょう。

> you can clearly see differences in the colors used.
> S   V~   ~V

副詞節の主語は「私が〜すると」とIで始まっていますが、後に続く主節の主語は you なので、「一般的に〜する」という意味にとりましょう。「下の角を〜すれば、使われている色の違いがよくわかる」という意味なので、正解は「下の角を拡大すれば」です。

問題文

A: Have you concluded whether this painting is original?
B: I'm sorry to say it is a fake. When I magnify this lower corner, you can clearly see differences in the colors used.

A：この絵がオリジナルかどうか、結論は出ているのですか。
B：残念ですが偽物です。この下の角を拡大すると、使われている色の違いがよくわかります。

正解 ☐ magnify …を拡大して見せる、…を誇張する
誤答 ☐ replicate …を複写する
    ☐ oversee (仕事や労働者など)を監督する
    ☐ uphold …を持ち上げる、(法・決定)を支持する
英文 ☐ conclude …だと結論を下す　☐ sorry to say 残念ながら　☐ fake 偽物、いんちき
    ☐ lower 下の方の

問題文

(2) The deadline to apply for the job opening at the embassy is next Friday. Only those who pass the (　　　) screening process will be invited to participate in an interview.

1	initial	**2**	invasive
3	inaudible	**4**	inherent

1文目

The deadline to apply for the job opening at the embassy is next Friday.
　　S　　　　　　　　　　　　　　　　　　　　　　　　　　　　　　　V

まず、1文目で「大使館の求人の応募の締め切りは、来週金曜日です」と言っているので、この文は大使館の求人に関連するものだとわかります。

2文目

Only those who pass the (　　　) screening process will be invited to
　　　S　　　　　　　　　　　　　　　　　　　　　　　V

participate in an interview.

2文目は、Only those who の箇所「～する人だけ」が主語です。
「何かしらのスクリーニングプロセスを通った人たちだけが、面接に参加するように招待されます」とあります。
1文目の情報からこの場面に合うものを考えましょう。

求人に関するプロセスだということを念頭におきながら、それぞれの選択肢を当てはめていきます。
1「最初の」プロセス？
2「侵略的な」プロセス？
3「聞こえない」プロセス？
4「本来備わっている」プロセス？
screening「審査」の意味がわかって「『最初の』選考プロセス」の意味になるとわかれ

ばよいのですが、screening の意味がわからなくても、1文目をしっかり理解していけば、「求人に関する何かのプロセスに通れば、面接に参加できる」という流れがつかめるはずです。したがって、「求人に関する『侵略的な』プロセス、求人に関する『聞こえない』プロセス、求人に関する『本来備わっている』プロセス」はどれも当てはまらないと判断でき、「求人に関する『最初の』選考プロセス」が正解だとわかるでしょう。

問題文

The deadline to apply for the job opening at the embassy is next Friday. Only those who pass the initial screening process will be invited to participate in an interview.

大使館の求人の応募は、来週金曜日が締め切りです。最初の書類選考を通過した方のみ、面接に来ていただきます。

正解 ☐ initial 初めの、最初の
誤答 ☐ invasive 侵略的な
☐ inaudible 聞こえない、聞き取れない
☐ inherent 固有の、本来の
英文 ☐ deadline 締め切り ☐ apply for …に応募する・申し込む ☐ job opening 求人
☐ screening 審査、選考 ☐ invite X to *do* Xに…するよう求める・促す
☐ participate in …に参加する

問題文

(3) As a manager, Tara tried to be a good role model for her staff and always showed (　　　) when handling difficult customers.

  1 affirmation   **2** blaze

  3 empathy   **4** fright

> As a manager,

前置詞句 **As a manager** のところで「マネジャーとして」と理解します。

> As a manager, <u>Tara</u> <u>tried</u> to be a good role model for her staff
>   S   V①

主語は **Tara** なので「タラはスタッフにとって良い模範になろうとした」と、まずはここで英文を区切って意味をとることができますね。

> <u>and</u> always <u>showed</u> (　　　) when handling difficult customers.
> ↑注意   V②

断言 　…をみせる　×
まばゆいもの　…をみせる　×
恐怖 　…をみせる　×
共感 　…をみせる　◎

この **and** 以降の空所を含む部分で構造があいまいになりがちです。**and** まで読んだ時点で並列されるものの候補としては、**tried** か **tried to be** か **a good role model** か **her staff** などいくつか浮かんでいるでしょう。**and** に続く **always** で解釈を急がずに **showed** まで目を進めたところで前半の **tried** が動詞①で、**showed** が動詞②だと推測すると、読みがあいまいになるのを避けることができます。

「タラはスタッフにとって良い模範になろうとした」「そして、タラは～を見せた」「難しいお客さんに対処するときに」という文のパーツがつかめれば、単語の意味から空所に

は「難しいお客さんに対処するときに見せると、良い模範になるもの」が入るとわかります。

選択肢の中だと難しいお客さんへの対応方法としては「断言」「まばゆいもの」「恐怖」ではなく、「共感」を見せることが他のスタッフにとっての模範になりそうだと考えられますね。

問題文

As a manager, Tara tried to be a good role model for her staff and always showed empathy when handling difficult customers.

タラはマネジャーとして、スタッフの模範となるように努め、気難しいお客さまには常に共感を示すようにした。

正解 □ empathy 共感、感情移入

誤答 □ affirmation 断言、確認
　　 □ blaze 火災、まばゆいもの、(名声の) 発揚
　　 □ fright 恐怖

英文 □ role model 手本　□ handle …を扱う・担当する

問題文

(4) The teacher led the schoolchildren through the park while keeping a careful eye on Rudy, who had (　　　) from the group and become lost on their last trip.

1 strolled **2** strayed
3 pinched **4** relocated

最初の単語から文を見てみると、

前半

The teacher led the schoolchildren through the park
　　S　　V

まず、前半で「先生は、公園の中をとおりながら園児たちを導いていた」と言っているので、この文は幼稚園児たちに関するものだとわかります。

後半では、先生がルディを注意深く見ていたことが書かれています。

後半

while keeping a careful eye on Rudy,　「ルディを用心深く見守りながら」

who had (　　　) from the group and become lost on their last trip.
　S'　　V'①　　　　　　　　　　　　　V'②

ここでも、あいまいになりやすいポイントは and が何と何を同格として並べているのかです。had が and をまたいで become にもつながっていると判断でき、そこから空所が動詞①で become が動詞②の関係だとわかります。ここから、
「ルディはグループから〜してしまい、」
「そして、前回の旅行では迷子になってしまった」
という構造だとわかるので、選択肢を当てはめていくと、「はぐれた」and「迷子になった」の形で正解だとわかります。

問題文

The teacher led the schoolchildren through the park while keeping a careful eye on Rudy, who had strayed from the group and become lost on their last trip.

先生は、前回の旅行で集団から外れて迷子になってしまったルディを用心深く見守りながら、園児たちを公園で誘導した。

正解 ☐ **stray** はぐれる、迷う
誤答 ☐ **stroll** ぶらつく、散歩する、巡業する
　　 ☐ **pinch** 締め付ける、切り詰める
　　 ☐ **relocate** 新しい場所に移る
英文 ☐ **lead A through B**（主語の案内で）AがBを通り抜ける　☐ **schoolchildren** 学童
　　 ☐ **keep an eye on** …から目を離さないでいる　☐ **lost** 道に迷った

問題文

(5) We provide (　　) training for all of our part-time employees to
ensure they are well-prepared for even the most difficult situations.

  1 hesitant   **2** hollow

  3 premature   **4** comprehensive

文にざっと目を通して全体のイメージを把握しようという方法もありますが、空所に遠いところから意味をわかろうとして「どんな研修なのか」について知りたいのに、「ensure ってなんだっけ？」「大変な状況のために準備するってどんな意味？」のようにあちこちの情報について考えてしまい、らちがあかなくなってしまうことがたびたび起こります。そうならないように、やはり文頭から英文を理解して構文を捉えていきましょう。

$$\underset{\text{S}}{\underline{\text{We}}}\ \underset{\text{V}}{\underline{\text{provide}}}\ (\quad)\ \text{training for all of our part-time employees}$$

まず、主語は We、動詞は provide なので、「私たちは～な研修をすべてのパートタイマーに実施する」という意味がわかりますね。

to ensure they are well-prepared for even the most difficult situations.

そして、副詞句 to ensure 以下は、「困難な状況にも対応できる準備を整えるために」の意味だとわかります。どんな研修を行うと、困難な状況に対応できるようになるかを選択肢を見ながら考えると、「ためらいがちな」「うつろな」「時期尚早の」ではなく、「包括的な」研修だとわかりますね。

問題文

We provide comprehensive training for all of our part-time employees to ensure they are well-prepared for even the most difficult situations.

当社はパート従業員全員を対象に総合的な研修を実施し、困難な状況にも対応できるような体制を整えています。

正解 ☐ comprehensive 包括的な、網羅的な

誤答 ☐ hesitant 躊躇した、ためらいがちな
☐ hollow うつろな、内容のない、くぼんだ
☐ premature 早すぎる、早産の、時期尚早の

英文 ☐ part-time パートタイムの　☐ ensure (that 節) …を確実にする・保証する
☐ well-prepared 用意周到な

問題文

(6) By the age of 18, Peter had gained international recognition for his jazz music. He was (　　) the most successful musician his university had ever seen.

1　unwittingly　　2　doubtfully
3　viciously　　　4　arguably

By the age of 18,

副詞句 By the age of 18で始まっているので、「18歳になる頃までには」の意味だとわかります。

Peter had gained international recognition for his jazz music.
 S　　　V

主語は Peter、動詞は had gained で「ピーターはジャズ音楽で世界的な評価を得ていた」と言っています。

He was (　　) the most successful musician (his university had ever seen).
 S　V

2文目は He「彼は」で始まっているので、同じ人物についての補足や言い換えた文になると考えられます。文の意味は「彼は大学の中で今までで一番成功した音楽家だった」で、これをふまえて選択肢を見ていくと、空所には「無意識に」「疑わしく」「意地悪く」ではなく、「『間違いなく』一番成功した」という意味が入るとわかります。

問題文

By the age of 18, Peter had gained international recognition for his jazz music. He was arguably the most successful musician his university had ever seen.

18歳になる頃には、ピーターはジャズ音楽で世界的な評価を得ていた。彼は、出身大学の卒業生の中で最も成功したミュージシャンだったと言っても過言ではない。

正解 ☐ arguably おそらく間違いなく

誤答 ☐ unwittingly 無意識に、知らず知らずに
　　 ☐ doubtfully 疑わしく、疑わしげに
　　 ☐ viciously 意地悪く、邪険に、凶暴に

英文 ☐ by the age of …歳までに　☐ gain recognition for …を認めている
　　 ☐ ever (最上級の後で強調して) これまでで、今までで

問題文

(7) Researchers recently discovered ruins deep in a jungle, so they brought back several (　　) to analyze how old the site is.

1 artifacts 2 deficits

3 nostrils 4 calamities

前半

Researchers recently discovered ruins deep in a jungle,
　　　S　　　　　　　　V

まず、前半で「最近、研究者がジャングルの奥で遺跡を発見した」とあります。

so　接続詞の so で、前半と後半がつながっています。

後半

they brought back several (　　　　) to analyze how old the site is.
　S　　　V

後半部分は、「彼ら（研究者たち）」が主語です。

「彼らはその遺跡がどれくらい古いのか分析するためにいくつかの〜を持ち帰った」とあるので、空所には、どれくらい古いのかを分析するためのもので、いくつか持ち帰ることができるものが入るとわかります。

そこで、「いくつかの〜を持ち帰る」に選択肢を当てはめて合うものを考えましょう。いくつかの「欠損」は持ち帰ることができません。「鼻孔」は遺跡に動物の鼻孔の化石など、落ちていそうなイメージもありますが、そう判断するにはもう少し動物などに関連する情報がないと、ここでは想像の飛躍が過ぎてしまうことになります。「大災害」も持ち帰るものとして不適切ですね。

したがって、「いくつかの『文化遺物』を持ち帰る」が正解だとわかります。「文化遺物」のイメージとしては土器や彫刻、宝飾などが浮かんでいればよいでしょう。

空所以降の to 不定詞（to analyze）の目的語が how old から始まる名詞節になっていることもチェックしておきましょう。

問題文

Researchers recently discovered ruins deep in a jungle, so they brought back several artifacts to analyze how old the site is.

最近、研究者がジャングルの奥で遺跡を発見し、その遺跡がどのくらい古いものかを分析するためにいくつかの遺物を持ち帰った。

正解 ☐ artifact 人工遺物、文化遺物

誤答 ☐ deficit 欠損、赤字、不足(額)、(機能の)障害
☐ nostril 鼻孔、小鼻
☐ calamity 大きな不幸、惨禍、大災害

英文 ☐ researcher 研究者、研究員　☐ recently 最近(現在完了と過去時制で用いられる)
☐ ruins (複数形で)遺跡、廃墟　☐ bring back …を持ち帰る　☐ analyze …を分析する

問題文

(8)　A: Grant's proposal sounds like our best solution to this crisis. Shall we take a vote?

　　B: It may be wise to (　　) until the president returns from his meeting.

　　1　hold off　　　　**2**　set in
　　3　get ahead　　　**4**　pass out

イディオムの問題です。そもそものイディオムの意味がわからない場合に、文脈とイディオムの中の副詞から、何とか正解にたどり着けるような考え方ができるように、問題を解き進んでみましょう。

A: Grant's proposal sounds like our best solution to this crisis.
　　　　　S　　　　　　　V

Shall we take a vote?
　　　S　　V

まず、A が「グラントの提案はこの重大局面に対する最良の解決策のように思えます。決を採りましょうか」と提案しています。

B: It may be wise to
　　S　　　　V

It may be wise to で、「～するのが賢明でしょう」が空所の前の意味です。

(　　) until the president returns from his meeting.
　　　　　　S'　　　　V'

その後ろに「社長が会議から戻るまで～する」とあります。

空所に入る語を考えると、「進める」「がんばる」「放っておく」「やめる」のような動詞が思い浮かぶでしょうか。その中で積極的に進めない方向性の「放っておく」「今は考えない」といった意味のイディオムを入れるのが妥当だと考えられます。「進める」という発想もありそうですが、A の「決を採るか」に答えていないため、会話が成立しているとは考えにくいでしょう。

選択肢の中の4つの副詞のうち、幅広い用法のすべてを正確にはカバーできないにしても、なんとなくあるイメージは次のようなものでしょう。

in（内部に包含するイメージ）

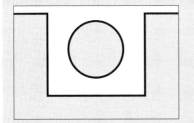

off（放っておくイメージ）

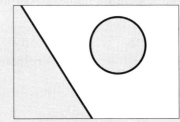

out（外に出すイメージ）

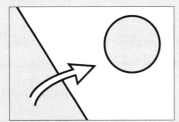

ahead（前に進むイメージ）

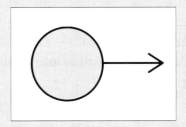

このヒントからでも、hold off を正解として選ぶことができますね。

問題文

A: Grant's proposal sounds like our best solution to this crisis. Shall we take a vote?

B: It may be wise to hold off until the president returns from his meeting.

A：グラントの提案は、この危機に対する最良の解決策のように思えます。投票を行いましょうか。

B：社長が会議から戻るまで保留にするのが賢明かもしれません。

正解 □ hold off …を遅らせる、…を先延ばしにする

誤答 □ set in（好ましくないことが）始まる、進行し始める
  □ get ahead 進む、進歩する、成功する
  □ pass out 意識を失う、立ち去る

英文 □ sound like …のような印象を与える　□ solution 解決（策）　□ take a vote 決を採る
  □ wise 賢明な

(1) With no oxygen and its extremely low temperatures, space is a (　　) environment for humans. Astronauts rely on a variety of equipment to survive.

1 hostile	**2** lofty
3 brisk	**4** responsive

(2) Few foods are as (　　) as cheese. It comes in a variety of colors and flavors and is used in many dishes around the world.

1 conditional	**2** obedient
3 hardy	**4** versatile

(3) The doctor told Chris that not wearing a seatbelt had ironically saved his life as the rescue team easily (　　) him from the car before it caught on fire.

1 extracted	**2** saluted
3 smashed	**4** imprinted

(1) 🔍 With で始まる前置詞句は、1文目の文全体の説明となります。「酸素がなく、極度に低温である宇宙」は「人間にとって〜な環境である」の空所に当てはまる形容詞を選びましょう。「過酷な」「厳しい」「適さない」の意味の形容詞を入れると、後の「(だから) 宇宙飛行士はさまざまな機器に頼って生きている」につながります。

📝 酸素がなく、極度に低温である宇宙は、人間にとって過酷な環境だ。宇宙飛行士は、さまざまな機器に頼って生きている。

✏️
- 正解 ☐ hostile (環境や条件などが) 過酷な、適さない
- 誤答 ☐ lofty (目的などが) 高尚な、(態度などが) 高慢な
  - ☐ brisk (人・態度などが) 活発な、(空気が) 心地よい、(商売が) 好調な、きびきびした
  - ☐ responsive すぐ応答する、敏感な、答えの
- 英文 ☐ oxygen 酸素　☐ astronaut 宇宙飛行士　☐ rely on …に頼る
  - ☐ equipment 機器、設備、装具　☐ survive 生き抜く、生き残る

(2) 🔍 Few foods are で始まっていて、ここだけでは理解が難しいと思う方も多いでしょう。「たいへん少ない数の食べ物がチーズと同じくらい〜だ」と理解します。続く文は「さまざまな色や風味があり、世界中の多くの料理に使われている」なので、選択肢のうち、「万能な」「用途の広い」の意味を持つものを選びましょう。チーズには「固い」ものもあるので、なんとなくのイメージから、hardy と誤答しないように注意。

📝 チーズほど万能な食品はなかなかない。さまざまな色や風味があり、世界中の多くの料理に使われている。

✏️
- 正解 ☐ versatile (物が) 用途の広い、(人が) 多才の
- 誤答 ☐ conditional 条件付きの、暫定的な
  - ☐ obedient 従順な、素直な
  - ☐ hardy 苦難に耐えられる、丈夫な、耐寒性の
- 英文 ☐ few 少しの(…しかない)、ほとんどない　☐ come in …の形がある、…として供給される
  - ☐ dish 料理、皿に盛った食べ物

(3) 🔍 文の前半は「医師がクリスに告げたことは、シートベルトをしていなかったことが皮肉にも彼の命を救ったということだ」とあります。接続詞 as 以下には、その説明が書かれていて、「火がつく前にレスキュー隊が彼を車から〜したから」とあるので、空所には「引き出す」「取り出す」の意味の語を入れます。何か交通事故に関わる語彙かもしれないというイメージから smash「粉砕する」を選ばないように注意しましょう。

📝 シートベルトをしていなかったことが、皮肉にもクリスの命を救ったと、医師はクリスに告げた。車に火がつく前にレスキュー隊が彼をその中から容易に救い出すことができたからだ。

✏️
- 正解 ☐ extract …を引き抜く、…を取り出す
- 誤答 ☐ salute …に挨拶する
  - ☐ smash …を粉砕する
  - ☐ imprint (心や記憶などに) …を強く印象づける、(判など) を押す
- 英文 ☐ ironically 皮肉なことに　☐ catch on fire 火がつく

🚩 **(1)** 1　**(2)** 4　**(3)** 1　29

(4) Daniel had difficulty with (　　) of his refrigerator because he didn't understand the city's recycling procedure.

   1 disposal   **2** downfall

   3 dilemma   **4** deduction

(5) Sarah tried to (　　) her excitement when she was declared the winner. She accepted her award with a smile, and thanked her family and friends for their support.

   1 conform   **2** conceal

   3 condemn   **4** convene

(6) Shawn's visits to his grandfather's farm left him completely exhausted. His first (　　) required him to wake up at sunrise to feed the animals and clean out the barn where they lived.

   1 remedy   **2** chore

   3 depot   **4** flock

(4)

🔍 接続詞 because の前に「ダニエルは冷蔵庫の〜に苦労した」とあります。ここだけでも「冷蔵庫」に関して苦労するのは「落下」「ジレンマ」「推論」ではなくて、「処分」がしっくりくるとわかるでしょう。because 以下で「ダニエルは市のリサイクルの手続きを理解していなかったため」と言っているので、disposal を選ぶのが適切だと確認できます。

📝 ダニエルは、市のリサイクルの手続きを理解していなかったため、冷蔵庫の廃棄に苦労した。

✏️ 正解 ☐ disposal 処分、廃棄
　　誤答 ☐ downfall 落下、急激な衰退、失脚
　　　　　☐ dilemma 板挟み、ジレンマ
　　　　　☐ deduction 控除、推論、演繹
　　英文 ☐ recycling 再生利用、リサイクル　☐ procedure 手続き、手順

(5)

🔍 前半に「サラは受賞が決まった時、興奮を〜しようとした」とあります。この文だけでも「興奮」は「順応させる」「非難する」「招集する」のではなく、「隠す」のが適切だとわかります。続く文を読んで、サラは興奮を「隠して」、笑顔で賞を受け取り、家族や友人に感謝の気持ちを伝えたのだと確認することができます。

📝 受賞が決まったとき、サラは興奮を隠そうとした。笑顔で賞を受け取り、支えてくれた家族や友人に感謝の気持ちを伝えた。

✏️ 正解 ☐ conceal …を見せないようにする、…を隠す
　　誤答 ☐ conform …を模範にならわせる、…を順応させる
　　　　　☐ condemn …を非難する、…に刑を宣告する
　　　　　☐ convene …を招集する
　　英文 ☐ declare A B A が B だと発表する・宣言する　☐ award 賞

(6)

🔍 前半に「ショーンが祖父の農場を訪ねて疲れ果ててしまった」とあり、続く文ではその理由について書かれています。「彼の最初の〜は早起きして、動物にエサをやり、動物小屋を掃除すること」とあるので、空所には「仕事」「雑用」の意味の名詞が入るとわかるでしょう。flock「家畜の群れ」や depot「倉庫」「貯蔵所」などは「農場」と関連があるように感じますが、選ばないように注意しましょう。2文目の最後にある the barn where they lived は関係副詞 where で導かれる形容詞節が barn を修飾しています。

📝 祖父の農場を訪ねたショーンは、すっかり疲れ果ててしまった。夜明けとともに起きて動物に餌をやり、動物小屋を掃除するのが最初の仕事だったのだ。

✏️ 正解 ☐ chore 日常的な仕事、雑用
　　誤答 ☐ remedy 治療、矯正法、救済策
　　　　　☐ depot 貯蔵所、倉庫、駅、発着所
　　　　　☐ flock（家畜、特に羊の）群れ、人の群れ
　　英文 ☐ leave X exhausted X を疲れ果てさせる　☐ require X to do X に…するよう要求する
　　　　　☐ at sunrise 日の出の時間に　☐ feed …に餌を与える　☐ clean out すっかりきれいにする
　　　　　☐ barn 家畜小屋、納屋

(7) Cultivating tomatoes requires careful consideration of outdoor conditions. The plant (　　) in warm, sunny climates with soil that drains easily, resulting in larger fruit.

1 mobilizes **2** grazes

3 evaporates **4** flourishes

(8) A: Why did we choose this city for our holiday? It's too hot and everything is expensive.

B: Could you please stop (　　) and try to enjoy our vacation?

1 defending **2** praying

3 grumbling **4** shattering

(9) Penguins are a group of (　　) birds that cannot fly. They may spend up to 75% of their time in the water, only coming on land to breed.

1 dormant **2** pious

3 trivial **4** aquatic

(7)

前半で「トマトの栽培は屋外の条件を十分に考慮する必要がある」と言っているので、トマト栽培の条件についての文章だとわかります。後半の文では「トマト」を「その植物」と言い換えて、「その植物は、水はけのよい土壌で、暖かく、日当たりの良い場所だと、〜して大きな実をつける」とあるので、「動員される」「草を食べる」「蒸発する」の意味ではなくて、「繁茂する」の意味の動詞が入るとわかります。

トマトの栽培は、屋外の条件を十分に考慮する必要がある。水はけのよい土壌で、暖かく日当たりのよい場所だと、葉が茂り、実は大きく育つ。

正解 ☐ flourish (草木が) 繁茂する
誤答 ☐ mobilize 動員される
　　 ☐ graze (家畜が) 草を食べる
　　 ☐ evaporate 蒸発する、消えてなくなる
英文 ☐ cultivate …を栽培する　☐ require …を必要とする　☐ consideration 考慮
　　 ☐ drain 排水される　☐ result in …という結果になる

(8)

人物Aが「なぜこの町を旅行先に選んだの？」と聞いています。主語がweであり、Why did we...? の形をとっているため、単純な疑問ではなく、多少の不満や、文句のニュアンスが含まれています。人物Aが「ここは暑いし、物価も高いし」と不満を言っているのに対して、人物Bは「〜をやめて、休暇を楽しみましょう」と言っているので、〜にはやめるべきものが入ります。「文句を言うのをやめる」が正解です。

A：なぜこの町を旅行先に選んだの？　暑いし、物価も高いし。
B：文句を言っていないで、休暇を楽しもうよ。

正解 ☐ grumble 不平を言う
誤答 ☐ defend (スポーツの試合で) 防御する、弁護する
　　 ☐ pray 祈る、懇願する
　　 ☐ shatter 粉々になる、(植物が) 実を落とす
英文 ☐ try to *do* …しようとする

(9)

前半では「ペンギンは飛べない〜の鳥の一種です」とあります。ここで選択肢の「冬眠中の」「敬虔な」「ささいな」ではなく aquatic「水生の」が当てはまるとわかります。続く文で「繁殖のために陸に上がってくるだけで、最長で75%の時間を水の中で過ごすこともある」と説明している点で「水生の鳥」についてだと確認できますね。

ペンギンは水鳥の一種で、空を飛ぶことができない。繁殖のために陸に上がってくるだけで、最長で75%の時間を水の中で過ごすこともある。

正解 ☐ aquatic 水中にすむ
誤答 ☐ dormant 休眠中の、冬眠中の
　　 ☐ pious 敬虔な、偽善的な、感心な
　　 ☐ trivial 取るに足りない、ささいな、当たり前の
英文 ☐ up to …まで　☐ only (動詞の前で) …するだけだ　☐ breed 繁殖する

筆記 1

(10) As a child, Natasha's father was often away on business trips and her mother worked night shifts, so she became responsible for her younger siblings' (   ).

    1 inheritance   **2** upbringing

    3 drawback   **4** exploration

(11) The general was considered to be a (   ) genius of his time, inventing strategies to reduce risks to his soldiers' lives.

    1 tactical   **2** superficial

    3 dismal   **4** competitive

(12) Jane (   ) a variety of language learning activities in her class to help her English students. Last week, students interviewed each other to practice asking and answering questions.

    1 implements   **2** alters

    3 suspends   **4** boasts

(10) 🔍 接続詞 so の前までの部分に「子どもの頃、父親は出張が多く、母親は夜勤が多かった」とあります。この後の「だから」を意味する順接の接続詞 so で続く文は「ナターシャは弟妹たちの〜に対して責任を負うようになった」とあるので、空所には弟妹に対して行うこととして「養育」を表す語が入るとわかります。

📝 子どもの頃、父親は出張が多く、母親は夜勤が多かったので、ナターシャは弟妹たちの養育を任されるようになった。

✏️ 正解 ☐ upbringing 養育、しつけ
誤答 ☐ inheritance 相続、相続財産、遺伝
☐ drawback 欠点、障害、控除、払い戻し
☐ exploration 探検、踏査、探究、診査
英文 ☐ as a child 子どもの頃　☐ be away on business trip 出張で不在である
☐ work night shifts 夜勤をする　☐ sibling 兄弟姉妹

筆記
1

(11) 🔍 前半は「その司令官は〜の天才と言われた」とあります。その後の inventing 以下では「兵士の命の危機を減らすための戦略を考案した」と説明しているので、司令官は何の天才かというと、「表面的な」「みじめな」「競争力のある」ではなく、「戦術の」で修飾すると意味が通ります。

📝 司令官はその時代の戦術の天才と言われ、兵士の命の危険を減らすための戦略を考案した。

✏️ 正解 ☐ tactical 戦術的な
誤答 ☐ superficial 表面の、見かけの、表面的な、中身のない
☐ dismal 陰気な、みじめな
☐ competitive 競争的な、競争心の強い、競争力のある
英文 ☐ general 軍司令官　☐ consider A to be B A を B だとみなす　☐ genius 天才
☐ invent …を考え出す　☐ strategy 戦略、戦術

(12) 🔍 前半は「ジェーンは英語を学ぶ生徒のために言語学習活動を〜する」とあります。ジェーンは学習活動をどうするのかに関する動詞を選びます。後半に「先週、生徒たちはお互いにインタビューをして、質問をしたり、答えたりする練習をした」とあり、実際に行ったことについて説明をしています。「実施する」の意味を表す動詞を選びましょう。

📝 ジェーンは英語を学ぶ生徒に役立ててもらおうと、クラスでさまざまな言語学習活動を実施している。先週、生徒たちはお互いにインタビューをして、質問をしたり答えたりする練習をした。

✏️ 正解 ☐ implement （計画など）を実行する
誤答 ☐ alter …を変える、…を変更する
☐ suspend …を保留にする、…を一時停止する、…を停職（停学）にする、…をつるす
☐ boast …と自慢する、…を（誇りとして）もつ

🚩 **(10)** 2 **(11)** 1 **(12)** 1

(13) The doctor was unable to ( ) my mother's illness and ended up referring her to a specialist.

1 diagnose **2** disorder
3 demolish **4** decorate

(14) Most experts believe that categorizing human groups by race has no biological basis, but Dr. Jean is confident genetic ( ) prove otherwise.

1 assaults **2** factors
3 buildups **4** memoirs

(15) Zack was surprised when the reporter took out a pen and paper to ( ) his answers. He thought that using a voice recorder would be easier than taking notes by hand.

1 seize on **2** lay over
3 jot down **4** stick with

(13) 🔍 「医師」が主語で始まっています。選択肢を見ると「医師」がすることは「乱す」「取り壊す」「飾る」ではなく、「診断する」が適当だと考えられます。文の意味を考えても、「医師は母の病気を～することができなくて、専門医を紹介することになった」とあることで、確認できますね。

🔤 医師は母の病気を診断することができず、結局、専門医を紹介してくれることになった。

✏️ 正解 ☐ diagnose（病気）を診断する
誤答 ☐ disorder …を乱す、…を乱雑にする、(心身)の調子を狂わせる
☐ demolish …を取り壊す、(主張や理論)を覆す、(相手)をやっつける、…に圧勝する
☐ decorate …を飾る、…にペンキを塗る、…に壁紙を張る、…に(勲章を)授ける
英文 ☐ end up *doing* 結局…することになる ☐ refer A to B A を B に紹介する

(14) 🔍 前半に「多くの専門家が信じているのは、人種による人類の分類は生物学的根拠がないことだ」とあります。接続詞 but の後は、「ジーン博士は遺伝的～がその逆のことを証明していると確信している」とあるので、genetic「遺伝的な」で修飾される名詞は何か、選びましょう。遺伝的な「襲撃」「増強」「自伝」ではなく、遺伝的な factor「要素」が当てはまることがわかるでしょう。

🔤 多くの専門家は、人種による人類の分類には生物学的根拠がないと考えているが、ジーン博士は遺伝的要因によってその逆のことが証明されると確信している。

✏️ 正解 ☐ factor 要因、要素
誤答 ☐ assault 襲撃、急襲、批判、(困難なことへの)挑戦
☐ buildup 増強、蓄積、準備、事前の宣伝、(物語などの)盛り上がり
☐ memoir 回顧録、自伝、研究論文
英文 ☐ categorize 分類する ☐ biological 生物学上の
☐ be confident (that 節) …だと確信している ☐ genetic 遺伝上の
☐ prove (…だと)わかる ☐ otherwise 異なって、違って

(15) 🔍 前半は「ザックは記者がペンと紙を取り出して、自分の答えを～したことに驚いた」とあります。その後の「彼は手でメモを取るより、ボイスレコーダーを使う方が簡単だと思った」というのが、ザックが驚いた理由だと書かれていると考えられます。「ザックは、ボイスレコーダーを使う方が簡単なのに、どうして～したのかと驚いた」と言い換えると、ペンと紙で「書き留める」が正解だとわかります。

🔤 ザックが驚いたのは、記者がペンと紙を取り出して、自分の答えを書き留めたことだ。手でメモを取るより、ボイスレコーダーの方が簡単だろうとザックは思った。

✏️ 正解 ☐ jot down …をちょっと書き留める
誤答 ☐ seize on (機会や欠点など)をつかむ、捕らえる (考えなど)に飛びつく
☐ lay over 延期する、かぶせる、飾る
☐ stick with 人から離れないでいる、忠実である、人の記憶に残る
英文 ☐ take out …を取り出す ☐ take notes 記録する、メモを取る ☐ by hand 手書きで

(16) Billy glanced at the clock and realized he needed to ( ) his work quickly so he wouldn't be late for the meeting.

1 size up   **2** roll by

3 wrap up   **4** get by

(17) A: I apologize for my frequent tardiness, but today's circumstances were simply out of my control.

B: You have exhausted my patience and I can no longer ( ) your excuses.

1 put up with   **2** opt out of

3 lash out at   **4** make away with

(18) Philip's close friends invited well-known artists from around the world to a grand event in order to ( ) his long career as the art museum's founder.

1 commemorate   **2** reconcile

3 intimidate   **4** overwhelm

(16) 🔍 前半は「ビリーは時計に目をやると、気づいた」とあり、realized の後は彼が気づいた内容について述べています。「彼は会議に遅れないように仕事を早く～する必要があった」の～に当てはまるイディオムを選択肢から探すと、「評価する」「流れていく」「通り過ぎる」ではなく「終わらせる」の意味の wrap up を選ぶとわかります。

🔁 ビリーは時計に目をやると、会議に遅れないように早く仕事を終わらせなければならないことに気づいた。

✏️ 正解 ☐ wrap up (仕事など) を終える、(レポートなど) を書き上げる
　　誤答 ☐ size up (人・状況) を判断する・評価する、…の型に合う、…の水準に達する
　　　　 ☐ roll by (車・雲などが) 流れていく、(時が) どんどん過ぎる
　　　　 ☐ get by (…のそば) を通り過ぎる、…の目を逃れる、…に認められる
　　英文 ☐ glance at …をちらりと見る　☐ be late for …に遅れる

(17) 🔍 人物 A が「遅刻が多いことは申し訳ないのですが、今日は私の力ではどうにもならない状況でした」と言っているので、人物 A は遅刻が多く、今日も遅刻をしたとわかります。それに対して人物 B が「あなたには堪忍袋の緒が切れてしまいました。もうあなたの言い訳には～できません」と言っているので、「避けられない」「非難できない」「持ち去れない」ではなく、「我慢できない」の意味の語が入ると考えられるでしょう。

🔁 A：遅刻が多いことは申し訳ないと思っていますが、今日は私の力ではどうにもならない状況でした。
　　B：あなたには堪忍袋の緒が切れてしまいました。もうあなたの言い訳なんか聞いていられません。

✏️ 正解 ☐ put up with …に耐える、…を我慢する
　　誤答 ☐ opt out of …を避ける、…から逃れる、…から身を引く
　　　　 ☐ lash out at …を激しく非難する、…に殴りかかる
　　　　 ☐ make away with …を持ち去る、…を滅ぼす、(お金) を使い果たす
　　英文 ☐ apologize for …について謝る　☐ tardiness 遅刻　☐ out of control なすすべがない
　　　　 ☐ exhaust …を疲弊させる、…を消耗させる　☐ no longer もう…でない
　　　　 ☐ excuse 弁解、言い訳

(18) 🔍 Philip's close friends が主語です。前半は「フィリップの親しい友人たちが世界各国の著名なアーティストを盛大なイベントに招待した」とあり、in order to の後は彼らが何のために招待したのかが書かれています。盛大なイベントとあるので、フィリップの長いキャリアを「記念する、祝う」を意味する単語が当てはまるとわかりますね。

🔁 美術館の創設者としての長いキャリアをたたえるため、フィリップの親しい友人たちが世界各国の著名なアーティストを招いて盛大なイベントを開催した。

✏️ 正解 ☐ commemorate …を記念する、…を祝する、…をたたえる
　　誤答 ☐ reconcile …を調和させる、…を仲直りさせる
　　　　 ☐ intimidate …を脅す、…を怖がらせる、…を威圧する
　　　　 ☐ overwhelm …を圧倒する、…を困惑させる、…に覆いかぶさる
　　英文 ☐ well-known 有名な、よく知られた　☐ founder 創設者、創立者

🚩 **(16)** 3　**(17)** 1　**(18)** 1

(19) A: Please explain your motivation for studying nursing at our university.

B: Well, your school was my first choice since it has the most (　　) program in the country.

1 ceaseless **2** dormant
3 cumulative **4** prestigious

Date
／ ① ② ③ ④
／ ① ② ③ ④
／ ① ② ③ ④

(20) Among Tom's many (　　) are truthfulness, loyalty, and courage. He is eager to lend a helping hand to those in need and fights for justice.

1 preferences **2** revelations
3 virtues **4** flaws

Date
／ ① ② ③ ④
／ ① ② ③ ④
／ ① ② ③ ④

(19) 🔍 人物Aが「あなたが本学で看護を学ぼうと思った動機を教えてください」と聞いていることから、ここが学校の面接の場であると推測できます。人物Bも「貴校は私の第一志望でした」と言っているので、ここが面接の場であり、人物Bは受験者だとわかります。since以下はこの学校が第一志望であった理由について述べているので、学校の良い面を表す「名声のある」のような意味の形容詞が入ると考えられます。

　✒️ A：あなたが本学で看護を学ぼうと思った動機を教えてください。
　　 B：ええ、国内で最も名声のあるプログラムが貴校にはありますので、第一志望としました。

　✏️ 正解 ☐ prestigious 名声のある、格式の高い
　　 誤答 ☐ ceaseless 絶え間のない
　　　　 ☐ dormant 睡眠状態の、休止状態にある、未発動の
　　　　 ☐ cumulative 累積する
　　 英文 ☐ motivation 動機 ☐ nursing 看護、介護 ☐ first choice 第一希望

(20) 🔍 主語が前置詞で始まることはないので、Amongは主語ではありません。文頭から読んで、「トムの多くの〜は」で始まり、ピリオドまでで3つの名詞が並んでいるので、「誠実さ、忠誠心、勇気」の3つをまとめて表現している名詞を選ぶと「長所」が適切だとわかります。これはtruthfulness, loyalty, courageの3つが主語である倒置の文になっています。その文法事項を知らなくても、続く「彼は困っている人に手を差し伸べたいと強く思っており、正義のために奮闘する」から正答にたどり着くことができます。

倒置が起こる場合はいくつかありますが、ここではそのうちの3つのパターンを挙げます。問題英文にあるAmongで始まる文は次のパターンの3番目に当てはまります。

1. 否定語で始まる文の倒置（強調のためと考えるとわかりやすいです）
   Never has she seen her cousin before.（彼女はいとこに会ったことがない）
2. Ifの省略による倒置（助動詞が前に来ます）
   Had I known about the movie, I would have joined you.（映画のことを知っていたら、一緒に行ったのに）
3. 副詞、または副詞句が前に来る倒置
   Behind the monitor sat the salesperson.（モニターの下で営業スタッフが座っている）

　✒️ トムには、誠実さ、忠誠心、勇気といった多くの長所がある。困っている人に手を差し伸べたいと強く思っており、正義のために奮闘する。

　✏️ 正解 ☐ virtue 長所、美徳
　　 誤答 ☐ preference 好むこと、好み、選択物、優先（権）
　　　　 ☐ revelation 明らかにすること、暴露、意外な新事実、啓示
　　　　 ☐ flaw 欠点、欠陥、きず、突風
　　 英文 ☐ among …の中で ☐ truthfulness 誠実 ☐ loyalty 誠実さ ☐ courage 勇気
　　　　 ☐ be eager to *do* しきりに…したがっている ☐ those in need 困っている人々
　　　　 ☐ justice 正義

(21) Professor Green's lectures are fairly ( ). He always begins by reviewing the previous material, followed by a short discussion to transition into the day's main topic.

   1 frail   **2** straightforward

   3 valid   **4** outrageous

(22) Mr. Walsh warned the employee not to make the same mistake again, ( ) keeping his voice low to try and stay calm.

   1 deliberately   **2** blissfully

   3 ironically   **4** solely

(23) When Todd resigned from his position, his supervisor asked him not to leave, saying the company would ( ) the loss of such a valuable employee.

   1 discredit   **2** lament

   3 compile   **4** evoke

(21) 🔍 1文目は「グリーン教授の講義は、かなり〜である」という意味です。この時点で「講義」という主語に対して形容詞 frail「もろい」と outrageous「不法な」は、補語としておそらく当てはまらないだろうと予想できます。2文目は「いつも前回の復習から始まり、短いディスカッションを経て、その日のメイントピックに移行する」とあり、いつも講義の流れが決まっているということを「わかりやすい」で表すことができると考えられるでしょう。

📄 グリーン教授の講義は、いたってシンプルである。いつも前回の復習から始まり、短いディスカッションを経て、その日のメイントピックに移行する。

✏️ 正解 ☐ straightforward 簡単な、わかりやすい
誤答 ☐ frail (体が) 弱い、もろい、(根拠が) 薄弱な、誘惑に負けやすい
☐ valid 有効な、根拠の確実な、正当な
☐ outrageous 不法な、常軌を逸した、無礼な、突飛な
英文 ☐ fairly かなり ☐ review …を復習する ☐ previous 以前の ☐ material 資料
☐ followed by その後に…が続く ☐ transition into …への移行

(22) 🔍 選択肢はすべて副詞です。前半は、「ウォルシュ氏は、同じ過ちを繰り返さないように従業員に注意した」とあります。その後に「声を小さくして、冷静でいようとした」と言っているため、どのように声を小さくして、冷静になろうとしたのかを表す副詞を選びます。「幸いにも」「皮肉にも」「一人で」よりも、「意識的に」を表す語がしっくりと当てはまりますね。

📄 ウォルシュ氏は、同じ過ちを繰り返さないようにと、意識的に小さい声で冷静でいようと努め、従業員に注意した。

✏️ 正解 ☐ deliberately 意識的に
誤答 ☐ blissfully 幸いにも、この上なく
☐ ironically 皮肉にも
☐ solely 一人で、単に
英文 ☐ warn X to *do* Xに…するよう注意を与える

(23) 🔍 When で始まる従属節は「トッドが退職したとき」で、続いて主節に「上司は退職しないように頼んだ」とあります。saying からは分詞構文で、上司がトッドに頼んだときに伝えた内容が書かれていると推測できます。上司が懇願して言った「会社はこんなに貴重な社員がいなくなることを〜するだろう」に当てはまる動詞を選択肢から選ぶと、「嘆き悲しむ」が正解だとわかります。

📄 トッドが退職するとき、上司は「こんな貴重な社員がいなくなったら会社が困る」と言って退職しないでくれと言った。

✏️ 正解 ☐ lament …を嘆き悲しむ
誤答 ☐ discredit …を疑う、…の信用を傷つける
☐ compile …を編集する、(資料) を集める、…を記録する
☐ evoke …を呼び起こす、…を喚起する、(笑いなど) を引き起こす
英文 ☐ resign from/as …を退職する、…を辞職する ☐ supervisor 上司、監督者
☐ ask X to *do* Xに…するよう頼む ☐ valuable 貴重な、大切な

(24) Learners of foreign languages often encounter many ( ) at the beginning of their studies. For example, slang expressions that are different from what is learned from textbooks is one major problem.

1 obstacles **2** captions
3 downfalls **4** rituals

(25) Richard became ( ) when his professor accused him of cheating. He explained that any similarities with his friend's essay were simply a coincidence.

1 conspicuous **2** disadvantaged
3 hypothetical **4** defensive

(24) 🔍 1文目で「外国語の学習者は、学習開始当初に多くの～に遭遇することが多い」とあります。ここでおそらく「障害、難しいこと」を表す語が当てはまるとわかるので、正解を選べるでしょう。2文目で、空所に当てはまる名詞に含まれるものの例として「俗語表現」が挙げられています。俗語表現と教科書の表現の違いは困難な障害になり得るので、obstacles が正解だと確認できますね。

🔁 外国語の学習者は、学習開始当初に多くの障害に遭遇することが多い。例えば、教科書で習うものとは異なる俗語表現も大きな問題の一つである。

✏️ 正解 ☐ obstacle 障害
誤答 ☐ caption 説明、字幕、表題
☐ downfall 失脚、転落、失墜、(雨や雪などの) 大降り
☐ ritual 儀式、慣例、(日常の) 決まった習慣
英文 ☐ encounter …に遭遇する ☐ at the beginning of …のはじめに
☐ slang expression 俗語表現 ☐ different from …と異なって

📣
For example, slang expression
　　　　　　　　　S

(that are different from what is learned from textbook)
　S'　　　　V'　　　　名詞節 (from の目的語) what = thing that

is one major problem.
V　　C

(25) 🔍 文頭から空所までで「リチャードは～になった」とあるので、空所には補語となる形容詞が入るとわかります。空所の後は「教授が彼の不正を非難したとき」と続くので、非難された場合に人がとる行動、感じることは何かを考えます。2文目では「彼は、友人のエッセイとの類似点は単なる偶然だと説明した」と、彼がとった行動が書かれているので、彼は自身を守った、つまり「保身的」になったと言えるでしょう。

🔁 リチャードは、教授から不正を非難され、保身的になった。彼は、友人のエッセイとの類似点は単なる偶然だと説明した。

✏️ 正解 ☐ defensive 保身的な
誤答 ☐ conspicuous 目立つ、人目につく、顕著な、異彩を放つ
☐ disadvantaged 恵まれない、不利な境遇の
☐ hypothetical 仮説の、仮定の、仮説を立てるのが好きな
英文 ☐ accuse A of B A を B のことで非難する ☐ cheat 不正をする
☐ explain that 節 …だと説明する ☐ similarity with …との類似点
☐ coincidence 偶然の一致

(26) Tim emphasized the need to stay under budget. His project manager ( ) his suggestion of changing the materials for the statue.

1 preceded 2 embraced
3 transplanted 4 blushed

(27) Throughout many parts of the world, gender ( ) is recognized as an urgent social issue. Northern European countries rank the highest in terms of women's well-being.

1 infrastructure 2 negligence
3 participation 4 disparity

(28) Over the past half a century, the global ( ) rate of adults has risen almost 20 percent. Data suggests even developing nations have better access to tools and resources for learning.

1 hospitalization 2 conscience
3 literacy 4 bravery

(26) 🔍 1文目は「ティムは、予算内に収めることの必要性を訴えた」です。続く2文目でティムの訴えに相手がどう対処したかについて書かれています。「プロジェクトマネジャーは、像の素材を変更するという提案を〜した」とあるので、提案を「先んじた」でも「移植した」でも「赤くした」でもなく「受け入れた」を意味する embraced が当てはまるとわかるでしょう。

🔁 ティムは、予算内に収めることの必要性を訴えた。プロジェクトマネジャーは、像の素材を変更するという提案を受け入れた。

✏️ 正解 ☐ embrace (考え・提案など) を受け入れる
誤答 ☐ precede …に先んずる、…に優先する、…の前置きにする
☐ transplant (臓器) を移植する、(植物) を移植する、…を移転する、…を移住させる
☐ blush …を赤くする、…を赤く染める
英文 ☐ emphasize …を力説する ☐ under budget 予算内で ☐ material 材料、素材
☐ statue 彫像

(27) 🔍 gender disparity は「男女格差」という語句です。gender に続く語が何なのかすぐにひらめかなくても、2文目で北欧諸国での女性の幸福度について書かれているので、gender「性」の何について、社会問題となっているのか考え、「格差」の意味の disparity を答えましょう。

🔁 世界の多くの地域で、男女間の格差が喫緊の社会問題として認識されている。北欧諸国は女性の幸福度が最も高くなっている。

✏️ 正解 ☐ disparity 格差、相違、不均衡
誤答 ☐ infrastructure インフラ、社会基盤
☐ negligence 怠慢、不注意 過失
☐ participation 参加、関与
英文 ☐ gender 社会的・文化的に見た性別 ☐ recognize A as B A を B であると認識する
☐ rank 順位を占める ☐ in terms of …の見地から、…に関して
☐ well-being 幸福 (な状態)

(28) 🔍 literacy rate は「識字率」の意味で頻繁に用いられます。これを知らない場合は、文頭の「過去半世紀の間に」から読み進めて、「世界の成人の〜の比率は20%近くも上昇した」とあることを確認し、2文目で、開発途上国で学習ツールへアクセスしやすくなっていることを読み取って、世界で上がったのは「文字を読む能力」の割合だと推測しましょう。

🔁 過去半世紀の間に、世界の成人の識字率は20%近くも上昇した。開発途上国でも、学習のためのツールやリソースへアクセスしやすくなっていることを示すデータもある。

✏️ 正解 ☐ literacy 識字能力
誤答 ☐ hospitalization 病院収容、入院加療、入院期間
☐ conscience 良心、善悪の観念、罪の意識
☐ bravery 勇敢、勇壮、華美、華やかさ
英文 ☐ rate 一定の割合、率 ☐ suggest (that 節) …だと示唆する
☐ developing nations 開発途上国 ☐ access to …を利用する機会
☐ resource リソース、資料、供給源

(29) Children often become upset when they do not receive ( ) attention from their parents as they believe the world revolves around them.

  1 ample   **2** insufficient

  3 solemn   **4** operational

(30) Many citizens called for the politician to clearly state his position on shutting down the factory. His previous comments had been ( ) and caused concern, especially among factory workers.

  1 rectangular   **2** adjacent

  3 ambiguous   **4** punctual

(31) Although Thomas promised that he would exercise and avoid sweets, a visit to the bakery on the way home was too ( ) to pass up.

  1 responsible   **2** irresistible

  3 unbearable   **4** humble

(29) まず、「子どもはしばしば怒ってしまう」とあり、続く when 以下は「親から～な関心を持たれないと」という意味です。as 以下にはその理由として「自分を中心に世界が回っていると信じているから」とあるので、自分中心の子どもは親からどんな関心を持たれないと怒るかを考えると、「十分な」を意味する形容詞が入るとわかります。insufficient は「不十分な」という意味なので、この文に not が含まれているのを見落とすと、選んでしまう可能性があります。

子どもは、自分を中心に世界が回っていると思い込んでいるため、親から十分気にかけてもらえないと怒ってしまうことがよくある。

正解 □ ample 余るほど十分な
誤答 □ insufficient 不十分な、不足している、不適当な
　　 □ solemn 厳粛な、まじめな、まじめくさった、宗教上の
　　 □ operational 使用できる、運転中の、操作上の、経営上の
英文 □ upset 腹を立てて　□ revolve around …を中心にして回る

(30) 「多くの市民が、工場閉鎖について立場を明確に表明するよう政治家に求めた」とあるので、政治家が多くの市民に詰め寄られている場面が想像できます。「彼のこれまでの発言は～で、特に工場労働者に不安を与えていた」の空所に当てはまるものとして、どんな発言だと労働者に不安を与えるか考えましょう。選択肢から「あいまいな」を意味する形容詞が入りますね。

多くの市民が、工場閉鎖について立場を明確に表明するよう政治家に求めた。彼のこれまでの発言はあいまいで、特に工場労働者に不安を与えていた。

正解 □ ambiguous あいまいな
誤答 □ rectangular 長方形の、直角の
　　 □ adjacent 隣接した、近隣の
　　 □ punctual 時間・期日を守る、遅滞のない
英文 □ call for X to do Xに…するよう求める　□ politician 政治家
　　 □ clearly はっきりと、明瞭に　□ state one's position 態度を明らかにする
　　 □ shut down (操業など)を停止する　□ cause concern 懸念を生じさせる

(31) 譲歩の副詞節を導く接続詞で始まる前半は「トーマスは運動して甘いものを控えると約束したけれども」という意味です。これに続く主節はそれができなかったという内容だと推測できます。後半に「帰り道にあるパン屋に寄ることがとても～だったので無視して通り過ぎることができなかった」とあるので、甘いパンを買って食べてしまったのでしょう。ここから、「パン屋に寄ることは～だった」に当てはまる形容詞は「実に魅力的」だとわかりますね。unbearable は受け入れるには苦痛だったり不愉快だったりすることなので不適切です。

運動をして、甘いものを控えると約束したトーマスだったが、帰り道にパン屋に寄らずにはいられなかった。

正解 □ irresistible 感情などを抑えられない、実に魅力的な
誤答 □ responsible 責任のある、…の原因である、信用できる
　　 □ unbearable 耐えられない、我慢できない
　　 □ humble 謙虚な、つつましい、(身分・地位が)低い、質素な
英文 □ promise that 節 …すると約束する　□ avoid …を避ける
　　 □ on the way (…へ行く)途中に　□ pass up …のそばを通り過ごす、…を無視する、…を見送る

(32) The CEO invited Tony and his family to dinner as a (   ) of appreciation for successfully managing his business investments over the years.

1 surplus   2 token

3 curfew   4 jeopardy

(33) Experts say both biological and social factors play a role in women (   ) men by up to five years on average. Aggressive behavior is one reason for men's disadvantage.

1 outliving   2 exhaling

3 convincing   4 immigrating

(34) Although experiments showed a significant difference in terms of flexibility, experts could not (   ) the artificial fabric from the natural one simply based on its appearance.

1 scramble   2 restrain

3 mimic   4 discern

(32) 🔍 「CEO は感謝の〜としてトニーとその家族を夕食に招待した」とあるので、この時点で「感謝の〜として」に当てはまる名詞は「しるし」を意味する語だとわかります。続く for 以下で「長年にわたって事業投資を成功させてきたこと」に対する「感謝のしるし」だと、内容を確認しましょう。

🔄 CEO は、長年にわたって事業投資を成功させてきたトニーとその家族を、感謝の気持ちを込めて夕食に招待した。

✏️ 正解 ☐ token しるし、記念
　　誤答 ☐ surplus 余り、余剰、黒字
　　　　　☐ curfew (夜間の)外出禁止令、門限、晩鐘
　　　　　☐ jeopardy 危険
　　英文 ☐ invite A to B AをBに招待する　☐ appreciation 感謝
　　　　　☐ successfully うまく、首尾よく　☐ investment 投資

(33) 🔍 空所を含む1文目は「専門家によると、平均で5年女性が男性〜であるのには、生物学的要因と社会的要因の両方が関わっている」とあります。by up to から数値的に比較されていると推測できます。続いて2文目で、攻撃的な行動が男性が不利になる理由だと書かれているので、これを踏まえて選択肢を見ると「長生きである」を意味する動詞が入るとわかります。

🔄 専門家によると、女性が男性より平均で5年も長生きすることには、生物学的要因と社会的要因の両方が関わっている。攻撃的な行動は、男性が不利になる理由の一つである。

✏️ 正解 ☐ outlive …より長生きする
　　誤答 ☐ exhale (息や言葉)を吐き出す、(ガス・におい)を発散する、(怒りなど)を爆発させる
　　　　　☐ convince …に確信させる、…に納得させる、(説得して)…に〜させる
　　　　　☐ immigrate (人)を(他国から)移住させる
　　英文 ☐ biological 生物学上の　☐ play a role in …で役割を果たす　☐ on average 平均で
　　　　　☐ aggressive 攻撃的な、けんか腰の　☐ disadvantage 不利

(34) 🔍 Although で始まる前半には「実験では柔軟性に大きな差が出たけれども」とあり、後半には「専門家は見た目だけでは〜ができなかった」とあります。artificial fabric と natural one の間が from でつながれているので、人工素材の生地と天然素材の生地を比較しているとわかります。したがって、空所には「〜を見分ける」を意味する語が入ると考えられます。

🔄 実験では柔軟性に大きな差が出たが、専門家にも見た目だけでは人工素材の生地と天然素材の生地の区別がつかなかった。

✏️ 正解 ☐ discern …を識別する
　　誤答 ☐ scramble …を急いでかき集める、(トランプなど)をかき混ぜる、…をごちゃ混ぜにする
　　　　　☐ restrain …を抑える、…を抑制する、…を制限する、…を拘束する
　　　　　☐ mimic (笑わせるために)…をまねる、…のまねをしてばかにする、…の擬態をする
　　英文 ☐ in terms of …の点から見て　☐ flexibility 柔軟性　☐ artificial 人工の
　　　　　☐ fabric 織物、生地　☐ based on …をもとに　☐ appearance 外観

(35) Stacey has a strange ( ) with rare diseases. Since a young age, she has read countless books on medical conditions.

  1 recession   **2** proportion
  3 equation   **4** fascination

(36) A: I know it sounds strange, but I've been ( ) chocolate with cheese lately.

   B: That reminds me of when my wife was pregnant and couldn't stop eating spicy foods.

  1 craving   **2** catering
  3 agitating **4** discarding

(37) Jennifer is at the top of her class. She spends most of her time in the library where she ( ) books on any subject.

  1 halts   **2** devours
  3 infects **4** lodges

(35)

空所を含む1文目は「ステイシーは、珍しい病気に対して変わった～をもっている」とあります。選択肢を見ると、strange が修飾する名詞として、「後退」「割合」「等式」ではなく、fascination「魅せられること」が当てはまると考えられます。続く2文目の「幼い頃から、病状に関する本を数え切れないほど読んできたから」からも確認することができますね。

ステイシーは、珍しい病気に不思議な魅力を感じる。幼い頃から、病気の症状に関する本を数え切れないほど読んできたという。

正解 □ fascination 魅せられること
誤答 □ recession （一時的な）景気の後退、不景気、退去
　　 □ proportion 割合、比率
　　 □ equation 等式、複雑な問題
英文 □ disease 病気　□ countless 数えきれない　□ medical condition 病気の症状

(36)

まず、人物Aが「変に聞こえるかもしれませんが、最近チーズ入りのチョコレートを～しています」と言っています。それを受けて人物Bが「それを聞いて、妻が妊娠中に辛いものを食べるのをやめられなかったのを思い出しました」と言っていることから、妊娠中の味覚の変化についての会話だと推測できます。人物Aの発言の中の「チーズ入りのチョコレート」はおかしな食べ物として表現されていて、妊娠中だった人物Bの妻が辛いものばかり食べていたのと同じように、人物Aがそれを欲していると考えると会話が成り立つので、空所には「切望している」を表す語が適しています。

A：おかしな話ですが、最近チーズ入りのチョコレートが食べたくなってきました。
B：それを聞いて、妻が妊娠中に辛いものを食べるのをやめられなかったのを思い出しました。

正解 □ crave …を切望する
誤答 □ cater 出向いて（パーティーなど）の仕出しをする、料理を提供する
　　 □ agitate …を揺り動かす、（人）を不安にする、…を動揺させる
　　 □ discard …を捨てる、…を放棄する、…を解雇する
英文 □ remind A of B AにBを思い出させる　□ pregnant 妊娠した

(37)

devour は「むさぼり読む」の意味の動詞なので、空所の後に続く名詞が books であることを確認したら、選択肢の中にこの動詞が入っているのを見た瞬間に「本をむさぼり読む」しかないという思考で解答できるのが理想でしょう。devour の意味があやふやな場合でも、1文目で「ジェニファーはクラスのトップである」とあり、2文目に「彼女は多くの時間を図書館で過ごし、あらゆるジャンルの本を～している」とあることから、空所には「止める」「感染する」「提出する」のどれも当てはまらないことがわかりますね。

ジェニファーはクラスのトップである。彼女は多くの時間を図書館で過ごし、あらゆるジャンルの本を読みあさる。

正解 □ devour …をむさぼり読む
誤答 □ halt …を止める
　　 □ infect …に感染する、…に侵入する
　　 □ lodge （訴状・申告書など）を提出する、（人）を泊める
英文 □ at the top 首位に　□ subject テーマ

(38) One of the more ( ) aspects of working as a programmer is checking for errors. It is similar to searching through a textbook for a single spelling mistake.

  1 painstaking   **2** sturdy

  3 discreet   **4** improper

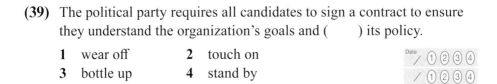

(39) The political party requires all candidates to sign a contract to ensure they understand the organization's goals and ( ) its policy.

  1 wear off   **2** touch on

  3 bottle up   **4** stand by

(40) A: I'm worried about what to do if the university doesn't accept my application.

    B: You shouldn't ( ) it. It's smart to have a backup plan.

  1 bank on   **2** aspire to

  3 pass through   **4** hang around

(38) 🔍 空所を含む1文目は「プログラマーとして働いていて〜な点のひとつは、エラーのチェックである」と言っています。2文目は「教科書の中にあるスペルミス1つを探し出すのに似ている」とあるので、これが1文目の「〜な点」についての説明だと考えられます。字がたくさんある教科書の中のスペルミスを探すのは大変骨の折れる仕事であると考え、選択肢から「骨の折れる」を意味する語を選びましょう。

🔁 プログラマーとして働いていて苦労する点のひとつは、エラーのチェックである。教科書の中からスペルミス1つを探し出すのに似ている。

✏️ [正解] ☐ painstaking 骨の折れる
　　　[誤答] ☐ sturdy (物) 丈夫な、(体) たくましい
　　　　　　 ☐ discreet (人・考えなど) 思慮深い、分別のある、慎重な、控えめな、目立たない
　　　　　　 ☐ improper (場所・目的などに) 不適当な、(事実・規則などに) 合わない、不道徳な
　　　[英文] ☐ aspect 側面、状況、見方　☐ check for …がないか調べる・確認する

(39) 🔍 文頭から contract までで「その政党は、すべての候補者に契約書への署名を求めている」と言っています。それに続く to は「〜するために」という目的を表す用法で、「組織の目標を理解し、その方針を〜することを確認するために」という意味になるので、空所には「守る」を意味するイディオムが入ります。

🔁 その政党は、組織の目標を理解し、その方針に従うことを約束させるために、すべての候補者に契約書への署名を求めている。

✏️ [正解] ☐ stand by (約束や方針を) 堅く守る
　　　[誤答] ☐ wear off …をすりへらす、…を徐々になくす
　　　　　　 ☐ touch on …に簡単に触れる、…に関係する、(行為・態度などが) …に近い
　　　　　　 ☐ bottle up (怒り・不平など) を抑える、…を隠す、(交通など) を封鎖する、…を瓶に密封する
　　　[英文] ☐ political party 政党　☐ require X to *do* Xに…するよう求める　☐ candidate 候補者
　　　　　　 ☐ ensure (that 節) …を確実にする

(40) 🔍 人物 A が「大学が願書を受理しなかったらどうしよう」と心配しています。それに対し、人物Bの応答は「〜するべきでないですよ」から始まり、「代替案を考えておくのが賢明です」と、述べています。代替案を考える方がいいと言っているので、「〜すべきでない」の空所には「あてにする、頼る」の意味のイディオムが入ります。日本語訳だけを考えると、「期待する」の意味で aspire to も入りそうですが、to の後には本人が達成したいと強く望んで行動するような内容がくるので、「(相手方の) 願書の受理」は不適当と考えられます。

🔁 A：大学が私の願書を受理しなかったらどうしようかと心配しています。
　　 B：そんなことは当てにしない方がいいですよ。万一の場合の計画を立てておくのが賢明です。

✏️ [正解] ☐ bank on …を当てにする・頼る (= count on, rely on)
　　　[誤答] ☐ aspire to …を熱望する
　　　　　　 ☐ pass through …を通り抜ける
　　　　　　 ☐ hang around …のあたりをぶらぶらする、(人) と一緒にいる
　　　[英文] ☐ be worried about …が心配である　☐ smart 賢明な　☐ backup plan 代替案

(41) Although it was his birthday party, Jeff (　　) from all his guests to walk alone by the shore. He preferred the quiet beauty of nature to crowds of people.

1	singled out	**2**	slipped away
3	backed down	**4**	broke up

(42) While many tourists take a few photos and quickly move on to the next destination, Isabel usually sits in the same place for hours, (　　) the scenery.

1	taking in	**2**	tearing up
3	tipping off	**4**	tucking away

(43) A successful presentation is not simply about memorizing the script, but depends on how well the message is (　　) to the audience.

1	articulated	**2**	deported
3	betrayed	**4**	huddled

(41) 🔍 主語は Jeff で、Although で始まる1文目の冒頭は「彼の誕生日会だったのに」です。空所を含む1文目の主節は「ジェフは招待客から〜して、海岸を一人で歩いた」とあります。誕生日会にふさわしくない行動を選択肢から選ぶと、「こっそり離れる」の意味を表すものが正解だとわかります。2文目が「彼は大勢の人間よりも静かな自然の美しさを好んだ」と、1文目の行動の理由を説明していることからも、文脈を確認することができますね。

🔁 自分の誕生日会であるにもかかわらず、ジェフは招待客から逃れるように海岸を一人で歩いた。彼は、大勢の人間よりも静かな自然の美しさが好きだったのだ。

✏️ [正解] ☐ slip away こっそり去る
[誤答] ☐ single out …を選び出す
☐ back down 手を引く、引き下がる
☐ break up ばらばらになる、終わりになる、企業が分割される
[英文] ☐ shore 海岸 ☐ prefer A to B Bより Aの方をむしろ好む ☐ crows of たくさんの…

(42) 🔍 接続詞 While で始まる従属節は「多くの観光客が数枚の写真を撮ったら、すぐに次の目的地に移動する一方で」という意味です。後半の「イザベルはいつも同じ場所に何時間も座って景色を〜している」から、景色に対して座って行うことを考えると空所に当てはまるのは「眺めている」だとわかります。

🔁 多くの観光客が数枚の写真を撮ったら、すぐに次の目的地に移動するのに対し、イザベルはいつも同じ場所に何時間も座って、景色を眺めている。

✏️ [正解] ☐ take in …をじっくり見る
[誤答] ☐ tear up …をずたずたに引き裂く、(床・道路など)を掘り起こす、…に穴をあける、(協定など)を破棄する
☐ tip off (人)に密告する、(人)にこっそり教える、(人)に密告して逃亡させる
☐ tuck away …をしまい込む、…を人目につかない場所に隠す
[英文] ☐ move on to (次の場所)へ移る ☐ destination 目的地、行き先 ☐ scenery 景色、風景

(43) 🔍 A successful presentation is not 〜 but …とあるので、「〜ではなくて…」の構文だとわかります。「成功しているプレゼンというのは、単に原稿を暗記するものではなく、メッセージがどのように聴衆に〜するかにかかっている」とあるので、「伝わる」の意味の語が入ります。空所の前には be 動詞の is があるので、「どのようにメッセージが明らかに表現されるか」のように受け身で意味を考えるとわかりやすいでしょう。

🔁 プレゼンテーションの成功は、単に原稿を暗記できるかではなく、メッセージをいかに聞き手に明確に伝えるかにかかっている。

✏️ [正解] ☐ articulate …を明確に表現する
[誤答] ☐ deport (外国人など)を国外に追放する
☐ betray (人・約束・信頼など)を裏切る
☐ huddle 身を寄せ合う、うずくまる
[英文] ☐ presentation プレゼンテーション、発表 ☐ memorize …を記憶する
☐ script 原稿、台本 ☐ depend on …による

筆記 1

(44) There are several (　　) kinds of mushrooms in this region, but their poisonous counterparts look extremely similar.

   1 gracious   **2** legitimate

   3 edible   **4** nomadic

(45) Michael felt (　　) to his co-workers for all they had done for him during his career, so he carefully considered the perfect thank-you gift for each of them.

   1 indispensable   **2** indifferent

   3 indebted   **4** inevitable

(46) Climate scientists recognize that plastic waste is causing harm to the environment. To address this issue, researchers are developing new materials that (　　) more quickly.

   1 decompose   **2** extinguish

   3 collaborate   **4** merge

(44) 🔍 空所を含む前半は「この地域には～なキノコが何種類かある」です。but から始まる後半の文に poisonous counterparts「有毒な対応するもの」、つまり「毒のあるキノコ」は「それらとよく似ている」とあるので、前半では「毒のないキノコ」について説明しているとわかり、空所には「毒のない、食べられる」を意味する語が入ると確認できます。

🔄 この地域には食用のキノコが何種類かあるが、毒キノコはそれらとよく似ている。

✏️
- 正解 ☐ edible 食べられる
- 誤答 ☐ gracious 思いやりのある、(目下に対して) 寛大な、(生活などが) 優雅な
  - ☐ legitimate 理にかなった、合法な
  - ☐ nomadic 遊動の、遊牧 (生活) の
- 英文 ☐ poisonous 有毒な　☐ counterpart 対応するもの　☐ extremely きわめて

(45) 🔍 空所を含む前半は「マイケルはこれまでのキャリアで同僚たちが色々としてくれたことに～を感じた」とあるので、「恩義」を表す語が入るとわかります。選択肢はすべて in- がついていてまぎらわしいですが、落ち着いて単語の意味を考えて、ミスをしないように気をつけましょう。実際に何をしたのかは so 以下の「一人一人に最適なお礼の品を慎重に検討した」から明らかになります。

🔄 マイケルは、これまでのキャリアでお世話になった同僚たちに恩義を感じ、一人一人に最適なお礼の品を慎重に検討した。

✏️
- 正解 ☐ indebted 恩義を受けて
- 誤答 ☐ indispensable 絶対必要な、なくてはならない
  - ☐ indifferent (人が) 無関心な、(物事が) 重要でない
  - ☐ inevitable 避けられない
- 英文 ☐ co-worker 同僚　☐ consider …をよく考える　☐ thank-you お礼の

(46) 🔍 1文目には「気候学者は、プラスチック廃棄物が環境に害を及ぼしていることを認識している」とあり、2文目には「この問題に対処するため、研究者はより早く～する新素材を開発している」とあります。プラスチックに代わり、環境に害を及ぼさない新素材の特徴を選択肢から選ぶと、「消す」「共同して働く」「併合する」ではなく「分解する」が最も適切だと考えられるでしょう。

🔄 気候学者は、プラスチック廃棄物が環境に害を及ぼしていることを認識している。この問題に対処するため、研究者はより早く分解する新素材を開発している。

✏️
- 正解 ☐ decompose 分解する
- 誤答 ☐ extinguish (火・光など) を消す
  - ☐ collaborate 共同して働く
  - ☐ merge 併合する、合体する
- 英文 ☐ recognize (that 節) (事実として) …を認める　☐ harm 害　☐ cause …の原因となる
  - ☐ address …に取り組む　☐ issue 問題点　☐ develop …を開発する
  - ☐ material 物質、素材

(47) Some regions of the country are experiencing a severe (   ).
Restrictions will be enforced until the summer's end to ensure all
citizens have enough water for drinking and washing.

1 drought **2** surplus
3 utility **4** raffle

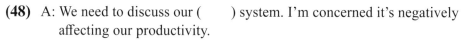

(48) A: We need to discuss our (   ) system. I'm concerned it's negatively
affecting our productivity.
B: Yes, I've been trying to set up a meeting with Carrie from the IT
department about a big upgrade.

1 pending **2** secular
3 eloquent **4** outdated

(49) The research team (   ) Rick as their leader since he had more than
10 years of experience in the industry.

1 decayed **2** expedited
3 incurred **4** designated

(47) 🔍 1文目には「その国のいくつかの地域は深刻な〜に見舞われている」とあります。空所には起こっては困るようなことが入ると推測できるでしょう。続く2文目の「すべての国民が飲料水や洗濯に十分な水を確保できるよう、夏の終わりまで制限が実施される予定である」から、水が足りない状況について書かれているとわかるので、空所には「干ばつ」を表す語が入ると確認できるでしょう。

🔄 その国には深刻な干ばつに見舞われている地域もある。すべての住民が飲料水や洗濯に十分な水を確保できるよう、夏の終わりまで制限が実施される予定である。

✏️ 正解 ☐ drought 干ばつ
誤答 ☐ surplus 余剰、余り
　　 ☐ utility 効用、有用性、有益
　　 ☐ raffle （慈善や購入資金調達のために売り出す）福引くじ
英文 ☐ restriction 制限、規制　☐ enforce …を実施する
　　 ☐ ensure（that 節）…を確実にする、…を保証する

(48) 🔍 人物 A が「〜のシステムについて相談する必要があります。生産性に悪影響を及ぼしているのではと心配しています」と言っていて、その解決法として、人物 B は「IT 部門のキャリーと大規模なアップグレードについての会議を設定しようとしています」と答えているので、人物 A の示した問題点はシステムが古いことからくるものと考えられます。したがって空所には「古い、旧式の」を表す形容詞が入ります。

🔄 A：当社の旧式のシステムについて相談する必要があります。生産性に悪影響を及ぼしているのではと心配しています。
B：はい、IT 部門のキャリーと大規模なアップグレードについての会議の日時を決めようとしています。

✏️ 正解 ☐ outdated 旧式の
誤答 ☐ pending 未決定の、審理中の
　　 ☐ secular 世俗的な、非宗教的な
　　 ☐ eloquent （人が）雄弁な、（文体など）人を動かす力のある、表情豊かな
英文 ☐ be concerned（that 節）…だと心配している　☐ negatively 悪く
　　 ☐ affect …に影響を及ぼす　☐ productivity 生産性　☐ upgrade アップグレード

(49) 🔍 「その調査チームはリックをリーダーとして〜した」とあるので、空所には「任命する、指名する」を表す語を入れるのが適切です。since 以下ではその理由として「この業界において10年以上の経験があるから」と言っていることから、文意が確認できます。

🔄 調査チームは、この業界で10年以上の経験があることからリックをリーダーに指名した。

✏️ 正解 ☐ designate …を指名する（designate A as B A を B に指名する）
誤答 ☐ decay （物が徐々に・自然に）腐敗する、（建物などが）老朽化する
　　 ☐ expedite （行動・計画など）をはかどらせる、…を促進する、（仕事など）を手早く片づける
　　 ☐ incur （負債・損害など）を負う、（危険・非難・怒りなど）をまねく
英文 ☐ have X years of experience X 年の経験がある

🚩 **(47) 1　(48) 4　(49) 4**

(50) Robert chooses the most luxurious hotels for his vacations. Rooftop pools and a large dining hall are (　　　) that make his stays more enjoyable.

1　catastrophes　　2　resolutions
3　fragrances　　　4　amenities

(51) The largest storm of the century ended (　　　). One moment the wind was roaring, but the next moment the sun was shining.

1　invariably　　2　primarily
3　abruptly　　　4　keenly

(52) Roberto had an exceptional (　　　) for languages from a young age. He could memorize new vocabulary much more quickly than other students.

1　ration　　　2　limitation
3　aptitude　　4　coverage

(50)

🔍 1文目は「ロバートは、休暇を過ごすホテルは最高級のものを選んでいる」と言っています。2文目にその理由として、「屋上プールや大食堂が滞在をより楽しくしてくれる〜である」とあるので、空所にはホテルにあれば、滞在が楽しくなるものである「設備、アメニティー」の意味の語を入れましょう。

📖 ロバートは、休暇を過ごすホテルには最高級のものを選んでいる。屋上プールや大食堂が滞在をより楽しくしてくれる設備である。

✏️ 正解 □ amenity 快適な設備
誤答 □ catastrophe (突然の)大惨事、大災害、大失敗
□ resolution (議会などの)決議、決心、(問題などの)解決
□ fragrance 芳香、香水
英文 □ luxurious 一流の、豪華な □ dining hall 食堂 □ stay 滞在 □ enjoyable 楽しい

(51)

🔍 空所を含む1文目は「今世紀最大の暴風雨は〜終わった」です。空所には動詞 end を修飾する副詞が入ります。続く文がその状況について説明しています。「風が唸ったかと思うと、次の瞬間には太陽が輝き出した」とあるので、暴風雨がどのように終わったかというと、「変わることなく」でも「主として」でも「鋭く」でもなく、「突然に」終わったという意味が当てはまると考えることができます。

📖 今世紀最大の暴風雨は突然終わった。風が唸っていたかと思うと、次の瞬間には太陽が輝き出した。

✏️ 正解 □ abruptly 突然
誤答 □ invariably 変わることなく、常に
□ primarily 主として、第一に、初めは
□ keenly (感覚・洞察力など)鋭く、(風・寒さなど)厳しく、(苦痛など)強烈に
英文 □ the(最大級) X of the century その世紀で最も…の X □ roar 轟音を立てる
□ one moment ..., but the next moment 〜 …かと思うと次の瞬間には〜

(52)

🔍 1文目には「ロベルトは、幼い頃から語学に並外れた〜を持っていた」とあります。この時点で当てはまるのは「配給量」「制約」「適用範囲」ではなく、「才能」を表す選択肢だと推測できます。2文目の「彼は他の生徒よりもずっと早く単語を覚えることができたから」で、1文目の内容に関して理由を述べていることからも当てはまる語を確認することができますね。

📖 ロベルトは、幼い頃から語学に並々ならぬ才能を持っていた。彼は他の生徒よりもずっと早く新出語を覚えることができた。

✏️ 正解 □ aptitude 才能、素質
誤答 □ ration (食料・燃料・衣料などの一定)配給量
□ limitation 制約、規制
□ coverage (保険の)適用範囲、保証範囲、(報道・取材の)範囲
英文 □ exceptional 並外れた □ memorize …を覚える

(53) The doctor was (　　) by the results of his patient's surgery. He had never seen anyone recover so quickly before.

    1 bewildered   **2** alleviated

    3 accused   **4** disrupted

(54) The emergency system was activated shortly after the earthquake, prompting the local government to call for the (　　) of residents living near the coast.

    1 leverage   **2** distraction

    3 evacuation   **4** breakout

(55) Life in modern society is (　　) and stressful, but we rarely find ourselves in the kind of mortal danger that our ancestors often experienced.

    1 rapt   **2** savvy

    3 martial   **4** hectic

(53) 🔍 1文目で「医師は、患者の手術の結果によって〜された」とあります。続く文には「彼はこれほど早く回復した人を見たことがなかった」という理由が書いてあることから、空所には「びっくりした、当惑した」を表す語が適切だとわかります。

🔁 医師は、患者の手術の結果に困惑していた。彼はこれほど早く回復した人を見たことがなかった。

✏️ 正解 ☐ **bewilder** …を当惑させる
誤答 ☐ **alleviate** (苦痛など)を軽くする、(問題など)を緩和する
☐ **accuse** (人)を(…のかどで)告発する (accuse A (人) of B の形)、…を非難する
☐ **disrupt** …の構造を破壊する、(会議・集会など)を混乱させる、(交通・通信など)を中断させる
英文 ☐ **surgery** 手術 ☐ **see X do** X が…するのを見る

(54) 🔍 「地震発生後すぐに緊急システムが作動した」の後、prompting ではじまる分詞構文の句が続きます。「沿岸に住む住民に〜を呼びかけるよう地元の自治体に促した」と言っているので、地震発生後に住民に呼びかける内容として、「避難」だと考えることができるでしょう。

🔁 地震発生後すぐに緊急システムが作動し、沿岸に住む住民に避難を呼びかけるよう地元の自治体に指示を送った。

✏️ 正解 ☐ **evacuation** 避難
誤答 ☐ **leverage** てこの作用、影響力
☐ **distraction** 気の散ること、気晴らし、心の混乱
☐ **breakout** 内訳、明細、(病気などの)突然の発生、吹き出物、(囚人などの)集団脱走
英文 ☐ **activate** …を作動させる ☐ **shortly after** …のすぐ後に
☐ **prompt X to do** X を促して…させる ☐ **call for** …を必要とする、…を要請する

(55) 🔍 前半の「現代社会の生活は〜で、ストレスも多い」より、空所には「ストレスが多い」と同じようにネガティブな意味の形容詞が入ると予想できます。逆接の but から続く節「しかし、私たちの祖先がしばしば経験したような命の危険にさらされることはほとんどない」では、「〜だけれども、命の危険にさらされることはない」と情報を追加していると読み取ることができます。選択肢の中から空所には「慌ただしい」を表す語を選ぶことができると考えられるでしょう。

🔁 現代社会の生活は慌ただしく、ストレスも多いが、私たちの祖先がしばしば経験したような命の危険にさらされることはほとんどない。

✏️ 正解 ☐ **hectic** 慌ただしい
誤答 ☐ **rapt** 心を奪われた、熱中した
☐ **savvy** (事情に)精通している
☐ **martial** 戦争の、軍事の、勇ましい
英文 ☐ **stressful** ストレスの多い、精神的に疲れる ☐ **rarely** まれにしか…しない
☐ **find oneself** 自分が…だと気づく ☐ **mortal** 命にかかわる ☐ **ancestor** 先祖

(56) Before visiting a foreign country, (   ) yourself with the local culture and customs is recommended to avoid misunderstandings and provide a more enjoyable experience.

1 acquainting   **2** compelling

3 disclosing   **4** browsing

(57) A: Your apartment certainly is (   ) for a university student.

B: Actually, it's my uncle's, so I don't even have to pay rent. There's no way I could afford to live here otherwise.

1 obtainable   **2** luxurious

3 questionable   **4** harmonious

(58) Lisa (   ) for the community center's preservation after listening to a number of complaints presented by locals who valued the institution.

1 grieved   **2** advocated

3 substituted   **4** integrated

(56) 🔍 文頭の副詞句は「外国を訪問する前に」という修飾をしています。「誤解を防ぎ、楽しい体験をもたらすので、自分自身を地元の文化と習慣に〜することが推奨されます」とあるので、「慣れさせる、知らせる」を表す語が文意に当てはまると考えられます。

📲 外国を訪問する前にその国の文化や習慣を知ると、誤解を避けられ、より楽しい体験ができるようになるため、そうすることをお勧めします。

✏️ 正解 ☐ acquaint（人）に精通させる（acquaint oneself with で「…に精通する」）
誤答 ☐ compel（人・もの）に無理に…させる
☐ disclose（隠れた物、秘密など）を明らかにする、…を発表する、…を開示する
☐ browse（本など）を拾い読みする、（ウェブページ・データなど）を閲覧する
英文 ☐ avoid …を避ける ☐ misunderstanding 誤解 ☐ provide …を与える
☐ enjoyable 楽しい

(57) 🔍 人物Aは「あなたのアパートは大学生としては〜ですね」と人物Bに話しています。それに対して人物Bは Actually, 「実は」と人物Aの予想に反することを切り出す前置きをして、「叔父の家なので家賃もかからないんです。そうでなければ、ここに住めるわけがありません」と言っています。otherwise は「別のやり方だと、そうでなければ」で、「ここがもし叔父の家ではなく、家賃がかかってしまうのであれば」の意味だと理解します。人物Aは学生にとってお金がかかるものを予想しながら発話したと考えられるので、「高価な、豪華な」の意味の形容詞を正解に選びましょう。

📲 A：あなたのアパートは大学生にしては豪華ですね。
B：実は、叔父の家なので家賃もかからないんです。そうでなければ、ここに住めるわけがありません。

✏️ 正解 ☐ luxurious 豪華な
誤答 ☐ obtainable 得られる、入手できる
☐ questionable（真実性など）疑わしい、（正直さ、礼儀などに）問題のある
☐ harmonious 調和した、仲のよい
英文 ☐ rent 家賃 ☐ There is no way ＋節 …するのは無理だ・到底できない
☐ can afford to *do* …する余裕がある ☐ otherwise そうでなければ

(58) 🔍 主語は Lisa で空所には過去形の動詞が入ります。全体は「リサは、公民館を大切にする地元の人たちから出される数々の苦情を聞いた後で、公民館の保存を〜した」の意味です。公民館を大切にしている人たちの意見を聞いてからすることは、公民館の保存を推し進める方向性の事柄だと考えられるので、空所には「悲しんだ」「交代した」「統合した」ではなく、「主張した」の意味の語を入れると文意が成り立ちます。

📲 リサは、公民館を大切にしている地元の人たちから出された数々の苦情を聞き、公民館を保存すべきだと主張した。

✏️ 正解 ☐ advocate 主張する（ここでは自動詞。advocate for …を主張する）
誤答 ☐ grieve 深く悲しむ
☐ substitute 代わりになる、交代する
☐ integrate 統合する、まとまる、人種（宗教）差別を廃止する
英文 ☐ preservation 保存 ☐ a number of 多くの ☐ complaint 苦情、不満
☐ present …を提出する、…を寄せる ☐ locals 地元の人 ☐ value …を大切にする
☐ institution 公共の建物、施設

(59) Having spent a week away from his garden, Scott returned to find his plants (   ). But he knew they would return to their previous state after plenty of water and some nutrients.

1 swapped   **2** withered

3 dictated   **4** incriminated

(60) Laura's (   ) all respect her as an authority on genetics and often look to her for support with their own research papers.

1 outsiders   **2** peers

3 assets   **4** blades

(61) The meeting experienced (   ) from the start due to miscommunication about the time and location, as well as mistakes with the day's agenda.

1 venues   **2** tributes

3 diplomas   **4** setbacks

(59) 🔍 1文目では「一週間、庭を離れた後に、スコットは戻って、植物が～であることに気づいた」とあります。ここで空所に入る語を選択肢から選ぶとおそらく「交換した」「指図した」「罪を負わせた」ではなく、「枯れた」だと推測できるでしょう。続く「しかし、水をたっぷりやり、栄養を与えれば、また元の状態に戻ることを知っていた」を読んで、文意が成立することを確認しましょう。

📝 一週間庭から離れたスコットは、戻ってくると植物がしおれていることに気づいた。しかし、水をたっぷりやり、栄養を与えれば、また元の状態に戻ることはわかっていた。

✏️ 正解 ☐ wither …をしおれさせる
　　誤答 ☐ swap …を交換する、…を取り換える
　　　　 ☐ dictate (用件) を書き取らせる、…を指図する
　　　　 ☐ incriminate (人) に罪を負わせる、(証拠・証言などが) …が有罪であることを示す、…を (害悪などの) 原因とみなす
　　英文 ☐ find X ＋過去分詞 X が…されているのを見つける　☐ previous 以前の
　　　　 ☐ nutrient 栄養分、栄養剤

(60) 🔍 「ローラの～は皆、彼女を遺伝学の権威として尊敬していて、自分たちの研究論文のサポートを求めることもしばしばある」という内容です。「ローラを尊敬していて、助けを求める」のはおそらくローラに近い関係で、仲間であると考えられるので、選択肢より「同僚」の意味を表す語句を選べばいいことがわかるでしょう。

📝 ローラの仲間は皆、彼女を遺伝学の権威として尊敬しており、自分たちの研究論文のサポートを求めることもしばしばある。

✏️ 正解 ☐ peer 同僚、仲間
　　誤答 ☐ outsider 外部の人、よそ者、のけ者
　　　　 ☐ asset 有益な人、利点、強み
　　　　 ☐ blade (刃物の) 刀身、(草の) 葉
　　英文 ☐ authority 権威　☐ genetics 遺伝学　☐ look to A for B A (人) の B を頼りにする
　　　　 ☐ research paper 研究論文

(61) 🔍 「そのミーティングは最初から時間や場所の連絡ミスによって～があり、その日のアジェンダにも間違いがあった」という内容です。「時間や場所の連絡ミス」というのはおそらく、良くないことであり、アジェンダにも間違いがあった、と続いているので、空所には、何らかの困りごとが入ると考えられます。選択肢から「妨げ」を表す setbacks を選ぶとしっくりくるでしょう。

📝 会議は最初から時間や場所の連絡ミスによって進行が妨げられ、その日のアジェンダにも間違いがあった。

✏️ 正解 ☐ setback 妨げ
　　誤答 ☐ venue (競技・会議などの) 開催指定地、会場
　　　　 ☐ tribute 敬意のあかしとしてささげるもの、賛辞
　　　　 ☐ diploma 卒業証書、資格証明書
　　英文 ☐ due to …が原因で　☐ miscommunication 誤った連絡
　　　　 ☐ A as well as B A と同様に B も　☐ agenda 協議事項、検討議題

(62) Karl traveled across a number of countries to try and (　　) himself in different cultures. He became fluent in several languages and now works as an interpreter.

1　pinch 　　　　　　2　enforce
3　supervise 　　　　4　immerse

(63) A: The locals say their parks are particularly beautiful at this time of year.
B: Actually, I was hoping to visit the (　　) garden for the new desert exhibition.

1　botanical 　　　　2　curable
3　lunar 　　　　　　4　ongoing

(64) A: I'm sorry to call you so early, but can you (　　) Jaden today? He took the day off.
B: I wish I could help you, but I have other plans today.

1　figure out 　　　　2　count in
3　cover for 　　　　4　stir up

(62) 🔍 空所を含む1文目には「カールは、彼自身を異文化に〜ために多くの国々を旅した」とあります。続いて、彼がその結果、「数カ国語を流暢に操れるようになり、現在は通訳として働いている」ことが書かれているので、空所には「異文化に浸る、没頭する」の意味になるように語を入れるのが適切だと考えられます。

🔁 カールは、異文化に浸るために多くの国々を旅した。数カ国語を流暢に操れるようになり、現在は通訳として働いている。

✏️ 正解 ☐ immerse …を没頭させる
誤答 ☐ pinch（体の一部）をつねる、…をつまむ、（靴・帽子などが）…を締めつける
☐ enforce（法律など）を施行する、…を実施する、（服従・行動など）を強いる、…を強要する、（要求など）を強く主張する
☐ supervise（人・仕事など）を監督する、…を指揮する、…を管理する
英文 ☐ a number of 多くの ☐ fluent 流暢な ☐ interpreter 通訳者

(63) 🔍 人物 A は「地元の人は、この時期の公園は特に美しいと言います」と人物 B に話しています。それに対して人物 B は「実は、新しい砂漠の展示を見に〜庭に行きたかったのです」と答えていることから、空所には庭を修飾する形容詞が入ります。選択肢より「植物の」という意味の語を選びましょう。

🔁 A：地元の人は、この時期の公園は特に美しいと言います。
B：実は、植物園の新しい砂漠の展示を見に行きたかったんです。

✏️ 正解 ☐ botanical 植物の
誤答 ☐ curable 治癒できる、治せる
☐ lunar 月の、月の作用による、（光など）青ざめた
☐ ongoing 続いている、進行中の
英文 ☐ locals 地元の人 ☐ at this time of year この時期には ☐ desert 砂漠
☐ exhibition 展示

(64) 🔍 人物 A が人物 B に「こんなに早く電話して申し訳ありません」と謝罪しつつ、but 以下で「今日、ジェイデン〜ができますか」と質問しています。ジェイデンは休暇を取ったと言っているので、空所には「〜の代わりを務める」の意味の語が入るとわかります。続いて人物 B が「お手伝いできればいいのですが、今日は別の予定があります」と、丁寧に断っていることも確認しておきましょう。

🔁 A：こんなに朝早く電話して申し訳ないのですが、今日ジェイデンの代わりをしてくれませんか。彼は今日休みを取ったんです。
B：お手伝いできればいいのですが、今日は別の予定があります。

✏️ 正解 ☐ cover for …の代わりを務める
誤答 ☐ figure out（問題など）を解決する、（理由など）がわかる、（経費など）を計算して出す
☐ count in …を勘定に入れる、…を仲間に入れる
☐ stir up（騒ぎなど）を引き起こす、（人・気持ちなど）を奮起させる、…をかきたてる
英文 ☐ day off 休暇

(65) While other companies profit from installation fees, GAD keeps additional expenses to a minimum. Therefore, customers that (　　　) the monthly plan can expect to halve their current costs.

1　show off 　　　2　play along

3　opt for 　　　　4　tone down

(66) The speaker thanked the audience for attending his presentation, and said, "Please don't hesitate to (　　　) me. For urgent matters, call the telephone number listed on my business card."

1　reach out to 　　2　break in on

3　work up to 　　　4　follow up with

(67) Since George moved out, his parents hope to turn his bedroom into a study. They intend to (　　　) most of his childhood belongings to make space.

1　step down 　　　2　toss out

3　block up 　　　　4　chip in

(65) 🔍 1文目は「他の企業が設置費用で利益を得ているのに対し、GAD は追加費用を最小限に抑えている」です。続いて「それゆえに、月額プランを~する顧客は、現在のコストが半減することが期待できる」とあります。空所には「設定、選択する」の内容を表すイディオムを選ぶと、GAD の月額プランを選んだ顧客が得をするという内容が成立します。Therefore から始まる2文目の主語は customers を that ... plan までが修飾していて長めです。

🔄 他社が設置費用で利益を得ているのに対し、GAD は追加費用を最小限に抑えている。そのため、月額プランを選択した顧客は、現在のコストが半減することが期待できる。

✏️ 正解 ☐ opt for …を選ぶ
誤答 ☐ show off (力量・富・知識など) を見せびらかす、…を引き立てる
☐ play along 調子を合わせる、協力する
☐ tone down (語気・調子など) を和らげる、(ラジオなど) の音量を下げる
英文 ☐ profit from …から利益を得る ☐ installation 設置 ☐ halve …を半減させる

(66) 🔍 講演者が、聴衆が講演に出席したことに感謝して、伝えた内容が「遠慮なく~してください。緊急の場合は、名刺に記載されている電話番号に電話してください」なので、空所には「連絡をして」の意味が入るとわかります。listed ... が直前の number を修飾していることも意識して理解しましょう。

🔄 講演者は、聴衆が講演にきてくれたことに感謝し、「遠慮なく声をかけてください。緊急の場合は、名刺に記載されている電話番号に電話してください」と述べた。

✏️ 正解 ☐ reach out to …に連絡を取ろうとする
誤答 ☐ break in on …を襲う、(話など) に割り込む
☐ work up to …ができるように準備する、盛り上がって…に達する
☐ follow up with …の後に続ける
英文 ☐ presentation 発表、プレゼンテーション ☐ urgent 緊急の ☐ business card 名刺

(67) 🔍 1文目で「ジョージが引っ越していなくなったので、両親は彼の寝室を書斎にするつもりだ」と言っています。study の意味がすぐにわからなくても、a がついているので何か具体的なものだと判断します。空所を含む2文目は「両親はジョージの子どもの頃の持ち物はほとんど~して、スペースを確保しようと考えている」とありますので、スペースを確保するためにすることは何かと考えましょう。子どもの頃の持ち物を「捨てる」の意味になる語を入れると文意が成り立ちます。

🔄 ジョージが引っ越したので、両親は彼の寝室を書斎にするつもりだ。子どもの頃の持ち物はほとんど捨てて、スペースを確保しようと考えている。

✏️ 正解 ☐ toss out (不要なもの) を捨てる
誤答 ☐ step down 車から降りる、(電圧) を下げる、…のスピードを落とす、(地位) から降りる〈from〉、(議論) から引き下がる
☐ block up …をふさぐ、…のじゃまをする
☐ chip in (金・時間など) を出し合う、(話・議論などに) 口を出す
英文 ☐ move out 引っ越して出ていく ☐ study 書斎 ☐ belongings 所持品、財産

🚩 **(65) 3 (66) 1 (67) 2**

(68) Harry went from shop to shop searching for an old-fashioned perfume to please his wife, thinking it would be a suitable ( ) of their younger days.

1 reminder 2 baseline
3 detour 4 controversy

(69) The most difficult part of Sam's ( ) class was trying to memorize the names of the many bones and muscles in the human body.

1 emission 2 chronology
3 anatomy 4 organism

(70) Paul's mother told him to be ( ) when applying for a job. She said that frequently inquiring about his application status would attract the recruiter's attention.

1 persistent 2 tolerant
3 mischievous 4 disgraceful

(68) 🔍 文の前半は「ハリーは、妻を喜ばせようと何軒も店を回って、昔流行った香水を探した」です。その後ろに thinking ... と分詞構文が続き、「その香水は若い頃の、相応しい～だろうと考えたので」とあります。「若い頃の～」との関連を考えると、「ほうふつとさせるもの、思い出させるもの」の意味が当てはまるので、選択肢から「思い出させるもの」を意味する語を選びましょう。

🔄 ハリーは、若い頃を思い出すのにふさわしいと思い、妻を喜ばせようと何軒も店を回って、昔流行った香水を探した。

✏️ 正解 ☐ reminder 思い出させるもの
　　誤答 ☐ baseline 基準線、(テニスや野球の)ベースライン
　　　　☐ detour 遠回り、回り道、迂回路
　　　　☐ controversy (長期にわたる公の)論争、論議
　　英文 ☐ old-fashioned 古風な、昔流行した　☐ perfume 香水　☐ please …を喜ばせる
　　　　☐ younger days 若かりし頃、青春時代

(69) 🔍 「サムの～の授業で一番難しかったのは、人体にあるたくさんの骨や筋肉の名前を覚えることだった」とあるので、空所には授業の科目名が入り、その授業の中では人体の骨や筋肉の名前を覚えるということがわかります。ここから、空所には人体について学ぶ科目名を選びましょう。organism には「有機体、動物」の意味がありますが、人体について学ぶ学問としては、もっと適した選択肢がありますね。

🔄 サムの解剖学の授業で一番難しかったのは、人体にあるたくさんの骨や筋肉の名前を覚えることだった。

✏️ 正解 ☐ anatomy 解剖学
　　誤答 ☐ emission (光・熱・におい・電磁波などの)放射、(煙突・車のエンジンなどからの)排気
　　　　☐ chronology 年代順配列、年表、年代記
　　　　☐ organism 有機体、動物・植物
　　英文 ☐ try to *do* …しようとする　☐ human body 人体

(70) 🔍 空所を含む1文目は「ポールの母親は、求人に応募するときは～ようにと言った」とあり、続く2文目ではその理由として、「頻繁に応募状況を問い合わせると、採用担当者の目に留まる」と言っています。ここから、頻繁に応募状況を問い合わせることは「寛容な」「いたずら好きな」「不名誉な」行動ではなく、「根気強い」行動だと考えられるので、これが当てはまります。

🔄 ポールの母親は、求人に応募するときは根気強くやるようにと言った。頻繁に応募状況を問い合わせると、採用担当者の目に留まるというのだ。

✏️ 正解 ☐ persistent 根気強い
　　誤答 ☐ tolerant (他人の意見などに対して)寛容な
　　　　☐ mischievous いたずら好きな、ちょっと意地の悪い
　　　　☐ disgraceful 恥になる、不名誉な
　　英文 ☐ apply for …に申し込む　☐ inquire about …について問い合わせる
　　　　☐ application status 応募の現状　☐ attract …を引きつける　☐ recruiter 新人採用担当者

(71) Zoe emailed customer service about the product she had recently purchased. She was not sure whether it was (   ) or she simply did not understand how to use it correctly.

1	boundless	2	faulty
3	adverse	4	enviable

(72) Hundreds of sports cars (   ) as their proud owners let them dry in the sun, having just been washed for the sporting event.

1	gleamed	2	manipulated
3	reinforced	4	tumbled

(73) John was unprepared for his trip abroad and seriously (   ) his business partners because he was ignorant of the differences between their cultures.

1	offended	2	clutched
3	broadened	4	retained

(71) 1文目に「ゾーイは、最近購入した製品についてカスタマーサービスにメールを送った」とあることから、ゾーイが何らかの理由でカスタマーサービスを必要としていたことがわかります。2文目で「～なのか、単に使い方がわからないだけなのか、よくわからなかったのだ」と、その理由を述べていると考えられるので、選択肢の中から「欠陥のある」を選び出すことができるでしょう。

ゾーイは、最近購入した製品についてカスタマーサービスにメールを送った。不良品なのか、単に使い方がわからないだけなのか、よくわからなかったのだ。

正解 ☐ faulty 欠陥のある
誤答 ☐ boundless 無限の、限りのない
　　 ☐ adverse 反対の、不利な
　　 ☐ enviable うらやましい
英文 ☐ email …にEメールを送る　☐ customer service お客様対応係
　　 ☐ be not sure whether 節 …かどうかはっきりしない・自信がない

(72) 主語は Hundreds of sports cars で、空所には動詞が入るので、「何百台ものスポーツカーが～した」という文になります。接続詞 as 以降は「誇らしげな所有者たちがそれらを日なたで乾かしているから」で、having 以降に「スポーツイベントのために洗車を終えて」とあります。したがって、洗車後の車が乾かされている状態の描写として適切なのは「きらめいた」となります。

スポーツイベントのために洗車を終え、誇らしげな所有者たちが日なたで乾かしている何百台ものスポーツカーがきらめいていた。

正解 ☐ gleam きらめく
誤答 ☐ manipulate …を巧みに扱う、(問題・事件など) を巧みに処理する、
　　 ☐ reinforce …を強化する、…を補強する
　　 ☐ tumble …を倒す、…をひっくり返す、…を投げ散らす、(建物) を取り壊す
英文 ☐ hundreds of 数百の…　☐ dry 乾く

(73) 空所を含む前半は「ジョンが海外出張の準備をしておらず、取引先の人たちを深刻に～した」という意味です。この時点で、空所には良くない意味の語が入ると推測できます。文の後半に「なぜなら、ジョンは文化の違いを知らなかったからだ」とあるので、選択肢から「怒らせる」の意味を表す語を選ぶとしっくりくるでしょう。

ジョンが海外出張の準備をしておらず、取引先の人たちをひどく怒らせてしまったのは、文化の違いを知らなかったからだ。

正解 ☐ offend …を怒らせる
誤答 ☐ clutch …をぐいとつかむ、…をしっかり握る
　　 ☐ broaden …を広げる、(知識・経験など) を広める
　　 ☐ retain …を保つ、…を保持する、…を維持する
英文 ☐ be unprepared for …に準備ができていない　☐ be ignorant of …を知らない

(74) A: Do you want me to renew our (　　) to that cooking magazine you like?

B: Actually, I noticed the monthly fees increased since last year, so let's cancel it.

1　subscription　　2　capability
3　eternity　　　　4　provocation

(75) A: Director, how would you like me to (　　) my character in this scene?

B: He is losing the war and public opinion is turning against him. You need to express how troubled he is.

1　retain　　　　2　conserve
3　portray　　　4　discriminate

(76) This survey is completely (　　). We will not collect any of your personal information, so please give us your honest opinion about the facilities.

1　anonymous　　2　explicit
3　drastic　　　　4　substantial

(74) 🔍 人物 A は「あなたのお気に入りの料理雑誌についての〜を更新しましょうか」と聞いています。それに対して人物 B は「実は去年から月額料金が上がったそうなので、やめようと思います」と答えています。ここから、A が B に雑誌の何かを更新するかどうか質問していることがわかるので、選択肢から「定期購読」を選びましょう。

🔁 A：あなたのお気に入りの料理雑誌の定期購読を更新しましょうか。
B：実は去年から月額料金が上がったそうなので、やめようと思います。

✏️ 正解 ☐ subscription 定期購読
誤答 ☐ capability 能力、才能、可能性
☐ eternity 永遠、永久不変の真理
☐ provocation 怒らせるもの、挑発、刺激
英文 ☐ renew …を更新する ☐ notice (that 節) …に気がつく ☐ monthly fee 月額料金

筆記 1

(75) 🔍 人物 A の発言は空所を含み、「監督、このシーンでは私のキャラクターをどう〜するべきですか」と人物 B に尋ねています。人物 B は「彼は戦争に負けそうで、世論も彼に敵対しています。どれほど悩んでいるかを表現する必要があります」と答えていることから、人物 A の空所には人物 B の express「表現する」とほぼ同様の意味の「演じる」が入るとわかります。

🔁 A：監督、このシーンでは私のキャラクターをどう演じるべきですか。
B：彼は戦争に負けそうで、世論も彼に敵対しています。どれほど悩んでいるかを表現する必要があります。

✏️ 正解 ☐ portray …を演じる
誤答 ☐ retain …を保持する、…を維持する、…を忘れないで記憶している
☐ conserve …を保存する、…を維持する、（資源など）を節約して使う
☐ discriminate …を識別する、…を区別する、…を差別する
英文 ☐ public opinion 世論 ☐ turn against …に敵対する、…に反発する
☐ troubled 困ったような、悩んで

(76) 🔍 空所を含む1文目は「このアンケートは完全に〜です」という意味です。続いて2文目で、「個人情報を収集することはありませんので、施設に関する率直なご意見をお聞かせください」と説明していることから、空所には「個人情報を収集することはない」によって説明されている、ほぼ同じ意味の語が入ります。

🔁 このアンケートは完全に匿名です。個人情報を収集することはありませんので、施設に関する率直なご意見をお聞かせください。

✏️ 正解 ☐ anonymous 匿名の
誤答 ☐ explicit（言葉が）明示的な、はっきりした、（人・性質などが）率直な、（性・暴力の表現が）露骨な
☐ drastic（薬などが）強烈な、思いきった、抜本的な、徹底的な
☐ substantial 中身のある、実質的な
英文 ☐ personal information 個人情報 ☐ facilities（複数形で）施設、設備

(77) Educational institutions such as universities may be expensive, but they are key to (　　) young people's social and mental abilities.

   1 abolishing   **2** fostering

   3 colonizing   **4** reckoning

(78) Companies that show (　　) towards employees may invest in entertainment facilities, offer social gatherings, and provide more flexible hours to raise productivity in the workplace.

   1 generosity   **2** occupancy

   3 sincerity   **4** residency

(79) Zach is obsessed with his health and well-being. He exercises almost every day, avoids (　　) foods, and doesn't drink alcohol or smoke.

   1 processed   **2** possessive

   3 affluent   **4** hasty

(77) 🔍 前半は「大学などの教育機関は、お金がかかるかもしれない」という意味です。その後に逆接の接続詞 but が続いて、「しかし、それらの教育機関は若者の社会性や精神力を〜する重要な存在である」の「〜する」に当てはまる語を選択肢から考えると「廃止する」「植民地化する」「みなす」ではなく、「育成する」が適切だとわかります。

🔄 大学などの教育機関は、お金はかかるかもしれないが、若者の社会性や精神力を育む重要な存在である。

✏️ 正解 ☐ foster …を育成する
誤答 ☐ abolish (制度・習慣など)を廃止する
☐ colonize (土地)に入植する、(土地)を植民地化する
☐ reckon …と思う、…を(〜と)みなす、…を数える、…を勘定に入れる
英文 ☐ educational institution 教育機関　☐ key to …の秘訣、…の手がかり

(78) 🔍 「従業員に〜を見せている企業は、娯楽施設に投資したり、懇親会を開いたり、職場の生産性を高めるためにフレックスタイムを導入したりすることができる」の空所に当てはまる語を選択肢から考えると「占有」「居住」ではなく「気前のよさ」が適切だと考えられます。日本語の訳からは「誠実さ」も当てはまりそうですが、娯楽施設や懇親会が挙げられていることから、「誠実さ」よりも「気前のよさ」が文脈に合うと考えられます。

🔄 従業員のために出費を惜しまない企業は、娯楽施設に投資したり、懇親会を開いたり、職場の生産性を高めるためにフレックスタイムを導入したりすることができる。

✏️ 正解 ☐ generosity 出し惜しみしないこと、気前のよさ
誤答 ☐ occupancy (土地・建物などの)占有、収容人数、稼働率
☐ sincerity 誠実さ、誠意
☐ residency 居住、外国での居住許可
英文 ☐ entertainment facilities 保養所、娯楽施設　☐ social gathering 懇親会、親睦会
☐ flexible hours フレックスタイム、柔軟な勤務時間　☐ productivity 生産性
☐ workplace 仕事場、職場

(79) 🔍 1文目は「ザックは、自分の健康と幸福にこだわっている」という意味です。具体的な内容は2文目に書かれていて、「彼はほぼ毎日運動をし、〜の食品を避け、酒も飲まず、タバコも吸わない」の空所に入るのは、「健康に悪い」ことを表す形容詞だと推測できます。したがって選択肢より「加工された」を選びましょう。

🔄 ザックは、自分の健康と幸福のことしかかんがえられなくなっている。ほぼ毎日運動をし、加工食品を避け、酒も飲まずタバコも吸わない。

✏️ 正解 ☐ processed 加工された
誤答 ☐ possessive 所有の
☐ affluent 裕福な、豊富な
☐ hasty 急いだ、早まった、そそっかしい
英文 ☐ be obsessed with (考えなど)に取りつかれている　☐ well-being 幸福

🚩 **(77) 2　(78) 1　(79) 1**

(80) With no other strong evidence available, the lawyer hired a professional photographer to (　　) a dark image taken from a security camera at the crime scene.

1 certify　　　　2 enhance
3 prescribe　　　4 shoplift

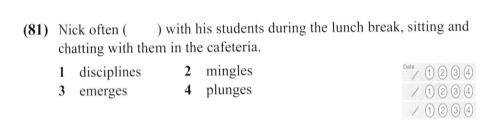

(81) Nick often (　　) with his students during the lunch break, sitting and chatting with them in the cafeteria.

1 disciplines　　2 mingles
3 emerges　　　4 plunges

(82) Fans were certain the previous year's champions would (　　) over their rival team again this year, but the race was closely matched until the very end.

1 splash　　　　2 bleach
3 rebound　　　4 prevail

(80) 🔍 「他に有力な証拠がないため、弁護士はプロのカメラマンに依頼し、犯行現場の防犯カメラが撮影した暗い画像を〜してもらった」の空所には「明るくする、見えやすくする」を意味する語が入ると考えられます。選択肢から、その両方の意味を含む「画質を向上させる」の意味になる語を選びましょう。

🔄 他に有力な証拠がないため、弁護士はプロのカメラマンに依頼し、犯行現場の防犯カメラが撮影した暗い画像を補正してもらった。

✏️ 正解 ☐ enhance …の質を向上させる
誤答 ☐ certify (文書で)…を証明する、…に免許を与える
☐ prescribe (薬・療法など)を処方する、(規則・方針として)…を定める
☐ shoplift (品物)を店頭から盗む
英文 ☐ evidence 証拠 ☐ security camera 防犯カメラ ☐ crime scene 犯行現場

(81) 🔍 「ニックは昼休みに、よく生徒と〜して、カフェテリアで座っておしゃべりをする」という意味です。空所の動作に伴うものとして、カフェテリアで生徒と座っておしゃべりをするということから考えると、「生徒に混ざる」の意味になる語が入るとわかります。生徒の輪の中に「飛び込む」という発想もあり得ますが、その場合は plunge ではなく get in among のように言います。

🔄 ニックは昼休みに、よく生徒に混ざってカフェテリアで座っておしゃべりをする。

✏️ 正解 ☐ mingle 混ざる、交際する、加わる
誤答 ☐ discipline (人)を訓練する
☐ emerge (暗闇などから)現れる、(事実などが)現れる、明らかになる
☐ plunge 飛び込む、急落する
英文 ☐ lunch break 昼休み ☐ chat 雑談する、おしゃべりする
☐ cafeteria カフェテリア、学生食堂

(82) 🔍 まず冒頭から certain までは、Fans が主語、were が動詞で「ファンは確信していた」という意味です。確信していた内容は「今年も前年度王者がライバルのチームに〜する」ことでしたが、but 以降で「しかし最後まで拮抗したレースが展開された」と説明されているので、空所には、「勝つ」を表す語が入るとわかります。

🔄 今年も前年度王者がライバルのチームに勝つとファンは確信していたが、最後まで拮抗したレースが展開された。

✏️ 正解 ☐ prevail 勝つ
誤答 ☐ splash (水・泥などが)はねる
☐ bleach 白くなる
☐ rebound (ボールなどが)はね返る、(減少・下落などから)回復する
英文 ☐ be certain (that 節)…だと確信している ☐ closely 接戦で ☐ matched 互角の

🏳️ **(80) 2 (81) 2 (82) 4**

(83) One tip for becoming a successful salesperson is to avoid being (　　) aggressive. Remaining friendly is more effective than pushing a product too hard.

　　1　collectively　　　**2**　excessively

　　3　arguably　　　　　**4**　hastily

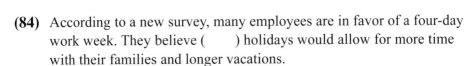

(84) According to a new survey, many employees are in favor of a four-day work week. They believe (　　) holidays would allow for more time with their families and longer vacations.

　　1　obscure　　　　　　**2**　consecutive

　　3　insistent　　　　　　**4**　overdue

(85) The (　　) period for next semester begins this week for new students, while seniors may sign up the following week.

　　1　construction　　　　**2**　engagement

　　3　resignation　　　　　**4**　enrollment

(83) 🔍 空所を含む1文目は「セールスパーソンとして成功するコツの一つは、〜強引な態度を取らないことである」です。空所には aggressive を修飾する副詞が入ります。その後の2文目に「強引に商品を売り込むよりも、親しみやすい態度を維持する方が効果的である」と続いているので、than 以下の「強引に商品を売り込むこと」が1文目が述べている避けるべきことに対応すると考え、選択肢のうちの「過度に」を表す副詞を選びましょう。

📝 セールスパーソンとして成功するコツの一つは、過度に強引な態度を取らないことである。強引に商品を売り込むよりも、親しみやすい態度を維持する方が効果的である。

✏️ 正解 ☐ excessively 過度に
　　 誤答 ☐ collectively 集合的に、ひとまとめにして
　　　　 ☐ arguably おそらく、間違いなく
　　　　 ☐ hastily 急いで、あわてて
　　 英文 ☐ tip (ためになる)助言　☐ salesperson 店員、セールスパーソン
　　　　 ☐ avoid *doing* …するのを避ける　☐ aggressive 強引な、押しの強い

(84) 🔍 1文目は「新しい調査によると、多くの従業員が週4日労働制に賛成している」という意味です。2文目で「〜な休暇であれば、家族と過ごす時間が増え、休暇も長くなるという効果があると考えているのだ」と続いているので、週4日労働制により、休暇がどうなるかを考えて、「連続した」を意味する語を入れましょう。

📝 新しい調査によると、多くの従業員が週4日労働制に賛成している。連休になれば、家族と過ごす時間が増え、休暇も長くなるという効果があると考えているのだ。

✏️ 正解 ☐ consecutive 連続する
　　 誤答 ☐ obscure (形などが)はっきりしない、(意味などが)あいまいな
　　　　 ☐ insistent (人が)しつこい、(色などが)目立つ
　　　　 ☐ overdue 支払い [返却] 期限の過ぎた、遅れた
　　 英文 ☐ according to …によれば　☐ be in favor of …に賛成する　☐ work week 週間労働時間
　　　　 ☐ allow for …という効果がある

(85) 🔍 「来学期の〜期間は新入生向けが今週から始まり、上級生は翌週登録する」という意味です。semester、new students などの語から、大学の履修についての文だとわかるので、選択肢から「登録」を意味する語を選びましょう。

📝 来学期の登録手続きは新入生向けが今週から始まり、上級生は翌週登録する。

✏️ 正解 ☐ enrollment 登録手続き
　　 誤答 ☐ construction 建設工事、建造物
　　　　 ☐ engagement (会合などの)約束、契約による雇用
　　　　 ☐ resignation 辞職、断念
　　 英文 ☐ semester 学期　☐ sign up 手続きをする、署名をする　☐ following 次に続く

(86) Similar to humans, many animal communities are organized in a strict social ( ), with powerful leaders at the top and the weak and young at the bottom.

1 enclosure   **2** federation

3 inheritance   **4** hierarchy

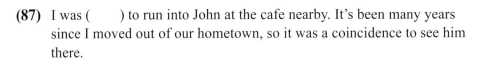

(87) I was ( ) to run into John at the cafe nearby. It's been many years since I moved out of our hometown, so it was a coincidence to see him there.

1 dedicated   **2** underdressed

3 astonished   **4** distinguished

(88) Outsourcing production to foreign countries is a ( ) arrangement which provides employment and stimulates the country's economy, while also cutting company costs.

1 maritime   **2** chronic

3 beneficial   **4** subjective

(86) 🔍 空所を含む前半に「動物の社会の多くは、人間と同じように厳しい社会的～を形成している」とあります。続く後半に「力のあるリーダーを頂点に、弱者や若者を底辺とする」とあるので、その内容から選択肢には「階層制度」が入るとわかります。ちなみに最初の Similar to ... はその前につく Being が省略された分詞構文です。

📝 動物の社会の多くは、人間と同じように、力のあるリーダーを頂点、弱者や若者を底辺とする厳しい階層制度を形成している。

✏️ 正解 ☐ hierarchy 階層制度
誤答 ☐ enclosure 囲い込み、封入物
☐ federation 連合組合、連邦政府
☐ inheritance 相続、遺産
英文 ☐ be similar to …に似ている　☐ organize …を組織する、…を準備する
☐ strict 厳しい、厳格な

(87) 🔍 空所を含む1文目は「近くのカフェでジョンに出会って私は～でした」という意味です。2文目には「地元を離れて何年も経つので、偶然の再会でした」と、その出会いについて説明しているので、選択肢より「びっくりした」を意味する語を入れましょう。

📝 近くのカフェでジョンに出会ってびっくりしました。私が地元を離れて何年も経つので、偶然の再会でした。

✏️ 正解 ☐ astonish …を驚かす
誤答 ☐ dedicate （時間など）をささげる、（書物など）を献呈する
☐ underdress （場にそぐわない）簡単すぎる服装をする
☐ distinguish …を見分ける
英文 ☐ run into …に思いがけず会う　☐ move out of 引っ越して…を出ていく
☐ coincidence 偶然の出来事

(88) 🔍 「海外に生産を委託することは、雇用機会を創出し、その国の経済を活性化するとともに、企業のコスト削減にもつながる～な活動である」という文です。「雇用機会を創出し、その国の経済を活性化する」ことが外国にとってどういう意味を持つのかを考えて、「有益な」を意味する語を選びましょう。

📝 海外に生産を委託することは、雇用機会を創出し、その国の経済を活性化するとともに、企業のコスト削減にもつながる有益な活動である。

✏️ 正解 ☐ beneficial 有益な
誤答 ☐ maritime 海事の、海の
☐ chronic 長期にわたる、（病気が）慢性の
☐ subjective 主観の、主観的な、想像上の
英文 ☐ outsource …を外部に委託する　☐ arrangement 準備、用意、手配
☐ stimulate …を活性化する、…を刺激する

(89) A: Do you have any advice regarding how I should talk about myself at my job interview next week?

B: I suggest you emphasize your strengths and (   ) your weaknesses.

1	shake up	**2**	play down
3	draw up	**4**	flag down

(90) Daryl's attempt at being a vegetarian failed because he couldn't resist bacon, so as an alternative he decided to (   ) on his overall meat consumption.

1	fall behind	**2**	lay down
3	cut back	**4**	walk out

(91) Tourists should be careful about getting (   ) at local markets. Locals will often raise the price if they think they can trick ignorant foreigners.

1	rounded out	**2**	ripped off
3	pushed on	**4**	tilted forward

(89) 🔍 人物 A は「来週の就職面接で自分についてどのように話せばいいか、何かアドバイスをいただけませんか」と人物 B に質問しています。それに対して人物 B は「自分の長所を強調し、短所を～することをお勧めします」と言っているので、短所は「重要ではないように言う」という意味を持つイディオムを選びましょう。

📋 A：来週の就職面接で自分についてどのように話せばいいか、何かアドバイスをいただけませんか。

B：自分の長所を強調し、短所にあまり触れないことをお勧めします。

✏️ 正解 ☐ **play down** …は重要ではないように言う
誤答 ☐ **shake up** (びんなど)を振ってまぜる、…を刷新する
☐ **draw up** (文書・案など)を作成する、…を引き寄せる
☐ **flag down** (乗り物・運転者など)を合図で停止させる
英文 ☐ **regarding** …に関しては　☐ **talk about oneself** 自身について話す
☐ **job interview** 就職の面接　☐ **suggest** (that 節)…を提案する
☐ **emphasize** …を強調する　☐ **strength** 長所、強み　☐ **weakness** 短所

(90) 🔍 文の前半は「ダリルのベジタリアンになるという試みはベーコンを我慢できなかったことにより失敗した」という意味です。空所を含む後半は「よって、代替手段として、ダリルは全体的な肉の消費量を～すると決めた」ですので、選択肢より「減らす」を意味するイディオムを選びましょう。

📋 ダリルはベーコンを食べずにいられず、ベジタリアンになるという試みに失敗したため、その代わりとして肉の消費量を全体的に減らすことにした。

✏️ 正解 ☐ **cut back** 削減する
誤答 ☐ **fall behind** 仕事などで遅れる、支払いが遅れる
☐ **lay down** …を下に置く、(規則など)を規定する、(基礎など)を築く
☐ **walk out** (抗議の意思表示として)退場する、ストをする、放棄する
英文 ☐ **attempt** 試み　☐ **vegetarian** ベジタリアン、菜食主義者　☐ **fail** 失敗する
☐ **resist** …を我慢する　☐ **alternative** 代わりの手段　☐ **overall** 全体の
☐ **consumption** 消費量

(91) 🔍 空所を含む1文目は「観光客は地元のマーケットで～にならないように気をつけなければならない」という意味です。観光客が気をつけなければいけない行為として適切な選択肢は「締めくくられる」「せかされる」「前に傾く」ではなくて、「ぼったくりにあう」でしょう。続く2文目の内容「現地の人は、無知な外国人をだませると思えば、しばしば値段をつり上げる」からも、選んだ選択肢が合っているかどうか確認できますね。

📋 観光客は地元のマーケットでぼったくりに遭わないように気をつけなければならない。現地の人は、無知な外国人をだませると思えば、しばしば値段をつり上げる。

✏️ 正解 ☐ **rip off** …からだまし取る
誤答 ☐ **round out** …の最後の仕上げをする、…を締めくくる
☐ **push on** (人)をせかす、(人)をせきたてて…させる
☐ **tilt forward** …を前に傾ける
英文 ☐ **get** ＋過去分詞 …される　☐ **locals** 地元の人　☐ **trick** …をだます
☐ **ignorant** 無知な、知らない

(92) Dean witnessed the thief leaving the house and promptly called the police to give an accurate description of the man so he could not ( ) his crime.

1 hold forth about 2 turn aside from
3 look up to   4 get away with

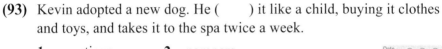

(93) Kevin adopted a new dog. He ( ) it like a child, buying it clothes and toys, and takes it to the spa twice a week.

1 sanctions   2 pampers
3 endows   4 compliments

(94) Rosetta began to feel ( ) 30 minutes after taking the pain medicine, so she lay down on her bed for a short nap.

1 weary   2 bulky
3 daring   4 infectious

(92) 🔍 文の前半は「ディーンは、泥棒が家を出て行くのを目撃し、すぐに警察に通報してその人の人相を正確に伝えた」です。続いて「だからその泥棒は罪を〜することができなかった」とあるので、「逃れる」を意味する選択肢を選びましょう。イディオムの意味が正確にわからなくても、イディオムに含まれる away などの語のイメージがヒントになります。

📝 ディーンは、泥棒が家を出て行くのを目撃し、すぐに警察に通報してその人相を正確に伝えたため、泥棒は罪を逃れることができなかった。

✏️ 正解 ☐ get away with …の罰を逃れる
　　誤答 ☐ hold forth about（軽蔑的な表現として）…について長々と話す
　　　　 ☐ turn aside from …からわき道に入る、…を見ないようにわきを向く
　　　　 ☐ look up to …（の方）を見上げる、（人）を尊敬する
　　英文 ☐ witness …を目撃する　☐ promptly 即座に　☐ accurate 正確な
　　　　 ☐ description 描写、説明　☐ crime 犯罪

(93) 🔍 「ケヴィンは新しい犬を飼い始めた」に続く、主語が He の2文目には、「彼はそれを子どものように〜」という形で空所があります。「かわいがる」や「大切にする」を意味する語を選びましょう。続く「洋服やおもちゃを買い与え、週に2回はスパに連れて行く」より、「かわいがって」「甘やかしている」様子がわかりますね。

📝 ケヴィンは新しい犬を飼い始めた。洋服やおもちゃを買い与え、週に2回はスパに連れて行き、子どものように甘やかしている。

✏️ 正解 ☐ pamper …を甘やかす
　　誤答 ☐ sanction …を認可する、…を承認する、…を制裁する
　　　　 ☐ endow （学校・病院など）に基金を寄付する
　　　　 ☐ compliment …に敬意を表する、…をほめる、…にお世辞を言う
　　英文 ☐ adopt …を引き取る

(94) 🔍 空所を含む前半は「ロゼッタは鎮痛剤を飲んで30分経つと〜を感じ始めた」です。続いて、「彼女はベッドに横になって少し仮眠をとった」とあるので、「疲れ」や「眠気」を感じたため、横になったという意味になるように空所に語を入れると文意が成り立つでしょう。

📝 鎮痛剤を飲んで30分経つと疲れが出てきたので、ロゼッタはベッドに横になって少し仮眠をとった。

✏️ 正解 ☐ weary 疲れた
　　誤答 ☐ bulky かさばった、体の大きい
　　　　 ☐ daring 勇敢な、大胆な、斬新な
　　　　 ☐ infectious 感染性の、伝染病の
　　英文 ☐ pain medicine 痛みに効く薬　☐ lie down 横になる（lie – lay – lain の活用に注意）
　　　　 ☐ nap 昼寝、仮眠

(95) Both the liberal and conservative parties agree that the military must
( ) to rapidly end the conflict and promote stability in the region.

1	collapse	**2**	intervene
3	render	**4**	devastate

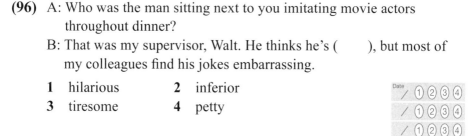

(96) A: Who was the man sitting next to you imitating movie actors
throughout dinner?
B: That was my supervisor, Walt. He thinks he's ( ), but most of
my colleagues find his jokes embarrassing.

1	hilarious	**2**	inferior
3	tiresome	**4**	petty

(97) Hoping to accelerate development of its new spacecraft, the company
allocated a ( ) amount of funds to expand the project's team.

1	sizeable	**2**	compact
3	traumatic	**4**	precarious

(95) 🔍 Both A and B の形で主語になっていて、動詞 agree の後に目的語となる that 節が続いています。「リベラル派も保守派も、紛争を迅速に終結させ、地域の安定を促進するために軍が～する必要があることに賛成している」と言っているので、どちらの派も合意している内容は、紛争を終結させることだとわかります。「そのために軍が～する必要がある」の空所に当てはまるのは選択肢より「介入する」だとわかるでしょう。

📝 リベラル派も保守派も、紛争を迅速に終結させ、地域の安定を促進するために軍が介入する必要があることに賛成している。

✏️ 正解 ☐ intervene 介入する
　　誤答 ☐ collapse （建物が）崩れる、（疲労や病気で）倒れる、衰弱する、（希望が）砕かれる、（計画が）失敗する、（価値などが）急落する、（家具などが）折りたためる
　　　　 ☐ render …を～にする、（援助）を与える、（敬意を）示す、（芸術的に）表現する、翻訳する、（報告書や回答など）を提出する
　　　　 ☐ devastate （国土）を荒廃させる、…を圧倒する、…を打ちのめす、…を困惑させる
　　英文 ☐ conservative 保守的な　☐ conflict 紛争、衝突　☐ stability 安定(性)

(96) 🔍 人物 A は「夕食中、あなたの隣に座って映画俳優の真似をしていたのは誰ですか」と聞いています。それに対して人物 B は「あれは私の上司のウォルトです」と答えてから、「本人は～と思っていますが、ほとんどの同僚は彼のジョークが恥ずかしいと思っています」とあるので、ものまねをしている本人はジョークが「面白い」と思っているという意味を入れるのが適切だと考えられるでしょう。

📝 A：夕食のとき、ずっとあなたの隣に座って映画俳優の真似をしていたのは誰ですか。
　　B：あれは私の上司のウォルトです。本人は面白いと思っていますが、同僚のほとんどは彼のジョークは恥ずかしいと思っています。

✏️ 正解 ☐ hilarious すごくおもしろい
　　誤答 ☐ inferior 劣った、下位の、下級の
　　　　 ☐ tiresome 厄介な、面倒な、飽き飽きする、うんざりする
　　　　 ☐ petty 取るに足らない、些細な、わずかな、心の狭い、けちな
　　英文 ☐ supervisor 上司、監督者　☐ colleague 同僚　☐ find A B A を B だと感じる・知る
　　　　 ☐ embarrassing 恥ずかしい、当惑させるような

(97) 🔍 「新型宇宙船の開発を加速させようと思うので」という理由を表す分詞構文に続いて、主節は「その会社はプロジェクトチームの拡充に～な額の資金を投入した」と言っているため、前半と関連づけて、選択肢より「かなり大きな」意味する語を選びましょう。

📝 新型宇宙船の開発を加速させようと思い、会社はプロジェクトチームの拡充に多額の資金を投入したのだ。

✏️ 正解 ☐ sizeable かなり大きな
　　誤答 ☐ compact 小型の
　　　　 ☐ traumatic 心理的外傷を与える、外傷性の
　　　　 ☐ precarious 事情次第の、あてにならない、不安定な、危険な
　　英文 ☐ accelerate …を促進する、…を速める　☐ spacecraft 宇宙船　☐ allocate …を配分する
　　　　 ☐ expand …を拡充する・広げる

(98) The entrepreneur's business outline sounded promising, but when asked to (　　) on his plan, he was unable to give any concrete details.

1 applaud **2** elaborate
3 displace **4** batter

Date
／ ① ② ③ ④
／ ① ② ③ ④
／ ① ② ③ ④

(99) The new (　　) proposed by the Liberal Party aims to increase taxes on businesses that pollute the environment.

1 nuisance **2** competence
3 obligation **4** legislation

Date
／ ① ② ③ ④
／ ① ② ③ ④
／ ① ② ③ ④

(100) The historic play centers around a family of four slaves who escape from a Southern plantation and have to survive with the constant (　　) of being captured and returned to their owner.

1 aspiration **2** retailer
3 threat **4** submission

Date
／ ① ② ③ ④
／ ① ② ③ ④
／ ① ② ③ ④

(98) 🔍 前半は「この起業家の事業概要は有望と思われた」です。その後に逆接の接続詞 but が続き「しかし、計画について~することを求められると、彼は具体的な内容を説明することができなかった」とあるので、選択肢より「詳しく説明する」の語が入ると文意がつながります。elaborate が自動詞で使われるときは、on と結びついて「…について詳しく述べる」という意味になります。面接試験の質問で使われるときもあるので覚えておきましょう。

📝 この起業家の事業概要は有望と思われたが、計画の詳細を尋ねられても、具体的な内容を説明することができなかった。

✏️ 正解 ☐ elaborate 詳細に述べる
誤答 ☐ applaud 拍手喝采する、ほめる
　　 ☐ displace …に取って代わる、…を取り除く、…を退去させる
　　 ☐ batter 何度もたたく、乱打する
英文 ☐ entrepreneur 起業家、事業家　☐ outline 概要、計画案
　　 ☐ promising 将来有望な、見込みがある　☐ concrete 具体的な

(99) 🔍 「自由党が提案した新しい~は、環境を汚染する企業への課税を強化することを目的としている」という内容で、「課税を強化する」とあることから、政党が提案するのは選択肢からおそらく「法案」だと推測できるでしょう。空所に入る名詞は直後の proposed by「…によって提案された」に修飾されていることもヒントになります。

📝 自由党が提案した新法は、環境を汚染する企業への課税を強化することを目的としている。

✏️ 正解 ☐ legislation 法律、法案
誤答 ☐ nuisance 迷惑な行為、困ったこと、不快なもの
　　 ☐ competence 能力、適性、技能
　　 ☐ obligation 義務、責任、義理、恩義
英文 ☐ aim to do …するのを目指す　☐ pollute …を汚染する

(100) 🔍 主語は play で動詞は centers（自動詞で「集中する」という意味）です。「この歴史劇は、4人の奴隷の家族を中心に展開する」という前半に、関係代名詞の who が続き「彼らは南部の農園から逃亡し、捕らえられて所有者に返されるという絶え間のない~がある中で生きていかねばならない」とあります。奴隷の家族がどんな状況の中で生きていかなければいけないのかを考えると、空所に当てはまるのは「恐れ、脅威」の意味を持つ語だとわかります。

📝 この歴史劇は、南部の農園から逃亡し、捕らえられて所有者の元に送り返される恐怖におびえながら生きていかなければならない4人の奴隷の家族を中心に展開する。

✏️ 正解 ☐ threat 恐れ
誤答 ☐ aspiration 抱負、向上心、熱望
　　 ☐ retailer 小売り商人
　　 ☐ submission 服従、言いなりになること、意見の提起、提出物
英文 ☐ play 劇　☐ center around …を軸として展開する
　　 ☐ plantation 大農園、プランテーション　☐ survive 生き延びる　☐ constant 絶えず続く…
　　 ☐ capture …を捕らえる

(101) The long working hours at the office were only ( ) for Tina because she got along well with her boss and colleagues.

   1 comparable   **2** adorable

   3 fashionable   **4** bearable

(102) In order to help prevent future pandemics, Ronald developed a computer program which ( ) the rate of infection based on historical data.

   1 simulates   **2** vows

   3 penetrates   **4** intercepts

(103) Favorable economic conditions such as low production costs have attracted businesses from across the world, transforming the country's largest port area into a ( ) city.

   1 transparent   **2** stern

   3 cosmopolitan   **4** tentative

(101) 🔍 「ティナの長時間労働は、上司や同僚とうまくいっているという理由でのみ～だった」の空所に入るものを、長時間労働を形容するのに適当かどうか考えながら選びましょう。選択肢の中では、文脈より「比較できる」「魅力的な」「流行の」ではなく「我慢できる」が適切だとわかります。

⚡ ティナが事務所での長時間労働に耐えられた訳は、上司や同僚とうまくいっていたからだけのことだ。

✏️ [正解] ☐ bearable 耐えられる
[誤答] ☐ comparable 比較できる、相当する、匹敵する
☐ adorable 魅力的な、かわいらしい、崇拝に値する
☐ fashionable 流行の、流行を追っている、上流の、流行を追う・上流の人々が集まる
[英文] ☐ working hours 労働時間 ☐ get along with …と良い関係にある、…と仲良くやっていく
☐ colleague 同僚

(102) 🔍 前半は「将来のパンデミック防止に役立てるために」で、その後に「ロナルドはコンピュータープログラムを開発した」とあります。program を which 以降の形容詞節で「そのプログラムは過去のデータをもとに感染率を～する」と説明しています。パンデミック防止に役立てるためには、過去のデータをもとに感染率を「知る」「再現する」という意味になると文意が通るでしょう。

⚡ ロナルドは、将来のパンデミック防止に役立てるために、過去のデータをもとに感染率をシミュレーションするコンピュータープログラムを開発した。

✏️ [正解] ☐ simulate …を模擬的に再現する、…のシミュレーションをする
[誤答] ☐ vow …を誓う、誓って…と言う
☐ penetrate …に突き通る、…を貫通する、…に潜入する、…に浸透する
☐ intercept …を途中で捕らえる、…を横取りする、(通信)を傍受する、…を遮る、…を妨害する
[英文] ☐ in order to do …するために、…する目的で ☐ pandemic 全国的な流行病
☐ develop …を開発する ☐ infection 伝染、感染 ☐ based on …に基づいて

(103) 🔍 前半は「生産コストの低さなどの好条件が世界中の企業を惹きつけた」とあり、後半は「その国の最大の港湾地域は～都市へと変貌を遂げた」とあります。世界中の企業を惹きつけた結果どうなったかを考え、「国際的な都市」という意味になるように単語を当てはめましょう。

⚡ 生産コストの低さなどの好条件が世界中の企業を惹きつけ、その国の最大の港湾地域は国際都市へと変貌を遂げた。

✏️ [正解] ☐ cosmopolitan 国際的な
[誤答] ☐ transparent 透明な
☐ stern 厳格な、(外観や顔つきが)人を寄せ付けない、恐ろしい、(状況や境遇が)苦しい、苛酷な
☐ tentative 仮の、試験的な、ためらいがちな、控えめな
[英文] ☐ favorable 好都合な、有利な ☐ production cost 生産費用 ☐ business 会社
☐ transform A into B A を B へと一変させる

(104) Based on Maria's questionnaire, roughly half of the study participants were dissatisfied with the new (　　), while a quarter said they would buy it once available.

1　workforce　　　　2　predecessor

3　scheme　　　　　4　prototype

(105) HMC offers guided mountain tours across 100 countries. Experienced staff provide all necessary equipment so customers may (　　) at their own speed and enjoy the natural scenery.

1　retrace　　　　　2　exceed

3　trek　　　　　　4　intrude

(106) Adam always looked forward to visiting his wealthy uncle, who never failed to present him with (　　) gifts such as the latest designer clothing.

1　counterfeit　　　　2　extravagant

3　indecisive　　　　4　messy

(104) 🔍 空所を含む前半は「マリアのアンケートによると、約半数の人が新型の〜に不満を持っている」です。後半は while「一方では」で始まり、前半と対比して「一方、4分の1は発売されたら買いたいと答えている」と述べています。したがって空所には「デザイン」「製品」などの意味の言葉が入ると考えられます。選択肢より「試作品」を選びましょう。

📝 マリアが行ったアンケートによると、回答者の約半数が新型の試作品に不満を持っている。一方、4分の1は発売されたら買いたいと答えている。

✏️ 正解 ☐ prototype 試作品
誤答 ☐ workforce 全従業員、総労働力、労働力人口
☐ predecessor 前任者、先輩、前にあったもの
☐ scheme たくらみ、陰謀、計画、組織、機構、配列
英文 ☐ based on …に基づいて ☐ questionnaire アンケート ☐ roughly およそ、約
☐ participant 参加者 ☐ be dissatisfied with …に対して不満を持つ ☐ quarter 4分の1

(105) 🔍 1文目は「HMCは世界100カ国で山岳ガイドツアーを行っています」とあり、この「山岳ガイドツアー」が正解を導く手がかりとなります。2文目は「経験豊富なスタッフが必要な道具をすべて用意しますので、お客様はご自分のスピードで〜を行い、自然の景色を楽しむことができます」とあります。前半で「山岳」という言葉が出てきたので、「山歩きをする」の意味の語を選ぶことができるでしょう。

📝 HMCは世界100カ国で山岳ガイドツアーを行っています。経験豊富なスタッフが必要な道具をすべて用意しますので、お客様はご自分のペースでトレッキングを行い、自然の景色を楽しむことができます。

✏️ 正解 ☐ trek 山歩きをする、トレッキングをする
誤答 ☐ retrace …を引き返す、…を後戻りする、…のもとを訪ねる、…をさかのぼって調べる
☐ exceed …を超える、超過する、上回る、卓越する
☐ intrude 割り込む、じゃまをする、立ち入る、押しかける
英文 ☐ offer …を提供する ☐ provide …を供給する ☐ equipment 装具、用品
☐ scenery 景色、風景

(106) 🔍 前半は「アダムは、裕福な叔父の家に行くのがいつも楽しみだった」とあり、後半は関係代名詞の who で叔父を修飾しています。「（叔父は）デザイナーの最新の洋服など、〜な贈り物をアダムに欠かさずプレゼントした」とあり、前半の「裕福な叔父」であることもふまえ、プレゼントするのは「豪勢な」ものだと考えて、選択肢を選びましょう。

📝 アダムは、裕福な叔父の家に行くのがいつも楽しみだった。叔父は、一流デザイナーの最新の洋服など、高級な贈り物を必ずプレゼントしてくれた。

✏️ 正解 ☐ extravagant 豪勢な
誤答 ☐ counterfeit 偽造の、模造の、虚偽の、心にもない
☐ indecisive 決断力のない、優柔不断な、決定的でない、不明確な
☐ messy 取り散らかした、きたない、(仕事などが)厄介な、手の汚れる、いいかげんな
英文 ☐ look forward to *doing* …するのを楽しみにする ☐ wealthy 裕福な
☐ fail to *do* …するのを怠る ☐ latest 最新の

(107) Mr. Greene explained that the investment has a high probability of profits, but ( ) some risk. He said, "Taking chances is a necessary step to becoming a successful investor."

1 endorses   **2** entails

3 enacts   **4** emigrates

(108) Student debt has hit record highs in recent years. Previous generations, however, were able to pay their ( ) by working part-time during the summer.

1 prescription   **2** administration

3 tuition   **4** unification

(109) If the economic situation ( ) any further, the company will need to consider implementing more serious cuts.

1 corresponds   **2** interacts

3 deteriorates   **4** subtracts

(107) 🔍 1文目は「グリーン氏は、この投資について、利益が出る確率は高いがリスクを～と説明した」ですので、この時点で、空所には「含む」「持っている」の意味の語が入ると推測できます。続いて2文目で「彼は『危険を承知でやってみることは、成功した投資家になるために必要なステップである』と述べた」と、情報を付け加えています。ここで文意が成立するかどうか確認しましょう。

筆記1

📝 グリーン氏は、この投資について、利益が出る確率は高いがリスクも伴うと説明した。そして、「危険を承知でやってみることは、成功した投資家になるために必要なステップである」と述べた。

✏️ 正解 ☐ entail …を必然的に伴う
誤答 ☐ endorse …を支持する、…を是認する、…を裏書する、…を保証する
☐ enact （法律）を制定する、…を規定する、（劇）を上演する、（役）を演ずる
☐ emigrate （他国へ）移住する、転居する
英文 ☐ explain that 節 …であることを説明する　☐ probability 見込み
☐ take chances 賭けに出る　☐ investor 投資家

(108) 🔍 「近年、学生の借金は過去最高を記録している」という1文目と対比し、2文目は「しかし、以前の世代は」で始まり、「夏休みにアルバイトをすることで～を支払うことができた」と続いています。学生の借金の原因であり、学生がアルバイトをして支払おうとするものは選択肢のどれかを考えると、「処方箋」「管理」「統一」ではなくて、「学費、授業料」が適切だと判断できます。

📝 近年、学生の借金は過去最高を記録している。しかし、以前の世代は、夏休みにアルバイトをすることで学費を支払うことができた。

✏️ 正解 ☐ tuition 学費、授業料
誤答 ☐ prescription 処方箋、規定、指示、解決法
☐ administration 管理、運営、行政、執行、本部、政府、（薬の）投与
☐ unification 統一、単一化
英文 ☐ debt 借金、負債　☐ record high 最高値、過去最高　☐ previous 以前の
☐ part-time 非常勤で

(109) 🔍 If で始まる従属節は条件を表し、「経済状況がこれ以上～すれば」であるのに対して、主節は「会社はさらに本格的な削減を検討する必要がある」となっています。経済状況がどうなった場合に削減することになるかを考えると選択肢より、「一致する」「影響しあう」「引き算をする」ではなくて、「悪化する」が当てはまると考えられるでしょう。

📝 経済状況がこれ以上悪化すれば、会社はさらに本格的な削減を検討する必要がある。

✏️ 正解 ☐ deteriorate 悪化する
誤答 ☐ correspond 一致する、調和する、相当する、文通する
☐ interact 相互に作用する、影響し合う、交流する
☐ subtract 引き算をする
英文 ☐ economic situation 経済状況　☐ consider *doing* …するのを検討する・熟考する
☐ implement …を実行する、…を施行する

(110) Experts agree that based on available data, it is an (　　) fact that most of the increase in global temperatures over the last several decades has been due to human activity.

1　adhesive　　　　2　inadequate
3　obstructive　　　4　undeniable

Date
／ ① ② ③ ④
／ ① ② ③ ④
／ ① ② ③ ④

(111) A new study shows that a majority of businesses find dedication to be the most desirable (　　) among new hires, followed by confidence and good communication skills.

1　proponent　　　　2　commission
3　vendor　　　　　 4　trait

Date
／ ① ② ③ ④
／ ① ② ③ ④
／ ① ② ③ ④

(110) 🔍 「専門家は見解が一致している」の後に、一致している内容について書かれています。「入手可能なデータによれば、過去数十年間の地球気温の上昇のほとんどが人間活動によるものであることは〜な事実である」の空所に当てはまる形容詞を選ぶので、「(明白な)」「(確実な)」のような意味の語が入ると推測できるでしょう。選択肢より、「粘着性の」「不十分な」「妨害する」ではなくて、「否定しがたい」が正解だとわかります。

🔁 専門家は、入手可能なデータによれば、過去数十年間の地球気温の上昇のほとんどが人間活動によるものであることは否定できない事実であるという点で見解が一致している。

✏️
正解 ☐ undeniable 否定しがたい
誤答 ☐ adhesive 粘着性の、くっついて離れない、いつまでも頭に残る
☐ inadequate 不十分な、不足な、不適格な、…する力がない
☐ obstructive 妨害する、邪魔となる
英文 ☐ agree that 節 …ということで意見が一致する ☐ based on …に基づいて
☐ available 利用できる ☐ fact that 節 …であるという事実 ☐ decade 十年間
☐ due to …が原因で

(111) 🔍 冒頭の A new study shows より、この文では新しい調査の結果が書かれているとわかります。「新しい調査によると、大多数の企業が、新入社員に対して最も望ましい〜は献身性であり、次いで自信と優れたコミュニケーション能力であると回答している」の空所に入るのは「性格」「素質」のような意味の語だと推測できます。選択肢より「特性」を意味する語を選ぶことができますね。

🔁 新しい調査によると、大多数の企業が新入社員に最も望む特性は献身性であり、次いで自信を持つことと優れたコミュニケーション能力であると回答している。

✏️
正解 ☐ trait 特性
誤答 ☐ proponent 提議者、提案者、弁護者、支持者
☐ commission 委員会、手数料、(任務の)委託、(委託された)任務、命令、委任事項
☐ vendor 売る人、売り主、行商人、販売会社
英文 ☐ show that 節 …であることを示す ☐ a majority of 大多数の… ☐ business 会社
☐ dedication 献身 ☐ desirable 望ましい ☐ new hire 新入社員
☐ followed by 続いて ☐ confidence 自信、確信、信頼

(112) A: The new CEO ( ) annual bonuses and less overtime for all
employees.

B: I think it's highly unlikely. Last time we were promised more
vacation time, but that never happened.

1 envisions **2** advances

3 pledges **4** objects

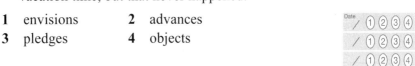

(113) Having been a city ( ) for most of his life, Teddy experienced
many difficulties upon moving to the countryside for his new work
assignment.

1 lodging **2** pilgrim

3 spectator **4** dweller

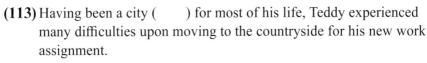

(114) Alyssa was aware that the future of her company ( ) successful
negotiations with the potential investor waiting in the next room.

1 coughed up **2** brought about

3 hinged on **4** spelled out

(112) 🔍 人物 A の発言は空所を含み、「新しい CEO は、全社員に年間ボーナスと残業の削減を〜しています」とあります。それに対して人物 B は「その可能性は極めて低いと思います」と述べ、「前回は休暇を増やすと約束されたけど、実現しませんでした」とその根拠を示しています。新しい CEO がしたことは全社員に年間ボーナスと残業の削減を「示す」「約束する」のような意味だと考えられるので、選択肢の中から「誓約する」を表す語を選びましょう。

📖 A：今度の CEO は、全社員に対して、毎年ボーナスを支給し、残業を削減すると約束しています。
B：そうなる能性は極めて低いと思います。前の人は休暇を増やすと約束したけど、実現しませんでした。

✏️ 正解 ☐ pledge …を誓約する
誤答 ☐ envision（将来のことを）心に描く、…を想像する、…をもくろむ
☐ advance …を進める、…を進捗させる、昇進させる、前払いする、（予定を）早める
☐ object …と言って反対する、反対して…だと言う
英文 ☐ CEO (chief executive officer) 最高経営責任者 ☐ annual 年 1 回の
☐ bonus ボーナス、賞与 ☐ overtime 時間外労働、超過勤務
☐ unlikely ありそうにない、見込みのない ☐ promise A B A（人）に B を約束する

(113) 🔍 空所を含む従属節は ing の形で始まり、「人生の大半を都会の〜だったので」の分詞構文となっています。主節は「テディは田舎への転勤で多くの困難を経験した」なので、空所には city と組み合わせると田舎の環境に不慣れな者の意味になる名詞を選ぶと文意がつながります。

📖 人生の大半を都会で暮らしてきたテディは、田舎へ転勤した直後から、多くの困難を経験した。

✏️ 正解 ☐ dweller 住人、居住者
誤答 ☐ lodging 宿泊所
☐ pilgrim 巡礼者、放浪者、旅人
☐ spectator 見物人、観客
英文 ☐ work assignment 仕事の割り当て、職務

(114) 🔍 冒頭は「アリッサは、気づいていた」という意味です。続いて、気づいていた内容について「隣の部屋で待っている投資家候補との成功した交渉に、自分の会社の将来が〜していること」とあり、まだ投資家に決まっていない候補との交渉が成功することに会社の将来がどう関わるかを考えると、空所には「かかっている」を表すイディオムが当てはまるとわかります。

📖 アリッサは、隣の部屋で待っている投資家候補との交渉がうまくいくかどうかに、自分の会社の将来がかかっていることを自覚していた。

✏️ 正解 ☐ hinge on …次第で決まる、…にかかる
誤答 ☐ cough up せきをして…を吐き出す、…をしぶしぶ渡す
☐ bring about …を引き起こす、…を成し遂げる
☐ spell out …を詳細に説明する、…のつづりを略さずに書く、…を理解する
英文 ☐ be aware that 節 …だと気づいている・知っている ☐ negotiation 交渉
☐ investor 投資家

(115) A: My son (   ) that game you got him for his birthday. I'm a little
concerned.

B: Maybe you should set a time limit on how often he can play.

1   burns off   **2**   melts away

3   puts forward   **4**   obsesses over

(116) The team's star player is (   ) for a new contract, but with their
current budget issues they might not be able to afford him anymore.

1   holding out   **2**   looking out

3   setting up   **4**   sticking up

(117) A: Here's the money I owe you from a few weeks ago. I meant to pay
you back, but I never (   ) it.

B: I thought you completely forgot! Thanks so much for remembering.

1   got around to   **2**   ended up with

3   held out for   **4**   backed off of

(115) 🔍 人物Aは「息子が、あなたが誕生日にプレゼントしたゲームに〜です。少し心配しています」と言っています。この時点で、恐らく、息子がゲームばかりやっていることを親が心配していると推測できますね。それに対して人物Bは「お子さんがどのぐらい遊べるか時間制限を設けた方がいいかもしれませんね」と提案しています。時間制限が必要になる状況をふまえて「…ばかりやっている」「取りつかれている」を表すイディオムを選択肢から選びましょう。

🔁 A：息子はあなたが誕生日にプレゼントしてくれたゲームに夢中なんです。少し心配しています。
B：お子さんがどのぐらい遊べるか時間制限を設けた方がいいかもしれませんね。

✏️ 正解 ☐ **obsess over** …に取りつかれる、…に執着する
誤答 ☐ **burn off** …を焼き払う、(エネルギー、脂肪、カロリーなど)を消費する
☐ **melt away** …を消失させる
☐ **put forward** …を提案する、推薦する、(名前)を挙げる、(時計の針)を進ませる
英文 ☐ **concerned** 心配している ☐ **time limit** 時間制限 ☐ **set a limit on** …に制限を設ける

(116) 🔍 空所を含む前半は「チームのスター選手は新しい契約を〜している」です。後半は接続詞のbutで始まり、「しかし、現在の予算問題では、もう彼にお金を払うことはできないかもしれない」とあるので、空所には予算の問題で危ぶまれる契約に対する動作として「望んでいる」「求めている」の意味のイディオムが入ると文意が成立することがわかります。

🔁 そのチームのスター選手は新しい契約の締結を要求しているが、現在の予算の問題がある限り、もう彼を雇うことはできないかもしれない。

✏️ 正解 ☐ **hold out for** …をあくまで要求する
誤答 ☐ **look out for** …を用心する、探す、世話をする
☐ **set up** 商売を始める、公言する、(機械などが)据えられる
☐ **stick up for** …を支持する
英文 ☐ **star player** スター選手、花形選手 ☐ **current** 現在の ☐ **budget** 予算 ☐ **issue** 問題点
☐ **afford** …を持つ余裕がある

(117) 🔍 人物Aは「数週間前に借りたお金です。返そうと思っていたのですが、決して〜しませんでした」と人物Bに話しています。それに対して人物Bは「完全に忘れていると思っていました！ 覚えていてくれて、本当にありがとうございます」と答えていることから、空所にはお金を返すまでの時間が長くなった理由になる文を成立させるものとして「時間をつくる」「機会を得る」の意味のイディオムが入るとわかります。選択肢より「手が回る」を表すイディオムを選びましょう。

🔁 A：数週間前に借りたお金です。返そうと思っていたのですが、なかなか返せませんでした。
B：完全に忘れられていると思っていました！ 覚えていてくれて、本当にありがとうございます。

✏️ 正解 ☐ **get around to** …に手が回る
誤答 ☐ **end up with** …で終わる、最後には…になる、ついには…となる
☐ **hold out for** 妥協せず断固として…を要求する
☐ **back off** 後退して離れる、引き下がる
英文 ☐ **owe A B** A(人)にBを借りている(ここでは money I owe you の money が B、you が A)
☐ **mean to** *do* …するつもりである

筆記 2

長文空所補充問題

Unit 1 …… チャレンジしよう！

Unit 2 …… 練習しよう！

アイコン一覧

 解説　 和訳　 語注　 正解　 構造解析

問題英文の読み方 P.112　解説・正解 P.118　訳・語句 P.120

The Baader-Meinhof Phenomenon

Otherwise known as the frequency bias, the Baader-Meinhof phenomenon is a trick our brains play on us. A common example is that we learn a new word and suddenly we see and hear that word everywhere. Another name for the phenomenon is "red car syndrome." We decide to buy a red car to stand out from the crowd, but every time we pull into a parking lot, all we see is red cars. What actually happens is that when we direct our attention to something, our awareness of it increases. In line with this trend, we then (**1**).

This is perfectly natural, and has happened to humans since the earliest civilizations. Its origin can be traced back to evolution: our ancestors had to be responsive to the objects and happenings around them, such as food sources or presence of dangerous animals, in order to stay alive. The frequency bias, our brain's ability to focus on what we are interested in, is a key part of our development. (**2**) paranoia, a mental condition in which a person tends to see objects, people or phenomena that are not there.

The frequency bias affects our brains in two consecutive stages. First, we sense that a certain event is frequent. Then, our brain makes us believe that that event did not occur as frequently before and we wonder what may have caused this change. People who do not know that these events are not happening more frequently—only our attention is more focused on them—are often drawn to wrong conclusions. (**3**), understanding how our mind works can prevent us from forming false ideas.

(1)　1　begin to see it as essential
　　　2　make an effort to find it
　　　3　learn to understand it better
　　　4　start noticing it more often

Date
／①②③④　／①②③④　／①②③④

(2)   **1**   That is a simpler way to explain
      2   It should not be confused with
      3   A common example of this is
      4   This could be a result of

(3)   **1**   So far
      2   In sum
      3   Incidentally
      4   Otherwise

筆記②

第1段落

The Baader-Meinhof Phenomenon

❶Otherwise known as the frequency bias, the Baader-Meinhof phenomenon is a trick our brains play on us. ❷A common example is that we learn a new word and suddenly we see and hear that word everywhere. ❸Another name for the phenomenon is "red car syndrome." ❹We decide to buy a red car to stand out from the crowd, but every time we pull into a parking lot, all we see is red cars. ❺What actually happens is that when we direct our attention to something, our awareness of it increases. ❻In line with this trend, we then (　1　).

❶ 1文目の冒頭は Otherwise で始まっていますが、主語はコンマの後の the Baader-Meinhof phenomenon です。しっかりと頭の中で「別の知られ方は～だが、バーダーマインホフ現象は…である」と主語を明らかにして読み始めましょう。また、「バーダーマインホフ現象はトリックだ」の trick とは、どのような意味でしょう。trick ということは「脳が私たちをだましているトリック」なのだと理解して、この現象やトリックについて展開されるのだろうと予測しながら読み進めます。

❷ 「よくある例は」で始まっています。さて、何の例でしょうか？ 1文目はバーダーマインホフ現象について言っていたので、バーダーマインホフ現象の例ですね。「バーダーマインホフ現象の例は、私たちが新しい単語を覚えると、すぐにその単語を色々なところで見たり聞いたりするようになるということだ」という意味です。

❸ 3文目の the phenomenon はバーダーマインホフ現象を言い換えています。英文では、このように、同一段落での各文で同じ事象を言い方を変えて示すことがよくあります。the のついた語を見つけたら毎回「あれ？ 今度はこんな風に言い換えているのか」と確認しながら読み進めましょう。「バーダーマインホフ現象の他の言い方は～です」と言っています。

❹ 4文目では他の言い方である「red car syndrome」の由来を説明しています。赤い車を意識するようになると、赤い車しか目に入らなくなる状況のことを言っています。

❺ 5文目では赤い車しか目に入らないときに何が起こっているのか説明しています。「実際に起こっていることは」で始まっています。最初の what を疑問詞の「何が～？」の意味にとらないように注意しましょう。What は関係代名詞です。「実際に起こっていることは」の後の that 節は「何かに注意を向けたら、それに対する意識が高まる」です。

❻ この段落の最後の文は空所があり、「この傾向（何かに注意を向けたら気づくようになること）とともに、私たちは（1）」という意味です。this は何を指しているのか、しっかりイメージできているかどうかを確認しながら読み進めましょう。
この段落ではバーダーマインホフ現象について説明していました。

第2段落

❶This is perfectly natural, and has happened to humans since the earliest civilizations. ❷Its origin can be traced back to evolution: our ancestors had to be responsive to the objects and happenings around them, such as food sources or presence of dangerous animals, in order to stay alive. ❸The frequency bias, our brain's ability to focus on what we are interested in, is a key part of our development. ❹(2) paranoia, a mental condition in which a person tends to see objects, people or phenomena that are not there.

❶ 「このことは完全に自然なことだ」で始まっています。そして、This が主語のまま、2つ目の動詞は現在完了形となり、「〜以来、人類に起こってきた」と続いています。

This は前の段落の内容、つまり、バーダーマインホフ現象を指しています。バーダーマインホフ現象が起こることは自然であり、太古の文明を築いてからずっと起こってきた現象であることを示しています。

❷ バーダーマインホフ現象について、さらに「進化にさかのぼることができる」と言って、それが人類にとってどんなに自然なことかを示しています。：（コロン）は「つまり」の意味で解釈しましょう。our ancestors had to be responsive の responsive を responsible「責任がある」と間違って解釈しないようにしましょう。「私たちの祖先は生きるために食料や、危険な動物たちなど、まわりの事象に反応しなければならなかった」と言っています。

❸ 今度もバーダーマインホフ現象をまた別の言い方に変えて、この現象が自然であることについてさらに説明を加えています。「この、頻度バイアス（注意が集中して頻度が高いと感じられる傾向）つまり、自分の興味のある対象に集中する傾向は、人間の進化に重要な役割を果たしている」と言っています。

❹ 4文目では、空欄の後に paranoia とあり、カンマに続く部分で paranoia は「ありもしないものが見える傾向」だと説明しています。ここで新しく出てきた用語、paranoia についてのイメージを自分なりに当てはめて作っておきましょう。パラノイアは、実際は悪口を言われていないのに、悪口を言っているに違いないと思い込んだり、他人が常に自分を批判していると思い込んだりすることです。

この段落では、バーダーマインホフ現象はごく自然に起こることだと説明していました。

筆記②

第3段落

❶The frequency bias affects our brains in two consecutive stages. ❷First, we sense that a certain event is frequent. ❸Then, our brain makes us believe that that event did not occur as frequently before and we wonder what may have caused this change. ❹People who do not know that these events are not happening more frequently—only our attention is more focused on them—are often drawn to wrong conclusions. ❺(3), understanding how our mind works can prevent us from forming false ideas.

❶❷❸ もう一度、バーダーマインホフ現象のことを「頻度バイアス」と言い換えて文を始めています。「このバイアス（注意が集中して頻度が高いと感じられる傾向）は、2段階で脳に影響する」と言っています。続く文でおそらくその2段階について説明していると予想して読み進めましょう。

　すると直後に First, とあり、第一段階についての説明であるとわかります。「（私たちは）ある出来事が頻繁に起こると思う」。続いて Then, とあるので、ここから第二段階についての説明として「その出来事は前はそんなに頻繁に起こらなかったけれども、どうして頻繁に起こり始めるのかと疑問に思う」と述べられています。

❹ この文は長いので、文頭からピリオドまで一瞬目を通して、主語がどこまでか確認しましょう。「出来事が前よりも頻繁に起こり始めたのではなくて、私たちが前よりも注意を向け始めただけということがわかっていない人」までが主語だとわかります。ダーシ（—）で挟まれた部分を取り払っても文が通じることを知っておけば慌てずに済みます。ここでは、つまり、「頻度バイアスがあると知らずに実際の出来事が増え始めたと思うと、勘違いを引き起こす」と言っています。

- -

❺ 主語は「我々の心がどのように働いているかを理解すること」です。つまり「バーダーマインホフ現象を例に出して説明した、我々の心の仕組みを理解すると、間違った考えを起こさずに済む」と述べて、この文章の全体をまとめています。

この段落単体としてはバーダーマインホフ現象が起きるときに脳が受けている影響について説明していました。

筆記 2

(1)　1　begin to see it as essential
　　　2　make an effort to find it
　　　3　learn to understand it better
　　　4　start noticing it more often

(2)　1　That is a simpler way to explain
　　　2　It should not be confused with
　　　3　A common example of this is
　　　4　This could be a result of

(3)　1　So far
　　　2　In sum
　　　3　Incidentally
　　　4　Otherwise

(1) 📝
1 それが不可欠であると考え始める
2 それを見つけるために努力する
3 それをよりよく理解することを学ぶ
4 より頻繁にそれに気づくようになる

🔍 第1段落の**⑤**にある「何かに注意を向けると、それに対する意識が高まる」という空所の直前の内容を理解できていれば、「より頻繁にそのことに気づくことになる」という意味の4 start noticing it more often を選択することができます。1は「それが不可欠である」では**②**〜**④**にあるバーダーマインホフ現象の例と違う意味になってしまうので不正解。2は赤い車を見るのにわざわざ「努力」する必要はなく、自然に目に入ってくるので不正解。3も「理解する」かどうかについては語られていないので不正解となります。

✏️ □ essential …必須の

. . . .

(2) 📝
1 それは…を説明するのに簡単な方法だ
2 それは…と混同されるべきではない
3 このよくある例は…だ
4 これは…の結果となる可能性がある

🔍 空所を含む文の直前にあたる第2段落の**❸**で、バーダーマインホフ現象は興味のあることに集中する脳の働きだと説明しています。そして、空所を含む文では、パラノイアについて書いてあり、興味の対象が自然と目に入ってくるバーダーマインホフ現象はパラノイアの症状とは違うとわかるので、2つを区別しなければいけないという意味になる2 It should not be confused with が正解です。1は第2段落がパラノイアについて説明しているわけではないので、不正解。3は paranoia は一つの例ではないので不正解。4もバーダーマインホフ現象と paranoia は、原因と結果の関係にはないので不正解となります。

✏️ □ confuse A with B AをBと混同する

. . . .

(3) 📝
1 これまでのところ
2 まとめて
3 ちなみに
4 そうでなければ

🔍 第3段落の最後の文**⑤**で、心の仕組みを理解することでどのような効果があるか、まとめの説明をしているので、2 In sum「要するに」が正解となります。1 So far「ここまでは」ではこれから何か続きそうですが、この文は最終文であり、課題を投げかけるような結びにもなっていないので、不正解。3 Incidentally「ちなみに」も一部の追加情報を言っているわけではないので、不正解。4「そうでなければ」は逆説を述べるときに使いますが、この文は特に読者への問いを投げかけるのでもなく、まとめの説明をしており、逆接は当てはまらないため、不正解となります。

🚩 **(1)** 4 **(2)** 2 **(3)** 2

The Baader-Meinhof Phenomenon

第1段落

❶ Otherwise known as the frequency bias, the Baader-Meinhof phenomenon is a trick our brains play on us.

❷ A common example is that we learn a new word and suddenly we see and hear that word everywhere.

❸ Another name for the phenomenon is "red car syndrome."

❹ We decide to buy a red car to stand out from the crowd, but every time we pull into a parking lot, all we see is red cars.

❺ What actually happens is that when we direct our attention to something, our awareness of it increases.

❻ In line with this trend, we then start noticing it more often.

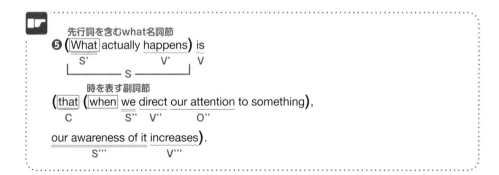

バーダー・マインホフ現象

第1段落

❶ 「頻度バイアス」という別名でも知られるバーダー・マインホフ現象（Baader-Meinhof phenomenon）は、私たちの脳が仕掛けるトリックだ。

❷ よくある例としては、新しい単語を知ると、突然その単語があちこちで見えたり聞こえたりするようになることが挙げられる。

❸ この現象の別名は、「赤い車症候群」だ。

❹ 目立つようにと赤い車を買うことにしたが、駐車場に車を止めるたびに赤い車ばかりが目についてしまうのだ。

❺ 実際に起こっているのは、何かに注意を向けると、それに対する意識が高まるということだ。

❻ それに伴い、私たちはその後、より頻繁にそのことに気づくようになる。

❶□ phenomenon 現象
□ otherwise known as 別名…と知られているが（otherwise は「別な方法で」） □ frequency 頻度
□ bias 偏向、偏り □ trick 錯覚 □ play A on B A（いたずらなど）を B（人）にする
❸□ syndrome 症候群 ❹□ stand out 目立つ □ crowd 群衆、人込み □ pull into 車を…に入れる
□ parking lot 駐車場 ❺□ direct A to B A を B に向ける □ awareness 意識、認識
❻□ in line with …と一致して、…に従って □ notice …に気がつく

筆記②

第2段落

❶ This is perfectly natural, and has happened to humans since the earliest civilizations.

❷ Its origin can be traced back to evolution: our ancestors had to be responsive to the objects and happenings around them, such as food sources or presence of dangerous animals, in order to stay alive.

❸ The frequency bias, our brain's ability to focus on what we are interested in, is a key part of our development.

❹ It should not be confused with paranoia, a mental condition in which a person tends to see objects, people or phenomena that are not there.

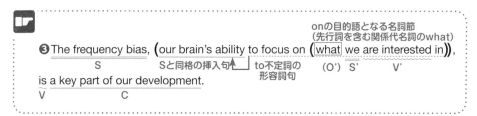

第3段落

❶ The frequency bias affects our brains in two consecutive stages.

❷ First, we sense that a certain event is frequent.

❸ Then, our brain makes us believe that that event did not occur as frequently before and we wonder what may have caused this change.

❹ People who do not know that these events are not happening more frequently—only our attention is more focused on them—are often drawn to wrong conclusions.

❺ In sum, understanding how our mind works can prevent us from forming false ideas.

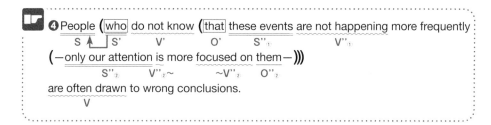

第2段落

❶ これはごく自然で、人類が太古の文明を築いて以来、ずっと続いていることだ。

❷ その起源は進化にさかのぼる。つまり、私たちの祖先は、生きていくために、食料源や危険な動物の存在など、身の回りの物や出来事に敏感に反応する必要があったのだ。

❸ 頻度錯誤という、興味のあることに集中する脳の働きは、私たちの進化に重要な役割を果たしている。

❹ ありもしない物や人、現象が見える傾向がある精神状態であるパラノイアと混同しないようにしなければならない。

❶ □ civilization 文明社会　❷ □ origin 起源　□ trace …の跡をたどる　□ evolution 進化
□ ancestor 祖先　□ responsive 敏感な　□ object 物体　□ presence 存在
❸ □ development 発達、進化　❹ □ confuse A with B A と B を混同する
□ paranoia 偏執病、妄想症　□ phenomena 現象（phenomenon の複数形）

第3段落

❶ 頻度錯誤は、2段階連続して私たちの脳に影響を及ぼす。

❷ まず、ある事象が頻繁に起こることを感じ取る。

❸ すると、脳は、その出来事が以前ほど頻繁には起こらなかったと思い込み、何がこのような変化をもたらしたのだろうかと考える。

❹ このような現象が頻繁に起こるようになったわけではなく、自分たちの注意力が高まっただけだとわかっていない人は往々にして誤った結論を導き出してしまう。

❺ つまり、心の仕組みを理解することで、誤った考えを抱くのを防ぐことができるのである。

❶ □ affect …に影響を及ぼす　□ consecutive 連続的な　❷ □ sense that 節 …だと感じる
□ frequent 頻繁な　❸ □ cause …を引き起こす　❹ □ conclusion 結論　□ draw …を引き寄せる
❺ □ in sum 要するに　□ prevent X from *doing* X が…するのを防ぐ　□ false 誤った、不正確な

問題英文の読み方 P.126　解説・正解 P.132　訳・語句 P.134

Making Water from Air

　　Arizona and New Mexico are located in the southwestern region of the United States and are the second and fourth-driest states in the country. They have a desert climate, which means extremely hot summers, mild winters, and only about 250 millimeters of rain per year. Climatologists (experts in climate science) predict that, because of climate change, these regions will become even drier and warmer over the coming decades. (**1**), rising temperatures will cause longer droughts—long periods without any rain—and water will be even harder to obtain for the native tribes, such as the Navajo, that live there.

　　An American company, along with some nonprofit organizations and a generous grant from a venture capitalist group, has started a project to help solve the problem. A set of "hydropanels" has been installed in a Navajo community, enabling fifteen households to get access to clean drinking water. The hydropanels are powered by solar energy—the most efficient and affordable independent power source in a dry and hot territory. The company operates the system in fifty countries worldwide, and confidently asserts that an installed system (**2**). This level of independence is important for remote areas like desert villages.

　　The technology behind the panels is relatively straightforward. Solar energy powers the fans inside the hydropanels that draw in air from the atmosphere. The air is then pushed through a water-absorbing material, which traps its water vapor content. The vapor is then condensed into water. A container collects the water and then some vital minerals are added (**3**). This is important in an area where the human body needs all the help it can get. The panels can be directly linked to faucets or home plumbing to provide maximum convenience.

(1)　　**1**　However
　　　　2　Furthermore
　　　　3　Otherwise
　　　　4　For example

Date ／ ①②③④ ／ ①②③④ ／ ①②③④

(2) **1**   can operate alone for many years
      2   will soon move out of the testing phase
      3   may bring some new research benefits
      4   is only for demonstration purposes

(3) **1**   to monitor the quality of the water
      2   because of the high heat they can generate
      3   as a way to make the liquid healthier
      4   to remove toxins from the hydropanels

Making Water from Air

❶Arizona and New Mexico are located in the southwestern region of the United States and are the second and fourth-driest states in the country. ❷They have a desert climate, which means extremely hot summers, mild winters, and only about 250 millimeters of rain per year. ❸Climatologists (experts in climate science) predict that, because of climate change, these regions will become even drier and warmer over the coming decades. ❹(1), rising temperatures will cause longer droughts—long periods without any rain—and water will be even harder to obtain for the native tribes, such as the Navajo, that live there.

❶ 「アリゾナ州とニューメキシコ州は〜に位置しています」で始まっています。Arizona や New Mexico のように「州」の名前だけを使うことが普通です。アメリカの地図が頭に入っていない人は地図で州の場所を把握しておくことをお勧めします。他の問題で出ることもありますし、特徴や位置関係がつかめると読解の助けになります。the second and fourth-driest states は文頭の順番のとおりに読むと、「アメリカの南西部に位置し、全米で2番目に乾燥している州がアリゾナで、4番目に乾燥している州がニューメキシコだ」ということです。

❷ 主語の They は「アリゾナ州とニューメキシコ州」です。「アリゾナ州とニューメキシコ州は砂漠気候を持っている」の後に主格の関係代名詞 which が来て、動詞は means なので、「それ（a disert climate）は、極端に暑い夏と、マイルドな冬と、1年あたりたった250ミリの雨を意味する」と言っています。

❸ 最初の語が明らかに難解な場合、きっとそれを何らかの方法で説明している部分があります。ここでは最初の Climatologists の直後に（　）があり、そこで「気候科学の専門家」と説明してくれています。「気候学者が予測している」内容は that 以下に出てきます。that 以下は because of climate change が前置詞句で、these regions が主語、will become が動詞です。「気候変動の理由により、これらの地域は今後数十年の間にさらに乾燥し、気温が上昇する」とあります。

❹ （1）の選択肢を見ると、ここには文と文をつなぐ言葉が入ることがわかります。前の文に「気候変動の理由により、これらの地域はさらに乾燥し、気温が上昇する」とあり、そして空所の後には「気温の上昇がさらに長い干ばつを引き起こす、そして水は先住民にとってより確保するのが難しくなる」と続いています。native tribes, such as the Navajo, の the Navajo は「ナバホ族」のことです。「水の確保は難しくなることが予想される」で段落が終わっているので、その解決策が次の段落で展開されるだろうと考えられます。
この段落では砂漠地帯での水の確保が難しくなることについて述べていました。

第2段落

❶An American company, along with some nonprofit organizations and a generous grant from a venture capitalist group, has started a project to help solve the problem. ❷A set of "hydropanels" has been installed in a Navajo community, enabling fifteen households to get access to clean drinking water. ❸The hydropanels are powered by solar energy—the most efficient and affordable independent power source in a dry and hot territory. ❹The company operates the system in fifty countries worldwide, and confidently asserts that an installed system (　2　). ❺This level of independence is important for remote areas like desert villages.

❶「あるアメリカの企業」が主語です。「アメリカの企業が非営利団体とともにベンチャーキャピタルのグループから得た多額の助成金をもって、この問題を解決するためのプロジェクトを始めた」と言っています。コンマで挟まれた along with some nonprofit organizations and a generous grant from a venture capitalist group の部分をじっくり一語一語訳すことに気を取られると全体の流れを見失ってしまうので、目を通す範囲を少し先まで広げて、まず「主語」と「動詞」をしっかりと捉えましょう。ここの場合だと、まず「アメリカの企業が問題解決のためのプロジェクトを始めた」の部分を把握して、その後で補足部分を理解するのです。

❷ この文を読み始める前から、前の文で述べられた、アメリカの企業が始めたプロジェクトについて詳細に語られると推測できます。実際、A set of "hydropanels" という、この文章では初めて見る単語で始まっています。「ハイドロパネル」とは何だろう？ と疑問に思うはずですが、詳しくは続く文で説明されていると考えて、「ハイドロパネルとは何か」は頭の隅に置いておきましょう。この文章では「ハイドロパネルのセットがナバホコミュニティーに設置された」とあり、それにより15世帯がきれいな飲み水にアクセスすることを可能にしたと言っています。

❸ ハイドロパネルについての説明が続きます。「ハイドロパネルは太陽エネルギーで動いている」のところで、何の資源により動いているのかがわかります。そして、―（ダーシ）以下で「太陽エネルギー」を具体的に説明しています。「乾燥した暑い地域で最も効率的かつ安価な独立したエネルギー資源である（太陽エネルギーでハイドロパネルは動いている）」という意味になります。しかし、まだハイドロパネルがどのような働きをするか説明されていません。

❹ The company というのは、この段落の最初に出てきた「アメリカのとある企業」ですね。この企業が「このシステムを世界中の50か国で運用しており、その設置システムは（2）である、と自信をもって言っている」とあります。

❺「このくらいの（高い）レベルに自立していることが、遠隔地では重要である」と言っています。
この段落では、砂漠気候の州において、水を確保しようとするプロジェクトによるハイドロパネルがどこに設置され、どのように活躍しているかについて書かれているということを確認しておきましょう。

筆記
②

第3段落

❶The technology behind the panels is relatively straightforward. ❷Solar energy powers the fans inside the hydropanels that draw in air from the atmosphere. ❸The air is then pushed through a water-absorbing material, which traps its water vapor content. ❹The vapor is then condensed into water. ❺A container collects the water and then some vital minerals are added (　3　). ❻This is important in an area where the human body needs all the help it can get. ❼The panels can be directly linked to faucets or home plumbing to provide maximum convenience.

❶ 第2段落ではハイドロパネルが多くの国で運用可能であることを言っていました。しかし、ハイドロパネルが何であるかという疑問は解けていませんね。この段落の冒頭は「このハイドロパネルを動かしている技術は」で始まっているので、疑問が解けると推測して、読み進めましょう。「ハイドロパネルを動かしている技術は straightforward だ」と言っているので、単語の意味が万一わからなくても、「ストレートだ」→「まっすぐだ」→「すなおだ」→「簡単だ」のように連想して解釈しておきましょう。

❷ 前の文とのつながりから、ハイドロパネルを動かしている技術が簡単であることについて話が展開されていると予測しながら読みましょう。実際、ハイドロパネルの技術について説明されています。主語は Solar energy、動詞は powers「動力を供給する」で、「太陽エネルギーはハイドロパネル内のファンに動力を与え、それが大気中の空気を取り込む」と言っています。

❸❹ 3文目と4文目はハイドロパネルを動かしている技術の説明を続けています。「そして空気は吸水性のある素材の中に取り込まれ、それが水蒸気を閉じ込める。そしてその水蒸気は凝縮して水になる」という文の流れになっています。

❺ 5文目でもハイドロパネルを動かしている技術の説明が続き、「容器がその水を集め、重要なミネラルが加えられる」とあります。

❻ 5文目にあった「容器が水を集め、ミネラルを加える」という説明に続いて6文目には「このことは手に入る限りのサポートを人体が必要とするような環境では重要なことだ」とあります。

❼ 最後の文では「パネルは、蛇口や家庭の配管に直接接続することができ、最大限の利便性を提供することができる」と言って、パネルの仕組みが簡単であり、家庭の配管につなぐことも簡単であるため使いやすいということを述べて、文を締めくくっています。
この段落では、ハイドロパネルの仕組みが簡単であることを説明していました。

筆記②

131

(1) 1 However
2 Furthermore
3 Otherwise
4 For example

(2) 1 can operate alone for many years
2 will soon move out of the testing phase
3 may bring some new research benefits
4 is only for demonstration purposes

(3) 1 to monitor the quality of the water
2 because of the high heat they can generate
3 as a way to make the liquid healthier
4 to remove toxins from the hydropanels

(1) 🔲 1 しかし
       2 さらに
       3 そうでなければ
       4 例えば

🔍 第1段落の空所 (1) の前にある文❸を見ると気候変動が原因で起こることが述べられていて、空所のある文❹でも同様に気候変動によってもたらされる問題が述べられています。したがって、空所以下は、「気候変動によって起こることの追加情報」だと考えられるので、Furthermore が正解です。1 However は「けれども」、3 Otherwise は「そうでなければ」、4 For example は「例えば」なので、いずれも追加情報を導くことにはならず、不正解です。

(2) 🔲 1 何年も単独で運用できる
       2 すぐにテスト段階を終えるだろう
       3 新たな研究成果が得られる可能性がある
       4 実証実験のためだけである

🔍 第2段落の空所 (2) を含む文❹の「このシステムが世界50か国で使用されている」の部分で、この企業によるシステムは世界中で使用されるほど成功していることがわかります。したがって、「その設置システムは〜」の空所に入るのは利点や優れている点であると考えられます。また空所を含む文の次❺で「このレベルで自立していることが重要だ」と述べていることから、程度が確立されているものだと判断することができます。これに合う選択肢は「何年も単独で運用できる」の意味の1 can operate alone for many years です。2は実際に使用されているので「テスト段階」は間違い。3は新たな研究成果が得られるという将来性だけでは、自立していることにはならないので不正解。4「デモンストレーションのためだけ」では意味がつながらないので不正解となります。

✏️ ☐ operate 稼働する、作動する ☐ phase 段階 ☐ move out of …から出ていく
☐ demonstration 実演説明、証明

(3) 🔲 1 水質を常にチェックするため
       2 高熱を発生させることができるため
       3 体にいい液体にする方法として
       4 ハイドロパネルから有害物質を除去するため

🔍 第3段落の❺で「容器が水を集め、ミネラルを加え」、❻で「これは、手に入る限りのサポートを人体が必要とするような環境では重要なこと」と言っています。人体が必要とする補助を選択肢の中から選んでいくと、最もふさわしいのは3「体にいい液体にする方法」だとわかります。1はミネラルが加えられても水質をチェックすることにならないので不正解。2は温度については言っていないので間違い。4は有害物質に関しては他に言及している場所がないので、不正解となります。

✏️ ☐ monitor …を検査する、…を観察する ☐ generate …を発生させる ☐ toxin 毒素

🚩 (1) 2 (2) 1 (3) 3

筆記2

Making Water from Air

第1段落

❶ Arizona and New Mexico are located in the southwestern region of the United States and are the second and fourth-driest states in the country.

❷ They have a desert climate, which means extremely hot summers, mild winters, and only about 250 millimeters of rain per year.

❸ Climatologists (experts in climate science) predict that, because of climate change, these regions will become even drier and warmer over the coming decades.

❹ Furthermore, rising temperatures will cause longer droughts—long periods without any rain—and water will be even harder to obtain for the native tribes, such as the Navajo, that live there.

第2段落

❶ An American company, along with some nonprofit organizations and a generous grant from a venture capitalist group, has started a project to help solve the problem.

❷ A set of "hydropanels" has been installed in a Navajo community, enabling fifteen households to get access to clean drinking water.

❸ The hydropanels are powered by solar energy—the most efficient and affordable independent power source in a dry and hot territory.

❹ The company operates the system in fifty countries worldwide, and confidently asserts that an installed system can operate alone for many years.

❺ This level of independence is important for remote areas like desert villages.

空気から水をつくる

第1段落

❶ アリゾナ州とニューメキシコ州は、アメリカの南西部に位置し、全米で2番目と4番目に乾燥している州だ。

❷ この2つの州は砂漠気候で、夏は非常に暑く、冬は温暖で、年間降水量は約250mm しかない。

❸ 気候変動により、これらの地域は今後数十年の間にさらに乾燥し気温が上昇すると気候学者（気候科学の専門家）は予測している。

❹ さらに、気温の上昇によって干ばつ（延々と続く雨が降らない期間）が長くなり、そこに住むナバホ族などの先住民にとって、水の確保がさらに難しくなることが予想される。

❶□ be located in …に位置する　❷□ desert 砂漠　❸□ climatologist 気候学者
□ predict that 節 …を予測する、…を予報する　□ coming 来たるべき　□ decade 10年間
❹□ drought 干ばつ　□ obtain …を得る　□ tribe 部族

第2段落

❶ アメリカのある企業が、この問題を解決するために非営利団体と共同でベンチャーキャピタルのグループから多額の助成金を得て、プロジェクトをスタートさせた。

❷ ナバホ族の集落に「ハイドロパネル」を設置し、15世帯が清潔な飲み水を手に入れることができるようになった。

❸ このハイドロパネルは、乾燥した暑い地域で最も効率的かつ安価な独立したエネルギー資源である太陽エネルギーで駆動している。

❹ 同社は世界50カ国でこのシステムを運用しており、設置したシステムは何年も単独で運用できる、と自信をもって言う。

❺ 砂漠の村のような遠隔地では、このような自立性が重要なのだ。

❶□ along with …と一緒に　□ nonprofit 非営利の　□ generous たくさんの、豊富な
□ grant 助成金　□ venture 投機、投機的事業　□ capitalist 資本家
□ help do …するのを助ける（do の前の to はよく省略される）　❷□ hydro- 水の
□ enable X to do X が…できるようにする　□ household 世帯　□ get access to …を手に入れる
❸□ power …を稼働させる・動かす　□ efficient 効率のいい　□ affordable 手ごろな、入手可能な
❹□ confidently 自信をもって　□ assert that 節 …と主張する　❺□ remote 遠隔の

第3段落

❶ The technology behind the panels is relatively straightforward.

❷ Solar energy powers the fans inside the hydropanels that draw in air from the atmosphere.

❸ The air is then pushed through a water-absorbing material, which traps its water vapor content.

❹ The vapor is then condensed into water.

❺ A container collects the water and then some vital minerals are added as a way to make the liquid healthier.

❻ This is important in an area where the human body needs all the help it can get.

❼ The panels can be directly linked to faucets or home plumbing to provide maximum convenience.

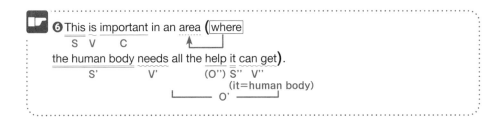

❶ パネルの仕組みは比較的簡単だ。

❷ 太陽エネルギーを動力源として、ハイドロパネル内のファンが大気中の空気を取り込む。

❸ その空気を吸水性のある素材の中に通し、水蒸気を閉じ込める。

❹ そして、その水蒸気を凝縮させて水にする。

❺ その水を容器に溜め、さらに重要なミネラルを加えることで、体にいい液体にする。

❻ これは、手に入る限りのサポートを人体が必要とするような環境では重要なことだ。

❼ パネルは、蛇口や家庭の配管に直接接続することができ、最大限の利便性を提供することができる。

❶□ panel パネル　□ relatively 比較的に　□ straightforward 簡単な、わかりやすい
❷□ fan 扇形のもの、ファン　□ draw in …を吸い込む、…を引き入れる
❸□ water-absorbing 吸水性の　□ trap （ガス・エネルギーなど）を逃がさない、…をためる
□ vapor 蒸気（water vapor content で「水蒸気量」）　❹□ condense …を凝縮する、…を圧縮する
❺□ container 容器　□ vital 生命の維持に必要な　❼□ faucet （水道の）蛇口　□ plumbing 配管

筆記②

The Vienna Vegetable Orchestra

Experimental music began in the middle of the 20th century, mainly in Europe and North America. (**1**) traditional music, which follows a highly structured pattern laid down in minute detail, experimental music is unique. It is not composed beforehand. An experimental musician will begin to play without any plan or expecting a specific outcome. Experimental music is not written out in notes, so it is difficult for one musician to pass on a piece to another.

Experimental musicians may use traditional instruments such as pianos or trumpets but also non-traditional ones, such as glass, wood or pots and pans. The Vienna Vegetable Orchestra may fall within this music genre. The Vegetable Orchestra players use all sorts of vegetables to make music. On performance days, they first go out to the market to choose the vegetables. They then carefully handcraft the vegetables into various instruments to suit their purpose. This means they must (**2**).

The music itself may not be experimental from a strict point of view, since the musicians play from sheet music and perform known classical pieces. The orchestra has played on several famous stages around the world, entertaining the audience with the unique sounds the vegetables make. However, they need to get new vegetables every time, because the ones used for playing (**3**). Unlike their metal counterparts, these instruments cannot survive more than an hour or two of rough handling.

(1)　**1**　Unaware of
　　　2　Aside from
　　　3　Contrary to
　　　4　In addition to

(2)
1   be detailed in their plans
2   choose stores carefully
3   enjoy a variety of items
4   be skilled as carvers

(3)
1   have to be returned to the market later
2   are destroyed by the end of the show
3   get preserved for future musical events
4   are in great demand by the audience

The Vienna Vegetable Orchestra

❶Experimental music began in the middle of the 20th century, mainly in Europe and North America. ❷(　1　) traditional music, which follows a highly structured pattern laid down in minute detail, experimental music is unique. ❸It is not composed beforehand. ❹An experimental musician will begin to play without any plan or expecting a specific outcome. ❺Experimental music is not written out in notes, so it is difficult for one musician to pass on a piece to another.

❶ 1文目の冒頭は Experimental music で始まっています。おそらく音楽に詳しくなければ、この意味がわからないですし、「Experimental＝実験の」と訳せても、イメージするのは難しいですね。ひとまず、「実験音楽」と直訳して読み進めましょう。「実験音楽は20世紀半ばに始まった」の後に修飾語が続いているので「実験音楽は主にヨーロッパや北米で20世紀半ばに始まった」と理解しておきます。

❷ 空所（1）の後に traditional music, とあります。コンマの後は関係代名詞の which が続くので、関係代名詞節については traditional music を主語とし、follows を動詞とした「伝統的な音楽（→主語）は細部にわたって表現され、高度な構成パターンに従っている（→動詞）」という構造になっていることを理解しましょう（P.148参照）。「細部にわたって表現され、高度な構成パターンにしたがっている伝統的な音楽」という仮の訳が頭に浮かびます。detail, までがこの文の修飾語句で、その後に experimental music is unique という SVC の構造の文が続いています。「実験音楽は独特である」と言っています。

❸ 3文目は「それは前もって作曲されていない」と言っています。It が指すものは experimental music です。

❹ 通常、英文を読む際に意識すべきことは、1文目、2文目…と進んでも主語に変化はあまりなく、言い方を変えて同じものを表していることが多いということです。4文目の主語は、今度は「実験音楽」ではなく、「実験音楽家」ですので、ここで少し変化があることに気づきましょう。「実験音楽家は何の計画もなく、ある結果を期待することもしないで演奏を開始する」と言っています。なお、ここの will は未来のことではなく、「いつも決まって～する」ということを表します。

❺ 5文目の主語はまた「実験音楽」です。「実験音楽は音符として書き出されていない」と言っています。つまり3文目から続く流れでは「実験音楽は、前もって作曲されていないし、計画もなく、結果を期待されず、譜面に書かれてもいない」と、実験音楽にないものばかりを並べていますね。だから、「音楽家が音楽を誰かに引き継ぐことが困難なのだ」と言っています。
この段落では「実験音楽」について紹介していました。

第2段落

❶Experimental musicians may use traditional instruments such as pianos or trumpets but also non-traditional ones, such as glass, wood or pots and pans. ❷The Vienna Vegetable Orchestra may fall within this music genre. ❸The Vegetable Orchestra players use all sorts of vegetables to make music. ❹On performance days, they first go out to the market to choose the vegetables. ❺They then carefully handcraft the vegetables into various instruments to suit their purpose. ❻This means they must (2).

❶ 1文目の主語は「実験音楽家」です。「実験音楽家はピアノやトランペットのような伝統的な楽器を使うこともあるが、伝統的でないものも使う」と言っています。読み手は前のパラグラフで実験音楽が「伝統的なものではなく、ユニークなものだ」と理解していますので、「実験音楽家は伝統的でないものも使う」と書いてあると、しっくりくるでしょう。「伝統的でない楽器」として「ガラスや、木や、鍋やフライパン」が挙げられています。

❷ タイトルにある The Vienna Vegetable Orchestra という用語が、ようやくここで登場してきました。Vienna とはオーストリアの首都、ウィーンのことです。英文を読むときにわからない人名や地名にフォーカスするのではなく、構造を理解し、わからないところをわからないと確認するだけで、とりあえずは読み進めることができます。構造のまま素直に「ウィーン・ベジタブル・オーケストラは、このミュージックジャンルの中に落ちるかもしれない」と読み、意味が具体的でない部分は、周りの文をヒントにして浮かんだイメージを当てはめて考えます。つまり「ウィーン・ベジタブル・オーケストラは、このミュージックのジャンルに入るかもしれない」と解釈すればいいのです。

❸ 3文目の主語は、「ベジタブル・オーケストラの演奏家たち」です。動詞は「使う」です。ベジタブルオーケストラの奏者たちは、音楽を作るために、あらゆる種類の野菜を使う」と言っています。

❹ 4文目の主語は they、つまり、3文目の「ベジタブル・オーケストラの演奏家たち」を指しています。動詞は go なので、「彼らは、行く」の骨格部分の解釈は変えないでください。「演奏の日には、彼らは野菜を選ぶために、最初に市場に出かけていく」と言っています。

❺ 5文目は They が主語、handcraft が動詞です。They は「ベジタブル・オーケストラの演奏家たち」を指していて、handcraft は「手細工で作る」です。単語の意味がわからなくても handcraft が動詞だと認識できれば、hand で craft するのだから、「手で作る」とわかります。「演奏家たちは、その野菜を丁寧に手で加工し、さまざまな楽器に仕上げる、目的にかなうように」と解釈しましょう。

❻ This が主語、means が動詞です。「これが意味するのは彼らが〜すべきだということだ」と言っています。
この段落では、実験音楽に使われる楽器へと話が発展していました。

第3段落

❶The music itself may not be experimental from a strict point of view, since the musicians play from sheet music and perform known classical pieces. ❷The orchestra has played on several famous stages around the world, entertaining the audience with the unique sounds the vegetables make. ❸However, they need to get new vegetables every time, because the ones used for playing (　3　). ❹Unlike their metal counterparts, these instruments cannot survive more than an hour or two of rough handling.

❶ 文全体の構造を見てみると、since の前までが主節、since の後が「〜なので」という意味の従属節となります。主節の文構造は SVC の2文型です。「音楽家はクラシックの楽譜に書いてある音楽を演奏するので、音楽そのものは、厳密には実験的とはいえないかもしれない」の意味になります。from a strict point of view は from という前置詞で始まっているので、文の骨格に関わらない「修飾語句」です。「厳密な見方をすると」と解釈しておきましょう。(P.152参照)

❷ この文の主語は The orchestra で「ウィーン・ベジタブル・オーケストラ」を指しています。world, までの部分には「このオーケストラは世界中でいくつもの有名なステージで演奏した」とあります。後半の entertaining 以降は分詞構文です。entertaining 以降は「(オーケストラは) それらの野菜が奏でるユニークな音で観客を楽しませてきた」という意味です。

❸ 3文目は However で始まっていることに注意して読みましょう。the ones は vegetables を指していて、「けれども、演奏に使った野菜は (3) なので、彼らは新しい野菜がいつも必要である」となります。

❹ 最後の文の主語は these instruments、動詞は cannot survive で直訳すると「これらの楽器は生きていくことができません」となります。their metal counterparts は金属の楽器のことを指しています。「これらの (野菜の) 楽器は、金属の楽器と違って、雑な扱いを受けると1、2時間以上は耐えられない」と言っています。
この段落ではウィーン・ベジタブル・オーケストラの音楽についてまとめていました。

筆記②

(1)　1　Unaware of
　　　　2　Aside from
　　　　3　Contrary to
　　　　4　In addition to

(2)　1　be detailed in their plans
　　　　2　choose stores carefully
　　　　3　enjoy a variety of items
　　　　4　be skilled as carvers

(3)　1　have to be returned to the market later
　　　　2　are destroyed by the end of the show
　　　　3　get preserved for future musical events
　　　　4　are in great demand by the audience

(1) 🔲 1 …に気がつかずに
2 …はさておき
3 …とは対照的に
4 …に加えて

🔍 第1段落❷の空所の後ろに traditional「伝統的な、昔ながらの、因習の」とあり、これを unique「独特の」と反対の性質のものだと捉えることができます。選択肢で逆接を表すのは3 Contrary to なので、これが正解です。1「…に気がつかずに」は気づいていないわけではないので不正解。2「…はさておき」は逆接の立場をとっていないので間違い。4「…に加えて」だと同じ性質のものの追加情報となってしまうので不正解です。

･･･

(2) 🔲 1 計画の中で詳しく説明される
2 お店を慎重に選ぶ
3 いろいろなものを楽しむ
4 彫刻の技術がある

🔍 前の文に「演奏家たちが野菜を手で加工し、目的にかなうように楽器に仕上げる」とあります。空所を含む文の This は前の文の内容を受けているので、それを最も的確に表現している選択肢を選ぶと、4の「彫刻の技術」が当てはまります。1は「計画」の話をしていないので間違い。2は「お店」ではなく、自分で加工する話なので間違い。3は野菜の種類の多さは重要視していないので不正解となります。

✏️ ☐ be skilled as …として熟練している　☐ carver 彫刻者

･･･

(3) 🔲 1 後でマーケットに戻さねばならない
2 公演が終わるまでに破損してしまう
3 将来の音楽イベントのために保存される
4 観客が大いに求めている

🔍 空所を含む文に「彼らは新しい野菜がいつも必要である」とあります。新しい野菜が必要になる状況を考えて選択肢を見ると、2の演奏に使った野菜が「壊れてしまう」が文意に合います。1はマーケットに戻さなければならないことの説明がないので不正解。3「将来のために保存される」だと後の文と矛盾するので不正解。4 観客が求めていることに関しても説明がないので不正解となります。最後の文の「これらの（野菜の）楽器は、金属の楽器と違って、雑な扱いを受けると1、2時間以上は耐えられない」からもヒントを得ることができます。

✏️ ☐ be in demand 需要がある、売れ行きがよい

The Vienna Vegetable Orchestra

第1段落

❶ Experimental music began in the middle of the 20th century, mainly in Europe and North America.

❷ Contrary to traditional music, which follows a highly structured pattern laid down in minute detail, experimental music is unique.

❸ It is not composed beforehand.

❹ An experimental musician will begin to play without any plan or expecting a specific outcome.

❺ Experimental music is not written out in notes, so it is difficult for one musician to pass on a piece to another.

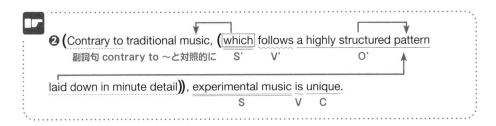

❷ (Contrary to traditional music, (which follows a highly structured pattern
　　副詞句 contrary to 〜と対照的に　　S'　　V'　　　　　　　O'

laid down in minute detail)), experimental music is unique.
　　　　　　　　　　　　　　　　　S　　　　　　　V　　C

ウィーン・ベジタブル・オーケストラ

❶ 実験音楽は、20世紀半ばに欧米を中心に始まった。

❷ 伝統的な音楽が、微に入り細をうがって緻密に構成されたパターンに従って演奏されるのとは対照的に、実験音楽はユニークである。

❸ 事前に作曲されることはないのだ。

❹ 実験音楽家は、何の計画もなく、特定の結果を期待することなく演奏を開始する。

❺ 実験音楽は音符で書かれていないので、ある音楽家から他の音楽家に曲を引き継ぐことは困難である。

❶□ experimental 実験的な ❷□ contrary to …に反して □ follow …に従う □ highly 大いに
□ structured 構造化された □ lay down …を規定する □ in minute detail こと細かに
❸□ beforehand 事前に、あらかじめ ❹□ expect …を待ち受ける・予期する □ specific 特定の
□ outcome 結果 ❺□ write out …をきちんと書く、…を清書する □ note 楽譜
□ pass on …を伝える、…を贈る □ piece 作品、曲

筆記②

第2段落

❶ Experimental musicians may use traditional instruments such as pianos or trumpets but also non-traditional ones, such as glass, wood or pots and pans.

❷ The Vienna Vegetable Orchestra may fall within this music genre.

❸ The Vegetable Orchestra players use all sorts of vegetables to make music.

❹ On performance days, they first go out to the market to choose the vegetables.

❺ They then carefully handcraft the vegetables into various instruments to suit their purpose.

❻ This means they must be skilled as carvers.

---

❶ Experimental musicians may use
　　　　　　S　　　　　　　　　V
traditional instruments such as pianos or trumpets
　　　　　　　　　　　　O₁
but also non-traditional ones, such as glass, wood or pots and pans.
　　　　　　　　　　　　O₂

第2段落

❶ 実験音楽家はピアノやトランペットのような伝統的な楽器を使うこともあるが、ガラスや木、鍋やフライパンなどの非伝統的な楽器も使用する。

❷ ウィーン・ベジタブル・オーケストラは、このジャンルに入るかもしれない。

❸ ベジタブルオーケストラの奏者たちは、あらゆる種類の野菜を使って音楽を奏でる。

❹ 演奏の日には、まず市場に出かけていって野菜を選ぶ。

❺ そして、その野菜を目的に合わせて丁寧に手で加工し、さまざまな楽器に仕上げる。

❻ つまり、彫刻の技術が必要なのだ。

❶ ☐ instrument 楽器　☐ A but also B A であり B もまた…　❷☐ fall within …の中に含まれる
☐ genre 様式、種類　❺☐ handcraft …を手細工で作る　☐ suit …に合う
☐ skilled 熟練した、腕のいい　☐ carver 彫刻師

第3段落

❶ The music itself may not be experimental from a strict point of view, since the musicians play from sheet music and perform known classical pieces.

❷ The orchestra has played on several famous stages around the world, entertaining the audience with the unique sounds the vegetables make.

❸ However, they need to get new vegetables every time, because the ones used for playing are destroyed by the end of the show.

❹ Unlike their metal counterparts, these instruments cannot survive more than an hour or two of rough handling.

---

❶ The music itself may not be experimental from a strict point of view,
　　　　S　　　　　V　　　　　　　C

([since] the musicians play from sheet music and perform known classical pieces).
副詞節(理由)　S'　　V'₁　　　　　　　　　　　　V'₂　　　　　O'₂

❷ The orchestra has played on several famous stages around the world,
　　　　S　　　　　V　　　　場所の副詞句

entertaining the audience with the unique sounds the vegetables make.
分詞構文　entertain A with B　　　　　O'　　　　　　S'　　　　V'

第3段落

❶ 奏者は楽譜を見ながらクラシックの有名な曲を演奏するので、音楽そのものは、厳密には実験的とはいえないかもしれない。

❷ このオーケストラは、世界中の有名な舞台で公演を行い、野菜が奏でるユニークな音で観客を楽しませてきた。

❸ しかし、演奏に使った野菜は公演が終わるまでに破損してしまうため、毎回新しい野菜を調達する必要がある。

❹ 金属製の楽器と違って、1、2時間の手荒な扱いに耐えられないのだ。

❶ □ from a ... point of view …的な観点から見れば　□ sheet music 一枚刷りの楽譜
□ known 一般に知られている　❷ □ entertain A with B A（人）を B で楽しませる
❹ □ counterpart 対応するもの、相対物

問題英文の読み方 P.156　解説・正解 P.158　訳・語句 P.160

Somalia, a Nation of Poets

Poetry has been at the heart of Somalian culture for centuries. The African country has been called a "nation of poets," first by Canadian scholar Margaret Lawrence, and later by several others familiar with its strong tradition of oral verse. While in most Western countries poetry (　1　) and is enjoyed by a somewhat narrow audience, the same is not true in Somalia. There, the love and appreciation of poems are a core part of everyday life. People gather around radios to listen to poems and have long discussions about their merits and problems.

Somali poetry follows strict metric rules and is filled with detailed references and other poetic devices. The poems can be divided into two main categories. *Maanso* are poems that have known authors and are concerned with serious social and political issues. They are composed with a specific goal in mind: to persuade their audience of the truth of their creators' side of a story. *Hees*, on the other hand, (　2　) and are often sung accompanied by music. They have been orally passed down generations and include work songs, rain songs, and lullabies.

To keep poetry alive in the often war-torn country, a nonprofit initiative called "Home of Somali Poetry" was created in 2021. Its website hosts a library of poems that contains everything from classics to modern literature. The organization also gives out annual awards to the most talented poets. (　3　), it intends to promote peace and human rights by uniting all Somalis and giving their voice an online platform.

(1)　**1**　is heavily commercialized
　　　2　has gained rapidly in popularity
　　　3　appeals mainly to the more educated
　　　4　is used broadly as a teaching tool

Date ／①②③④　／①②③④　／①②③④

(2) 1 can be found in ancient documents
    2 are of old but unknown authorship
    3 lack any sort of rhythm or tone
    4 are designed only for priests

(3) 1 In spite of that
    2 As a response
    3 Be that as it may
    4 Furthermore

筆記2

第1段落

Somalia, a Nation of Poets

❶Poetry has been at the heart of Somalian culture for centuries. ❷The African country has been called a "nation of poets," first by Canadian scholar Margaret Lawrence, and later by several others familiar with its strong tradition of oral verse. ❸While in most Western countries poetry (1) and is enjoyed by a somewhat narrow audience, the same is not true in Somalia. ❹There, the love and appreciation of poems are a core part of everyday life. ❺People gather around radios to listen to poems and have long discussions about their merits and problems.

第2段落

❶Somali poetry follows strict metric rules and is filled with detailed references and other poetic devices. ❷The poems can be divided into two main categories. ❸*Maanso* are poems that have known authors and are concerned with serious social and political issues. ❹They are composed with a specific goal in mind: to persuade their audience of the truth of their creators' side of a story. ❺*Hees*, on the other hand, (2) and are often sung accompanied by music. ❻They have been orally passed down generations and include work songs, rain songs, and lullabies.

第3段落

❶To keep poetry alive in the often war-torn country, a nonprofit initiative called "Home of Somali Poetry" was created in 2021. ❷Its website hosts a library of poems that contains everything from classics to modern literature. ❸The organization also gives out annual awards to the most talented poets. ❹(3), it intends to promote peace and human rights by uniting all Somalis and giving their voice an online platform.

この段落は❶の「詩は何世紀にもわたってソマリアの文化の中心であった」で始まっています。❷ではソマリアを「このアフリカの国」と言い換え、「このアフリカの国はマーガレット・ローレンスや、他の人々に『詩人の国』と呼ばれた」と言っています。❸には空所1が含まれていて「欧米の多くの国では詩は〜だけれども、ソマリアではそうではない」とあります。続く❹❺では「ソマリアでは、詩を愛し、鑑賞することが日常生活の中核をなしている。人々はラジオを囲んで詩を聞き、議論する」と、ソマリアでは詩は日常とともにあることが書かれています。

第2段落

第2段落は、❶で「ソマリ語の詩は厳格な韻律法則に沿っていて、入り組んだ引用などの詩的な仕掛けに満ちている」とあり、この後の❷で詩について2つに分類できると言っています。❸❹では、その1つとして「Maanso は作者がわかっている詩で、深刻な社会的、政治的問題を扱い、作者側の主張が正しいことを聞き手に納得させる」と説明され、次の❺では空所2を含み、もう一つの「Hees」について書かれています。Hees, on the other hand, で始まっているので、Maanso と違う点について書かれていると考えることができ、「一方、Hees は〜で、音楽を伴って歌われ、口承で代々受け継がれてきた」という点が特徴だとわかります。❻では Hees の伝承の形と扱うテーマについて述べています。

第3段落

第3段落は、❶で詩に関する新たな取り組みとして「戦乱の続くこの国で詩を守り続けるために『Home of Somali Poetry』という取り組みが始まった」という話から始めています。❷で「そのウェブサイトで古典から現代文学までを含む詩のライブラリーを公開している」とあり、❸で「才能のある詩人に賞を授与している」と、取り組みの内容について書いています。空所3の後、❹は「すべてのソマリ人を団結させることで、平和と人権を促進させることを目指している」と、この取り組み全体の方向性を示して、この文章を締めくくっています。

(1)　**1**　is heavily commercialized
　　　　2　has gained rapidly in popularity
　　　　3　appeals mainly to the more educated
　　　　4　is used broadly as a teaching tool

(2)　**1**　can be found in ancient documents
　　　　2　are of old but unknown authorship
　　　　3　lack any sort of rhythm or tone
　　　　4　are designed only for priests

(3)　**1**　In spite of that
　　　　2　As a response
　　　　3　Be that as it may
　　　　4　Furthermore

(1) 🔲 1 かなり商業化されている
2 急速に人気を得た
3 主に教養の高い人にアピールしている
4 教材として広く使われている

🔍 第1段落❸の空所を含む文には「ソマリアではそうではない」とあり、続く❹❺でソマリアでは詩は日常とともにあると書かれています。これらをヒントに詩が広く親しまれているソマリアとは逆の状況を考えると、空所には「（欧米では、日常的なものではなく）教養の高い人にアピールしている」が当てはまるとわかります。「the ＋分詞（educated）」で人を表していることも注意しておきましょう。

....

(2) 🔲 1 古文書で見ることができる
2 古いが作者不詳である
3 リズムや調子に欠ける
4 司祭のためにのみ書かれている

🔍 第2段落❸❹で Maanso について説明した後に、空所を含む❺が「一方、Hees は」という対比をする表現で始まっているので、Maanso とは異なる内容を選択肢から選びます。❸の Maanso の説明にある「作者がわかっている」と、❻の Hees の説明の「口承で代々受け継がれてきた」という点が対照になると考えると、「古く、作者不詳である」が入るとわかります。

✏️ □ ancient 古代の、古くからの　□ authorship 原作者　□ lack …を欠いている　□ priest 聖職者、司祭

....

(3) 🔲 1 それにもかかわらず
2 応答として
3 それはともかくとして
4 さらに

🔍 第3段落❹の「すべてのソマリ人を団結させることで、平和と人権を促進させることを目指している」は、❷「そのウェブサイトで古典から現代文学までを含む詩のライブラリーを公開している」と❸「才能のある詩人に賞を授与している」といった活動と同様に、文化の保護と発展に関する取り組みの内容についての追加情報だと考えられるので、空所には「さらに」を表す語が入るとわかります。❷の Its website、❸の The organization、❹の it が同一のものを指していると捉えることができれば、文章全体の動詞の連続性がつかめるでしょう。

Somalia, a Nation of Poets

第1段落

❶ Poetry has been at the heart of Somalian culture for centuries.

❷ The African country has been called a "nation of poets," first by Canadian scholar Margaret Lawrence, and later by several others familiar with its strong tradition of oral verse.

❸ While in most Western countries poetry appeals mainly to the more educated and is enjoyed by a somewhat narrow audience, the same is not true in Somalia.

❹ There, the love and appreciation of poems are a core part of everyday life.

❺ People gather around radios to listen to poems and have long discussions about their merits and problems.

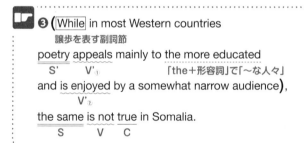

❸ (While in most Western countries
　　譲歩を表す副詞節
poetry appeals mainly to the more educated
　S'　　V'①　　　　　　　　　　「the＋形容詞」で「～な人々」
and is enjoyed by a somewhat narrow audience),
　　　V'②
the same is not true in Somalia.
　S　　　V　C

詩人の国　ソマリア

第1段落

❶ ソマリアでは、何世紀にもわたって詩が文化の中心であった。

❷ カナダの学者マーガレット・ローレンスが最初に、このアフリカの国を「詩人の国」と呼び、その後、伝統的な優れた口承詩に精通した他の人々もそう呼んでいる。

❸ 欧米の多くの国では、詩は主に教養の高い人にアピールし、狭い範囲の人々によってのみ楽しまれているが、ソマリアではそうではない。

❹ ソマリアでは、詩を愛し、鑑賞することが日常生活の中核をなしている。

❺ 人々はラジオを囲んで詩を聴き、その良しあしについて長い議論を交わす。

❷□ familiar with …をよく知っている　□ oral □頭の、口述の　□ verse 詩
❸□ appeal to …の興味をそそる　□ educated 教養のある (the educated で「教養のある人々」)
□ somewhat やや、幾分か　□ the same 同じこと・もの　❹□ appreciation 鑑賞　□ core 中核
❺□ merit 長所、美点、価値

第2段落

❶ Somali poetry follows strict metric rules and is filled with detailed references and other poetic devices.

❷ The poems can be divided into two main categories.

❸ *Maanso* are poems that have known authors and are concerned with serious social and political issues.

❹ They are composed with a specific goal in mind: to persuade their audience of the truth of their creators' side of a story.

❺ *Hees*, on the other hand, are of old but unknown authorship and are often sung accompanied by music.

❻ They have been orally passed down generations and include work songs, rain songs, and lullabies.

第3段落

❶ To keep poetry alive in the often war-torn country, a nonprofit initiative called "Home of Somali Poetry" was created in 2021.

❷ Its website hosts a library of poems that contains everything from classics to modern literature.

❸ The organization also gives out annual awards to the most talented poets.

❹ Furthermore, it intends to promote peace and human rights by uniting all Somalis and giving their voice an online platform.

第2段落

❶ ソマリ語の詩は厳格な韻律法則に則っており、入り組んだ引用などの詩的な仕掛けに満ちている。

❷ 詩は大きく2つに分類される。

❸ Maanso は作者がわかっている詩で、深刻な社会的、政治的問題を扱う。

❹ 作者側の主張が正しいことを聴き手に納得させるという、具体的な目標を持って詠まれている。

❺ 一方、Hees は、作者不詳の古い歌であり、音楽を伴って歌われることが多い。

❻ 口承で代々受け継がれてきたもので、労働歌、雨乞い歌、子守歌などがある。

❶□ metric 韻律　□ be filled with …で満たされる　□ detailed 詳細な、精密な
□ reference 引用、言及　□ device 手法、趣向　❷□ divide into …に分類する
❸□ be concerned with …に関係がある　□ issue 問題、論点　❹□ compose (詩・曲など) を作る
□ with X in mind X を念頭に置いて　□ persuade A of B A に B を信じさせる
❺□ authorship 原作者　□ accompanied by …を伴って　❻□ orally 口頭で
□ pass down …を代々伝える　□ lullaby 子守歌

第3段落

❶ 戦乱の続くこの国で詩を守り続けるために、2021年に「Home of Somali Poetry」という非営利の取り組みが始まった。

❷ そのウェブサイトでは、古典から現代文学までを含む詩のライブラリーが公開されている。

❸ また、最も才能のある詩人に対して毎年賞を授与している。

❹ さらに、すべてのソマリ人を団結させ、彼らの声をオンラインで伝えることで、平和と人権を促進することを目的としている。

❶□ keep X alive X を存続させる　□ war-torn 戦争で荒廃した　□ nonprofit 非営利の
□ initiative 働きかけ、(問題に対するための) 行動計画　❷□ host …を提供する、…を管理する
□ contain …を含む　❸□ give out …を支給する、…を配付する　□ annual 年に一度の　□ award 賞
□ talented 才能のある　❹□ intend to *do* …することを目的とする　□ promote …を促進する
□ unite …を団結させる

Life on Venus?

Astronomers and others have long wondered whether humanity is alone in the universe. Mars had first been the primary target of investigations in this respect, though scientists have also examined the moons of Jupiter and Saturn. (**1**), researchers often look for these across space. In 2020, researchers believed they had identified the presence of the chemical phosphine in the atmosphere of Venus. This gave a new direction to space research focused on the possibility of extraterrestrial life, or forms of life outside earth.

Phosphine can be found in abundance on Earth and is produced in environments that have very low oxygen levels. Its existence often suggests organic processes or existence of life—since only bacteria (tiny living organisms) are known to create it. (**2**), through 2020, the main scientific opinion seemed to be that the presence of phosphine was likely the result of bacteria that could somehow survive in the harsh atmosphere of Venus.

But by 2021, other ideas emerged to counter this narrative. Venus's atmosphere mainly consists of sulfuric acid, which is a substance that destroys cell structures. Therefore, it seems extremely unlikely that bacteria, or any other organism, (**3**). Moreover, the amount of phosphine supposedly discovered in the clouds of Venus was so small, it was not necessarily proof of life. Some scientists have suggested that it could actually be some other chemical, perhaps the result of volcanic activity, particularly when scientific equipment currently has limited capacity to measure such tiny amounts of chemicals over the vast distance of space.

(1) 1 Based on the fact organisms are adaptable
2 Since certain substances are indicators of life
3 Until microorganisms are encountered by accident
4 Whenever new life forms are discovered on earth

Date ／ ① ② ③ ④ ／ ① ② ③ ④ ／ ① ② ③ ④

(2)   **1**   Surprisingly
　　　　2   As a result
　　　　3   Nevertheless
　　　　4   At most

(3)   **1**   could survive in such an environment
　　　　2   could have any difficulty discovering it
　　　　3   wouldn't use these conditions to their advantage
　　　　4   would need protective structures to live there

筆記②

第1段落

Life on Venus?

❶Astronomers and others have long wondered whether humanity is alone in the universe. ❷Mars had first been the primary target of investigations in this respect, though scientists have also examined the moons of Jupiter and Saturn. ❸(1), researchers often look for these across space. ❹In 2020, researchers believed they had identified the presence of the chemical phosphine in the atmosphere of Venus. ❺This gave a new direction to space research focused on the possibility of extraterrestrial life, or forms of life outside earth.

第2段落

❶Phosphine can be found in abundance on Earth and is produced in environments that have very low oxygen levels. ❷Its existence often suggests organic processes—or existence of life—since only bacteria (tiny living organisms) are known to create it. ❸(2), through 2020, the main scientific opinion seemed to be that the presence of phosphine was likely the result of bacteria that could somehow survive in the harsh atmosphere of Venus.

第3段落

❶But by 2021, other ideas emerged to counter this narrative. ❷Venus's atmosphere mainly consists of sulfuric acid, which is a substance that destroys cell structures. ❸Therefore, it seems extremely unlikely that bacteria, or any other organism, (3). ❹Moreover, the amount of phosphine supposedly discovered in the clouds of Venus was so small, it was not necessarily proof of life. ❺Some scientists have suggested that it could actually be some other chemical, perhaps the result of volcanic activity, particularly when scientific equipment currently has limited capacity to measure such tiny amounts of chemicals over the vast distance of space.

第1段落

第1段落❶は「天文学者らは、長い間考えてきた」で始まっています。その天文学者らが考えてきた内容は「人類は宇宙で孤独な存在かどうか」ということです。❷からは、そのような考えから進められてきた調査の経緯について書いてあります。火星が主な調査対象で、その後、木星や土星の衛星も調査されてきたとあります。❸では、空所の後に「研究者はそれを宇宙空間で探すことが多い」とあり、空所には「それ」を指す語が含まれることになります。❹❺では2020年に研究者は金星の大気中に「ホスフィン」という化学物質が存在することを突きとめたと言っていて、これが宇宙の探索に新たな方向性を与えるものになったとあります。

第2段落

第2段落❶では「ホスフィンは地球上に豊富にあることが見受けられ、酸素濃度が低い環境で生成される」とあり、「ホスフィンの存在が生命の存在を示唆することが多い」と書かれているのが❷です。❸では空所の後に「2020年までの見解は、ホスフィンが存在しているのはバクテリアがいるためだろうということだった」と書かれています。

第3段落

第2段落では2020年までの見解（生命は存在している）を記しているのに対し、But by 2021で始まる第3段落では、別の考え方（生命は存在していないのでは？）について述べていることが第3段落❶からうかがえます。❷で「金星の大気の構成物質である硫酸は細胞を破壊する」と言っており、❸からは「それゆえに生物の何かの可能性が低い」とわかります。また❹では（生命が存在していないもう一つの理由として）「金星のホスフィンは微量であったため、生命体が存在したとは言えない」と述べたのに続けて、❺では「他の科学者は（ホスフィンではなく）他の物質だと指摘している」と、前の段落とは全く逆の内容でこの文章を締めくくっています。

(1) 1 Based on the fact organisms are adaptable
2 Since certain substances are indicators of life
3 Until microorganisms are encountered by accident
4 Whenever new life forms are discovered on earth

(2) 1 Surprisingly
2 As a result
3 Nevertheless
4 At most

(3) 1 could survive in such an environment
2 could have any difficulty discovering it
3 wouldn't use these conditions to their advantage
4 would need protective structures to live there

(1) 🔄 1 生物には順応性があるという事実に基づいて
　　　　2 ある種の物質が生命の指標となるため
　　　　3 偶然に微生物に遭遇するまで
　　　　4 地球上で新しい生命体が発見されるたびに

🔍 第1段落❹❺で「2020年に研究者が金星の大気中のホスフィンの存在を突き止め、これが地球外生命を求める宇宙探索に新たな方向性を与えた」と述べていることから、空所には「ある化学物質が何かを突き止めるカギになる」という意味の語が入るとわかります。

✏️ □ adaptable 順応性［適応力］がある　□ substance 物資　□ indicator of …の指標
　　□ microorganism 微生物　□ encounter …に遭遇する

----

(2) 🔄 1 意外にも
　　　　2 その結果
　　　　3 それでも
　　　　4 せいぜい

🔍 第2段落❶の「ホスフィンは地球上に豊富にあることが見受けられ、酸素濃度が低い環境で生成される」という説明と、❷の「ホスフィンの存在が生命の存在を示唆することが多い」という説明でホスフィンの性質を明らかにした後に、❸の「2020年までの見解は、ホスフィンが存在しているのはバクテリアがいるためだろうということだった」という内容が続いています。❷までと❸の内容の関係を考えると、空所には「つまり」のような、これまでの内容をまとめる語や因果関係を表す語が入るとわかります。

----

(3) 🔄 1 このような環境で生存できる
　　　　2 それを発見することが困難である
　　　　3 これらの条件をうまく利用しない
　　　　4 そこで生存するためには、身を守る構造が必要である

🔍 第3段落❷の「金星の大気の構成物質である硫酸は細胞を破壊する」という説明と、❹の「金星のホスフィンは微量であったため、生命体が存在したとは言えない」という説明から、生物が生存できる可能性は低いと考えられるため、選択肢の「そのような環境で生きること」が当てはまるとわかります。

✏️ □ to one's advantage …に有利になるように　□ protective 保護する

Life on Venus?

第1段落

❶ Astronomers and others have long wondered whether humanity is alone in the universe.

❷ Mars had first been the primary target of investigations in this respect, though scientists have also examined the moons of Jupiter and Saturn.

❸ Since certain substances are indicators of life, researchers often look for these across space.

❹ In 2020, researchers believed they had identified the presence of the chemical phosphine in the atmosphere of Venus.

❺ This gave a new direction to space research focused on the possibility of extraterrestrial life, or forms of life outside earth.

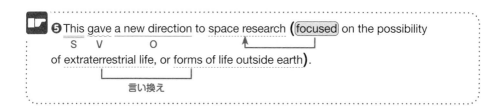

❺This gave a new direction to space research (focused on the possibility
  S   V   O
of extraterrestrial life, or forms of life outside earth).
          言い換え

金星に生命が存在する？

❶ 人類は宇宙で孤独な存在なのだろうかと、天文学者らは長い間考えてきた。

❷ この点については、まず火星が主な調査対象であったが、木星や土星の衛星も調査されてきた。

❸ ある種の物質が生命の指標となるため、研究者は宇宙空間でそれを探すことが多い。

❹ 2020年、研究者は金星の大気中にホスフィンという化学物質の存在を突き止めたと考えた。

❺ これは、地球外生命体すなわち地球の外の生き物の可能性を探る宇宙の探索に、新たな方向性を与えるものであった。

❶□ astronomer 天文学者　□ wonder whether …か否かと考える　□ humanity 人類
❷□ Mars 火星　□ investigation 調査、研究　□ in this respect この点で　□ examine …を調査する
□ moon 衛星　□ Jupiter 木星　□ Saturn 土星　❸□ look for …を探す
❹□ identify …を突きとめる、…の正体を確認する　□ presence 存在　□ phosphine ホスフィン
□ atmosphere（天体を取り巻く）ガス体　□ Venus 金星
❺□ give a new direction to …に新しい方向性を与える　□ extraterrestrial 地球外の
□ forms of life 生き物の種類

筆記②

171

第2段落

❶ Phosphine can be found in abundance on Earth and is produced in environments that have very low oxygen levels.

❷ Its existence often suggests organic processes—or existence of life—since only bacteria (tiny living organisms) are known to create it.

❸ As a result, through 2020, the main scientific opinion seemed to be that the presence of phosphine was likely the result of bacteria that could somehow survive in the harsh atmosphere of Venus.

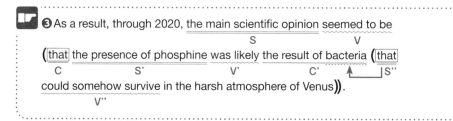

第3段落

❶ But by 2021, other ideas emerged to counter this narrative.

❷ Venus's atmosphere mainly consists of sulfuric acid, which is a substance that destroys cell structures.

❸ Therefore, it seems extremely unlikely that bacteria, or any other organism, could survive in such an environment.

❹ Moreover, the amount of phosphine supposedly discovered in the clouds of Venus was so small, it was not necessarily proof of life.

❺ Some scientists have suggested that it could actually be some other chemical, perhaps the result of volcanic activity, particularly when scientific equipment currently has limited capacity to measure such tiny amounts of chemicals over the vast distance of space.

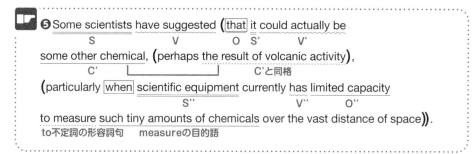

第2段落

❶ ホスフィンは地球上に豊富に存在し、酸素濃度が非常に低い環境で生成される。

❷ ホスフィンを生成するのはバクテリア（微小生物）だけであることがわかっているため、その存在は有機的なプロセス、つまり生命の存在を示唆することが多い。

❸ そのため、ホスフィンが存在しているのは、金星の厳しい大気の中で何とか生き延びることのできるバクテリアがいるためであろうというのが、2020年までの主な科学者の見解だったようだ。

❶ ☐ in abundance 豊富に、たくさん　☐ oxygen 酸素　❷ ☐ existence 存在、存在の事実
☐ suggest …を示唆する　☐ organic process 生きている有機体で起こる作用
☐ bacteria バクテリア、細菌　☐ tiny living organism 微生物　❸ ☐ likely おそらく、たぶん
☐ somehow 何とか、どうにかして　☐ harsh 厳しい、苛酷な

第3段落

❶ しかし、2021年までに、この説に対抗する別の考え方が浮上した。

❷ 金星の大気は主に硫酸で構成されているが、この硫酸は細胞の構造を破壊する物質である。

❸ したがって、バクテリアやその他の生物がこのような環境で生存できる可能性は極めて低いと思われる。

❹ さらに、金星の雲から発見されたとされるホスフィンの量は非常に微量であり、必ずしも生命体が存在する証拠とは言えない。

❺ 特に、現在の科学機器で、宇宙空間の広大な距離の中で微量の化学物質を測定するのは限界があるため、科学者の中には、火山活動で生じた他の化学物質である可能性を指摘する者もいる。

❶ ☐ emerge 現れる、持ち上がる　☐ counter …に対抗する　☐ narrative（出来事・体験などの）話
❷ ☐ consist of（部分・要素）から成る　☐ sulfuric acid 硫酸　☐ substance 物質
☐ cell structure 細胞の構造　❸ ☐ unlikely ありそうもない、本当らしくない
☐ organism 有機体、生物　❹ ☐ supposedly …と思われる、…とされている　☐ proof 証拠
❺ ☐ volcanic 火山の　☐ equipment 機器　☐ limit …を制限する
☐ tiny amounts of わずかな量の…　☐ vast 広大な、非常に大きな　☐ distance 距離

筆記②

問題英文の読み方 P.176　解説・正解 P.178　訳・語句 P.180

American Art in the 1960s

The 1960s brought significant changes in art in the United States. They were mainly guided by the era's somewhat extreme social and political trends. Between the 1940s and 1970s the country participated in several military conflicts, including World War II and the Korean and Vietnam wars. These events had a deep impact on the American population, and artists were more than willing to express their feelings through their works. (**1**), the achievements of the civil rights movements enabled women and minorities to contribute to art.

Several new art forms also emerged in the 1960s. Prosperity and consumer culture were on the rise in the decade and the imagery of advertisements and marketing (**2**). Pop art (new realism) originated from these trends, and this new art form used the techniques of commercial art to highlight everyday objects. Minimalism, another new style, reduced objects to basic geometric forms in single color.

The decade also saw a rise in the publicity of art, and larger audiences were able to view art pieces in museums and galleries, thanks to an influx of support from the government as well as private institutions and individuals. At the same time, efforts were made by new artists to take art out of these establishments and bring it to the streets. They held performances, which were unique and impressive. Conceptual art was born, which (**3**), no matter how messy that appeared. This was a sharp break from the standard of displaying refined and completed art pieces. All in all, because of the 1960s, art has become more open and the boundaries between fine art and popular art became less distinct.

(1)　1　To sum up
　　　2　Beyond that
　　　3　In contrast
　　　4　Sooner or later

Date
／① ② ③ ④　／① ② ③ ④　／① ② ③ ④

(2)   **1**   began to gradually disappear
         2   was disliked by traditional critics
         3   referred to events early in the century
         4   created a strong new influence

(3)   **1**   focused on the creative process of art
         2   offered discounted items to everyone
         3   promoted discussions on art theories
         4   relied on local sources of funding

筆記②

American Art in the 1960s

❶The 1960s brought significant changes in art in the United States. ❷They were mainly guided by the era's somewhat extreme social and political trends. ❸Between the 1940s and 1970s the country participated in several military conflicts, including World War II and the Korean and Vietnam wars. ❹These events had a deep impact on the American population, and artists were more than willing to express their feelings through their works. ❺(1), the achievements of the civil rights movements enabled women and minorities to contribute to art.

❶Several new art forms also emerged in the 1960s. ❷Prosperity and consumer culture were on the rise in the decade and the imagery of advertisements and marketing (2). ❸Pop art (new realism) originated from these trends, and this new art form used the techniques of commercial art to highlight everyday objects. ❹Minimalism, another new style, reduced objects to basic geometric forms in single color.

❶The decade also saw a rise in the publicity of art, and larger audiences were able to view art pieces in museums and galleries, thanks to an influx of support from the government as well as private institutions and individuals. ❷At the same time, efforts were made by new artists to take art out of these establishments and bring it to the streets. ❸They held performances, which were unique and impressive. ❹Conceptual art was born, which (3), no matter how messy that appeared. ❺This was a sharp break from the standard of displaying refined and completed art pieces. ❻All in all, because of the 1960s, art has become more open and the boundaries between fine art and popular art became less distinct.

第1段落

The 1960s brought で始まる第1段落❶は直訳すると「1960年代は変化を持ってきた」ですが、この形で「1960年代にはアメリカの美術に変化がおこった」という意味として読みます。第1段落は「アメリカの美術の変化」や「1960年代の出来事」について説明しているだろうと予測をしながら読み進めましょう。❷はその「変化」を They で受け、「変化は社会的、政治的傾向に導かれた」と言っていて、❸❹ではより具体的に「アメリカはいくつかの紛争に関わり、それが国民に深い衝撃を与え、アーティストは感情を表現することを望んだ」と述べています。これに続き、❺では「女性やマイノリティも芸術に貢献するようになった」と言っています。

第2段落

第2段落はアメリカの美術における変化の中から1960年代に範囲をしぼっていることが❶でわかります。❷は空所を含んで「この10年間で繁栄と文化レベルが上昇し、広告やマーケティングをイメージしたものが〜した」とあり、❸❹では、そこから生まれた新たな様式である「ポップアート」や「ミニマリズム」について紹介しています。

第3段落

第3段落は❶で「美術品の宣伝が盛んになり、さまざまなところからの支援によって、多くの人々が美術品を鑑賞することができるようになった」と言っていることから、美術品と鑑賞する人々との環境の変化について述べられるだろうと考えることができます。❷❸では、「これと同時にアートを外に持ち出そうという動きが起こり、そのパフォーマンスはユニークだった」とあります。❹は「コンセプチュアル・アートが生まれ、いかに雑多なものであろうとも、〜だった」で、❺は「完成された芸術作品を展示する時代は終わった」とあるので、空所にはそのつながりを成立させるものを当てはめます。❻の「1960年代のおかげで芸術はより開かれたものとなり、洗練された芸術と大衆的な芸術との隔たりが縮まった」で文章を締めくくっています。

(1)
1 To sum up
2 Beyond that
3 In contrast
4 Sooner or later

(2)
1 began to gradually disappear
2 was disliked by traditional critics
3 referred to events early in the century
4 created a strong new influence

(3)
1 focused on the creative process of art
2 offered discounted items to everyone
3 promoted discussions on art theories
4 relied on local sources of funding

(1) 🏴 1 まとめると
　　　　2 さらに
　　　　3 それに対して
　　　　4 いずれは

🔍 第1段落❸❹の「アメリカはいくつかの紛争に関わり、それが国民に深い衝撃を与え、アーティストは感情を表現することを望んだ」という流れに沿うように、❺で「女性やマイノリティも芸術に貢献するようになった」と言っているので、空所には「それに、加えて」などを表す語が入るとわかります。

(2) 🏴 1 徐々に消え始めた
　　　　2 伝統的な批評家に嫌われた
　　　　3 世紀の初頭の出来事に言及した
　　　　4 新たな強い影響力を生み出した

🔍 第2段落❷の「この10年間で繁栄と文化レベルが上昇し、広告やマーケティングをイメージしたものが〜した」とあり、❸でポップアートがその流れから生まれ、商業美術の技法を用いていたと述べ、❹でミニマリズムも同様に登場した様式であると述べていることから、「（広告やマーケティングをイメージ化したものがポップアートやミニマリズムのもとになるほどの）強い影響力を生み出した」を当てはめると意味がつながります。

✏️ ☐ disappear 見えなくなる、なくなる ☐ critic 批評家、評論家 ☐ refer to …に関連している

(3) 🏴 1 芸術の創造過程を重視した
　　　　2 誰にでも割引価格で商品を提供した
　　　　3 芸術理論に関する議論を促進した
　　　　4 地元の財源に依存した

🔍 第3段落❹の「いかに雑多なものであろうとも、〜だった」と、❺の「完成された芸術作品を展示する時代は終わった」から、「（完成品ではなく）作っていく過程を重視した」を当てはめると意味がつながります。

✏️ ☐ discounted 割引の ☐ promote …を促進する ☐ theory 理論 ☐ funding 資金、財政的支援

筆記②

🚩 **(1)** 2 **(2)** 4 **(3)** 1　179

American Art in the 1960s

第1段落

❶ The 1960s brought significant changes in art in the United States.

❷ They were mainly guided by the era's somewhat extreme social and political trends.

❸ Between the 1940s and 1970s the country participated in several military conflicts, including World War II and the Korean and Vietnam wars.

❹ These events had a deep impact on the American population, and artists were more than willing to express their feelings through their works.

❺ Beyond that, the achievements of the civil rights movements enabled women and minorities to contribute to art.

第2段落

❶ Several new art forms also emerged in the 1960s.

❷ Prosperity and consumer culture were on the rise in the decade and the imagery of advertisements and marketing created a strong new influence.

❸ Pop art (new realism) originated from these trends, and this new art form used the techniques of commercial art to highlight everyday objects.

❹ Minimalism, another new style, reduced objects to basic geometric forms in single color.

1960年代のアメリカ美術

筆記 2

第1段落

❶ 1960年代は、アメリカの美術に大きな変化がもたらされた。

❷ それは主に、この時代のやや極端な社会的、政治的傾向に導かれたものであった。

❸ 1940年代から1970年代にかけて、アメリカは第二次世界大戦、朝鮮戦争、ベトナム戦争など、いくつかの軍事的紛争に関わった。

❹ これらの出来事はアメリカ国民に深い衝撃を与え、アーティストは自分たちの感情を作品を通して表現することを強く望んだ。

❺ さらに、公民権運動の成果により、女性やマイノリティも芸術に貢献することができるようになった。

❶□ significant 重大な　❷□ somewhat やや、いくらか　❸□ participate in …に加わる
□ military 軍事の　□ conflict 紛争、戦闘　❹□ impact 衝撃、影響力
□ the American population アメリカ人　□ willing to *do* …する意向がある
❺□ achievement 成功、功績　□ enable X to *do* X が…できるようにする　□ minority 少数派
□ contribute to …で役割を果たす

第2段落

❶ また、1960年代には、いくつかの新しい芸術様式が生まれた。

❷ この10年間は繁栄と消費文化のレベルが上昇し、広告やマーケティングをイメージ化したものが新たな強い影響力を生み出した。

❸ ポップアート（ニューリアリズム）はこうした流れから生まれたもので、この新しい芸術様式は商業美術の技法を用いて、ありふれた品物を際立たせるものであった。

❹ もう1つの新しい様式であるミニマリズムは、対象物を単色の基本的な幾何学形態に変化させた。

❶□ emerge 現れる　❷□ prosperity 好況、経済的成功
□ be on the rise 上がりつつある、増加の傾向にある　□ decade 10年間　□ imagery イメージ、心像
❸□ realism 写実主義、現実主義　□ originate from …から起こる　□ technique 技法
□ highlight …を目立たせる　❹□ reduce A to B A を B（簡単なもの）に変える
□ geometric 幾何学の、幾何学的な

第3段落

❶ The decade also saw a rise in the publicity of art, and larger audiences were able to view art pieces in museums and galleries, thanks to an influx of support from the government as well as private institutions and individuals.

❷ At the same time, efforts were made by new artists to take art out of these establishments and bring it to the streets.

❸ They held performances, which were unique and impressive.

❹ Conceptual art was born, which focused on the creative process of art, no matter how messy that appeared.

❺ This was a sharp break from the standard of displaying refined and completed art pieces.

❻ All in all, because of the 1960s, art has become more open and the boundaries between fine art and popular art became less distinct.

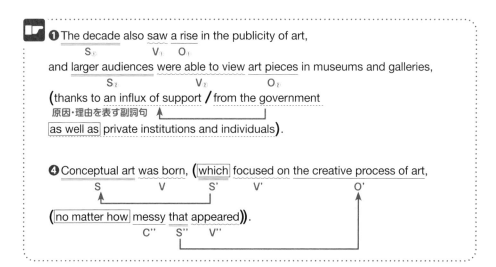

❶ また、この年代は美術品の宣伝が盛んになり、政府、民間団体、個人が盛んに支援したおかげで、美術館やギャラリーで多くの人々が美術品を鑑賞することができるようになった。

❷ その一方で、新しいアーティストたちが、アートをそういった施設の外に持ち出し、街角に持ち込もうと試みた。

❸ 彼らが行ったパフォーマンスはユニークで印象的だった。

❹ コンセプチュアル・アートが生まれ、いかに雑多なものであろうとも、芸術の創造過程を重視した。

❺ 洗練され、完成された芸術作品を展示するのが当たり前だった時代は完全に終わりを告げたのだ。

❻ 総じて言えば、1960年代のおかげで、芸術はよりオープンになり、ファインアートとポピュラーアートの境界はよりあいまいになったのである。

❶□ see（ある時代が）（出来事）の舞台となる　□ publicity 宣伝　□ gallery 画廊、美術品展示室
□ influx 流入、到来　□ institution 組織、施設　❷□ take A out of B A を B から取り出す
□ establishment 設立物、施設　❹□ conceptual 概念の　□ messy 乱雑な、取り散らかした
❺□ break 変わり目、決別　□ refined 洗練された　❻□ all in all 全体として、概して
□ boundary 境界　□ distinct 明確な

筆記②

問題英文の読み方 P.186　解説・正解 P.188　訳・語句 P.190

Infants and Learning

For most of the nineteenth century, it was commonly believed that a newborn's mind was a "blank slate." Psychologists thought that when infants were born, they possessed no knowledge whatsoever, but gained all their information gradually, as they got older. Given the fact that infants are limited in their movements and spend most of their days sleeping, it is no wonder that this concept prevailed for so long. With the advance of technology and a wider acceptance of new methodologies, however, (　**1**　).

Swiss psychologist Jean Piaget was the first expert to sharply break away from the "blank slate" approach. After studying hundreds of infants, he came to the conclusion that the human brain possesses complex learning mechanisms from the moment of birth. He also found that cognitive development, that is, the process of learning to think about and understand the world around us, happens in stages, and each stage is characterized by acquiring different skills. Most importantly, he discovered that infants actively seek environmental stimulation. (　**2**　), they want to learn and not just let people, objects, and events shape them.

Piaget's findings (　**3**　) for studying infant learning. Numerous hypotheses have succeeded his discoveries, but they all agree that young children are active learners who are capable of setting goals, planning, and revising what they know. They have shown that the human brain is a genetically prepared organ ready to absorb knowledge from one's first day of life.

(1)　**1**　psychological studies themselves lost credibility
　　　2　researchers began to focus on other areas of the brain
　　　3　this belief came under more and more criticism
　　　4　new analyses created more questions than answers

Date ／①②③④ ／①②③④ ／①②③④

(2)　**1**　In spite of that
　　　　2　As a case in point
　　　　3　To put it simply
　　　　4　At most

(3)　**1**　pioneered childcare techniques
　　　　2　proved to be an inspiration
　　　　3　confirmed what earlier scientists thought
　　　　4　seemed like a step backward

第1段落

Infants and Learning

❶For most of the nineteenth century, it was commonly believed that a newborn's mind was a "blank slate." ❷Psychologists thought that when infants were born, they possessed no knowledge whatsoever, but gained all their information gradually, as they got older. ❸Given the fact that infants are limited in their movements and spend most of their days sleeping, it is no wonder that this concept prevailed for so long. ❹With the advance of technology and a wider acceptance of new methodologies, however, (**1**).

第2段落

❶Swiss psychologist Jean Piaget was the first expert to sharply break away from the "blank slate" approach. ❷After studying hundreds of infants, he came to the conclusion that the human brain possesses complex learning mechanisms from the moment of birth. ❸He also found that cognitive development, that is, the process of learning to think about and understand the world around us, happens in stages, and each stage is characterized by acquiring different skills. ❹Most importantly, he discovered that infants actively seek environmental stimulation. ❺(**2**), they want to learn and not just let people, objects, and events shape them.

第3段落

❶Piaget's findings (**3**) for studying infant learning. ❷Numerous hypotheses have succeeded his discoveries, but they all agree that young children are active learners who are capable of setting goals, planning, and revising what they know. ❸They have shown that the human brain is a genetically prepared organ ready to absorb knowledge from one's first day of life.

第1段落

❶は「長い間、新生児の心は『空白の石板』だったと信じられてきた」で始まっています。この blank slate はどのようなものかと考えながら読み進めましょう。❷❸では、それについて「心理学者は、乳児は生まれた時には何の知識も持っていないが、年を重ねながら情報を獲得していくと考えていた。それは乳児は一日の大半を寝て過ごすという事実を踏まえれば、当然だ」と書かれています。❹は文の前半と後半の間に however があり、一見すると文の途中に逆接が入っていると思えるかもしれませんが、この文が With ... という前置詞句から始まることと、however が文のどこに来ても前の1文にかかることがあることを考慮に入れて読むと❸からのつながりが見えてきます。

第2段落

❶に「ピアジェはこの『空白の石板』の理論から脱却した最初の専門家だった」とあることから、この段落では、新たな説が展開されると推測できます。❷❸で、「人間の脳には生まれた瞬間から、複雑な学習メカニズムが備わっていて、認知機能の発達は段階的におこり、それぞれの段階で異なるスキルを獲得する」と、ピアジェの発見について書かれています。❺のはじめに空所がありますが、❹の「乳幼児は積極的に環境刺激を求めている」に続いて、❺「人や物、出来事によって自分自身を形作るだけではなく、自分から学びたいと思うのだ」と、ピアジェの発見の結論について述べています。

第3段落

❶には空所があり、「ピアジェの発見は、乳幼児の学習を研究する上での～」という意味になります。続く❷❸では、「多くの仮説が彼の発見を受け継いだが、どれも幼児は能動的な学習者であるという点で一致し、人間の脳は生後1日目から知識を吸収できるように遺伝的に準備された器官であると示した」とまとめています。

(1) 　1　psychological studies themselves lost credibility
　　　2　researchers began to focus on other areas of the brain
　　　3　this belief came under more and more criticism
　　　4　new analyses created more questions than answers

(2) 　1　In spite of that
　　　2　As a case in point
　　　3　To put it simply
　　　4　At most

(3) 　1　pioneered childcare techniques
　　　2　proved to be an inspiration
　　　3　confirmed what earlier scientists thought
　　　4　seemed like a step backward

(1) 📱 1 心理学の研究そのものが信頼性を失った
2 研究者は脳の他の部位に注目し始めた
3 この考え方は批判されるようになった
4 新たな分析によって、わかったこと以上に疑問が生み出された

🔍 第1段落❸までは「空白の石板」の考え方が長く普及していたことを述べていますが、空所を含む❹は「技術が進歩し、新しい方法論が受け入れられるにつれ、」で始まり、however の逆接でその流れに反する展開を導こうとしているので、後半の空所には「この考え方は批判されるようになった」という意味の節が入るとつながります。

✏️ □ credibility 信頼性

- -

(2) 📱 1 にもかかわらず
2 例として
3 つまり
4 せいぜい

🔍 第2段落❹の「乳幼児は積極的に環境刺激を求めている」に続いて、❺「人や物、出来事によって自分自身を形作るだけではなく、自分から学びたいと思うのだ」と、ピアジェの発見の内容について述べています。この2つの文の関係性を見ると、❹の内容を❺で言い換えていることがわかるので、空所には「簡潔に言うと、つまり」の意味を表す語を入れると文がつながります。

- -

(3) 📱 1 育児の技術の先駆者となった
2 大きな刺激となった
3 以前の科学者が考えていたことを確認した
4 一歩後退したように思えた

🔍 第3段落❶に「ピアジェの発見は、乳幼児の学習を研究する上での〜」とあるので、乳幼児の学習を研究する上でピアジェの発見がどう影響をしているかを、その後に続く文から探ります。❷に「多くの仮説が彼の発見を受け継いだが」とあることから、それが研究者らに研究の発想を与えたと読み取れます。

✏️ □ pioneer 率先する □ childcare 育児、保育 □ backward 後方に

Infants and Learning

❶ For most of the nineteenth century, it was commonly believed that a newborn's mind was a "blank slate."

❷ Psychologists thought that when infants were born, they possessed no knowledge whatsoever, but gained all their information gradually, as they got older.

❸ Given the fact that infants are limited in their movements and spend most of their days sleeping, it is no wonder that this concept prevailed for so long.

❹ With the advance of technology and a wider acceptance of new methodologies, however, this belief came under more and more criticism.

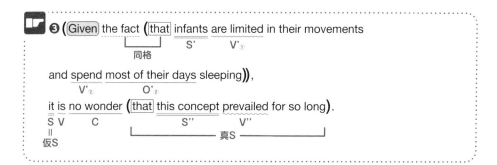

乳幼児と学習

第1段落

❶ 19世紀の大半の時期には、新生児の心は「白紙状態」だと信じられていた。

❷ 心理学者は、乳児は生まれたときには何の知識も持っておらず、情報はすべて歳を重ねながら獲得していくと考えていた。

❸ 乳児は動きが制限され、一日の大半を寝て過ごすという事実を踏まえれば、このような考え方が長く続いたのも不思議ではない。

❹ しかし、技術が進歩し、新しい方法論が広く受け入れられるようになると、この考え方は批判されるようになった。

❶ □ newborn 新生児　□ blank slate 白紙状態のもの　❷ □ possess（能力・性質など）を持つ
□ no ... whatsoever 少しの…もない（whatever の強調形）
❸ □ given the fact that 節 …という事実を考えると　□ spend X *doing* X（時間など）を…して過ごす
□ it is no wonder that 節 …というのは明らかだ　□ prevail 普及している、流行している
□ for so long 長年にわたって　❹ □ methodology 方法論　□ come under（批判など）にさらされる
□ criticism 批判

第2段落

❶ Swiss psychologist Jean Piaget was the first expert to sharply break away from the "blank slate" approach.

❷ After studying hundreds of infants, he came to the conclusion that the human brain possesses complex learning mechanisms from the moment of birth.

❸ He also found that cognitive development, that is, the process of learning to think about and understand the world around us, happens in stages, and each stage is characterized by acquiring different skills.

❹ Most importantly, he discovered that infants actively seek environmental stimulation.

❺ To put it simply, they want to learn and not just let people, objects, and events shape them.

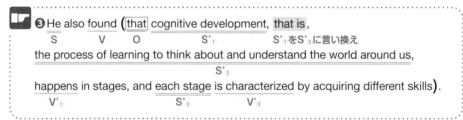

第3段落

❶ Piaget's findings proved to be an inspiration for studying infant learning.

❷ Numerous hypotheses have succeeded his discoveries, but they all agree that young children are active learners who are capable of setting goals, planning, and revising what they know.

❸ They have shown that the human brain is a genetically prepared organ ready to absorb knowledge from one's first day of life.

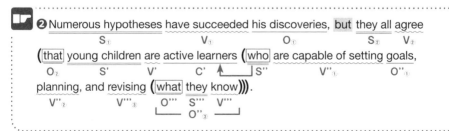

第2段落

❶ この「白紙状態」理論から脱却した最初の専門家が、スイスの心理学者ジャン・ピアジェだ。

❷ ピアジェは、何百人もの幼児を研究した結果、人間の脳には生まれた瞬間から複雑な学習メカニズムが備わっていると結論づけた。

❸ そして、認知機能の発達、つまり、私たちを取り巻く世界について考え、理解するための学習過程は段階的に行われ、それぞれの段階で異なるスキルを獲得するという特徴があることを発見した。

❹ そして、最も重要なことは、乳幼児が積極的に環境刺激を求めていることを発見したことだ。

❺ つまり、人や物、出来事によって自分自身を形作るだけではなく、自分から学びたいと思うのだ。

❶ □ sharply はっきりと　□ break away 離脱する
❷ □ come to the conclusion that 節 …という結論に達する　□ complex 複雑な
□ mechanism 仕組み　❸ □ cognitive 認識の　□ that is すなわち、つまり　□ in stages 段階的に
□ characterize …を特徴づける　□ acquire …を身に付ける　❹ □ stimulation 刺激
□ to put it simply 簡単に言うと　□ let X do X に…させる

第3段落

❶ ピアジェの発見は、乳幼児の学習を研究する上で大きな刺激となった。

❷ ピアジェの発見を受け継いだ仮説は数多くあるが、いずれも、幼児は目標を設定し、計画を立て、自分の知っていることを修正することができる能動的な学習者である、という点で一致している。

❸ そして、人間の脳が、生後1日目から知識を吸収できるように遺伝的に準備された器官であることを示したのである。

❶ □ prove to be …となる　□ inspiration 着想の源　❷ □ numerous 多数の
□ hypothesis 仮説、憶測　□ succeed …に続く、…の跡を継ぐ
□ be capable of doing …する能力がある　□ revise …を修正する
❸ □ show that 節 …ということを示す　□ genetically 遺伝学的に　□ prepared 準備ができた…
□ organ 臓器、器官　□ be ready to do …する用意ができている　□ absorb …を吸収する

On Public Goods

The concept of "public goods" has probably existed from the earliest civilizations. It is simply something that everyone—or the general public—can use at no direct cost. The Nobel Prize-winning economist Paul Samuelson defined public goods as something that neither excludes anyone nor competes with any products or services. (**1**), bridges, roads, and tunnels are typical public goods, since they offer easier transportation to everyone and do not compete with private companies.

Samuelson's definition of public goods is not accepted by all social scientists or economists, though. A public bridge must be paid for, usually through local taxes. Public projects typically gain strong support in their earliest phases, when broad outlines are proposed. Voters who (**2**) may, however, change their minds when informed of the tax cost and service details. In the end, a population that feels itself already overtaxed may decline any more public goods because they can become very expensive.

Also, it is sometimes difficult to determine what kind of product or service does not compete with public goods. Education or healthcare are often considered public goods, but public schools or hospitals compete with private ones. However, (**3**) remain popular among citizens. Citizens often like the idea of something open to anyone, especially when the total costs are unclear or far into the future. Therefore, leaders can usually gain support by promising them to a nation.

(1)　**1**　Apart from these
　　　　2　In return
　　　　3　Nevertheless
　　　　4　As cases in point

Date
／①②③④　／①②③④　／①②③④

(2)   **1**   were often critical of private initiatives

         2   can explain all the fine policy points

         3   were initially supportive of these programs

         4   fiercely oppose any kind of notable changes

(3)   **1**   presidents who firmly deny them

         2   what are essentially government projects

         3   companies that compete with public goods

         4   economists who support this spending

筆記 ②

第1段落

On Public Goods

❶The concept of "public goods" has probably existed from the earliest civilizations. ❷It is simply something that everyone—or the general public—can use at no direct cost. ❸The Nobel Prize-winning economist Paul Samuelson defined public goods as something that neither excludes anyone nor competes with any products or services. ❹(1), bridges, roads, and tunnels are typical public goods, since they offer easier transportation to everyone and do not compete with private companies.

第2段落

❶Samuelson's definition of public goods is not accepted by all social scientists or economists, though. ❷A public bridge must be paid for, usually through local taxes. ❸Public projects typically gain strong support in their earliest phases, when broad outlines are proposed. ❹Voters who (2) may, however, change their minds when informed of the tax cost and service details. ❺In the end, a population that feels itself already overtaxed may decline any more public goods because they can become very expensive.

第3段落

❶Also, it is sometimes difficult to determine what kind of product or service does not compete with public goods. ❷Education or healthcare are often considered public goods, but public schools or hospitals compete with private ones. ❸However, (3) remain popular among citizens. ❹Citizens often like the idea of something open to anyone, especially when the total costs are unclear or far into the future. ❺Therefore, leaders can usually gain support by promising them to a nation.

第1段落

①②では「公共財という概念は昔からあり、それは誰もが利用できるものだ」と説明し、③では、経済学者のサミュエルソンによる定義について述べています。④では空所の後にその具体例について「橋」「道路」「トンネル」などが挙げられています。

この段落では「公共財」という概念とその定義について書かれていました。

....

第2段落

第2段落の①ではサミュエルソンの「公共財」の定義がすべての学者たちに受け入れられているわけではないと述べています。続く文からそれについて説明していて、②では具体例として「公共の橋は地方税という形の利用料が必要である」と述べています。③では、また大きな括りに戻り、「公共事業は初期段階では賛同を得ている」とありますが、④では「しかし、詳細を知ると、〜の有権者は考えを変える」と、③の「初期段階」から先に進んだ状況について説明しています。つまり、「税金が高いと感じると、人は公共財を拒否することがある」と⑤で述べています。

この段落では前の段落にあった定義とは対照的な公共財の見方について説明していました。

....

第3段落

第3段落の①では、「公共財と競合しないことについては判断が難しい」とあるので、この段落では「公共財と競合しないことの判断の難しさ」についての具体的な説明があると予想できます。②では、教育も医療も公共財であるはずなのに、学校同士、病院同士の間にも競合が存在すると言っています。「しかし」で始まる③は空所に続く「評価が高い」につながるものを考えます。④では、市民の視点について「みんなが使えるものという考えが好まれる」と述べ、⑤はその them (みんなが使えるものと思われている公共財) を約束することという条件を by ... の形で付け加えて、「公共財について約束すると政治家は支持を得られやすい」で文章を締めくくっています。

(1)　1　Apart from these
　　　　2　In return
　　　　3　Nevertheless
　　　　4　As cases in point

(2)　1　were often critical of private initiatives
　　　　2　can explain all the fine policy points
　　　　3　were initially supportive of these programs
　　　　4　fiercely oppose any kind of notable changes

(3)　1　presidents who firmly deny them
　　　　2　what are essentially government projects
　　　　3　companies that compete with public goods
　　　　4　economists who support this spending

(1) 🔄 1 これらとは別に
2 見返りとして
3 それでも
4 例を挙げると

🔍 第1段落❹で空所の後に❶から❸で述べた公共財の具体例として「橋」「道路」「トンネル」などが挙げられているので、空所には「例を挙げると」を表す語句が入るとわかります。

....

(2) 🔄 1 民間企業による取り組みに批判的な意見が多かった
2 政策のあらゆる細かい点まで説明できる
3 当初は計画に賛成していた
4 著しい変化にはどんなものにも激しく反対する

🔍 第2段落❹の however をヒントに逆の関係になっているものを探します。❸の「公共事業は初期段階では賛同を得ている」状況であったものが、❹「有権者は詳細を知らされると考えを変える」という反応に変わり、その例となる❺の「人は税金が高いと感じると、公共財を拒否することがある」につながっているので、考えを変える前の有権者は公共財に対して拒否とは逆の意見であったと考えることができます。

✏️ ☐ critical of …を批判する ☐ initiative 主導 ☐ initially 初めは ☐ supportive of …を支持する
☐ fiercely 猛烈に、ひどく ☐ oppose …に反対する ☐ notable 著しい

....

(3) 🔄 1 それを断固として否定する大統領
2 本来は政府の事業であるもの
3 公共財と競合する企業
4 この支出を支持する経済学者

🔍 第3段落❶から❷で公共財と競合するかどうかの線引きの難しさについて述べているので、空所に1か4を入れると、それぞれ them と this の受ける要素がはっきりしません。3は後に続く❹の「誰にでも開かれている」の点で当てはまりません。2の「本来は政府の事業であるもの」を入れると、直前の文で述べたような競合している面があったとしても、それでも評価が高いという意味がつながります。

✏️ ☐ firmly 断固として ☐ essentially 本質的に、基本的に

🚩 **(1)** 4 **(2)** 3 **(3)** 2 199

On Public Goods

第1段落

❶ The concept of "public goods" has probably existed from the earliest civilizations.

❷ It is simply something that everyone—or the general public—can use at no direct cost.

❸ The Nobel Prize-winning economist Paul Samuelson defined public goods as something that neither excludes anyone nor competes with any products or services.

❹ As cases in point, bridges, roads, and tunnels are typical public goods, since they offer easier transportation to everyone and do not compete with private companies.

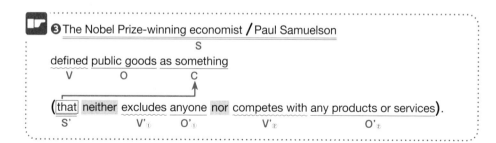

公共財について

第1段落

① 「公共財」という概念は、おそらく太古の文明から存在している。

② それは、誰もが、つまり一般の人々が、直接的には対価を払わずに利用できるものである。

③ ノーベル賞を受賞した経済学者ポール・サミュエルソンは、「誰も排除せず、いかなる製品やサービスとも競合しないもの」を公共財と定義した。

④ 例を挙げると、橋や道路、トンネルなどは、誰もが利用しやすい交通手段であり、民間企業とは競合しないので、典型的な公共財といえる。

① □ concept 概念　□ exist 存在する　□ civilization 文明社会
② □ the general public 一般人、市民　□ direct cost 直接費　③ □ define A as B A を B と定義する
□ neither A nor B A も B もどちらも…ない　□ exclude …を排除する
□ compete with …と競争する　④ □ as a case in point 例を挙げると

筆記②

第2段落

❶ Samuelson's definition of public goods is not accepted by all social scientists or economists, though.

❷ A public bridge must be paid for, usually through local taxes.

❸ Public projects typically gain strong support in their earliest phases, when broad outlines are proposed.

❹ Voters who were initially supportive of these programs may, however, change their minds when informed of the tax cost and service details.

❺ In the end, a population that feels itself already overtaxed may decline any more public goods because they can become very expensive.

---

❹ Voters (who were initially supportive of these programs)
　　S　↑　S'　　　　　V'　　　　　　　O'

may, however, change their minds
　　　　　　　　V　　　　O

(when informed of the tax cost and service details).
　　　　V''　　　　　　O''
　　　主節のSと主語が同じなため省略
　　　述語動詞がbe動詞のため省略

❺ In the end, a population (that feels itself already overtaxed)
　　　　　　　　S　　↑　S'　V'　O'　feel O done「Oが…されたと感じる」
　　　　　　　　　　　　　　　　　　　‖
may decline any more public goods　　a population
　　V　　　　　O

(because they can become very expensive).
　　　　　S''　　V''　　　　C''

第2段落

❶ しかし、サミュエルソンの言う公共財の定義が、すべての社会科学者や経済学者に受け入れられているわけではない。

❷ 公共の橋は、通常、地方税という形で利用料を払わなければならない。

❸ 公共事業は、その初期段階、つまり大枠が提案された段階では、強い賛同を得ているのが一般的である。

❹ しかし、当初は計画に賛成していた有権者も、税金やサービスの詳細を知らされると、考えを変えることもある。

❺ 結局、すでに税金が高すぎると感じた人々は、これ以上公共財を増やすと非常に高くつくので、それを拒否する可能性がある。

❶□ definition 定義　❷□ pay for …の代金を支払う　❸□ gain …を得る　□ phase 段階　□ outline 概要、計画案　❹□ initially 最初に　□ be supportive of …の支えになる　□ inform A of B A に B のことを知らせる　❺□ in the end 結局　□ population（一地域の）全住民　□ overtax …に重税をかける　□ decline …を断る

第3段落

❶ Also, it is sometimes difficult to determine what kind of product or service does not compete with public goods.

❷ Education or healthcare are often considered public goods, but public schools or hospitals compete with private ones.

❸ However, what are essentially government projects remain popular among citizens.

❹ Citizens often like the idea of something open to anyone, especially when the total costs are unclear or far into the future.

❺ Therefore, leaders can usually gain support by promising them to a nation.

❸ However, (what are essentially government projects)
              S' V'   C'
                           — S —

remain popular among citizens.
   V   C

① また、公共財と競合しないのはどんな商品やサービスか、判断が難しい場合がある。

② 教育や医療は公共財とみなされることが多いが、公立の学校や病院は私立のものと競合している。

③ しかし、本来は政府の事業であるものが、市民の間では変わらずに評価が高い。

④ 特に、費用の総合計が不明確であったり、ずっと先までわからないものだったりする場合、誰もが使えるものだという点を市民がプラスに評価することが多いのだ。

⑤ そういうわけで、国のリーダーが国民にそのような公共財の設置を約束すると支持を得られるのはよくある話である。

① ☐ determine …を決定する　② ☐ healthcare 保健医療　☐ consider A B A を B とみなす
③ ☐ essentially 本質的に　④ ☐ unclear 不明瞭　☐ far into the future はるか未来に
⑤ ☐ promise A to B A を B（人）に約束する

筆記②

205

問題英文の読み方 P.208　解説・正解 P.210　訳・語句 P.212

Improving Vocational Schools

Secondary school education has long been a complex concept. Students have been grouped in different types of schools depending on their abilities and their long-term life goals. Those who wish to pursue higher education go to academic high schools, whereas those who want to learn a trade choose vocational schools. While this, in itself, should not mean that students in vocational schools are worth less than (**1**), the general perception of society as well as vocational school students themselves is that they somehow rank lower.

It has been observed that most of these vocational students do develop certain irresponsible behaviors. They do not work hard, their grades tend to be low, they often miss classes and, even if present, act in a distracted way. Sociologists have been trying to figure out the main underlying reasons behind this. They think one reason for (**2**) is that vocational school students lack a sense of belonging in relation to both their school and their peers.

Several studies have shown that there is a close relationship between students' sense of belonging and their academic performance. Research by sociologist Mieke van Houtte suggests that the most important factor in developing a sense of connection in students is the trust of teachers. According to her, if teachers trusted vocational students more, they would also expect more of them. That would increase the level of confidence in students. And, (**3**), it would enhance academic performance and result in greater social acceptance.

(1)　**1**　those who did not attend secondary school
　　　　2　kids who come from poor backgrounds
　　　　3　their counterparts on another educational track
　　　　4　students who score the very lowest on exams

Date
／①②③④　／①②③④　／①②③④

(2)   **1**   investing more in these learners
         2   their negative school behaviors
         3   such a focus on their technical capabilities
         4   their searching for better opportunities

(3)   **1**   until then
         2   to be specific
         3   regardless
         4   sooner or later

筆記 ②

第1段落

Improving Vocational Schools

❶Secondary school education has long been a complex concept. ❷Students have been grouped in different types of schools depending on their abilities and their long-term life goals. ❸Those who wish to pursue higher education go to academic high schools, whereas those who want to learn a trade choose vocational schools. ❹While this, in itself, should not mean that students in vocational schools are worth less than (1), the general perception of society as well as vocational school students themselves is that they somehow rank lower.

第2段落

❶It has been observed that most of these vocational students do develop certain irresponsible behaviors. ❷They do not work hard, their grades tend to be low, they often miss classes and, even if present, act in a distracted way. ❸Sociologists have been trying to figure out the main underlying reasons behind this. ❹They think one reason for (2) is that vocational school students lack a sense of belonging in relation to both their school and their peers.

第3段落

❶Several studies have shown that there is a close relationship between students' sense of belonging and their academic performance. ❷Research by sociologist Mieke van Houtte suggests that the most important factor in developing a sense of connection in students is the trust of teachers. ❸According to her, if teachers trusted vocational students more, they would also expect more of them. ❹That would increase the level of confidence in students. ❺And, (3), it would enhance academic performance and result in greater social acceptance.

第1段落

第1段落の❶は「中等教育の概念は複雑だ」と言っており、その複雑さについて「生徒は能力や人生の目標に応じてさまざまな学校に分かれていく」と説明しているのが❷です。❸では「〜の人々は○○で、一方、〜の人々は△△」の形で具体例として、進学するタイプと職業訓練校に行くタイプを挙げています。❹では「職業訓練校に行くタイプが〜よりも価値が低いというわけではないが、格下と認識されている」とあります。
この段落では中等教育のタイプについて説明していました。

- -

第2段落

第2段落は❶に「職業訓練校の生徒に無責任な行動が見られる」とあり、前の段落での「格下と認識されている」の言及に関して一例を挙げ、❷ではさらに「職業訓練校の生徒は勉強しないし、成績は悪くなりがちで、たびたび欠席する」と書かれています。❸では「社会学者が理由を解明しようとしている」とあり、その考えられる理由として❹に「彼らの〜の理由は帰属意識がないこと」と言っています。

- -

第3段落

前のパラグラフの最終文で示唆された「職業訓練校の生徒の帰属意識の欠如」に関して、❶で「研究によると帰属意識と成績には関係がある」と述べています。❷から❹では具体的な要因と対策として「ある社会学者の研究によると、帰属意識を高めるのに重要なのは教師との信頼関係であり、教師が信頼すれば、もっと期待するようになり、それにより教師からの信頼感も高まる」という連鎖的に深まる関係性を説明しています。❺は「（そうすれば）社会の受け入れ態勢が整う」と、この文章を締めくくっています。

(1)
1 those who did not attend secondary school
2 kids who come from poor backgrounds
3 their counterparts on another educational track
4 students who score the very lowest on exams

(2)
1 investing more in these learners
2 their negative school behaviors
3 such a focus on their technical capabilities
4 their searching for better opportunities

(3)
1 until then
2 to be specific
3 regardless
4 sooner or later

(1) 📋 1　中学校に通わなかった人
　　　　2　貧しい環境にある子ども
　　　　3　他の教育課程の生徒
　　　　4　試験で最も低い点数を取った生徒

🔍 第1段落❹に「職業訓練校に行くタイプが～よりも価値が低いというわけではないが、格下と認識されている」とあるので、「職業訓練校に行くタイプ」と比較されているものが空所に入るとわかります。1つ前の❸で「職業訓練校に行くタイプ」と並べて「進学するタイプ」について述べられているので、これを言い換えて表した3が正解です。

✏️ □ counterpart 対応する人、同等の地位の人　□ track 習熟度別学級

· ·

(2) 📋 1　これらの学習者にもっと投資すること
　　　　2　学校での後ろ向きの行動
　　　　3　彼らの技術的な能力にそのように焦点を当てること
　　　　4　より良い機会を求めていること

🔍 第2段落❶❷では職業訓練校の生徒が勉強に積極的でないことが述べられ、❸ではその理由を社会学者が解明しようとしていることが書かれています。❹ではその理由として「帰属意識がないこと」が挙げられています。したがって、空所には職業訓練校の学生の「勉強しないし、成績は悪くなりがちで、欠席する」という様子を表している語句が当てはまります。

✏️ □ invest 投資する　□ capability 能力

· ·

(3) 📋 1　それまで
　　　　2　具体的に言うと
　　　　3　構わず
　　　　4　遅かれ早かれ

🔍 選択肢はどれも挿入句なので、まず第3段落の空所の後の「生徒の学業の成績を高める」という it が何なのかを前の文からつかんでおくことが大切です。❶では「帰属意識と成績に関係がある」と述べ、❷から❹では「教師との信頼関係が生徒に対する信頼感を高める」と述べています。ここから、「教師との信頼関係から帰属意識を持つこと」が生徒の学業の成績を高める it だとわかります。この因果関係に合うものとして空所には「いずれ」を表す語が入ると判断できます。空所の語句がなくても文が成立するため、誤答選択肢の不適切さが目立たないという難しさがあります。復習では、それぞれの語句の使われ方を確認しておきましょう。

筆記 ②

Improving Vocational Schools

❶ Secondary school education has long been a complex concept.

❷ Students have been grouped in different types of schools depending on their abilities and their long-term life goals.

❸ Those who wish to pursue higher education go to academic high schools, whereas those who want to learn a trade choose vocational schools.

❹ While this, in itself, should not mean that students in vocational schools are worth less than their counterparts on another educational track, the general perception of society as well as vocational school students themselves is that they somehow rank lower.

---

❸ Those (who wish to pursue higher education)
　　S　　S'　　　　V'　　　　　　　　O'
go to academic high schools,
　V　　　　　　O

(whereas those (who want to learn a trade)
　　　　　　S''　　S'''　　V'''　　O'''
choose vocational schools).
　V''　　　　　O''

❹ (While this, in itself, should not mean
　　　　　　S'　　　　　　　　V'
(that students in vocational schools are worth less than
　O　　S''　　　　　　　　　　　V''　　C''（目的語をとる形容詞）
their counterparts on another educational track)),
C''の目的語
the general perception of society
　　　　　S

as well as vocational school students themselves

is (that they somehow rank lower).
V　C　S'''　　　　V'''　C'''

職業訓練校の改善

第1段落

① 中等教育は、長い間、複雑な概念であり続けている。

② 生徒は能力や人生の長期的な目標に応じて、さまざまなタイプの学校に分かれていく。

③ 進学を希望する生徒はアカデミックな高校に進学する一方で、仕事の技能を身に付けたい生徒は職業訓練校を選択する。

④ このことは、職業訓練校の生徒が他の教育課程の生徒よりも価値が低いということではないはずだが、社会一般や職業訓練校の生徒自身の認識では、何となく格下であるということになっている。

□ vocational 職業訓練の　**①**□ secondary 中等教育の　□ complex 複雑な　□ concept 概念
②□ group …を分類する、…を群れにする　**③**□ pursue …を追求する、…を得ようとする
□ whereas …であるのに　□ trade 職業、仕事　**④**□ in itself それ自体、本質的に
□ worth less than …の価値に満たない　□ counterpart 対応するもの・人　□ track 能力別クラス
□ perception 認識　□ somehow どういうわけか　□ rank …に等級をつける、…を評価する

筆記②

213

第2段落

❶ It has been observed that most of these vocational students do develop certain irresponsible behaviors.

❷ They do not work hard, their grades tend to be low, they often miss classes and, even if present, act in a distracted way.

❸ Sociologists have been trying to figure out the main underlying reasons behind this.

❹ They think one reason for their negative school behaviors is that vocational school students lack a sense of belonging in relation to both their school and their peers.

---

❹ They think (one reason for their negative school behaviors
　　 S　　V　[that]　　S'
　　　　　　　　　　　O

is ([that] vocational school students lack a sense of belonging
V'　C'　　　　　S''　　　　　　V''　　　　O''

in relation to both their school and their peers)).

第2段落

❶ 職業訓練校の生徒の多くに、ある種の無責任な行動が見られてきた。

❷ 一生懸命に勉強せず、成績は悪くなりがちで、授業を欠席することも多く、出席していても注意散漫な行動を取ることもある。

❸ 社会学者たちは、このような状況の背後にある主な理由を解明しようとしている。

❹ 職業訓練校の生徒が学校と仲間の両方に対して帰属意識を持っていないことが、学校での後ろ向きの行動の理由の一つであると、社会学者たちは考えている。

❶☐ observe（観察によって）…に気づく　☐ develop（問題など）を生じさせる　☐ certain ある一定の
☐ irresponsible 無責任な　❷☐ grade 成績、評価　☐ miss …を欠席する　☐ distracted 気が散った
❸☐ sociologist 社会学者　☐ figure out …を理解する　☐ underlying 根底にある、基礎を成す
❹☐ lack …を欠く　☐ a sense of belonging 一体感、帰属意識　☐ in relation to …に関連して
☐ peer 仲間、同輩

筆記②

第3段落

❶ Several studies have shown that there is a close relationship between students' sense of belonging and their academic performance.

❷ Research by sociologist Mieke van Houtte suggests that the most important factor in developing a sense of connection in students is the trust of teachers.

❸ According to her, if teachers trusted vocational students more, they would also expect more of them.

❹ That would increase the level of confidence in students.

❺ And, sooner or later, it would enhance academic performance and result in greater social acceptance.

❷ Research by sociologist Mieke van Houtte
      S

suggests (that the most important factor in developing
   V   O   S'

a sense of connection in students is the trust of teachers).
                           V'   C'

❶ いくつかの研究により、生徒の帰属意識と学業成績には密接な関係があることが示されている。

❷ 社会学者のミーケ・ファン・ホウトの研究によると、生徒の帰属意識を高めるために最も重要なのは、教師との信頼関係であるという。

❸ 彼女によると、もし教師が職業訓練生をもっと信頼すれば、もっと期待するようになるだろうという。

❹ そうすれば、生徒に対する信頼感が高まる。

❺ そして、遅かれ早かれ、学業成績が向上し、社会的な受け入れ態勢が整うことになるという。

❶□ academic performance 学業成績　❷□ suggest that 節 …であることを示す
□ factor 要素、要因　□ a sense of connection 連帯感　□ trust 信頼、信用
❸□ according to …によると　□ trust …を信頼する　□ expect …を(当然のこととして)期待する
❹□ level of confidence in …に対する信頼度　❺□ sooner or later 遅かれ早かれ
□ enhance …を高める　□ acceptance 受容

筆記②

Returning to Sender

Parks worldwide struggle with pollution and litter. Many have put up signs around their grounds, warning people not to throw trash around. (**1**), the amount of such materials keeps rising. Experts say that one of the most important ways to prevent littering is to provide easy access to waste or recycling bins, so that people who have empty wrapping, cans or bottles can easily throw them away. Tough laws that place big fines on littering—when actually enforced—can also convince people not to litter.

Singapore, one of the cleanest countries on earth, uses a complex system to prevent littering, including cameras, enforcement officers, high fines, and even robot dogs to prevent people from polluting the city-state and encourage them to follow health rules. Khao Yai National Park has another approach to polluters. This large and beautiful park in Thailand has launched a program to shame parkgoers into behaving better: it is mailing litter (including food wrappers, empty cans, and other items) back to the litterers. The offenders (**2**), perhaps inviting additional shame.

While receiving trash at one's door and being criticized online may seem bad, the park still has other standard punishments it can give out, such as a $16,000 fine and up to five years in prison. People who litter often think, "it's just a can or a few scraps of paper." But when millions of people do that, it harms the location. Although it (**3**) to the offenders, park officers say that litter in the park is not only visually unpleasant, but harmful to plants, animals, and the whole local ecosystem.

(1)　**1**　Not only that
　　　2　Even so
　　　3　Provided that
　　　4　In addition

(2)　**1**　may have been sent warning letters
　　　　2　could be found on other properties
　　　　3　will also be profiled on social media
　　　　4　can seek some help from the police

(3)　**1**　would be very attractive
　　　　2　may prove to be convenient
　　　　3　was actually suggested
　　　　4　could seem rather harsh

第1段落

Returning to Sender

❶Parks worldwide struggle with pollution and litter. ❷Many have put up signs around their grounds, warning people not to throw trash around. ❸(1), the amount of such materials keeps rising. ❹Experts say that one of the most important ways to prevent littering is to provide easy access to waste or recycling bins, so that people who have empty wrapping, cans or bottles can easily throw them away. ❺Tough laws that place big fines on littering—when actually enforced—can also convince people not to litter.

第2段落

❶Singapore, one of the cleanest countries on earth, uses a complex system to prevent littering, including cameras, enforcement officers, high fines, and even robot dogs to prevent people from polluting the city-state and encourage them to follow health rules. ❷Khao Yai National Park has another approach to polluters. ❸This large and beautiful park in Thailand has launched a program to shame parkgoers into behaving better: it is mailing litter (including food wrappers, empty cans, and other items) back to the litterers. ❹The offenders (2), perhaps inviting additional shame.

第3段落

❶While receiving trash at one's door and being criticized online may seem bad, the park still has other standard punishments it can give out, such as a $16,000 fine and up to five years in prison. ❷People who litter often think, "it's just a can or a few scraps of paper." ❸But when millions of people do that, it harms the location. ❹Although it (3) to the offenders, park officers say that litter in the park is not only visually unpleasant, but harmful to plants, animals, and the whole local ecosystem.

第1段落

タイトルを見ただけだと、「差出人に戻すこと」とはいったい何のことなのか、メールの差出人か何かの話かと思うかもしれませんね。本文を読むと、❶に「世界中の公園が、汚染やごみの散乱に悩まされている」とあるので、ごみの問題なのだろうと推測できます。❷は「多くの公園ではごみを捨てないよう注意喚起している」、❸では「その量は増え続けている」とあります。❹ではそれを防ぐ方法として、「ごみ箱やリサイクルボックスを簡単に見つけられるようにすること」が挙げられ、また❺では「ポイ捨てに高額の罰金を科す法律を施行すること」も挙げられています。

第2段落

❶は「地球上でもっとも清潔な国の一つであるシンガポールではポイ捨てを防ぐために、カメラ、警察官、罰金、ロボット犬などを用いている」と言っています。❷❸では、別の例としてタイのKhao Yai 国立公園が取っているアプローチを挙げ、「Khao Yai 国立公園では、汚した人に恥をかかせるプログラム、つまりごみを郵便で送り返すことを始めた」と述べています。❹には空所2が含まれていて「違反者は〜して、さらに恥をかかされる」とあります。

第3段落

❶には「ごみを受け取ることだけでも嫌なことだが、公園には罰金や禁固刑などの懲罰が用意されている」と、さらなる罰則について書かれています。❷から❹では、「ポイ捨てをする人はたかが紙屑だと思うかもしれないが、何百万人がそうすると、公園に害が及ぶ。公園内のごみは景観を損なうだけではなく、地域の生態系全体にとっても有害だ」と、ポイ捨ての公共へ対する悪影響について、まとめています。

(1) 1 Not only that
2 Even so
3 Provided that
4 In addition

(2) 1 may have been sent warning letters
2 could be found on other properties
3 will also be profiled on social media
4 can seek some help from the police

(3) 1 would be very attractive
2 may prove to be convenient
3 was actually suggested
4 could seem rather harsh

(1) 🏴 1 それだけではなく
　　　　2 それでも
　　　　3 もし…とすれば
　　　　4 さらに

🔍 第1段落❷で「多くの公園ではごみを捨てないよう注意喚起している」と述べていますが、❸では「その量（＝ごみの量）は増え続けている」とあるので、この展開から空所には「しかし、それでもなお」の意味の語が当てはまるとわかります。

- -

(2) 🏴 1 警告書を送られていたかもしれない
　　　　2 他の敷地で発見される可能性がある
　　　　3 ソーシャルメディア上に掲載される
　　　　4 警察に何らかの助けを求めることができる

🔍 第2段落❷から❹までで違反者に対して罰として恥をかかせると説明しているので、空所には恥をかくことが入ると判断できます。選択肢のうち「ソーシャルメディアに掲載される」がそれに当てはまります。

✒ □ profile …の特徴や経歴を取り上げる

- -

(3) 🏴 1 非常に魅力的であろう
　　　　2 便利であることがわかるかもしれない
　　　　3 実際に提案された
　　　　4 かなり厳しいと思われるかもしれない

🔍 第3段落の空所がある文では、it が違反者に対して〜ではあるが、公園の職員はごみがいかに有害であるかについて語っています。❷で違反者がポイ捨てを問題視しないと述べていますが、これを選択肢の1や2のように捉えるには違反者の都合に焦点を当てた情報が足りません。3もここまでで違反者に提案されたものはなく、与えられるものは罰しか出てきていません。it が空欄の節に続く、park officers の発言を指すと考えると、4で文意が成立します。ポイ捨てする人にとって問題でないことを unpleasant かつ harmful と言っている点が「かなり厳しい」ということになります。

✒ □ harsh 厳しい

Returning to Sender

第1段落

❶ Parks worldwide struggle with pollution and litter.

❷ Many have put up signs around their grounds, warning people not to throw trash around.

❸ Even so, the amount of such materials keeps rising.

❹ Experts say that one of the most important ways to prevent littering is to provide easy access to waste or recycling bins, so that people who have empty wrapping, cans or bottles can easily throw them away.

❺ Tough laws that place big fines on littering—when actually enforced—can also convince people not to litter.

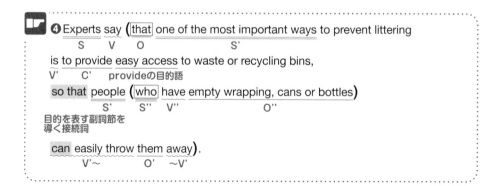

差出人に戻す

第1段落

① 世界中の公園が、汚染やごみの散乱に悩まされている。

② 多くの公園では看板を設置し、ごみを捨てないよう注意喚起している。

③ それでも、その量は増え続けている。

④ 専門家によると、ポイ捨てを防ぐ最も有力な方法の一つは、ごみ箱やリサイクルボックスを簡単に見つけられるようにし、空いた包装紙や缶、瓶を持っている人がすぐに捨てられるようにすることだそうだ。

⑤ また、ポイ捨てに高額の罰金を科す厳しい法律で（それが実際に施行されれば）ポイ捨てを防ぐことができる。

① □ struggle with （難題など）に苦闘する・取り組む　□ pollution 汚染、公害　□ litter 散らかったごみ
② □ put up …を掲示する　□ warn X not to *do* X に…しないように警告する
□ throw trash ごみを投げ捨てる　④ □ prevent …を防ぐ　□ litter ごみを散らかす
□ access to …への接近　□ so that X can *do* X が…できるように
□ throw X away X を投げ捨てる　⑤ □ tough 厳格な　□ place fines on …に罰金を科す
□ enforce （法律）を施行する　□ convince X to *do* X を説得して…させる

筆記②

第2段落

❶ Singapore, one of the cleanest countries on earth, uses a complex system to prevent littering, including cameras, enforcement officers, high fines, and even robot dogs to prevent people from polluting the city-state and encourage them to follow health rules.

❷ Khao Yai National Park has another approach to polluters.

❸ This large and beautiful park in Thailand has launched a program to shame parkgoers into behaving better: it is mailing litter (including food wrappers, empty cans, and other items) back to the litterers.

❹ The offenders will also be profiled on social media, perhaps inviting additional shame.

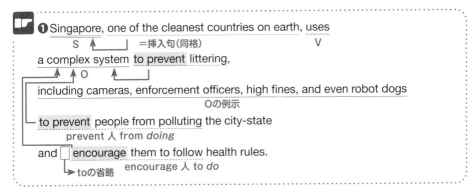

第3段落

❶ While receiving trash at one's door and being criticized online may seem bad, the park still has other standard punishments it can give out, such as a $16,000 fine and up to five years in prison.

❷ People who litter often think, "it's just a can or a few scraps of paper."

❸ But when millions of people do that, it harms the location.

❹ Although it could seem rather harsh to the offenders, park officers say that litter in the park is not only visually unpleasant, but harmful to plants, animals, and the whole local ecosystem.

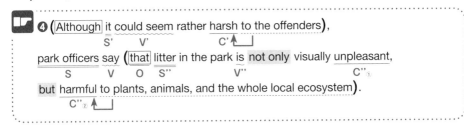

第2段落

❶ 地球上で最も清潔な国の一つであるシンガポールでは、カメラ、警察官、高額の罰金、さらにはロボット犬などの複雑なシステムを用いてポイ捨てを防止し、人々が都市を汚すのを防ぎ、衛生規則を守るように働きかけている。

❷ Khao Yai 国立公園は、汚した人に対する別のアプローチを取っている。

❸ タイにあるこの広大な美しい公園では、訪れる人たちによりよい行動をさせるために、汚した人に恥をかかせるプログラムを始めた。それは、ごみ（食べ物の包み紙や空き缶など）をポイ捨てした人に郵便で送り返すというものだ。

❹ ポイ捨てをした人は、ソーシャルメディア上に掲載され、さらに恥をかかされることになる。

❶☐ enforcement officer 警察官　☐ fine 罰金　☐ prevent X from *doing* X が…しないようにする
☐ pollute …を汚染する　☐ encourage X to *do* X に…するよう勧める　❷☐ polluter 汚染者
❸☐ launch …を始める　☐ shame X into *doing* X(人)を恥じ入らせて…させる
☐ parkgoer 公園に行く人　☐ mail A back to B A を B に郵便で送り返す
☐ litterer (公園などに)所かまわずごみを捨てる人　❹☐ offender 犯罪者, 違反者
☐ profile A on B A を B(メディアなど)で取り上げる　☐ invite (危険など)を引き起こす

第3段落

❶ ごみを玄関先で受け取ったりネットで批判されたりするだけでも嫌なことのように思えるが、公園には1万6千ドルの罰金や最長5年の禁固刑など、更に執行可能な標準的な罰則が用意されている。

❷ ポイ捨てをする人は、「たかが缶や紙くずだ」と思うことが多い。

❸ ただ、何百万人もの人がそういうことをすると、公園に害が及ぶのだ。

❹ 違反者にはかなり厳しいと思われるかもしれないが、公園内のごみは景観を損なうだけでなく、植物や動物、地域の生態系全体にとっても有害だと、公園の職員は言っている。

❶☐ criticize …を非難する　☐ punishment 処罰, 処分　☐ give out …を公表する
☐ in prison 刑務所に入って　❷☐ scrap 切れ端　❸☐ harm …を害する　❹☐ harsh 厳しい, 残酷な
☐ visually 視覚的に　☐ unpleasant 不愉快な　☐ harmful 有害な

筆記 3

長文内容一致問題

Unit 1 …… チャレンジしよう!

Unit 2 …… 練習しよう!

アイコン一覧

 解説 和訳 語注 正解 構造解析

問題英文の読み方 P.232　解説・正解 P.238　訳・語句 P.242

Hybrid Electric Vehicles: a Good Choice?

Hybrid Electric Vehicles (HEVs) are a category of cars and trucks designed to deal with some of the concerns and weak points of Electric Vehicles (EVs), while still being cleaner than Internal Combustion Engine (ICE) cars. "Hybrid" means the joining of two distinct things, in this case a combustion engine and an electric motor. This was to give HEVs longer range. Range is a special concern for drivers in rural areas, where public charging stations are fewer and drivers often have to regularly travel long distances. When the battery charge on the HEV runs low or the car itself reaches a certain speed, the vehicle automatically switches over to the combustion engine, both to extend vehicle range and recharge the battery— this results in higher overall energy efficiency.

However, some people feel HEVs are not as carbon-friendly as advertised. While many car companies claim that their HEVs emit no more than 44g of CO_2 per kilometer, independent experiments show that the true amount of emissions is closer to 120g per kilometer. Also, many HEV drivers do not operate their cars in an energy-efficient manner. Specifically, they over-rely on the combustion engine to charge their batteries, instead of hooking up to an electric outlet. That creates unnecessary carbon emissions that could be avoided if the driver took a few minutes out of his or her day to charge the car or truck before going to sleep.

Some people have gone so far as to claim that it is no use getting either an EV or HEV, since they are not much more nature-friendly than a compact car. However, studies of the Environmental Protection Agency over many years have shown that, despite these various factors, EVs are still the best cars for the environment. HEVs may perform as well as EVs when drivers take care as to how they drive and whether they refuel or recharge. HEV drivers should try to use their combustion engines as little as possible, for both fuel economy and clean energy reasons.

(1)　What is one thing the passage says about drivers in rural areas?

　　1　They need cars that are powerful enough to carry heavy loads over very long distances and therefore prefer EVs.

2 They require vehicles that do not need frequent charging because they may not have as many charging stations around as cities have.

3 They dislike the idea of switching from ICE cars and trucks to EVs or HEVs because they don't trust new technologies.

4 They are often driving in open areas and therefore do not care about reducing car emissions to protect the environment.

(2) As a result of independent field testing, it was determined that

1 the pollution measurements of HEVs based on CO_2 emissions per kilometer are much higher than the figures released by vehicle manufacturers.

2 although HEVs have much lower emission levels compared to EVs, they are both more polluting than ICE cars.

3 the current emission testing systems are unreliable on either electric cars or hybrid vehicles and have to be upgraded to give accurate results.

4 all types of cars and trucks need to become EVs or HEVs sooner or later in order to bring down carbon emissions.

(3) Which of the following statements would the author of the passage most likely agree with?

1 Most people who drive HEVs in rural areas constantly switch between engines, which potentially increases their total carbon emissions.

2 In spite of batteries being slightly more polluting than combustion engines, people should consider switching to EVs for the fuel savings they offer.

3 Since all vehicles are equally polluting regardless of the type of power source they have, it is better to continue with combustion engines.

4 Drivers of HEVs have some control over their vehicle emissions, so they should use the less polluting battery option as much as possible.

Hybrid Electric Vehicles: a Good Choice?

❶Hybrid Electric Vehicles (HEVs) are a category of cars and trucks designed to deal with some of the concerns and weak points of Electric Vehicles (EVs), while still being cleaner than Internal Combustion Engine (ICE) cars. ❷"Hybrid" means the joining of two distinct things, in this case a combustion engine and an electric motor. ❸This was to give HEVs longer range. ❹Range is a special concern for drivers in rural areas, where public charging stations are fewer and drivers often have to regularly travel long distances. ❺When the battery charge on the HEV runs low or the car itself reaches a certain speed, the vehicle automatically switches over to the combustion engine, both to extend vehicle range and recharge the battery—this results in higher overall energy efficiency.

この問題英文の長さは約300語です。

❶ 1文目の冒頭は私たちもすでに聞き慣れている「ハイブリッド車」の説明をしています。Hybrid Electric Vehicles (HEVs) が主語、are が動詞で「ハイブリッド車とは車とトラックの一つのカテゴリーです」と言っています。その後に、「電気自動車の弱点と問題点を克服して、内燃機関車よりもクリーンであるとして設計された車とトラックのカテゴリーだ」といって、「ハイブリッド車」の分類について詳しく説明しています。

❷ 主語が Hybrid、動詞が means で始まっている2文目は「ハイブリッド」について説明しています。「『ハイブリッド』とは、2つの異なるものを結合させること」と言っています。そして、コンマの後は in this case と続き、「(この場合のハイブリッドとは、)内燃エンジンと電気モーターの2つだ」と言っています。

❸ 主語の This は前の文を指していて、「このことは」と言っています。was to は be to「～することになっている」の過去形で、「このことは電気自動車に長い範囲（走行可能距離）を与えることになった」というのが直訳になります。つまり「このために HEV の走行可能距離は長くなった」と解釈しましょう。

❹ 前の文で「HEV の走行可能距離が長くなった」とあったので、それを受けて、「その『走行可能距離』は地方のドライバーたちの間で重要事項なのだ」と言っています。where は関係副詞で、後に主語、動詞が続きます。where の後の主語は public charging stations と drivers で、動詞は are と have to travel です。where 以下の関係副詞節で、どういう地方なのかについて説明しています。つまり「公共の充電ステーションが少なく、ドライバーたちは定期的に長距離を移動しなければならないことが多い」という環境なので、そんな地方のドライバーたちの間の重要な関心ごとが走行可能距離なのです。

❺ When で始まるこの文の主節の主語は it で、動詞は switches over です。When 以下は「HEV のバッテリーの充電量が少なくなったり、車自体が一定の速度に達すると」、主節は「車は自動的に内燃エンジンに切り替わり、走行可能距離の延長とバッテリーの充電を行う」と解釈しましょう。

第1段落では、ハイブリッド車について説明していました。

第2段落

❶However, some people feel HEVs are not as carbon-friendly as advertised. ❷While many car companies claim that their HEVs emit no more than 44g of CO_2 per kilometer, independent experiments show that the true amount of emissions is closer to 120g per kilometer. ❸Also, many HEV drivers do not operate their cars in an energy-efficient manner. ❹Specifically, they over-rely on the combustion engine to charge their batteries, instead of hooking up to an electric outlet. ❺That creates unnecessary carbon emissions that could be avoided if the driver took a few minutes out of his or her day to charge the car or truck before going to sleep.

❶ 新しい段落が始まってすぐに However があります。前の段落とは逆の視点で話が展開していくはずだと考え、心の準備をしましょう。「（前の段落ではハイブリッド車の良い点について述べたけれども、）しかしながら、何人かの人々は HEV は宣伝されているほど環境に優しくないと感じている」と述べています。

❷ 前の文で「何人かの人々は HEV は環境に優しくないと言っている」とあるので、この文では、その理由を挙げていると考えられます。While からの従属節は「多くの自動車会社が HEV の CO2排出量は1km あたり44g に過ぎないと主張しているが、その一方」、主節は「独自の実験によると、本当の排出量は1km あたり120g に近い」と述べています。なるほど、独自の研究から、自動車会社の発表する数値よりも環境に優しくないことが示されているわけですね。

❸ Also, で文が始まったら、前の文と同じ方向性の主張が別の例で挙げられると考えましょう。「（HEV は実際はあまり環境に優しくないし、）HEV ドライバーの多くは、エネルギー効率の良い運転をしていない」つまり、「だから HEV はそんなに環境に優しくない」という方向性の一致が読み取れます。

❹ Specifically で始まったら、その文は前の文の具体例を述べています。「HEV はそんなに良くない」という主張がさらに続きそうですね。「HEV ドライバーの多くはバッテリーを充電するために内燃エンジンに頼りすぎている／電気コンセントを使わずに」とあり、電気コンセントを使って充電する人は少ないと述べています。

❺ 主語は That、動詞は creates、目的語は unnecessary carbon emissions です。「それは不要な二酸化炭素の排出を生み出している」という意味で、「二酸化炭素の排出」を説明する that 節以下は、「もしドライバーが寝る前に数分間、車やトラックを充電していれば回避できるはずの（二酸化炭素の排出）」となっています。この段落の最後の5文目では、HEV ドライバーがエネルギー効率の良い使用法をしていないことについて、これでもかと、繰り返し述べることで主張の方向性を十分に明らかにして締めくくっています。
この段落ではハイブリッド車が一般に考えられているほど良いとは感じられない人の理由について書かれていました。

第3段落

❶Some people have gone so far as to claim that it is no use getting either an EV or HEV, since they are not much more nature-friendly than a compact car. ❷However, studies of the Environmental Protection Agency over many years have shown that, despite these various factors, EVs are still the best cars for the environment. ❸HEVs may perform as well as EVs when drivers take care as to how they drive and whether they refuel or recharge. ❹HEV drivers should try to use their combustion engines as little as possible, for both fuel economy and clean energy reasons.

❶ 主語は Some people、動詞は have gone です。直訳すると「何人かの人々は〜と主張するほど遠いところまで行ってしまった」となります。これは「〜とさえ主張する人々もいる」という極端な例を出していると解釈しましょう。that 以下は「EV も HEV も買う意味がない／それらはコンパクトカーよりもすごく環境に優しいわけではないから」という意味です。

❷ However で始まるので、前の文と反対の内容が展開されると考えて読み進めましょう。studies (~) have shown that の形を見たら、機械的に「研究によると」と解釈しましょう。「環境保護庁の長年の研究によると、こうしたさまざまな要因にかかわらず、EV は環境に最も優しいクルマであることがわかっている」となり、EV は環境に優しいという視点で話が展開しているとわかります。

❸ 前の段落で「良くない」理由を述べられていた HEV も「運転や給油・充電のしかたに気を付ければ EV と同等の性能を発揮する可能性がある」と述べられ、ここでようやく、肯定的な立場から論じられることになります。

❹ この文章全体の最後では「HEV のドライバーは、燃費とクリーンエネルギーの両方の理由からできるだけ内燃機関を使わないようにする必要があるのだ」とあり、結局、ハイブリッド車が環境に優しい車であるかは効果的な使用法次第なのだということが結論づけられるかたちで締めくくられています。
この段落は HEV の活用の仕方について書かれていました。

(1) What is one thing the passage says about drivers in rural areas?

1 They need cars that are powerful enough to carry heavy loads over very long distances and therefore prefer EVs.

2 They require vehicles that do not need frequent charging because they may not have as many charging stations around as cities have.

3 They dislike the idea of switching from ICE cars and trucks to EVs or HEVs because they don't trust new technologies.

4 They are often driving in open areas and therefore do not care about reducing car emissions to protect the environment.

(2) As a result of independent field testing, it was determined that

1 the pollution measurements of HEVs based on CO2 emissions per kilometer are much higher than the figures released by vehicle manufacturers.

2 although HEVs have much lower emission levels compared to EVs, they are both more polluting than ICE cars.

3 the current emission testing systems are unreliable on either electric cars or hybrid vehicles and have to be upgraded to give accurate results.

4 all types of cars and trucks need to become EVs or HEVs sooner or later in order to bring down carbon emissions.

(1) 📶 この文章で、地方のドライバーについて書かれているのはどんなことですか。

    1 重い荷物を長距離運ぶのに十分なパワーのある車を必要としており、そのため EV を好む。

    2 都市部と比べて充電スタンドが近くにないため、頻繁に充電する必要のない車を必要とする。

    3 新しい技術を信用せず、ICE 車や ICE トラックから EV や HEV に乗り換えることに抵抗がある。

    4 広々とした場所を走ることが多いので、環境保全のための排気ガス削減には関心がない。

🔍 第1段落❹に「公共の充電ステーションが少なく、定期的に長距離を移動しなければならないことが多い地方のドライバーにとって、走行可能距離は特に重要な関心事だ」とあります。ここから答えを確定しましょう。

- -

(2) 📶 独自のフィールドテストの結果判明したのは、

    1 HEV の1km あたりの CO_2排出量に基づく汚染の数値は、自動車メーカーが発表している数値よりもはるかに高いということだ。

    2 HEV は EV に比べて排出が大幅に少ないが、どちらも ICE 車よりは汚染度が高いということだ。

    3 現在の排出測定システムは、電気自動車とハイブリッド車のどちらにしても信頼性が低く、正確な結果を得るためには改良が必要だということだ。

    4 炭素排出量を減らすためには、すべてのタイプの自動車やトラックが遅かれ早かれ電気自動車またはハイブリッド車になる必要があるということだ。

🔍 第2段落❷で「多くの自動車会社が HEV の CO2排出量は1km あたり44g に過ぎないとしているが、独自の実験によると、本当の排出量は1km あたり120g に近いという」と独自のフィールドテストの結果に関する説明があります。ここで問2の正解を確定することができます。

✏️ ☐ unreliable 信頼できない ☐ sooner or later 遅かれ早かれ ☐ bring down …を下げる

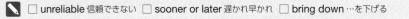

- -

筆記③

🚩 **(1)** 2 **(2)** 1 239

(3) Which of the following statements would the author of the passage most likely agree with?

1 Most people who drive HEVs in rural areas constantly switch between engines, which potentially increases their total carbon emissions.

2 In spite of batteries being slightly more polluting than combustion engines, people should consider switching to EVs for the fuel savings they offer.

3 Since all vehicles are equally polluting regardless of the type of power source they have, it is better to continue with combustion engines.

4 Drivers of HEVs have some control over their vehicle emissions, so they should use the less polluting battery option as much as possible.

(3) 🏳 この文章の筆者は、次のどの意見に最も同意すると考えられますか。

1　地方で HEV を運転する人の多くは、常にエンジンを切り替えて運転するため、CO_2 の総排出量が増える可能性がある。

2　バッテリーは内燃エンジンよりわずかに汚染度が高いとは言うものの、バッテリーが可能にする燃費の節約のために EV への乗り換えを検討すべきである。

3　どのような動力源であっても、すべての自動車が同じように大気を汚染するので、内燃エンジンを使い続けた方がよい。

4　HEV のドライバーは排ガスをある程度コントロールできるのだから、なるべく汚染度の低いバッテリーを使うべきだ。

🔍 第3段落❸❹に「HEV は、運転のしかたや給油・充電に気をつければ、EV と同等の性能を発揮する可能性がある。HEV のドライバーは、燃費とクリーンエネルギーの両方の理由から、できるだけ内燃エンジンを使わないようにする必要があるのだ」とあります。ここから問3の正解が確定できます。

🖊 ☐ potentially もしかすると　☐ regardless of …にかかわらず　☐ power source 動力源

Hybrid Electric Vehicles: a Good Choice?

第1段落

❶ Hybrid Electric Vehicles (HEVs) are a category of cars and trucks designed to deal with some of the concerns and weak points of Electric Vehicles (EVs), while still being cleaner than Internal Combustion Engine (ICE) cars.

❷ "Hybrid" means the joining of two distinct things, in this case a combustion engine and an electric motor.

❸ This was to give HEVs longer range.

❹ Range is a special concern for drivers in rural areas, where public charging stations are fewer and drivers often have to regularly travel long distances.

❺ When the battery charge on the HEV runs low or the car itself reaches a certain speed, the vehicle automatically switches over to the combustion engine, both to extend vehicle range and recharge the battery—this results in higher overall energy efficiency.

---

❹ Range is a special concern for drivers in rural areas, (where
S   V   C

public charging stations are fewer
S'①   V'① C'①

and drivers often have to regularly travel long distances).
S'②   V'②~   ~V'②   O'②

❺ (When the battery charge on the HEV runs low or
S'①   V'① C'①

the car itself reaches a certain speed),
S'②   V'②   O'②

the vehicle automatically switches over to the combustion engine,
S   V

both to extend vehicle range and recharge the battery
　　　結果を表す副詞句のto不定詞　　　to省略

—this results in higher overall energy efficiency.
S"   V"   O"

ハイブリッド車：良い選択か

第1段落

❶ ハイブリッド車 (HEV) は、電気自動車 (EV) の弱点と問題点を克服し、内燃エンジン (ICE) 車よりもクリーンだとして設計された乗用車やトラックの1つのカテゴリーだ。

❷ 「ハイブリッド」とは、2つの異なるものを結合させることを言うが、この場合のハイブリッド とは、内燃エンジンと電気モーターの2つを組み合わせたという意味である。

❸ これによって HEV の走行可能距離は長くなった。

❹ 公共の充電ステーションが少なく、定期的に長距離を移動しなければならないことが多い地 方のドライバーにとって、走行可能距離は特に重要な関心事だ。

❺ HEV のバッテリーの充電量が少なくなったり、車自体が一定の速度に達すると、車は自動的 に内燃エンジンに切り替わり、走行可能距離の延長とバッテリーの充電を行う。その結果、全 体的なエネルギー効率が高まる。

❶□ concern 心配、懸念材料　□ hybrid 混成の、雑種の　□ combustion 燃焼
❷□ distinct 異なった　❸□ range 走行距離　❹□ rural 田舎の、地方の
❺□ switch over 切り替える　□ extend …を延長する　□ overall 全体の

筆記③

第2段落

❶ However, some people feel HEVs are not as carbon-friendly as advertised.

❷ While many car companies claim that their HEVs emit no more than 44g of CO_2 per kilometer, independent experiments show that the true amount of emissions is closer to 120g per kilometer.

❸ Also, many HEV drivers do not operate their cars in an energy-efficient manner.

❹ Specifically, they over-rely on the combustion engine to charge their batteries, instead of hooking up to an electric outlet.

❺ That creates unnecessary carbon emissions that could be avoided if the driver took a few minutes out of his or her day to charge the car or truck before going to sleep.

---

❺ That creates unnecessary carbon emissions (that could be avoided
　　S　　V　　　　　　　O　　　　　　　　S'　　　　V'
(if the driver took a few minutes out of his or her day
　　　S''　　V''　　　O''
to charge the car or truck (before going to sleep))).
副詞句を表す　chargeの目的語　　時を表す副詞句
to不定詞

❶ しかし、HEV は宣伝されているほど環境に優しくないと感じる人もいる。

❷ 多くの自動車会社が HEV の CO2排出量は1km あたり44g に過ぎないとしているが、独自の実験によると、本当の排出量は1km あたり120g に近いという。

❸ また、HEV ドライバーの多くは、エネルギー効率の良い運転をしていない。

❹ 具体的には、バッテリーを充電するために電気コンセントを使わず、内燃エンジンに頼りすぎている。

❺ その結果、もしドライバーが一日のうちの寝る前の数分間を費やして、車やトラックを充電していれば回避できるはずの不要な二酸化炭素の排出が起こっているのである。

❶ ☐ -friendly …という害をひき起こさない　❷ ☐ claim that 節 …だと主張する　☐ emit …を放出する
☐ emission 放出　☐ energy-efficient エネルギー効率の良い　☐ hook up to …に接続する
☐ electric outlet コンセント

第3段落

❶ Some people have gone so far as to claim that it is no use getting either an EV or HEV, since they are not much more nature-friendly than a compact car.

❷ However, studies of the Environmental Protection Agency over many years have shown that, despite these various factors, EVs are still the best cars for the environment.

❸ HEVs may perform as well as EVs when drivers take care as to how they drive and whether they refuel or recharge.

❹ HEV drivers should try to use their combustion engines as little as possible, for both fuel economy and clean energy reasons.

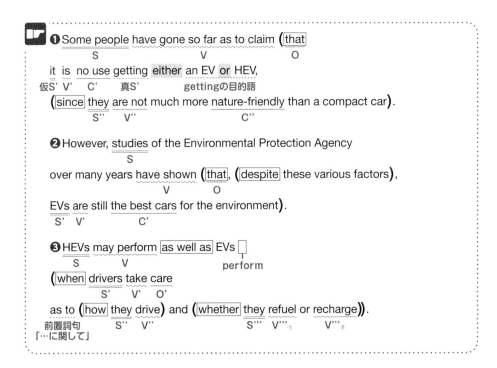

❶ EV も HEV もコンパクトカーに比べて、はるかに自然環境に優しいわけではないから買っても無駄だ、とさえ主張する人もいる。

❷ しかし、環境保護庁が研究によって長年示しているのは、こうしたさまざまな要因を考慮しても、EV が環境に最も優しい車であることに変わりないということである。

❸ HEV は、運転のしかたや給油・充電に気をつければ、EV と同等の性能を発揮する可能性がある。

❹ HEV のドライバーは、燃費とクリーンエネルギーの両方の理由から、できるだけ内燃エンジンを使わないようにする必要があるのだ。

❶ □ go so far as to *do* …しさえする　□ it is no use *doing* …しても無駄である
❷ □ studies show that 節 研究によると…ということを示している（定型表現）
□ despite …にもかかわらず　❸ □ A as well as B A と同様に B も　□ as to …に関して
□ refuel 給油する　□ recharge 充電する

問題英文の読み方 P.250　解説・正解 P.256　訳・語句 P.260

Should You Share Your DNA Profile?

DNA is a complex chemical structure that carries the specific genetic code of a person, so it acts as a sort of natural personal identifier. Although all humans share the same 99.9% of DNA, (and identical twins share 100%), the remaining 0.1% is unique to you. There is tremendous medical potential in the use of DNA. For example, doctors can use your DNA to predict and possibly prevent diseases that have long run in your family line. In the future, medical companies may produce customized medication based on DNA, so that treatments can be designed for each patient. Police use DNA to catch criminals while defense lawyers use it to free wrongly-accused people.

At the same time, not all DNA uses are beneficial. An insurance company that knows a DNA profile might decline to cover a person or charge him or her a higher rate if they are more likely to have a peculiar disease. A company might prefer to employ a person whose DNA indicates a long line of productive ancestors over one whose genes show a family history of laziness or crime. In a worst case, as some researchers warn, the United States or even the world could become a society ruled by genetic elites. Numerous American laws protect ordinary people's DNA privacy. In particular, a 2008 law called GINA protects Americans from employers, insurers, and others asking about one's genetic background or requiring DNA tests as a condition of work or insurance coverage.

However, one problem is that many Americans today willingly share their DNA information with companies that promise to trace their family histories. For a small fee, these firms can tell you whether you are related to an ancient prince or pirate. In a multi-ethnic society such as the US, this kind of tracking can be especially interesting. At the same time, experts warn against entrusting these companies with such critical personal information. This is because, while GINA protects you against being forced to provide genetic information, it says almost nothing about its use when it is voluntarily provided. The DNA tracing companies are therefore legally able to share it with an employer, insurer or marketer, or simply sell it on the open market. This is why many privacy experts discourage people from using these services. It might be interesting to find that Queen Victoria or George Washington was your ancestor, but it might not be worth the privacy cost. At the very least, privacy experts encourage people to carefully compare the terms and conditions of service of these businesses and choose those firms which offer more privacy.

(1) What does the author say about medical uses of DNA?

    1   DNA testing would allow doctors to trace your family line to see how certain diseases were treated in the past.

    2   The information from DNA tests could be used not only to prevent certain diseases but to create customized drugs.

    3   DNA of people with several diseases may prove to be useful in finding the origin of major illnesses.

    4   The DNA collected from people may be used by companies to make medicines in large quantities at lower cost.

(2) What do we learn about GINA?

    1   It shields people from being forced to give their DNA to companies that provide certain services or employment.

    2   It is a series of laws that enable both insurance companies and customers to keep their contracts private.

    3   It is a piece of legislation that ensures DNA can never be used for commercial purposes except with special government permission.

    4   It is a regulation framework that supports free and fair negotiation between companies for control of human DNA.

筆
記
③

(3) What should users of DNA tracing companies first do?

    1   Confirm that the company can track ancestors very precisely until your connection with a famous historical figure is proven.

    2   Review their policies on how they intend to handle the data they obtain from testing the DNA of their customers.

    3   Request the companies to change their terms and conditions to suit the DNA type you are providing.

    4   Insist on a written guarantee that the result of your DNA test will never be shared with any foreign governments.

第1段落

Should You Share Your DNA Profile?

❶DNA is a complex chemical structure that carries the specific genetic code of a person, so it acts as a sort of natural personal identifier. ❷Although all humans share the same 99.9% of DNA, (and identical twins share 100%), the remaining 0.1% is unique to you. ❸There is tremendous medical potential in the use of DNA. ❹For example, doctors can use your DNA to predict and possibly prevent diseases that have long run in your family line. ❺In the future, medical companies may produce customized medication based on DNA, so that treatments can be designed for each patient. ❻Police use DNA to catch criminals while defense lawyers use it to free wrongly-accused people.

この問題英文の長さは約400語です。

❶ 1文目は難しい単語に惑わされずに、「DNAは化学構造で、個人を特定できる情報を持っている」と解釈しましょう。主語はDNA、動詞はisで、「DNAは複雑な化学構造だ」。chemical structureをthat以下が修飾し、「人を特定する遺伝情報を持つ複雑な化学構造」と言っています。接続詞のso以下の節は「だから、それ（DNA）は人が生まれつき持っている個人を識別するものとしての役割を果たしている」という内容です。

❷ Althoughという接続詞で文が始まっています。Althoughの後に主語と動詞が続き、コンマまでで「～だけれども」の意味になります。「すべての人間が99.9%、（一卵性の双子は100%同じ）DNAを共有するけれども」の後に主節が続きます。「残りの0.1%は個人特有のものだ」とあることから、DNAとはすべての人間が99.9%も共有しているものだとわかりますね。

❸ 「このDNAを利用することは医学的に大いなる可能性を秘めている」と書いてあるので、この次には「医学的なDNAの可能性」の例がくるだろうと予想しながら読み進めましょう。

❹ 「例えば」で始まっています。「（DNAはどんな可能性を秘めているかというと、）例えば、医師はDNAを使ってその家系に古くから伝わる病気を予測し、予防できる」という内容です。

❺ In the futureで始まっており、「将来、製薬会社はDNAに基づいてカスタマイズした薬を製造することもできる」という別の可能性についても言っています。文の後半で「治療が個々の患者に合わせられるように」と説明を加えています。

❻ また、別の例として「警察」と「弁護士」のDNAの活用方法について述べられています。主節の主語がPoliceで、接続詞whileの後の主語がdefense lawyersなので、「警察は犯罪者を捕まえるために、弁護人は冤罪者を釈放させるためにDNAを活用している」という意味です。

この段落ではDNAの概要と、その遺伝情報により、どの分野にどのような活用方法があるかについて説明していました。

筆記③

第2段落

❶At the same time, not all DNA uses are beneficial. ❷An insurance company that knows a DNA profile might decline to cover a person or charge him or her a higher rate if they are more likely to have a peculiar disease. ❸A company might prefer to employ a person whose DNA indicates a long line of productive ancestors over one whose genes show a family history of laziness or crime. ❹In a worst case, as some researchers warn, the United States or even the world could become a society ruled by genetic elites. ❺Numerous American laws protect ordinary people's DNA privacy. ❻In particular, a 2008 law called GINA protects Americans from employers, insurers, and others asking about one's genetic background or requiring DNA tests as a condition of work or insurance coverage.

❶ 「同時に、すべての DNA 活用法が有益だとは限らない」で始まっているので、この段落の一つの方向性として「DNA の活用で、有益ではないこと」を例示していくものだろうと推測して読み進めます。

❷ 冠詞 An が付いた An insurance company で始まっているので、ある保険会社で好ましくない DNA の活用が行われている例について説明されていると予想できるでしょう。「DNA 情報を知っている保険会社は、例えばその人が特殊な病気にかかりやすいと判断した場合に保険の契約を拒否したり、高い保険料を請求したりするかもしれない」と、保険会社に有利で、顧客にとって不利になる可能性があると述べています。

❸ 前の文と同様に冠詞 A が付いて A company で始まっているので、また別の会社で DNA を活用できない例が挙げられることがわかります。「そして、またある会社では（怠け者や犯罪者の家系よりも）生産性が高い先祖の DNA を持った人物を雇いたいと思うかもしれない」と、さらに、企業に有利で、求職者に不利になる可能性がある例を示しています。

❹ 前の2つの A(An) …「ある〜」で始まる文からたたみかけるように、この文にも a が付いて「そして、最悪の場合には」で始まっています。主語は the United States (or even the world) で動詞は could become です。「最悪の場合、アメリカ、もしくは世界全体が遺伝子のエリートに支配された社会になるでしょう」と想像しています。

❺ 前の文までで展開された DNA の活用に関する悪い可能性と、最悪の場合を踏まえて、アメリカでは対策がされているという具体的な事例を述べています。「一般人の DNA プライバシーを保護する法律が多くある」と説明しています。

❻ 前の文を受けて、「特に2008年の法律は〜」と具体例を挙げています。ここで初めて GINA という用語が出てきます。「2008年に制定された GINA と呼ばれる法律では、労働や保険加入の条件として遺伝的背景を尋ねられたり DNA 検査を要求されたりすることのないよう、アメリカ人を保護している」と説明しています。アメリカ人の DNA プライバシーが法律によって保護されていることが、この後の内容にどう影響するのかをここから推測するのは難しいですが、ここまでの展開を頭に入れて次の段落に進みましょう。
この段落では、DNA の活用による危険性と、アメリカ人がその危険から保護されていることについて述べていました。

第3段落

❶However, one problem is that many Americans today willingly share their DNA information with companies that promise to trace their family histories. ❷For a small fee, these firms can tell you whether you are related to an ancient prince or pirate. ❸In a multi-ethnic society such as the US, this kind of tracking can be especially interesting. ❹At the same time, experts warn against entrusting these companies with such critical personal information. ❺This is because, while GINA protects you against being forced to provide genetic information, it says almost nothing about its use when it is voluntarily provided. ❻The DNA tracing companies are therefore legally able to share it with an employer, insurer or marketer, or simply sell it on the open market. ❼This is why many privacy experts discourage people from using these services. ❽It might be interesting to find that Queen Victoria or George Washington was your ancestor, but it might not be worth the privacy cost. ❾At the very least, privacy experts encourage people to carefully compare the terms and conditions of service of these businesses and choose those firms which offer more privacy.

❶ However で始まり、主語は one problem、動詞は is で「しかし、ある問題は～」なので、その後の that 節内で問題点が語られると予想できます。that 節内を見てみると、「多くのアメリカ人が家系をさかのぼって調べてくれる会社に自分の DNA 情報を抵抗なく共有している」とあります。この1文目を読んで、「どんな会社だろう？」「どうしてだろう？」のような問いを持つことができれば、上手く読み進められている証拠です。

❷ 英文を読んでいる間は脳が活発に動いていますが、その中でも前の文で浮かんだ問いを引き継いで「どんな会社かというと」「どうして多くのアメリカ人は情報をシェアしてしまうのかというと」と、頭の中で答えとなる要素を待ち受ける準備をしてから読み進めると、「わずかな料金で、これらの会社はあなたが古代の王子や海賊と血縁があるかどうかを教えてくれる」という意味がクリアになります。

❸ ここでも前の文で「なぜそんな会社があるのか」「そのサービスは何なんだ」という問いが浮かんでいると、本文にある「アメリカのような多民族社会では」の背景がすっきりと見え、「このような追跡調査は特に興味深い」という状況が理解できます。

❹ また、専門家は「これらの企業にこのような重要な個人情報を託してはいけない」と警告しています。

❺ この文では、前の文を受け、どうして個人情報を企業に託してはいけないのかについて述べています。理由は「GINA（という法律）は、遺伝情報の提供を強制されることからは保護するが、任意で提供する場合の利用については、ほとんど何も言っていないから」です。確かに、「家系をさかのぼって調べてくれるサービス」と聞けば自分のルーツを知ろうとDNA情報を与えてしまうかもしれませんが、DNA追跡会社の本当の目的は顧客のルーツを調べることではなく、雇用主や保険会社が欲しくても法的に保護されている顧客の遺伝子情報を、顧客側から提供してくれるように仕向けることなのかも知れないと考えることができますね。

❻ 主語はThe DNA tracing companies、動詞はare able to shareです。可能を表すare able toの間にtherefore「だから」とlegally「合法的に」が入っています。「だから、追跡会社は合法的にシェアできる」という構造を押さえた上で、「DNA追跡会社は、雇用主、保険会社、マーケティング会社と情報を共有したり、単に一般市場で販売したりすることが合法的に可能である」と解釈しましょう。

❼ This is whyは直訳だと「それが〜の（why以下の）理由だ」となりますが、This is whyを見たら機械的に「だから」と訳す習慣をつけるとよいでしょう。「だから、多くのプライバシー専門家は、こうしたサービスの利用をしないよう勧めている」と言っています。

❽ この文はbutをはさんでIt might be ...の形が繰り返されます。「ビクトリア女王やジョージ・ワシントンが自分の祖先だと知るのは面白いかもしれない／しかし／（いくら面白くても、それは）プライバシーの代償に見合うものではないのかもしれない」の流れから、筆者がDNAの提供に反対の立場で話を進めていることが見えてきますね。

❾ 最後の文はAt the very leastで始まっています。直訳では「少なくとも」ですが、ここに「できるだけやめた方がいいけれど」という意味が含まれていると解釈できます。このような前置きをした上で「個人情報保護の専門家が勧めている内容は、これらの企業のサービス利用規約を慎重に比較し、プライバシーについてより多く配慮している企業を注意深く選択することだ」と述べています。前置きに含まれる「本当は情報の提供はやめた方がいいけれども、それでももし自分のルーツを知るなどの目的で業者にDNA情報を提供するのであれば」という意味合いを取り入れて理解するには、ここまでの文の中から筆者のDNA情報提供に関する立場を捉えておく必要があります。

この段落では今日のアメリカ社会で、アメリカ人が直面している具体的な問題について述べていました。

筆記③

(1) What does the author say about medical uses of DNA?

1 DNA testing would allow doctors to trace your family line to see how certain diseases were treated in the past.

2 The information from DNA tests could be used not only to prevent certain diseases but to create customized drugs.

3 DNA of people with several diseases may prove to be useful in finding the origin of major illnesses.

4 The DNA collected from people may be used by companies to make medicines in large quantities at lower cost.

(2) What do we learn about GINA?

1 It shields people from being forced to give their DNA to companies that provide certain services or employment.

2 It is a series of laws that enable both insurance companies and customers to keep their contracts private.

3 It is a piece of legislation that ensures DNA can never be used for commercial purposes except with special government permission.

4 It is a regulation framework that supports free and fair negotiation between companies for control of human DNA.

(1) 🔲 筆者は、DNA の医学的利用についてどのように言っていますか。

　1　DNA 検査によって医師は家系をたどり、特定の病気が過去にどのように治療されたかを知ることができる。

　2　DNA 検査から得られる情報は、特定の病気を予防するためだけでなく、特別注文に合わせた薬を製造するためにも使われるかもしれない。

　3　複数の病気を持つ人の DNA は、主要な病気の原因を見つけるのに役立つかもしれない。

　4　人から採取した DNA を使って、企業が安価で大量に医薬品を作るかもしれない。

🔍 第1段落❹❺に「医師は DNA を使って、その家系に古くから伝わる病気を予測し、予防することができるかもしれない。将来的には、製薬会社が DNA をもとにカスタマイズした薬を製造し、患者一人一人に合った治療を行うことができるようになるかもしれない」とあります。ここから問1の正解がわかります。

✏️ ☐ treat (病気)を治療する　☐ in large quantities 大量に

. . . .

(2) 🔲 GINA についてわかることは何ですか。

　1　特定のサービスや雇用を提供する企業に、自分の DNA を提供することを強制されないようにする。

　2　保険会社と顧客の双方が契約を非公開に保てるようにするための一連の法律である。

　3　政府の特別な許可がない限り、DNA を商用目的に使用できないようにする法律である。

　4　ヒトの DNA を管理するための、企業間の自由で公正な交渉を支援する規制の枠組みである。

🔍 第2段落❻で「2008年に制定された GINA と呼ばれる法律により、雇用主や保険会社に、就労や保険加入の条件として遺伝的背景を尋ねられたり DNA 検査を要求されたりしないように、アメリカ人を保護している」と GINA について説明をしています。問2の答えはここで明らかになります。

✏️ ☐ shield …を保護する　☐ enable X to *do* X を…することができるようにする　☐ legislation 法律
　☐ ensure (that 節) …を保証する・確実にする　☐ framework 枠組み

. . . .

(3) What should users of DNA tracing companies first do?

1 Confirm that the company can track ancestors very precisely until your connection with a famous historical figure is proven.

2 Review their policies on how they intend to handle the data they obtain from testing the DNA of their customers.

3 Request the companies to change their terms and conditions to suit the DNA type you are providing.

4 Insist on a written guarantee that the result of your DNA test will never be shared with any foreign governments.

(3)　☑4　DNA 追跡会社の利用者がまずすべきことは何ですか。

1　有名な歴史上の人物との関係が証明されるまで、その会社が非常に正確に先祖を追跡できることを確認する。

2　顧客の DNA を検査して得たデータをどのように扱うつもりなのか、その会社の方針を確認する。

3　提供する DNA の種類に合わせて条件を変更するよう会社に求める。

4　DNA 検査の結果が外国のいかなる政府とも共有されないことを保証する書面を要求する。

🔍 第3段落❾に「個人情報保護の専門家は、これらの企業のサービス利用規約を慎重に比較し、プライバシーにより配慮した企業を選択するよう勧めている」とあります。ここで問3の答えがわかります。

✏️　□ precisely 正確に　□ figure 人物　□ intend to *do* …するつもりである　□ insist on …を要求する

Should You Share Your DNA Profile?

❶ DNA is a complex chemical structure that carries the specific genetic code of a person, so it acts as a sort of natural personal identifier.

❷ Although all humans share the same 99.9% of DNA, (and identical twins share 100%), the remaining 0.1% is unique to you.

❸ There is tremendous medical potential in the use of DNA.

❹ For example, doctors can use your DNA to predict and possibly prevent diseases that have long run in your family line.

❺ In the future, medical companies may produce customized medication based on DNA, so that treatments can be designed for each patient.

❻ Police use DNA to catch criminals while defense lawyers use it to free wrongly-accused people.

---

❹ For example, doctors can use your DNA
　　　　　　　　　　S　　　V　　　O

to predict and possibly prevent diseases (that have long run in your family line).
副詞句のto不定詞　　　　　　　　　predictと　　S'　V'~　　　~V'
　　　　　　　　　　　　　　　　preventの
　　　　　　　　　　　　　　　　目的語

❺ In the future, medical companies may produce
　　　　　　　　　　　S　　　　　　　V
customized medication (based on DNA),
　　　　O　　　　　　　　過去分詞での後置修飾

(so that treatments can be designed for each patient).
結果を表す　　S'　　　　　V'
副詞節

DNA の個人情報を共有すべきか

第1段落

❶ DNA は人を特定する遺伝情報を持つ複雑な化学構造であるため、人が生まれつき持っている一種の個人識別用の記号のような役割を担っている。

❷ すべての人間は99.9%の同じ DNA を共有している（一卵性の双子は100％同じ）が、残りの0.1%はその人特有のものだ。

❸ DNA を利用することは、医学的に非常に大きな可能性を秘めている。

❹ 例えば、医師は DNA を使って、その家系に古くから続いている病気を予測し、予防することができるかもしれない。

❺ 将来的には、製薬会社が DNA をもとにカスタマイズした薬を製造し、患者一人一人に合った治療を行うことができるようになるかもしれない。

❻ 警察は犯罪者を捕まえるために、弁護人は冤罪者を釈放させるために DNA を活用している。

□ profile 紹介、略歴　**❶**□ specific 特定の、明確な　□ genetic code 遺伝情報　□ a sort of 一種の
□ identifier 識別子　**❷**□ identical twin 一卵性双生児　□ remaining 残り
□ be unique to …に特有の　**❸**□ tremendous とてつもない　**❹**□ predict …を予測する
□ family line 家系　**❺**□ medication 薬　□ treatment 治療法　**❻**□ criminal 犯罪者
□ defense lawyer 被告側の弁護士　□ free …を解放する、…を自由にする　□ accused 罪に問われた

筆記③

261

第2段落

❶ At the same time, not all DNA uses are beneficial.

❷ An insurance company that knows a DNA profile might decline to cover a person or charge him or her a higher rate if they are more likely to have a peculiar disease.

❸ A company might prefer to employ a person whose DNA indicates a long line of productive ancestors over one whose genes show a family history of laziness or crime.

❹ In a worst case, as some researchers warn, the United States or even the world could become a society ruled by genetic elites.

❺ Numerous American laws protect ordinary people's DNA privacy.

❻ In particular, a 2008 law called GINA protects Americans from employers, insurers, and others asking about one's genetic background or requiring DNA tests as a condition of work or insurance coverage.

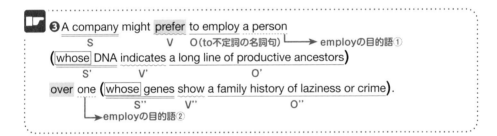

第2段落

❶ 一方で、DNA の活用法がすべて有益であるとは限らない。

❷ DNA の個人情報を知る保険会社は、その人が特殊な病気にかかりやすいと判断した場合、保険の契約を拒否したり、高い保険料を請求したりするかもしれない。

❸ また、ある企業では、怠け者や犯罪者の家系よりも、先祖の生産性の高さを示す DNA を持つ人物を雇いたいと思うかもしれない。

❹ 最悪の場合、一部の研究者が警告しているように、アメリカあるいは世界は、遺伝子エリートに支配される社会になるかもしれない。

❺ アメリカには、一般人の DNA のプライバシーを保護する法律が数多くある。

❻ 特に、2008年に制定された GINA と呼ばれる法律により、雇用主や保険会社などから就労や保険加入の条件として遺伝的背景を尋ねられたり DNA 検査を要求されたりしないように、アメリカ人を保護している。

❶ ☐ beneficial 有益な　❷ ☐ insurance 保険　☐ decline to *do* …するのを断る
☐ cover 保険をかける　☐ charge A B A（人）に B（金額など）を請求する
☐ be likely to *do* …するおそれがある　☐ peculiar 特殊な
❸ ☐ prefer to *do* A over B B よりは A を…したい　☐ long line of …の家系　☐ ancestor 祖先
☐ gene 遺伝子　☐ laziness 怠惰　❹ ☐ rule …を支配する　☐ genetic 遺伝上の
☐ elite 選ばれた者　❺ ☐ ordinary 普通の　❻ ☐ insurer 保険業者　☐ require …を要求する
☐ coverage 適用範囲

筆記 ③

第3段落

❶ However, one problem is that many Americans today willingly share their DNA information with companies that promise to trace their family histories.

❷ For a small fee, these firms can tell you whether you are related to an ancient prince or pirate.

❸ In a multi-ethnic society such as the US, this kind of tracking can be especially interesting.

❹ At the same time, experts warn against entrusting these companies with such critical personal information.

❺ This is because, while GINA protects you against being forced to provide genetic information, it says almost nothing about its use when it is voluntarily provided.

❻ The DNA tracing companies are therefore legally able to share it with an employer, insurer or marketer, or simply sell it on the open market.

❼ This is why many privacy experts discourage people from using these services.

❽ It might be interesting to find that Queen Victoria or George Washington was your ancestor, but it might not be worth the privacy cost.

❾ At the very least, privacy experts encourage people to carefully compare the terms and conditions of service of these businesses and choose those firms which offer more privacy.

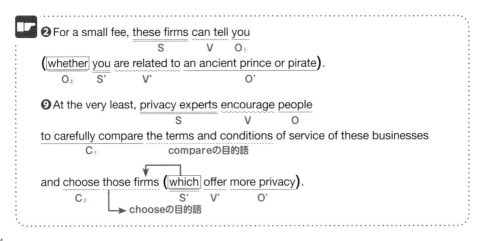

❷ For a small fee, these firms can tell you
  S   V   O₁
(whether you are related to an ancient prince or pirate).
 O₂   S'   V'   O'

❾ At the very least, privacy experts encourage people
                S   V   O
to carefully compare the terms and conditions of service of these businesses
      C₁   compareの目的語

and choose those firms (which offer more privacy).
    C₂   S'   V'   O'
        └→ chooseの目的語

第3段落

❶ しかし、今日、多くのアメリカ人が、家系をさかのぼって調べてくれる会社と、自分のDNA情報を抵抗感なく共有していることが問題になっている。

❷ これらの会社は、わずかな料金で、顧客が大昔の王子や海賊と血縁関係があるかどうかを教えてくれる。

❸ アメリカのような多民族社会では、このような追跡調査に対する関心は特に高い。

❹ 同時に専門家は、こうした企業に重要な個人情報を託すことについて警告を発している。

❺ なぜなら、GINAは遺伝情報の提供を強制されることからは保護するが、任意で提供する場合の利用については、ほとんど何も言っていないからだ。

❻ したがって、DNA追跡会社は、雇用主、保険会社、マーケティング会社と情報を共有したり、単に一般市場で販売したりすることが法的に可能である。

❼ このため、多くのプライバシー専門家は、こうしたサービスの利用を思いとどまるよう促している。

❽ ビクトリア女王やジョージ・ワシントンが自分の祖先だと知るのは面白いかもしれないが、プライバシーの代償に見合うものではないこともあるのだ。

❾ 少なくとも、個人情報保護の専門家は、これらの企業のサービス利用規約を慎重に比較し、プライバシーにより配慮した企業を選択するよう勧めている。

❶ □ willingly 喜んで　□ trace (出所など)をさかのぼる
❷ □ relate A to B A を B と関係させる (be related to で「…に関係している・結びついている」)
　□ ancient 大昔の　□ pirate 海賊　❸ □ multi-ethnic 多民族の
❹ □ entrust A with B A に B を預ける・任せる　□ critical 重要な
❺ □ force X to *do* X に強いて…させる　□ voluntarily 自発的に
❼ □ discourage X from *doing* X に…するのを思いとどまらせる
❽ □ worth ... …の価値がある (目的語を必要とする形容詞)　❾ □ at the very least 少なくとも
　□ encourage X to *do* X に…するよう奨励する　□ terms and conditions 諸条件

筆記③

問題英文の読み方 P.270　解説・正解 P.278　訳・語句 P.282

The Role of Student Clubs in USA

Millions of students in the United States participate in school clubs each year. These clubs range across a wide variety of topics and activities, from sports and science to charitable organizations and leisure. Most experts say that these school clubs provide an opportunity to gain social and leadership skills, as well as practical knowledge in various fields. Historically, many of the most successful Americans—from lawyers and doctors to governors and beyond—have participated in multiple clubs during their time in high school, often in leadership positions. As a result, until recently it seemed that parents and teachers unanimously believed that school clubs were always a good thing. However, some new scholarship suggests that these kinds of clubs can have negative effects as well.

Whether or not a club is a positive thing for a student depends on several factors. To begin with, it is ideal when a student wants to participate in a club and enjoys doing so. As one might imagine, students get the most out of clubs that they enjoy. It is not especially important to fully master a club skill. Even if the student does not become a talented football player or computer programmer, club participation itself develops more motivation, enthusiasm, and social skills. On the other hand, children who feel pressured to participate in a club will find it stressful and not look forward to participating after class or on weekends. Student clubs can bring immense academic, social or athletic benefits, but only when a child is there voluntarily.

Pressure to join clubs can come from multiple sources. Parents often want children to join certain clubs, especially those involved in advanced academics or sports, since these go onto a student's school record. It can increase their chances of getting accepted to top American universities, especially if they have served as club captains or presidents. Other students can be another source, especially since membership in some school clubs is a matter of pride among peers. Social media is another phenomenon that may push kids to join clubs, as some of the most successful and popular school clubs may have an extensive social media presence. Students who don't join these school clubs may therefore feel socially left out and then end up joining even though they don't really want to.

There is no need for this to be the case, however. Experts have advice as to how families can handle this issue. Firstly, families should look at the different clubs available at a school and see if any of these genuinely match the child's interest. Families should also check out the leadership opportunities within a club. Some clubs have many, while others have few. Children can also experience a variety of clubs, which may introduce them to new subjects or interests. Experts also encourage students to form their own clubs, if they do not see an interesting one on the list offered by the school. In the end, as long as a student is enjoying himself or herself, any school club can be just fine.

筆記③

(1) What is suggested about school clubs in the first paragraph?

   1 They were first formed at elite American schools and then gradually spread to other schools and universities.

   2 They were originally designed to help students who had fallen behind in academic subjects, but were later offered to everyone.

   3 They were filled mainly with students who wanted to avoid serious classwork and relax more during weekends.

   4 They were supported at first by almost all educators because they thought club participation was consistently beneficial.

(2) What does the author say about practical skills?

   1 These are not as important as gaining the personal and social skills that come with being part of an enjoyable group.

   2 They are taught more often in high school classes, even though a majority of younger children want to learn them.

   3 Children who master these skills early in life do much better than those who do so later.

   4 Some of these skills are far more useful and profitable to a child than others are.

(3) What is one thing we learn about elite American universities?

1 They usually only admit young people who show special interest in becoming leaders of their country in the future.

2 They want students who are excellent in several different academic areas so that they can teach as well as learn from others.

3 They are biased against students who joined sports and other non-academic activities which would negatively impact their academic performance.

4 They grant admission more easily to students who have been active in school clubs and have participated as their leaders.

(4) According to the author of the passage, how can parents help their children with school clubs?

1 They can get information about the types of future jobs that former members of each school club have received.

2 They should have open and honest discussions with former teachers of the school who were involved in club activities.

3 They must first find out which of the clubs offered at the school are in line with the real interests of their child.

4 They could search for schools that offer several clubs that ensure their child gets admitted into top universities.

The Role of Student Clubs in USA

❶Millions of students in the United States participate in school clubs each year. ❷These clubs range across a wide variety of topics and activities, from sports and science to charitable organizations and leisure. ❸Most experts say that these school clubs provide an opportunity to gain social and leadership skills, as well as practical knowledge in various fields. ❹Historically, many of the most successful Americans—from lawyers and doctors to governors and beyond—have participated in multiple clubs during their time in high school, often in leadership positions. ❺As a result, until recently it seemed that parents and teachers unanimously believed that school clubs were always a good thing. ❻However, some new scholarship suggests that these kinds of clubs can have negative effects as well.

この問題英文の長さは約500語です。

❶ 1文目の冒頭は Millions of students in the United States で始まっています。ここから、この文章はアメリカの生徒についての話だとわかります。Millions of は正確な数字としての「数百万人」よりも、「沢山の、多くの」というニュアンスで捉えましょう。「アメリカの生徒の多くはクラブ活動に参加している」を読んで、頭の中のフォーカスをアメリカの学校のクラブ活動に向けていきます。

❷ These clubs が主語で、range が動詞だとしっかり認識し、「これらのクラブは〜にわたる」と解釈しましょう。「これらのクラブは、さまざまなテーマや活動に及んでいる」の topics and activities「テーマや活動」を前置詞以降の具体例が修飾し、from と to でその範囲を「スポーツや科学から、慈善団体やレジャーまで」だと示しています。

❸ Most experts が主語、say が動詞でその後に that 節が続いています。文頭で「誰か（権威のある人や論文など）」が「言っている」の形を見たら、機械的に「〜によると」と頭の中で言い換えましょう。直訳は「専門家は言っている（専門家によると）／これらのクラブは、社会性やリーダーシップを得る機会を提供している／さまざまな分野における実践的な知識と同様に」となります。

❹ 前の文で「専門家はクラブが機会を提供していると述べている」とあるので、この文ではその歴史上の例を挙げています。文構造は「歴史的には、アメリカで成功した人たちの多くは、高校時代に多くのクラブに参加して、リーダーのポジションにいた」の「アメリカで成功した人たち」を「例えば、弁護士や医師、知事など」が後ろから修飾している形になっています。

❺ 文の主語は it、動詞は seemed です。As a result はここまでの内容から「専門家たちはクラブが良い機会を提供していると述べている」という流れを踏まえた上で、「その結果、最近まで学校のクラブ活動は常に良いものであると、親や教師が一致して信じていたようだ」と解釈します。

❻ 第1段落の締めくくりは However で始まり、「しかし、いくつかの研究は負の効果もあると言っている」と、反対の立場の視点を紹介して、次の段落の展開を想像させます。
この第1段落では、学校でのクラブ活動が生徒に与える良い効果について述べている専門家の意見を紹介し、それを親や教師がどのように受け止めていたのか（信じていたのか）について説明していました。

筆記③

271

第2段落

❶Whether or not a club is a positive thing for a student depends on several factors. ❷To begin with, it is ideal when a student wants to participate in a club and enjoys doing so. ❸As one might imagine, students get the most out of clubs that they enjoy. ❹It is not especially important to fully master a club skill. ❺Even if the student does not become a talented football player or computer programmer, club participation itself develops more motivation, enthusiasm, and social skills. ❻On the other hand, children who feel pressured to participate in a club will find it stressful and not look forward to participating after class or on weekends. ❼Student clubs can bring immense academic, social or athletic benefits, but only when a child is there voluntarily.

❶ 前のパラグラフの最後で示唆した「負の効果」の話が始まる前に、「クラブが生徒にとってプラスになるかどうか」、つまり、正の効果を得られるのかについても、いくつかの要因に左右されると言っています。

❷ To begin with「まずはじめに」とあるので、1つ目の要因がここで示されるとわかります。it is ideal when は「〜の時ならば理想的だ」と解釈しましょう。「生徒がクラブに参加したいと思って、それを楽しんでいる時ならば、理想的だ」と意味を取ります。

❸ students が主語、get が動詞です。直訳は「人がおそらくイメージするように、生徒は彼らが楽しむクラブを最大限に活用できるのである」になります。As one might imagine は「one（誰でもいいから一人＝誰もが）がイメージするように」という意味で、一般的な傾向について述べていると解釈します。

❹ クラブではスキルを身に付けられる機会はありますが、「その技能を完全に身に付けることは特に重要ではない」と述べています。

❺ 前の文を受けて、「クラブで技能を完全に身に付けることが重要ではない例として、つまり」と頭の中で付け加えてから読み進めましょう。Even if「たとえ〜でも」で始まる従属節の主語は the student、動詞は does not become です。主節の主語は club participation、動詞は develops で、「たとえ立派なサッカー選手やプログラマーにならなくても、クラブに参加すること自体が、意欲と熱意と社会性を発達させる」と言っています。

❻ On the other hand で始まる6文目は、前の文をふまえた内容で「（クラブに参加することで育まれる社会性があるが、）その一方」という意味で、ここでクラブがもたらす負の効果の1つ目について述べています。children が主語、will find が動詞で、「子どもたちはそれをストレスと感じる」という形になっています。文全体では「（負の効果としては）クラブに参加することをプレッシャーに感じている子どもは、クラブをストレスに感じ、楽しみだと思わない」という意味です。

❼ 第2段落のまとめとなる最終文です。Student clubs が主語、bring が動詞で「学校のクラブは、学業や社会生活、あるいはスポーツに多大な利益をもたらす」の後に but と入って節が続き、「しかし、それは子どもが自発的に参加した場合にだけである」と、自発的に参加することが大事だと締めくくっています。この段落の2文目の内容が一部言い換えられて再度述べられていることも読み取れます。
この段落では、クラブに参加することがプラスになるかどうかを左右する要因について簡単に分類し、その要因から、クラブに参加することの負の効果についても言及していました。

❶Pressure to join clubs can come from multiple sources. ❷Parents often want children to join certain clubs, especially those involved in advanced academics or sports, since these go onto a student's school record. ❸It can increase their chances of getting accepted to top American universities, especially if they have served as club captains or presidents. ❹Other students can be another source, especially since membership in some school clubs is a matter of pride among peers. ❺Social media is another phenomenon that may push kids to join clubs, as some of the most successful and popular school clubs may have an extensive social media presence. ❻Students who don't join these school clubs may therefore feel socially left out and then end up joining even though they don't really want to.

❶ 前の段落の6文目では、負の効果の1つ目として、「クラブ参加をプレッシャーと思うこと」とありました。第3段落の1文目では、「プレッシャーはさまざまなところから生じる」と言っているので、この段落ではそのプレッシャーはどこからくるかについて説明されるということが示されています。

❷ 前の文を読んで、次の文には「プレッシャーがどこからくるのか」について書いてあるはずだ、と心の準備ができているならば、文頭の Parents という主語を見ただけで、なるほど、親がプレッシャーをかけていると言っているのだろうと、文全体を読む前に内容を察することができます。各々の単語の意味はもちろん大切ですが、同時に「文章の流れ」や「予測」が長文読解には大切です。主語の後ろに目を移すと、「親はしばしば子どもが特定のクラブに参加することを望む／特に、レベルの高い学問やスポーツに関係するクラブであれば、子どもの学業成績に反映されるから」とあります。確かに、内申書に良いから、見栄えが良いから、などの理由で親が子どもを有名な部に入れたいと思い、プレッシャーをかけるかもしれませんね。

❸ It can increase を見て、すぐに「そうすれば、～できるようになる」のニュアンスをつかみましょう。「そうすれば、トップの大学に入学できるチャンスが増える」と言っています。「特に、キャプテンや部長をしていれば」と続いているので、高校の内申書を良く見せるために有名な部の部長をしてほしいという親の期待がここでも読み取れます。

❹ Other students can be another source は、何気なく文字面を追っても意味が取りにくいところです。Other students が主語で、can be が動詞ですので、「他の生徒はもう一つの（プレッシャーの）もとである」と理解します。especially 以下は「特に、ある学校のクラブに所属しているというのは友達のあいだでのプライドに関わる問題だから」という意味です。つまり、1つ目のプレッシャーの要因は「親」、2つ目は「友達」ということになります。

❺ Social media is another phenomenon でこれが3つ目のプレッシャーの要因だとわかります。「ソーシャルメディアも子どもたちをクラブに参加させる要因のひとつになる」という意味です。わかりやすく "The third source is ..." などで始めてくれればいいのに、と思う方もいるかも知れませんね。しかし、文章を書く人たちは単純に同じパターンを繰り返すよりも、より変化に富んだ、ウィットに富んだ表現を求めることもあるので、受験者である皆さんが、そういった書き手の趣向を察して読んでいく必要があります。ソーシャルメディアが要因の一つである理由は「人気のある学校のクラブは、広範囲のソーシャルメディアで存在感がある」からだと言っています。

❻ Students が主語で、may feel が動詞です。「このようなクラブに参加しない生徒は、社会的に取り残されたと感じる」とあり、そして「（参加しない生徒も、ソーシャルメディアのプレッシャーにより）本当は参加したくないのに参加することになるかもしれない」と理解できれば、プレッシャーのあまり、参加したくもないクラブに嫌々参加している生徒の様子が目に浮かぶでしょう。
この段落では負の効果が出る要因を3つ説明していました。

❶There is no need for this to be the case, however. ❷Experts have advice as to how families can handle this issue. ❸Firstly, families should look at the different clubs available at a school and see if any of these genuinely match the child's interest. ❹Families should also check out the leadership opportunities within a club. ❺Some clubs have many, while others have few. ❻Children can also experience a variety of clubs, which may introduce them to new subjects or interests. ❼Experts also encourage students to form their own clubs, if they do not see an interesting one on the list offered by the school. ❽In the end, as long as a student is enjoying himself or herself, any school club can be just fine.

❶ however が文末に来ても、文頭に来て
も、ほとんど意味は同じです。どちらにあっ
ても、前の文を受けて「しかし、そうである必
要はない」という意味になります。決して「そ
んな必要はない、しかし～（次の文）」と解釈
しないようにしましょう。

❷ Experts have advice as to で「専門家
が～についてのアドバイスを持っている」の
意味です。そのまま読み進めて、何について
のアドバイスを持っているのかを見ると、「家
族がこの問題を処理できるような方法」とあ
ります。

❸ Firstly「1つ目は」とあるので、2つ目も あ
るだろうと予測しておきましょう。ここから
専門家によるアドバイスがいくつか示される
とわかります。「家族が、学校にあるさまざま
なクラブを調べ、子どもの興味に合うものが
あるかどうかを見る」ことが1つ目です。

❹ 1つ目のアドバイスに付け加えて「クラブ
の中でリーダーシップを発揮する機会がある
かどうかも家族が調べる必要がある」と言っ
ています。

❺ 前の文についての説明が続き、「そのよう
な機会がたくさんあるクラブもあれば、ほと
んどないクラブもある」と述べているため、
リーダーシップを発揮できるクラブかどうか
も見極める必要があるとわかります。

❻ もう一つの可能性について話を展開しよ
うとしています。「また、さまざまなクラブを
経験することで、新しいテーマや趣味に出合
えるかもしれない」と述べています。

❼ 特に「2番目に」とは書いてありませんが、
この文の also が何に対応するかということ
や前の文までは families の中でも親の側の方
法だったのに対して、ここから students が
行動の中心になっていること、もう少しで段
落が終わることを考えると、ここからがもう
一つの専門家によるアドバイスではないかと
推測できます。専門家は「生徒が自分でクラ
ブを創設すること」を勧めていますね。

❽ この段落の最後の文です。「最終的には、
生徒が楽しめれば、どんなクラブでもいいの
だ」とあります。要するに、強制やプレッシャ
ーによりクラブに参加するよりも、自分が楽
しんでクラブに参加することが理想的である
と述べて、この文章を締めくくっています。
この段落では生徒がプレッシャーからクラブ
に参加しているという問題の解決法について
説明していました。

筆記③

(1) What is suggested about school clubs in the first paragraph?

1 They were first formed at elite American schools and then gradually spread to other schools and universities.

2 They were originally designed to help students who had fallen behind in academic subjects, but were later offered to everyone.

3 They were filled mainly with students who wanted to avoid serious classwork and relax more during weekends.

4 They were supported at first by almost all educators because they thought club participation was consistently beneficial.

(2) What does the author say about practical skills?

1 These are not as important as gaining the personal and social skills that come with being part of an enjoyable group.

2 They are taught more often in high school classes, even though a majority of younger children want to learn them.

3 Children who master these skills early in life do much better than those who do so later.

4 Some of these skills are far more useful and profitable to a child than others are.

(1) 📋 第1段落で学校のクラブについてどんなことが示唆されていますか。

1 最初はアメリカのエリート校で結成され、その後徐々に他の学校や大学に広まっていった。

2 もともとは学業で後れを取った生徒を助けるために作られたものだったが、後にすべての人を受け入れるようになった。

3 厳しい授業を避け、週末にもっとリラックスしたいという生徒で主にあふれ返った。

4 当初、ほぼすべての教育関係者が、クラブに参加することは常に有益であると考え、それを支持していた。

🔍 第1段落の❸❹で「専門家によるとクラブはさまざまな分野における実践的な知識と同時に社会性やリーダーシップを得る機会を提供していて、歴史的にアメリカで成功した人々は高校時代に複数のクラブにおいてリーダーのポジションにいた」とあり、その結果として❺で「最近まで学校のクラブは常に良いものであるという考えで親も教師も一致していた」と述べています。ここから問1の答えがわかります。

✏️ ☐ fall behind (人に) 後れを取る ☐ consistently 終始一貫して、矛盾なく ☐ beneficial 有益な

. . . .

(2) 📋 筆者は、実際に役立つ能力についてどのように言っていますか。

1 楽しいグループの一員になることで得られる個人的・社会的スキルの獲得ほど重要ではない。

2 低学年の子どもの大半が学びたがっているにもかかわらず、高校の授業で教えられることが多い。

3 これらの能力を人生の早い段階で習得した子どもは、そうでない子どもよりもずっと良い結果を残す。

4 これらの能力の中には、他の能力よりもはるかに子どもにとって有用で有益なものがある。

🔍 第2段落の❹で「クラブで技能を完全に身に付けることは特に重要ではない」と述べています。続く❺でも「参加すること自体が意欲、熱意、社会性を発達させる」とあることから、クラブでの技能の習得よりも参加することで伸びる他の面を重要視していることがわかります。ここから問2の解答がわかります。

. . . .

🚩 **(1)** 4 **(2)** 1

(3) What is one thing we learn about elite American universities?

1 They usually only admit young people who show special interest in becoming leaders of their country in the future.

2 They want students who are excellent in several different academic areas so that they can teach as well as learn from others.

3 They are biased against students who joined sports and other non-academic activities which would negatively impact their academic performance.

4 They grant admission more easily to students who have been active in school clubs and have participated as their leaders.

(4) According to the author of the passage, how can parents help their children with school clubs?

1 They can get information about the types of future jobs that former members of each school club have received.

2 They should have open and honest discussions with former teachers of the school who were involved in club activities.

3 They must first find out which of the clubs offered at the school are in line with the real interests of their child.

4 They could search for schools that offer several clubs that ensure their child gets admitted into top universities.

(3) 🏳 アメリカのエリート大学について、わかることは何ですか。

1 たいていは将来自国のリーダーになることに特別な関心を示している若者だけを入学させる。

2 他人から学び、教えることもできるよう、複数の学問分野に優れた学生を求めている。

3 学業成績に悪影響を及ぼすような、スポーツなどの課外活動に参加した学生には偏見を持つ。

4 学校のクラブで活動し、リーダーを務めた生徒には、簡単に入学許可を与える。

🔍 第3段落の❸で「そうすれば(＝特にレベルの高い学問やスポーツに関するクラブに参加していれば)、クラブのキャプテンや部長を務めた経験があればなおのこと、トップの大学に入学できるチャンスが増える」と述べています。ここで問3の正解がわかります。

✎ □ be biased against …に偏見をいだいている □ impact …に強い影響を与える □ grant …を与える

----

(4) 🏳 著者によると、子どもが学校のクラブ活動をする際に、親はどのように支援できますか。

1 それぞれの学校クラブの元メンバーが就いている職業の種類に関する情報を得ることができる。

2 部活に関わっていた元教師と率直に話し合いをするべきである。

3 学校で行われている部活動のうち、子どもの本当の興味に合ったものはどれかをまず知る必要がある。

4 子どもを一流大学に合格させることができるようなクラブがいくつもある学校を探すことができる。

🔍 第4段落の❷から❹で、家族で問題を解決するための専門家からのアドバイスとして「家族が学校にあるさまざまなクラブを調べ、子どもの興味に合うかどうかを見る」ことと合わせて「クラブの中でリーダーシップを発揮する機会があるかどうかも調べる」ことを挙げています。ここから問4の解答がわかります。

✎ □ in line with …と一致して □ ensure …を確実にする

The Role of Student Clubs in USA

第1段落

❶ Millions of students in the United States participate in school clubs each year.

❷ These clubs range across a wide variety of topics and activities, from sports and science to charitable organizations and leisure.

❸ Most experts say that these school clubs provide an opportunity to gain social and leadership skills, as well as practical knowledge in various fields.

❹ Historically, many of the most successful Americans—from lawyers and doctors to governors and beyond—have participated in multiple clubs during their time in high school, often in leadership positions.

❺ As a result, until recently it seemed that parents and teachers unanimously believed that school clubs were always a good thing.

❻ However, some new scholarship suggests that these kinds of clubs can have negative effects as well.

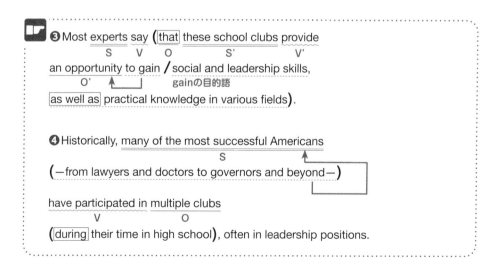

米国における学校のクラブの役割

第1段落

❶ 米国では、毎年数百万人の生徒が学校のクラブ活動に参加している。

❷ これらのクラブは、スポーツや科学、慈善団体やレジャーなど、さまざまなテーマや活動に及んでいる。

❸ ほとんどの専門家は、これらの学校クラブが、社会性やリーダーシップ、そしてさまざまな分野における実践的な知識を得る機会を提供していると述べている。

❹ 歴史的に見ても、弁護士や医師、知事など、アメリカで最も成功した人たちの多くは、高校時代に多くのクラブに参加し、しばしばリーダーシップを発揮してきた。

❺ そのため、つい最近まで、学校のクラブ活動は常に良いものであると、親や教師が一致して信じていたようである。

❻ しかし、いくつかの新しい研究は、この種のクラブが負の効果も持ち得ることを示唆している。

❷□ range 及ぶ　□ charitable organization 慈善団体　❺□ as a result その結果
□ unanimously 満場一致で、異議なく　❻□ scholarship 学問　□ suggest that 節 …だと示唆する

第2段落

❶ Whether or not a club is a positive thing for a student depends on several factors.

❷ To begin with, it is ideal when a student wants to participate in a club and enjoys doing so.

❸ As one might imagine, students get the most out of clubs that they enjoy.

❹ It is not especially important to fully master a club skill.

❺ Even if the student does not become a talented football player or computer programmer, club participation itself develops more motivation, enthusiasm, and social skills.

❻ On the other hand, children who feel pressured to participate in a club will find it stressful and not look forward to participating after class or on weekends.

❼ Student clubs can bring immense academic, social or athletic benefits, but only when a child is there voluntarily.

❶ (Whether or not a club is a positive thing for a student)
　　　　　　　　　S'　V'　　　C'
　　　　　　　　　　　　　S

depends on several factors.
　V　　　　　　O

❻ On the other hand, children (who feel pressured to participate in a club)
　　　　　　　　　　　　　　S　　　S'　V'　　　C'　　　　副詞句のto不定詞

will find it stressful and not look forward to participating
V①　O①　C　　　　　(will)　　V②　　　　　　O②

(after class) or (on weekends).
時を表す副詞句

284

第2段落

❶ クラブが生徒にとってプラスになるかどうかは、いくつかの要因に左右される。

❷ そもそも、生徒がクラブに参加したいと思い、それを楽しむことができるのが理想的だ。

❸ 容易に想像できるのが、生徒は自分が楽しいと思えるクラブで最も大きな力を発揮する。

❹ クラブで技能を完全に身に付けることは特に重要ではない。

❺ たとえ才能あるサッカー選手やコンピュータープログラマーにならなくても、クラブに参加すること自体が、意欲と熱意をかき立て、社会性を育む。

❻ 逆に、クラブに参加することをプレッシャーに感じている子どもは、それがストレスになり、授業後や週末に参加することを楽しめなくなる。

❼ 学校のクラブは、学業や社会生活、あるいはスポーツに多大な利益をもたらすが、それは子どもが自発的に参加した場合に限られる。

❶□ depend on …次第である　❷□ to begin with まず第一に
❸□ get the most out of …を最大限活用する　❺□ talented 才能のある　□ motivation 動機づけ
　□ enthusiasm 熱意　❻□ on the other hand 他方では　□ feel pressured ストレスを感じる
❼□ immense 莫大な、計り知れない　□ benefit 利益　□ voluntarily 自発的に

第3段落

❶ Pressure to join clubs can come from multiple sources.

❷ Parents often want children to join certain clubs, especially those involved in advanced academics or sports, since these go onto a student's school record.

❸ It can increase their chances of getting accepted to top American universities, especially if they have served as club captains or presidents.

❹ Other students can be another source, especially since membership in some school clubs is a matter of pride among peers.

❺ Social media is another phenomenon that may push kids to join clubs, as some of the most successful and popular school clubs may have an extensive social media presence.

❻ Students who don't join these school clubs may therefore feel socially left out and then end up joining even though they don't really want to.

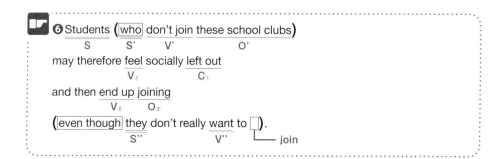

❻ Students (who don't join these school clubs)
　　S　　　 S'　 V'　　　　　　O'
may therefore feel socially left out
　　　　　　V₁　　　　　C₁
and then end up joining
　　　　V₂　　O₂
(even though they don't really want to ☐).
　　　　　　 S"　　　　　　V"　　└── join

❶ クラブに参加するようにというプレッシャーは、さまざまなところから生じる。

❷ 特に、レベルの高い学問やスポーツに関係するクラブは生徒の学業成績に反映されるため、親はしばしば子どもが特定のクラブに参加することを望む。

❸ しかも、クラブのキャプテンや部長を務めた経験があれば、アメリカの一流大学に合格する可能性が高くなる。

❹ 学校のクラブに所属していることは仲間内のプライドの問題でもあるから、なおさら、他の生徒がプレッシャーの原因になることもある。

❺ 最も成果を上げ、人気もある学校のクラブは、広範囲のソーシャルメディアで存在感があるので、ソーシャルメディアも子どもたちをクラブに参加させる要因のひとつになる。

❻ このようなクラブに参加しない生徒は、社会的に取り残されたと感じ、本当は参加したくないのに参加することになるかもしれない。

❶☐ multiple 多数の、多様の　☐ source 原因、情報源　❷☐ involve A in B A は B を伴う
☐ advanced 上級の　☐ school record 学績　❸☐ get + 過去分詞 …される
☐ accept …を受け入れる　☐ serve as …として務める　❹☐ a matter of …の問題
☐ peer 仲間、同等の者　❺☐ phenomenon 現象、事象　☐ extensive 広範囲にわたる
☐ presence 存在　❻☐ leave out …を除外する　☐ end up *doing* 結局…することになる

筆記③

第4段落

❶ There is no need for this to be the case, however.

❷ Experts have advice as to how families can handle this issue.

❸ Firstly, families should look at the different clubs available at a school and see if any of these genuinely match the child's interest.

❹ Families should also check out the leadership opportunities within a club.

❺ Some clubs have many, while others have few.

❻ Children can also experience a variety of clubs, which may introduce them to new subjects or interests.

❼ Experts also encourage students to form their own clubs, if they do not see an interesting one on the list offered by the school.

❽ In the end, as long as a student is enjoying himself or herself, any school club can be just fine.

❶ しかし、そのようなことをする必要はない。

❷ 家族がこの問題にどう対処すればいいか、専門家がアドバイスしている。

❸ まず、学校にあるさまざまなクラブを調べ、その中に子どもの興味に合うものがあるかどうかを家族が検討することだ。

❹ また、クラブの中でリーダーシップを発揮する機会があるかどうかも調べる必要がある。

❺ そのような機会がたくさんあるクラブもあれば、ほとんどないクラブもある。

❻ また、さまざまなクラブを経験することで、新しいテーマや趣味に出会えるかもしれない。

❼ 専門家は学校のクラブのリストに興味をそそられるものがない場合、生徒が自分でクラブを創設することも勧めている。

❽ 最終的には、生徒が楽しめれば、どんなクラブでもいいのだ。

❷□ as to …に関して ❸□ available 利用できる (ここでは後置修飾)
□ genuinely まぎれもなく、心から ❼□ encourage X to *do* X が…するよう奨励する
□ form …を創設する、…を組織する ❽□ as long as …である限りは

筆記③

問題英文の読み方 P.292　解説・正解 P.296　訳・語句 P.298

Self-Cloning Crayfish

Although most people like pets, releasing one into the wild is never a good idea. This is because they can have severe effects on a local ecosystem. For example, house cats released into the wild in Australia have become "super predators" there because the continent has no large competitors such as wolves or cougars that could keep the wild cat population down. Like hippos in Columbia or Asian carp in Canada, these animals are often classified as invasive species: animals taken to a new region where they have no natural enemies or environmental or seasonal controls.

Now, both Europe and the United States are struggling with a new invasive species: marbled crayfish. While they appear harmless, the crayfish consume nearly every living thing in water, including all insects and plants. This creature is so dangerous because it can lay large numbers of eggs, up to 700 or more, at a time. Moreover, the animal is self-cloning, meaning that it doesn't need a partner. The creatures do have one weakness: their health. Since the crayfish are self-cloning, they lack the strength that comes from genetic diversity. As a result, they may be killed off entirely by any new disease, pollution or change in water conditions.

Scientists cannot wait on some kind of environmental change to kill off the crayfish, though. Instead, they have searched for ways to remove the animal from bodies of water, although none of them are easy, cost-efficient or fast enough to match its high breeding rate. Most of the ways discovered to deal with the crayfish are expensive and require heavy manual labor, such as underwater cages or other trapping systems. Researchers are going to have to find other, more practical ways to deal with this invader. Otherwise, the threat from marbled crayfish may only grow.

(1) According to the author of the passage, pets released into the wild

    1 can disturb an existing ecosystem if they are in a new habitat without any predator animal that might attack them.

    2 will increase the diversity of species in the locality by competing with most of the native predators.

3 will not be able to survive for long because they do not know how to use the natural resources available in the area.

4 will stop breeding in large numbers once most of their prey and natural resources are gone from a given location.

(2) What do we learn about the marbled crayfish?

1 It mates several times a year and creates several hundred eggs in order to survive water pollution and diseases.

2 It cannot be killed even by some of the largest freshwater fish in American and Canadian waters because of its huge size.

3 It is a species that may not survive any substantial changes to its environment because it does not have genetic diversity.

4 It was released into the wild at the same time as the Asian carp, but has managed to multiply much faster.

(3) According to the author of the passage, what is true about species removal?

1 If done during breeding season and with the right technology, the removal of invasive animals can be an easy task.

2 It is typically very expensive and may take a lot of time, especially if the targeted species has a high breeding rate.

3 It requires experts to release a self-cloning variety of the invasive species to interrupt the natural reproduction process of the creature.

4 It is easier to carry out with land species than it is with water-based species because of the risk of water pollution.

Self-Cloning Crayfish

❶Although most people like pets, releasing one into the wild is never a good idea. ❷This is because they can have severe effects on a local ecosystem. ❸For example, house cats released into the wild in Australia have become "super predators" there because the continent has no large competitors such as wolves or cougars that could keep the wild cat population down. ❹Like hippos in Columbia or Asian carp in Canada, these animals are often classified as invasive species: animals taken to a new region where they have no natural enemies or environmental or seasonal controls.

❶Now, both Europe and the United States are struggling with a new invasive species: marbled crayfish. ❷While they appear harmless, the crayfish consume nearly every living thing in water, including all insects and plants. ❸This creature is so dangerous because it can lay large numbers of eggs, up to 700 or more, at a time. ❹Moreover, the animal is self-cloning, meaning that it doesn't need a partner. ❺The creatures do have one weakness: their health. ❻Since the crayfish are self-cloning, they lack the strength that comes from genetic diversity. ❼As a result, they may be killed off entirely by any new disease, pollution or change in water conditions.

この問題英文の長さは約300語です。

タイトルの単語の意味がわからなければ「自分でクローン化する何かの魚?」と思うかもしれません。そのように想像した場合、❶が「ほとんどの人々はペットが好きだが〜」で始まっているのを意外に感じるかもしれません。単語の意味から内容を推測できなくても、読み進められるようにしっかりと構文を捉えましょう。❶❷では「ペットを野生に帰してしまうと、その地域の生態系に深刻な影響を与え得る」と、問題を述べています。❸❹では「オーストラリアで野に放たれた家ネコが最強の捕食者になっており、それはコロンビアのカバやカナダのコイと同様に侵略的外来種と分類されることがある」と具体例を挙げています。

第2段落

前の段落の具体例に続いて、第2段落❶から現在欧米で出現した外来種について「それはミステリークレイフィッシュだ」と導入しています。❷から❹ではこの外来種の強い生殖力について「一見無害だが、水中のほとんどの生物を食べてしまい、卵は一度に700個以上産み、さらには単為生殖する」と説明をしています。❹ではタイトルを見たときにはわからなかった self-cloning の意味が確認できます。次の❺から❼では、反対にこの外来種の弱点について、「単為生殖するため、多様性がもたらす頑健さに欠け、少しの環境の変化で絶滅する可能性がある」と述べています。

第3段落

❶Scientists cannot wait on some kind of environmental change to kill off the crayfish, though. ❷Instead, they have searched for ways to remove the animal from bodies of water, although none of them are easy, cost-efficient or fast enough to match its high breeding rate. ❸Most of the ways discovered to deal with the crayfish are expensive and require heavy manual labor, such as underwater cages or other trapping systems. ❹Researchers are going to have to find other, more practical ways to deal with this invader. ❺Otherwise, the threat from marbled crayfish may only grow.

前段落の内容をふまえて第3段落❶❷では、人々による外来種への対処について「環境の変化を待つのではなく川や湖からこの動物を除去する方法が模索されているが、どの方法も高い繁殖率に対抗できるものではない」と述べています。その後も、❸から❺で「ミステリークレイフィッシュ駆除の方法のほとんどは高額で人手が必要であり、もっと実用的な方法を開発しないと、この動物による脅威は増すばかりだ」と、良い解決策がまだ開発されていないという内容で文章を終えています。

筆記③

(1) According to the author of the passage, pets released into the wild

1 can disturb an existing ecosystem if they are in a new habitat without any predator animal that might attack them.

2 will increase the diversity of species in the locality by competing with most of the native predators.

3 will not be able to survive for long because they do not know how to use the natural resources available in the area.

4 will stop breeding in large numbers once most of their prey and natural resources are gone from a given location.

(2) What do we learn about the marbled crayfish?

1 It mates several times a year and creates several hundred eggs in order to survive water pollution and diseases.

2 It cannot be killed even by some of the largest freshwater fish in American and Canadian waters because of its huge size.

3 It is a species that may not survive any substantial changes to its environment because it does not have genetic diversity.

4 It was released into the wild at the same time as the Asian carp, but has managed to multiply much faster.

(3) According to the author of the passage, what is true about species removal?

1 If done during breeding season and with the right technology, the removal of invasive animals can be an easy task.

2 It is typically very expensive and may take a lot of time, especially if the targeted species has a high breeding rate.

3 It requires experts to release a self-cloning variety of the invasive species to interrupt the natural reproduction process of the creature.

4 It is easier to carry out with land species than it is with water-based species because of the risk of water pollution.

(1) 📝 この文章の著者によると、野に放たれたペットは

1 ペットを襲う可能性のある捕食動物がいない場所が新しい生息地の場合、現存の生態系を乱す可能性がある。

2 在来の捕食動物のほとんどと競争することによって、その地域の種の多様性を高めるだろう。

3 その地域で得られる天然資源の利用方法を知らないため、長くは生存できない。

4 その場所から獲物や天然資源がほとんどなくなると、大量に繁殖することをやめてしまう。

🔍 第1段落❶❷で「ペットを野生に帰すとその地域の生態系に深刻な影響を与えるため良くない」と述べており、その例として❸で「最強の捕食者」となった家ネコが挙げられています。❹でそのような状況に至る原因として「天敵が不在で環境や季節による制御がない新しい地域に持ち込まれた動物は侵略的外来種に分類されることがある」と述べているため、これを言い換えた1が正解となります。

✏️ ☐ disturb …を乱す ☐ existing 現存の ☐ habitat 生息地 ☐ locality 地域 ☐ compete 競争する
☐ prey 獲物 ☐ given 一定の、特定の

· ·

(2) 📝 ミステリークレイフィッシュについてわかることは何ですか。

1 水質汚染や病気に負けないように、年に数回交尾をし、数百個の卵を産む。

2 アメリカやカナダにいる大型淡水魚でも、その巨大さゆえ殺すことができない。

3 遺伝的多様性がないため、環境が大きく変化すると生き残れない可能性がある種である。

4 コイと同時に自然界に放たれたが、はるかに速いスピードで増殖している。

🔍 第2段落❷以降でミステリークレイフィッシュの特徴が列挙されており、❺から❼で「単為生殖するため多様性がもたらす頑健さがなく、水質の変化などで絶滅する可能性がある」と弱点が説明されています。これを言い換えた3が正解です。1は「単為生殖のため環境の変化に弱い」という内容と合わないので不正解。2は、本文でミステリークレイフィッシュの大きさについての言及はないため不正解。4も本文中にコイと同時に自然界に放たれたという記載はないため不正解。

✏️ ☐ mate 交尾する ☐ freshwater 淡水の ☐ substantial 相当な、かなりの
☐ managed to *do* うまく…を成し遂げる ☐ multiply 繁殖する、増える

· ·

(3) 📝 この文章の著者によると、種の駆除について正しいのはどれですか。

1 繁殖時期に適切な技術で行えば、特定外来生物の駆除は簡単な作業になる。

2 一般的に非常にコストがかかり、特に対象となる種の繁殖率が高い場合は多くの時間を要することがある。

3 専門家が外来侵略種の単為生殖する品種を放ち、その生物の自然な繁殖プロセスを中断させることが必要である。

4 水質汚染のリスクがあるため、水生生物よりも陸生生物の方が、実行しやすい。

🔍 第3段落❶❷で答えることができます。種の駆除に関して、❷で「どの方法も高い繁殖率に対抗できるほど簡単ではなく、費用対効果も悪く、即効性もない」と述べているので、これを言い換えた2が正解です。1は❷で「どの方法も実用的ではない」とあり、❹でも「より実用的な方法を開発する必要がある」と述べていることから不正解。3、4は本文内に記述がないため不正解。

✏️ ☐ removal 除去 ☐ target …を目標とする、…を標的にする ☐ interrupt …を中断する
☐ reproduction 繁殖 ☐ carry out …を実行する ☐ water-based 水性の

🚩 **(1)** 1 **(2)** 3 **(3)** 2

Self-Cloning Crayfish

第1段落

❶ Although most people like pets, releasing one into the wild is never a good idea.

❷ This is because they can have severe effects on a local ecosystem.

❸ For example, house cats released into the wild in Australia have become "super predators" there because the continent has no large competitors such as wolves or cougars that could keep the wild cat population down.

❹ Like hippos in Columbia or Asian carp in Canada, these animals are often classified as invasive species: animals taken to a new region where they have no natural enemies or environmental or seasonal controls.

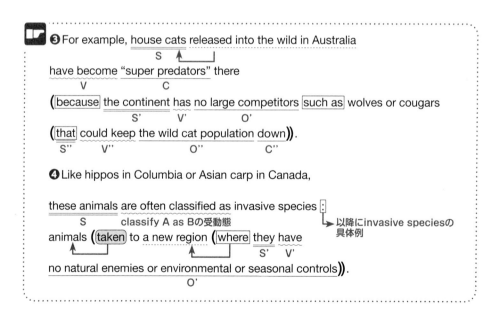

単為生殖するザリガニ

❶ ペットが好きな人は多いが、それを野生に帰すのは決して良いことではない。

❷ なぜなら、ペットはその地域の生態系に深刻な影響を与え得るからだ。

❸ 例えば、オーストラリアでは、野に放たれた家ネコが「最強の捕食者」になってしまっている。なぜなら、野生のネコの個体数を抑制し得るオオカミやクーガーといった大型の競争相手がこの大陸にはいないからだ。

❹ この動物は、コロンビアのカバやカナダのコイと同様に、天敵が不在で環境や季節による制御がない新しい地域に持ち込まれた動物で、しばしば侵略的外来種に分類される。

☐ cloning 無性的に繁殖する　☐ crayfish ザリガニ　❶☐ release …を放す
❷☐ have an effect on …に影響を与える　☐ ecosystem 生態系　❸☐ predator 捕食動物
☐ continent 大陸　☐ competitor 競争相手　☐ cougar クーガー
❹☐ hippo カバ（hippopotamus）　☐ carp コイ　☐ classify …を分類する
☐ invasive species 侵略的外来種　☐ enemy 敵　☐ seasonal 季節的な　☐ control 抑制力

筆記③

第2段落

❶ Now, both Europe and the United States are struggling with a new invasive species: marbled crayfish.

❷ While they appear harmless, the crayfish consume nearly every living thing in water, including all insects and plants.

❸ This creature is so dangerous because it can lay large numbers of eggs, up to 700 or more, at a time.

❹ Moreover, the animal is self-cloning, meaning that it doesn't need a partner.

❺ The creatures do have one weakness: their health.

❻ Since the crayfish are self-cloning, they lack the strength that comes from genetic diversity.

❼ As a result, they may be killed off entirely by any new disease, pollution or change in water conditions.

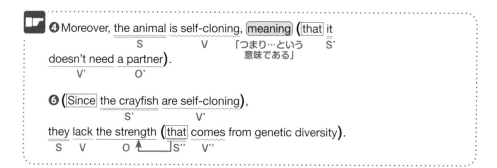

❶ そして今、欧米では新たな外来種であるミステリークレイフィッシュに悩まされている。

❷ 一見無害に見えるが、このザリガニは水中のあらゆる昆虫や植物など、ほとんどすべての生物を食べてしまう。

❸ この生物が非常に危険なのは、一度に700個以上もの大量の卵を産むことができるからだ。

❹ しかも、この生物は（メスだけで）単為生殖するため、オスを必要としない。

❺ （しかし、）この生物には1つだけ弱点がある。それは健康状態である。

❻ ミステリークレイフィッシュは単為生殖するので、遺伝子の多様性がもたらす頑健さがないのだ。

❼ そのため、新しい病気や汚染、水質の変化などがあれば、全滅する可能性がある。

❶ ☐ struggle with …と戦う、…と取っ組み合う ☐ marbled 大理石模様の
❷ ☐ consume …を食い尽くす ❸ ☐ creature 生き物 ☐ lay (卵) を産む ☐ up to …に至るまで
❻ ☐ strength 強み ☐ genetic 遺伝子の ☐ diversity 多様性
☐ kill off …を大量に殺す、…を絶滅させる

第3段落

❶ Scientists cannot wait on some kind of environmental change to kill off the crayfish, though.

❷ Instead, they have searched for ways to remove the animal from bodies of water, although none of them are easy, cost-efficient or fast enough to match its high breeding rate.

❸ Most of the ways discovered to deal with the crayfish are expensive and require heavy manual labor, such as underwater cages or other trapping systems.

❹ Researchers are going to have to find other, more practical ways to deal with this invader.

❺ Otherwise, the threat from marbled crayfish may only grow.

---

❷ Instead, they have searched for ways
             S   V   O

to remove the animal from bodies of water,
形容詞句のto不定詞 　┗➤removeの目的語

(although none of them are easy, cost-efficient or fast enough to match
　　　　　　S'　　　　V'　　　　　　　C'

its high breeding rate).
　　matchの目的語

❸ Most of the ways (discovered to deal with the crayfish)
　　　　　　S　　　　　　　　　　副詞句のto不定詞　　┗➤deal withの目的語

are expensive and require heavy manual labor,
V₁　　　C　　　　　V₂　　　　　　O

such as underwater cages or other trapping systems.
　　例示

❶ しかし、科学者は、ミステリークレイフィッシュを全滅させるような環境の変化をただ待ってはいられない。

❷ そんなことはせず、川や湖からこの動物を除去する方法が模索されている。しかし、どの方法もミステリークレイフィッシュの高い繁殖率に対抗できるほど簡単ではなく、費用対効果も悪く、また即効性もない。

❸ ミステリークレイフィッシュを駆除するために考案された方法のほとんどは、水中カゴなどの捕獲罠のように、高価で人手を要するものばかりだ。

❹ 研究者は、この侵入者に対処するための、もっと実用的な方法を今後も開発しなければならない。

❺ そうしなければ、ミステリークレイフィッシュの脅威は増すばかりであろう。

❷ □ remove …を除去する　□ body of water 水域　□ cost-efficient 費用対効果のよい
□ enough to *do* …するのに十分に　□ match …に匹敵する、…と一致する　□ breeding rate 繁殖率
❸ □ deal with …に対処する　□ require …を必要とする　□ heavy manual labor 激しい肉体労働
□ underwater 水中の　□ cage かご、おり　□ trap …をわなで捕らえる　❹ □ practical 実用的な
□ invader 侵入者　❺ □ otherwise そうでなければ

問題英文の読み方 P.306　解説・正解 P.310　訳・語句 P.312

Managing Time

Both children and adults spend a large amount of their lives studying or learning new things. At the same time, people usually want to learn as quickly as possible. Traditionally, most businesses or schools emphasized the basic idea of "the more time spent on something, the more achieved." But since at least the 19th century, these traditional concepts of academic and professional productivity have been questioned. This is because most people can see that, in reality, not everyone gets the same result out of the same time spent on a task.

One approach to improving personal productivity is called the Pomodoro Technique. This involves breaking up study into 25-minute periods. Each study period is called "1 pomodoro." The learner should take a 5-10-minute break after every pomodoro. A longer break of about 20-30 minutes should be taken after four pomodoros, before restarting the cycle. Timeboxing is another technique where a worker will set a maximum amount of time to be spent on a project before taking a break. Another approach is the Eisenhower Matrix, where tasks are arranged in squares based on their importance. These methods are supposed to be much more productive than simply studying or working oneself to exhaustion.

In most of these new study or work methods, a long or short break is necessary. Some schools and companies are giving students or employees more time away from desks—sometimes days—in order to boost innovation. Pomodoro and other techniques may be difficult for traditional managers or teachers to accept, especially those who feel that "real" productivity means going through books or manuals for hours without stop. It is important for modern teachers and managers to focus on what is actually done in a time period, rather than just measuring how long a student or worker has been behind a desk.

(1) In the years before the 19th century most people felt that

    1 those who were working should not waste time studying because not all people were considered capable of academic achievement.

2 anyone who was physically able to work should do so as much as possible to compensate for the weak.

3 people who regularly spent an excessive amount of time on a task were not suitable for continuing in that task.

4 spending as much time as possible on a particular task would certainly make a person better at doing it.

(2) One feature Pomodoro and similar productivity-enhancing approaches have in common is

1 using specific apps to learn different subjects in order to master each of them much faster.

2 taking the maximum time necessary for big projects that are assigned by senior managers or school teachers.

3 organizing a complex task in a way that makes it more manageable and easier to accomplish by a person.

4 being prepared to endure a mild level of exhaustion in order to create a perfect business or academic project.

(3) According to the author of the passage, why do some teachers or managers have difficulty accepting the Pomodoro method?

1 It conflicts with their belief that working hard continuously is the best way to get projects done by students or workers.

2 They feel that it makes people lose their focus when they stop and restart their work several times.

3 This technique was not taught to them in teaching or management schools, so they think it is against the rules to use it.

4 They require a few years of technical study to fully master the method before teaching it to others.

Managing Time

❶Both children and adults spend a large amount of their lives studying or learning new things. ❷At the same time, people usually want to learn as quickly as possible. ❸Traditionally, most businesses or schools emphasized the basic idea of "the more time spent on something, the more achieved." ❹But since at least the 19th century, these traditional concepts of academic and professional productivity have been questioned. ❺This is because most people can see that, in reality, not everyone gets the same result out of the same time spent on a task.

❶One approach to improving personal productivity is called the Pomodoro Technique. ❷This involves breaking up study into 25-minute periods. ❸Each study period is called "1 pomodoro." ❹The learner should take a 5-10-minute break after every pomodoro. ❺A longer break of about 20-30 minutes should be taken after four pomodoros, before restarting the cycle. ❻Timeboxing is another technique where a worker will set a maximum amount of time to be spent on a project before taking a break. ❼Another approach is the Eisenhower Matrix, where tasks are arranged in squares based on their importance. ❽These methods are supposed to be much more productive than simply studying or working oneself to exhaustion.

この問題英文の長さは約300語です。

タイトルから「時間管理」に関する文章だとわかります。❶は「子どもも大人も」で始まり、一般的に学ぶことに多くの時間をかけていると述べています。❷❸は「人はできるだけ早く学ぶことを望む一方、伝統的には時間をかけると成果が上がるという考えが重視されていた」と書かれています。続く❹は、前の文に対して「伝統的な概念には疑問が持たれるようになった」とあり、その理由として❺で「同じように時間を使っても同じ結果を得られるわけではない」と書かれています。

第2段落では、生産性を高める一つのアプローチとして❶に「ポモドーロ・テクニック」という語が出てきます。❷から❺では具体的な説明として、「25分ずつの区切りを『1ポモドーロ』と呼び、1ポモドーロごとに5〜10分の休憩を取り、4ポモドーロ勉強したら長い休憩を取るというサイクルを繰り返す」とあります。また、別のアプローチとして、❻の「タイムボックス」という、あるプロジェクトに費やす時間の上限を決めてから休憩を取る方法と、❼の「アイゼンハワー・マトリックス」という、重要度に応じて四角の中でタスクを整理する方法が述べられています。❽では「どちらの方法も、単に疲れるまで勉強したり、頑張ったりするよりも生産性が高い」とまとめています。

第3段落

❶In most of these new study or work methods, a long or short break is necessary. ❷Some schools and companies are giving students or employees more time away from desks—sometimes days—in order to boost innovation. ❸Pomodoro and other techniques may be difficult for traditional managers or teachers to accept, especially those who feel that "real" productivity means going through books or manuals for hours without stop. ❹It is important for modern teachers and managers to focus on what is actually done in a time period, rather than just measuring how long a student or worker has been behind a desk.

第3段落❶❷ではこれらの新しい方法について述べています。「これらの方法は休憩を必要としていて、机から長い間離れることを促進する学校や企業もある」と言っています。❸で「昔の管理職や教師には受け入れがたいかもしれない」と述べており、続く❹で「現代では『どれだけ長く机に向かったか』ではなく、『実際に何を行ったか』に注目すべきである」と締めくくっています。

(1) In the years before the 19th century most people felt that

1 those who were working should not waste time studying because not all people were considered capable of academic achievement.

2 anyone who was physically able to work should do so as much as possible to compensate for the weak.

3 people who regularly spent an excessive amount of time on a task were not suitable for continuing in that task.

4 spending as much time as possible on a particular task would certainly make a person better at doing it.

(2) One feature Pomodoro and similar productivity-enhancing approaches have in common is

1 using specific apps to learn different subjects in order to master each of them much faster.

2 taking the maximum time necessary for big projects that are assigned by senior managers or school teachers.

3 organizing a complex task in a way that makes it more manageable and easier to accomplish by a person.

4 being prepared to endure a mild level of exhaustion in order to create a perfect business or academic project.

(3) According to the author of the passage, why do some teachers or managers have difficulty accepting the Pomodoro method?

1 It conflicts with their belief that working hard continuously is the best way to get projects done by students or workers.

2 They feel that it makes people lose their focus when they stop and restart their work several times.

3 This technique was not taught to them in teaching or management schools, so they think it is against the rules to use it.

4 They require a few years of technical study to fully master the method before teaching it to others.

(1) 🔲 19世紀より前にほとんどの人が考えていたのは

1　働いている人は勉強などに無駄な時間を費やすべきではないということだ。なぜならすべての人が学問を究められるわけではないと考えられていたから。

2　体が丈夫で働ける人は、弱者の代わりにできるだけ働くべきであるということだ。

3　ある仕事に過剰な時間を費やしている人は、その仕事を続けるのに適していないということだ。

4　特定の仕事にできるだけ多くの時間を費やせば、その人は確実にその仕事をこなせるようになるということだ。

🔍 第1段落❸に「従来、ほとんどの企業や学校では、『時間をかければかけるほど成果が上がる』という基本的な考え方を重視してきた」とあり、この言い換えになっている4が正解です。

✒️ ☐ compensate for …を埋め合わせる　☐ excessive 過度の

----

(2) 🔲 ポモドーロと、それと同じような生産性向上のためのアプローチに共通する特徴の1つは

1　さまざまなテーマをより早く習得するために、特定のアプリを使うことだ。

2　上司や学校の先生から与えられた大きなプロジェクトに、必要な最大限の時間をかけることだ。

3　複雑なタスクを一人で管理しやすく、成し遂げやすいように整理することだ。

4　ビジネスや学問のプロジェクトを完璧に仕上げるために、軽い疲労に耐えられるようになっていることだ。

🔍 第2段落❷にポモドーロについて「25分ずつ区切って勉強をするものだ」とあり、❻❼では「タイムボックスは、あるプロジェクトに費やす時間の上限を決めてから休憩を取る方法だ。また、アイゼンハワー・マトリックスと呼ばれる、重要度に応じた四角の中にタスクを配置する方法もある」と他の方法の特徴を説明しています。これらの共通点を述べている3が答えだとわかります。

✒️ ☐ enhance（質や力など）を高める　☐ have X in common X が共通点としてある
☐ assign …を割り当てる　☐ endure …に耐える

----

(3) 🔲 この文章の著者によると、なぜ一部の教師や管理職はポモドーロ方式を受け入れにくいのでしょうか。

1　懸命に働き続けることが学生や労働者がプロジェクトを成し遂げるのに最良のやり方だという信念に反する。

2　何度も作業を中断したり再開したりすると、集中力が切れると感じる。

3　教員養成校や経営者養成校で教わらなかった手法なので、使うのはルール違反だと考えている。

4　人に教える前に、数年間技術的な勉強をして方法を完全にマスターする必要がある。

🔍 第3段落❸に「昔ながらの管理職や教師、特に、『本当の』生産性とは本やマニュアルに何時間も目を通すことだと考えている人たちには、ポモドーロやその他のテクニックは受け入れがたいかもしれない」とあり、それと前後の文で述べている現代の取り組み方との対比から解答しましょう。

✒️ ☐ conflict with …に相反する

Managing Time

第1段落

❶ Both children and adults spend a large amount of their lives studying or learning new things.

❷ At the same time, people usually want to learn as quickly as possible.

❸ Traditionally, most businesses or schools emphasized the basic idea of "the more time spent on something, the more achieved."

❹ But since at least the 19th century, these traditional concepts of academic and professional productivity have been questioned.

❺ This is because most people can see that, in reality, not everyone gets the same result out of the same time spent on a task.

第2段落

❶ One approach to improving personal productivity is called the Pomodoro Technique.

❷ This involves breaking up study into 25-minute periods.

❸ Each study period is called "1 pomodoro."

❹ The learner should take a 5-10-minute break after every pomodoro.

❺ A longer break of about 20-30 minutes should be taken after four pomodoros, before restarting the cycle.

❻ Timeboxing is another technique where a worker will set a maximum amount of time to be spent on a project before taking a break.

❼ Another approach is the Eisenhower Matrix, where tasks are arranged in squares based on their importance.

❽ These methods are supposed to be much more productive than simply studying or working oneself to exhaustion.

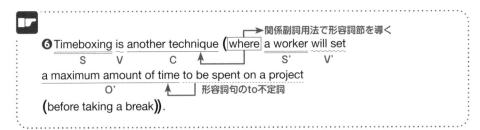

312

時間の管理

第1段落

❶ 子どもも大人も、人生の大半を勉強や新しいことを学ぶことに費やしている。

❷ 同時に、人はできるだけ早く学びたいと思うのが普通だ。

❸ 従来、ほとんどの企業や学校では、「時間をかければかけるほど成果が上がる」という基本的な考え方を重視してきた。

❹ しかし、少なくとも19世紀以降、学問や仕事の生産性に関するこうした伝統的な概念には疑問が持たれるようになった。

❺ なぜなら、現実には、ある課題に同じ時間を使っても誰もが同じ結果を得られるわけではない、ということをほとんどの人がわかっているからだ。

> ❶□ spend X *doing* …するのに X (時間や金)を費やす　❸□ business 会社、店
> □ emphasize …を強調する　□ spend A on B A(時間や金)を B に費やす
> □ achieve …を成し遂げる　❹□ concept 考え、概念　□ productivity 生産性
> □ question …に疑いをかける　❺□ get A out of B B から A を得る

第2段落

❶ 個人の生産性を向上させるアプローチの1つに、「ポモドーロ・テクニック」と呼ばれるものがある。

❷ これは、25分ずつ区切って勉強をするものだ。

❸ その勉強時間の区切りは「1ポモドーロ」と呼ばれる。

❹ 学習者は、1ポモドーロごとに5 〜 10分の休憩を取る必要がある。

❺ 4ポモドーロ勉強したら20 〜 30分程度の休憩を取り、また同じサイクルを繰り返す。

❻ 「タイムボックス」は、あるプロジェクトに費やす時間の上限を決めてから休憩を取るという別の方法だ。

❼ また、アイゼンハワー・マトリックスと呼ばれる、重要度に応じた四角の中にタスクを配置する方法もある。

❽ これらの方法は、単に疲れるまで勉強したり、頑張ったりするよりも、はるかに生産性が高いとされている。

> ❶□ improve …を改善する　❷□ involve …を意味する　□ break up A into B A を B に分割する
> ❼□ in a square 四角になって　❽□ be supposed to be X (世間では)X だと考えられている
> □ exhaustion 疲労困憊

筆記 ③

第3段落

❶ In most of these new study or work methods, a long or short break is necessary.

❷ Some schools and companies are giving students or employees more time away from desks—sometimes days—in order to boost innovation.

❸ Pomodoro and other techniques may be difficult for traditional managers or teachers to accept, especially those who feel that "real" productivity means going through books or manuals for hours without stop.

❹ It is important for modern teachers and managers to focus on what is actually done in a time period, rather than just measuring how long a student or worker has been behind a desk.

---

❸ Pomodoro and other techniques may be difficult
$\quad$ S $\qquad$ V $\quad$ C

for traditional managers or teachers to accept,
$\qquad$ to acceptの意味上のS

especially those (who feel (that "real" productivity means
同格 $\qquad$ S' V' O' $\qquad$ S'' $\qquad$ V''

going through books or manuals for hours without stop)).
$\qquad$ O''

❹ It is important for modern teachers and managers
仮S V $\quad$ C $\qquad$ to focus onの意味上のS

to focus on (what is actually done in a time period),
真S $\quad$ S' $\quad$ V'
$\qquad$ onの目的語①

(rather than just measuring (how long
$\quad$ → ここから副詞句 $\quad$ onの目的語②

a student or worker has been behind a desk)).
$\quad$ S'' $\qquad$ V'' $\qquad$ C''

314

❶ これらの新しい勉強法や仕事術の多くは、長短の休憩を必要としている。

❷ 学校や企業の中には、イノベーションを促進するために、学生や社員を更に長時間（ときには数日）、机から離れさせているところもある。

❸ 昔ながらの管理職や教師、特に、「本当の」生産性とは本やマニュアルに何時間も目を通すことだと考えている人たちには、ポモドーロやその他のテクニックは受け入れがたいかもしれない。

❹ 現代の教師や管理職にとって重要なのは、生徒や社員がどれだけ長く机に向かったかを測定するのではなく、ある期間に実際に何を行ったかに注目することなのだ。

❷☐ boost …を増加する　☐ innovation 革新　❸☐ go through …を通して読む
❹☐ focus on …を重視する　☐ measure （人物など）を評価する
☐ be behind a desk デスクワークをしている

問題英文の読み方 P.318　解説・正解 P.322　訳・語句 P.324

Are Dentures a Good Thing?

The French are generally credited with developing dentures (false teeth) in the 1700s, although new evidence suggests the ancient Etruscan civilization developed them in 700 B.C. The French, at least, were able to make more durable models that could be mass produced. Prior to this, people without teeth were reduced to eating soft foods such as soups, soft fruits, and vegetables, and other items that did not require the teeth to bite, chew, and grind. Without healthier, protein-rich foods, the elderly are at particular risk of growing weak. Dentures seemed to be a solution to this critical problem.

While dentures do enable one to chew, the amount of pressure one can bring to chewing—the bite force—is much reduced. Within 5 years of wearing dentures, people can lose up to 75% of their bite force. This means that they tend to avoid tough to eat but nutrient-rich foods such as nuts or celery. Denture-wearing senior citizens may therefore lose access to the foods they need most, resulting in muscle and bone loss that makes them prone to falls and fractures. Studies have found that people who are over 60 with dentures are 35% more likely to be frail than those having at least twenty of their natural teeth at that age.

Dentures need to be maintained in good condition, by removing them frequently for thorough brushing and cleaning. Implants, or artificial teeth, on the other hand, need not be removed once they are fixed. Since they are drilled directly into the jawbone, they are stronger and can deal with tougher foods. Nevertheless, they need to be maintained the same way as natural teeth and may even require occasional replacement. The easiest solution, as every dentist around the world says, is to take good care of your natural teeth, so that you can not only enjoy a range of delicious and healthy foods, but lead a long and healthy life.

(1)　When French dentures were invented it was initially thought that

　　1　these would solve the problem of people who had damaged teeth being restricted in their diets.

    2   the devices would remind people to take better care of their mouths and protect their natural teeth.

    3   they would improve over time and provide a lot more bite force that would enable people to eat harder foods.

    4   people would only use them when they wanted to eat hard foods such as nuts to stay healthy in old age.

(2)   What is one problem faced by denture wearers?

    1   Their jaw shape may change after a few months of wearing the dentures and that creates stress in the wearer.

    2   The food items people prefer to eat gradually change as they age and they do not want the dentures anymore.

    3   Muscles and bones in the mouth become weak when people fail to brush and clean the dentures properly.

    4   The amount of bite power that people originally had significantly decreases, making them avoid nutritious foods that are hard to chew.

(3)   What conclusion can be made about implants?

    1   Cleaning and maintenance costs of implants can be quite high, so they should be used as a last resort.

    2   Implants are impossible to remove once they are placed into the jaw, so they should be fixed only when absolutely necessary.

    3   Despite enabling people to eat harder foods compared to dentures, implanted teeth are still not a perfect replacement for natural teeth.

    4   They are more irritating to the wearer since they are screwed into the actual jawbone and may eventually weaken one's bite.

Are Dentures a Good Thing?

❶The French are generally credited with developing dentures (false teeth) in the 1700s, although new evidence suggests the ancient Etruscan civilization developed them in 700 B.C. ❷The French, at least, were able to make more durable models that could be mass produced. ❸Prior to this, people without teeth were reduced to eating soft foods such as soups, soft fruits, and vegetables, and other items that did not require the teeth to bite, chew, and grind. ❹Without healthier, protein-rich foods, the elderly are at particular risk of growing weak. ❺Dentures seemed to be a solution to this critical problem.

❶While dentures do enable one to chew, the amount of pressure one can bring to chewing—the bite force—is much reduced. ❷Within 5 years of wearing dentures, people can lose up to 75% of their bite force. ❸This means that they tend to avoid tough to eat but nutrient-rich foods such as nuts or celery. ❹Denture-wearing senior citizens may therefore lose access to the foods they need most, resulting in muscle and bone loss that makes them prone to falls and fractures. ❺Studies have found that people who are over 60 with dentures are 35% more likely to be frail than those having at least twenty of their natural teeth at that age.

この問題英文の長さは約300語です。

「入れ歯は良いものか」というタイトルです。良いという結論になるのか、良くないという結論になるのか、予想しながら読み進めましょう。❶では「一般的にフランス人が入れ歯を開発したと考えられているが、新しい証拠によると、紀元前700年にエトルリア文明で開発されていた」とあります。❷ではフランス人が少なくとも成し遂げたことについて、❸ではフランス人が入れ歯を開発する以前は歯のない人々は柔らかいものばかり食べていたことについて述べています。❹では高齢者が健康的で栄養価の高い食品をとる必要性について述べ、❺で「だから解決策として入れ歯が登場した」とあります。

この段落ではフランス人が入れ歯を開発した頃の状況について書かれていました。

第2段落の❶は While で始まり、「入れ歯で噛めるようにはできるが、その一方で、噛む力は弱められる」とあります。具体的には、❷❸で「入れ歯を装着して5年で噛む力が75％程度低下するため、食べにくいが栄養価の高い食品を敬遠しがちになる」と言っています。そのようなこともあり、❹❺では「入れ歯を装着している高齢者は必要な食べ物に手を伸ばさなくなり、筋力や骨が弱くなることで転倒や骨折を起こしやすくなり、60歳以上の自分の歯がある人と比べ、入れ歯をしている人は虚弱体質になる割合が35％高い」という研究例があることを挙げています。

この段落では、入れ歯の問題点について述べていました。

筆記 ③

第3段落

❶Dentures need to be maintained in good condition, by removing them frequently for thorough brushing and cleaning. ❷Implants, or artificial teeth, on the other hand, need not be removed once they are fixed. ❸Since they are drilled directly into the jawbone, they are stronger and can deal with tougher foods. ❹Nevertheless, they need to be maintained the same way as natural teeth and may even require occasional replacement. ❺The easiest solution, as every dentist around the world says, is to take good care of your natural teeth, so that you can not only enjoy a range of delicious and healthy foods, but lead a long and healthy life.

❶❷では、「入れ歯」と「インプラント」の違いについて、「入れ歯は掃除が必要だが、インプラントは取り外す必要がない」と言っています。❸❹ではインプラントの長所と短所について、「強度が高い」が、「自分の歯と同じようにメンテナンスする必要がある」と挙げています。最後の❺では「もっとも簡単な解決策は自分の歯を大切にすることだ」と、結局は入れ歯を使わない方がよいとまとめています。

この段落では入れ歯とインプラントの長短を挙げ、タイトルに関する考察の機会を提示する内容になっていました。

筆記③

(1) When French dentures were invented it was initially thought that

1 these would solve the problem of people who had damaged teeth being restricted in their diets.

2 the devices would remind people to take better care of their mouths and protect their natural teeth.

3 they would improve over time and provide a lot more bite force that would enable people to eat harder foods.

4 people would only use them when they wanted to eat hard foods such as nuts to stay healthy in old age.

(2) What is one problem faced by denture wearers?

1 Their jaw shape may change after a few months of wearing the dentures and that creates stress in the wearer.

2 The food items people prefer to eat gradually change as they age and they do not want the dentures anymore.

3 Muscles and bones in the mouth become weak when people fail to brush and clean the dentures properly.

4 The amount of bite power that people originally had significantly decreases, making them avoid nutritious foods that are hard to chew.

(3) What conclusion can be made about implants?

1 Cleaning and maintenance costs of implants can be quite high, so they should be used as a last resort.

2 Implants are impossible to remove once they are placed into the jaw, so they should be fixed only when absolutely necessary.

3 Despite enabling people to eat harder foods compared to dentures, implanted teeth are still not a perfect replacement for natural teeth.

4 They are more irritating to the wearer since they are screwed into the actual jawbone and may eventually weaken one's bite.

(1) 📋 フランス製の入れ歯が発明されたとき、当初考えられたのは
1 歯を傷めた人が食生活を制限される問題が解決するだろうということだ。
2 その器具によって、人が口の手入れをして自分の歯を守るようになるということだ。
3 時が経てば改良され、より強い力で噛めるようになり、硬いものも食べられるようになるということだ。
4 老後の健康維持のために、ナッツ類などの硬いものを食べるときだけ使用するということだ。

🔍 第1段落❸から❺で「それ以前は、歯のない人は、スープや柔らかい果物、野菜など、噛み切ったり咀嚼したりすり潰したりする必要のない柔らかいものを食べるしかなかった。健康的でタンパク質の豊富な食品を摂らなければ、高齢者は特に体が弱くなる危険性がある。この重大な問題を解決するために登場したのが、入れ歯である」と述べています。ここから問1の答えがわかります。

✏️ ☐ initially 初めに ☐ restrict …を制限する ☐ diet 日常の飲食物 ☐ protect …を守る

· ·

(2) 📋 入れ歯を装着している人が直面する問題点は何ですか。
1 義歯を装着して数か月経つと顎の形が変わり、装着者のストレスになることがある。
2 加齢とともに好みの食べ物が変化し、入れ歯を着けたくなくなる。
3 入れ歯の適切なブラッシングや清掃を怠ると、口の中の筋肉や骨が弱くなる。
4 もともと持っていた噛む力が著しく低下し、噛みにくいが栄養価の高い食品を避けるようになる。

🔍 第2段落❶から❸で述べている「入れ歯で噛めるようにはできるが、噛む力はかなり弱くなる。入れ歯を装着して5年もすると、噛む力が75％程度低下してしまう。そのため、ナッツやセロリなど、食べにくいが栄養価の高い食品を敬遠しがちになる」の内容が4で言い換えられています。

✏️ ☐ face …に直面する ☐ age 年をとる ☐ properly 適切に ☐ significantly 著しく
☐ nutritious 栄養分のある

· ·

(3) 📋 インプラントについて、どのような結論が出るのでしょうか。
1 インプラントの清掃やメンテナンスの費用はかなり高額になるため、最終手段として使用する必要がある。
2 インプラントは一度顎に埋め込むと取り外しができないので、どうしても必要な場合のみ固定する。
3 入れ歯に比べれば硬いものも食べられるが、本物の歯の完全な代替物とはいえない。
4 顎の骨自体にねじ込むため、インプラントの方が装着者にとって刺激が強くなり、やがて噛み合わせが弱くなる可能性がある。

🔍 第3段落❸❹で「顎の骨に直接穴を開けるので、強度が高く、硬い食べ物にも対応できる。とはいえ、自分の歯と同じようにメンテナンスする必要があり、時折交換が必要な場合もある」とインプラントの長所と短所を述べています。ここから問3に答えることができます。

✏️ ☐ conclusion 結論、断定 ☐ resort (訴える)手段、頼りにするもの ☐ irritating いらいらさせる
☐ screw …をねじで取り付ける、…をねじ込む ☐ eventually やがて、結局

🚩 **(1) 1 (2) 4 (3) 3**

Are Dentures a Good Thing?

第1段落

❶ The French are generally credited with developing dentures (false teeth) in the 1700s, although new evidence suggests the ancient Etruscan civilization developed them in 700 B.C.

❷ The French, at least, were able to make more durable models that could be mass produced.

❸ Prior to this, people without teeth were reduced to eating soft foods such as soups, soft fruits, and vegetables, and other items that did not require the teeth to bite, chew, and grind.

❹ Without healthier, protein-rich foods, the elderly are at particular risk of growing weak.

❺ Dentures seemed to be a solution to this critical problem.

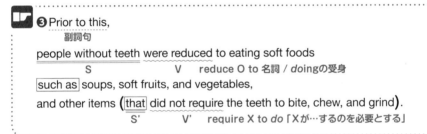

❸ Prior to this,
　　　副詞句
people without teeth were reduced to eating soft foods
　　　S　　　　　　　　　V　　reduce O to 名詞 / doingの受身
such as soups, soft fruits, and vegetables,
and other items (that did not require the teeth to bite, chew, and grind).
　　　　　　　　　　S'　　　V'　　require X to do「Xが…するのを必要とする」

第2段落

❶ While dentures do enable one to chew, the amount of pressure one can bring to chewing—the bite force—is much reduced.

❷ Within 5 years of wearing dentures, people can lose up to 75% of their bite force.

❸ This means that they tend to avoid tough to eat but nutrient-rich foods such as nuts or celery.

❹ Denture-wearing senior citizens may therefore lose access to the foods they need most, resulting in muscle and bone loss that makes them prone to falls and fractures.

❺ Studies have found that people who are over 60 with dentures are 35% more likely to be frail than those having at least twenty of their natural teeth at that age.

入れ歯は良いものなのか

第1段落

❶ 入れ歯（義歯）は、1700年代にフランス人が開発したというのが通説だが、新しい証拠によると、古代エトルリア文明では紀元前700年に開発されていたという。

❷ だが、フランス人は少なくともより丈夫で大量生産が可能な製品を作ることは成し遂げたと言える。

❸ それ以前は、歯のない人は、スープや柔らかい果物、野菜など、噛み切ったり咀嚼したりすり潰したりする必要のない柔らかいものを食べるしかなかった。

❹ 健康的でタンパク質の豊富な食品を摂らなければ、高齢者は特に体が弱くなる危険性がある。

❺ この重大な問題を解決するために登場したのが、入れ歯である。

☐ dentures 一組の義歯　❶☐ credit A with B A に B の性質があると信じる　☐ false 人工の
☐ evidence 証拠　☐ ancient 古代の　☐ Etruscan エトルリアの　☐ civilization 文明
❷☐ durable 丈夫な　☐ mass produced 大量生産された　❸☐ prior to …より前に
☐ be reduced to *doing* 余儀なく…することになる　☐ require X to *do* X が…するのを必要とする
☐ grind …をかみ砕く　❹☐ protein-rich たんぱく質が豊富な　☐ the elderly 年配の人
☐ be at risk of …の危険がある　☐ grow （次第に）…になる　❺☐ solution 解決策
☐ critical 重大な

第2段落

❶ 入れ歯は噛むことはできるが、噛む力（咬合力<ruby>咬合力<rt>こうごう</rt></ruby>）はかなり弱くなる。

❷ 入れ歯を装着して5年もすると、噛む力が75%程度低下してしまう。

❸ そのため、ナッツやセロリなど、食べにくいが栄養価の高い食品を敬遠しがちになる。

❹ 入れ歯を装着している高齢者は、最も必要な食べ物に手を伸ばさなくなり、筋肉や骨が減少して、転倒や骨折を起こしやすくなる可能性がある。

❺ 60歳以上で入れ歯をしている人は、その年齢で自分の歯が20本以上ある人に比べて、虚弱体質になる割合が35%高いという研究結果もある。

❶☐ enable X to *do* X が…できるようにする　❷☐ up to …に至るまで　☐ bite force 噛む力（咬合力）
❸☐ avoid …を避ける　☐ nutrient-rich 栄養が豊富な　☐ celery セロリ
❹☐ denture-wearing 入れ歯を装着している　☐ result in …という結果になる
☐ prone to …の傾向がある　☐ fall 転倒　☐ fracture 骨折　❺☐ frail （体質が）虚弱な
☐ be likely to *do* …しそう

筆記 ③

第3段落

❶ Dentures need to be maintained in good condition, by removing them frequently for thorough brushing and cleaning.

❷ Implants, or artificial teeth, on the other hand, need not be removed once they are fixed.

❸ Since they are drilled directly into the jawbone, they are stronger and can deal with tougher foods.

❹ Nevertheless, they need to be maintained the same way as natural teeth and may even require occasional replacement.

❺ The easiest solution, as every dentist around the world says, is to take good care of your natural teeth, so that you can not only enjoy a range of delicious and healthy foods, but lead a long and healthy life.

---

❷ Implants, (or artificial teeth), (on the other hand),
    S   Sの言い換え
need not be removed (once they are fixed).
    V   S' V'

❺ The easiest solution, (as every dentist around the world says),
    S   S'   V'
is to take good care of your natural teeth,
V   C

(so that) you can not only enjoy a range of delicious and healthy foods,
結果を表す S''   V''①   O''①
副詞節

but lead a long and healthy life).
(but also) V''②   O''②

第3段落

❶ 入れ歯は、こまめに外してブラッシングやクリーニングを行い、良好な状態を維持する必要がある。

❷ 一方、インプラント（人工歯）は、一度固定すると取り外す必要がない。

❸ 顎の骨に直接穴を開けるので、強度が高く、硬い食べ物にも対応できる。

❹ とはいえ、自分の歯と同じようにメンテナンスする必要があり、時折交換が必要な場合もある。

❺ 世界中の歯科医師が言うように、最も簡単な解決策は、自分の歯を大切にすることだ。そうすれば、おいしくて健康な食べ物をいろいろと楽しめるだけでなく、長く健康な生活を過ごせるのだ。

❶□ maintain …を保持する　□ remove …を取り外す　□ thorough 徹底的な　□ brushing 歯磨き
❷□ implant 歯科インプラント、人口歯根　□ artificial 人工の　□ on the other hand 他方では
□ fix …を固定する　❸□ drill …に穴を開ける　□ jawbone 顎の骨　□ deal with …を処理する
❹□ nevertheless それにもかかわらず　□ occasional 時折の　□ replacement 交換
❺□ a range of いくらかの範囲の　□ lead a life 人生・生活を過ごす

筆記③

問題英文の読み方 P.330　解説・正解 P.332　訳・語句 P.334

How Should We Write?

For native English speakers, it seems natural to read and write from left to right. However, it is certainly not the only way to do so. Arabic and Hebrew are written right to left, as is Kurdish. Writing horizontally is not standard, either. Classical Mongolian is written left to right, but in vertical columns, not horizontal lines. Some scholars think the direction might have been determined by how a language was originally written, whether it was imprinted on clay slabs or stones or drawn with ink on scrolls of animal skin or paper. In the end, it appears there is no set principle or logical reason for a language to be written one way or another.

Researchers say the scripts of languages, including their symbols, alphabets, and writing patterns, are the results of thousands of years of social evolution. Even two states existing right next to one another can have very different languages and writing styles. Vietnam had used Chinese writing for many centuries, but in the 17th century—under European influence and later colonial control—began gradually switching to a modified Roman alphabet, making the change complete by the mid 20th century. Swahili, a language common to much of East and Southern Africa, originally used Arabic script but then, as Africa fell under European control, gradually switched to the Roman alphabet. However, Swahili has kept a very large number of Arabic words and concepts.

The Roman alphabet is the same one used for English. Most European countries also use it, although Russia uses the Cyrillic alphabet, as do Serbia and Ukraine. Cyrillic, like the Korean alphabet "Hangeul," is unique in that its creator is known. While Hangeul was created in the mid 15th century by King Sejong the Great, Cyrillic dates further back to the 9th century and was named after St. Cyril, who is credited with its formation. Most other languages are so old that their alphabets or characters developed over time, instead of being the design of one person.

(1) What does the passage say about writing direction?

1　It frequently changes from left to right or vertical to horizontal as a nation switches from animal skins to paper or other materials.
2　Most of the older languages are now being written left to right despite the opposite direction being more logical.
3　The direction of writing is usually fixed by the creator of a language and should never be changed.
4　There is no evidence that any specific direction is the best way to read or write a language.

(2) What is suggested about Vietnam?

1　It replaced its long-used China-based written language with a script that was introduced from the West.
2　An entirely new writing script was created by its scholars and kings in the 9th and 15th centuries.
3　The country has influenced China through the promotion of certain language script techniques that it developed.
4　Its script is interestingly similar to that of the Swahili language used on the African continent.

(3) Cyrillic and Hangeul are similar to one another

1　as it is known who created these scripts and when they were made.
2　because they were both made around the same time and were created by rulers of the same country.
3　since they both use a very complex script that is difficult for almost any outsider to learn.
4　in that they are the only two scripts that use characters instead of alphabets on the European or Asian mainland.

第1段落

How Should We Write?

❶For native English speakers, it seems natural to read and write from left to right. ❷However, it is certainly not the only way to do so. ❸Arabic and Hebrew are written right to left, as is Kurdish. ❹Writing horizontally is not standard, either. ❺Classical Mongolian is written left to right, but in vertical columns, not horizontal lines. ❻Some scholars think the direction might have been determined by how a language was originally written, whether it was imprinted on clay slabs or stones or drawn with ink on scrolls of animal skin or paper. ❼In the end, it appears there is no set principle or logical reason for a language to be written one way or another.

第2段落

❶Researchers say the scripts of languages, including their symbols, alphabets, and writing patterns, are the results of thousands of years of social evolution. ❷Even two states existing right next to one another can have very different languages and writing styles. ❸Vietnam had used Chinese writing for many centuries, but in the 17th century—under European influence and later colonial control—began gradually switching to a modified Roman alphabet, making the change complete by the mid 20th century. ❹Swahili, a language common to much of East and Southern Africa, originally used Arabic script but then, as Africa fell under European control, gradually switched to the Roman alphabet. ❺However, Swahili has kept a very large number of Arabic words and concepts.

第3段落

❶The Roman alphabet is the same one used for English. ❷Most European countries also use it, although Russia uses the Cyrillic alphabet, as do Serbia and Ukraine. ❸Cyrillic, like the Korean alphabet "Hangeul," is unique in that its creator is known. ❹While Hangeul was created in the mid 15th century by King Sejong the Great, Cyrillic dates further back to the 9th century and was named after St. Cyril, who is credited with its formation. ❺Most other languages are so old that their alphabets or characters developed over time, instead of being the design of one person.

この問題英文の長さは約300語です。

「どのような書き方が良いだろうか」というタイトルの文章です。❶❷では、「英語が母国語の人にとっては左から右に書くのが自然なようだが、それは唯一の方法でない」と問題提起をしています。続く文では、言語によって文字の書かれる方向が異なる例が挙げられています。❸では「アラビア語、ヘブライ語、クルド語は右から左に書かれる」、❺では「古典のモンゴル語は縦書き」と言っています。そして❻では、ある学者によると文字の書かれる方向は「もともとその言語が粘土板や石に刻まれたのか、動物の皮や紙に書かれたのかによって決まった」とあります。この段落のまとめとして、❼では「結局、言語を書く方法について決まった原理や理由はない」と言っています。

前の段落で「決まった原理や理由はない」とまとめられた「書き方」について、❶で「言語の表記法は何千年にもわたる社会の進化の結果である」と述べられています。「隣り合う二つの国でも書き方が違うことがある」と書かれた❷の具体例として、❸で「ベトナムは17世紀のヨーロッパからの影響と植民地支配を受けて、変形させたローマ字の表記に移行した」とあります。続く❹には別の例として「スワヒリ語はアフリカがヨーロッパの支配下に置かれてから徐々にローマ字に変えた」とありますが、❺で「それでもスワヒリ語にはアラビア語の単語や概念が残っている」と言っています。

この段落からは社会的な変化にともなう表記の変遷がうかがえます。

第3段落の❶は「ローマ字は英語で使われているのと同じものだ」とあるので、この後の文では「文字」についての話が展開すると予測できます。❷では「ロシアやセルビアやウクライナはキリル文字を使っているが、ヨーロッパ諸国の多くはローマ字を使っている」と例を挙げています。❸ではキリル文字とハングルの共通点について書かれていて、❹でそれぞれの成立について「ハングルは15世紀半ばに世宗によって、キリル文字は9世紀に聖キュリロスによって」と述べています。❺は、第2段落1文目と同様に「それらの文字や記号は長い時間をかけて発展してきた」と一部の例外を交えながら述べて、この文章を結論づけています。

第3段落には文字の導入の起点が明らかであるものの例について書いてありました。

(1) What does the passage say about writing direction?

1 It frequently changes from left to right or vertical to horizontal as a nation switches from animal skins to paper or other materials.

2 Most of the older languages are now being written left to right despite the opposite direction being more logical.

3 The direction of writing is usually fixed by the creator of a language and should never be changed.

4 There is no evidence that any specific direction is the best way to read or write a language.

(2) What is suggested about Vietnam?

1 It replaced its long-used China-based written language with a script that was introduced from the West.

2 An entirely new writing script was created by its scholars and kings in the 9th and 15th centuries.

3 The country has influenced China through the promotion of certain language script techniques that it developed.

4 Its script is interestingly similar to that of the Swahili language used on the African continent.

(3) Cyrillic and Hangeul are similar to one another

1 as it is known who created these scripts and when they were made.

2 because they were both made around the same time and were created by rulers of the same country.

3 since they both use a very complex script that is difficult for almost any outsider to learn.

4 in that they are the only two scripts that use characters instead of alphabets on the European or Asian mainland.

(1) 📻 この文章では、書く方向についてどのように言っていますか。

1　国家が動物の皮から紙や他の素材に切り替えるときに、左方向から右方向へ、あるいは縦書きから横書きへと頻繁に変化する。

2　古い言語のほとんどは、右から左に書く方が論理的であるにもかかわらず、現在では左から右へ書かれる。

3　書く方向は通常、言語の創造者によって固定されており、決して変えてはならない。

4　特定の方向が、言語の読み書きに最適であるという証拠はない。

🔍 第1段落❻で書き方の源流についての説を挙げた後に、❼で「結局のところ、ある言語がある方法で書かれたことに決まった原理や論理的な理由はないようだ」と述べていることから答えがわかります。

✎ □ despite …にもかかわらず　□ opposite 逆の　□ evidence 証拠

・・

(2) 📻 ベトナムについて示唆されていることは何ですか。

1　長い間使っていた中国由来の書き言葉を改め、西洋の表記方法を取り入れた。

2　9世紀と15世紀に、学者や王によって全く新しい文字が作られた。

3　自国が開発した言語表記のテクニックを普及させて、中国に影響を与えた。

4　その表記法は、アフリカ大陸で使われているスワヒリ語の文字と興味深いほど似ている。

🔍 第2段落❸の「ベトナムは何世紀も前から漢字を使っていたが、17世紀のヨーロッパからの影響と植民地支配を受けてローマ字の表記に移行した」が解答の手がかりとなっています。

✎ □ entirely 全く　□ promotion 促進、振興　□ interestingly 興味深く

・・

(3) 📻 キリル文字とハングルが互いに似ているのは、

1　これらの文字は、誰がいつ作ったかがわかっているから。

2　どちらも同じ時期に、同じ国の支配者によって作られたから。

3　どちらも非常に複雑な文字を使用しており、部外者が習得するのは困難であるため。

4　ヨーロッパやアジア大陸で、アルファベットの代わりの文字を使っているのはこの2種類の文字だけである点。

🔍 第3段落❸❹「キリル文字は、韓国のアルファベット『ハングル』と同様に、その作成者が判明している点に特徴がある。ハングルは15世紀半ばに世宗によって創出されたが、キリル文字はさらに9世紀までさかのぼり、その成立に貢献したとされる聖キュリロスにちなんで命名された」から問3の答えを導くことができます。

✎ □ ruler 支配者、統治者　□ complex 複雑な　□ outsider 外部の人、よそ者

How Should We Write?

❶ For native English speakers, it seems natural to read and write from left to right.

❷ However, it is certainly not the only way to do so.

❸ Arabic and Hebrew are written right to left, as is Kurdish.

❹ Writing horizontally is not standard, either.

❺ Classical Mongolian is written left to right, but in vertical columns, not horizontal lines.

❻ Some scholars think the direction might have been determined by how a language was originally written, whether it was imprinted on clay slabs or stones or drawn with ink on scrolls of animal skin or paper.

❼ In the end, it appears there is no set principle or logical reason for a language to be written one way or another.

---

❸ Arabic and Hebrew are written right to left, (as is Kurdish).
S　　　　　　　　　V　　　　　　　　　as「…と同じく」節内の倒置

❻ Some scholars think (that the direction might have been determined
S　　　　V　　O　　　S'　　　　　　　V'

by (how a language was originally written),
S''　　　　　　V''

(whether it was imprinted on clay slabs or stones
S'''　V'''①

or drawn with ink on scrolls of animal skin or paper)).
V'''②

どのような書き方がよいのだろうか

第1段落

❶ 英語を母国語とする人にとって、左から右に文字を読み、そして書くのは自然なことのように思われる。

❷ しかし、それが唯一の方法でないことは確かだ。

❸ アラビア語やヘブライ語は右から左に書かれ、クルド語も同様だ。

❹ 横書きも標準ではない。

❺ 古典のモンゴル語は左から右へ書くが、横書きではなく縦書きだ。

❻ 文字の書かれる方向は、もともとその言語がどのように書かれたか、つまり粘土板や石に刻まれたか、動物の皮や紙の巻物に墨で書かれたかによって決まったのではないかと考える学者もいる。

❼ 結局のところ、ある言語がある方法で書かれたことに、決まった原理や論理的な理由はないようだ。

❸☐ Hebrew ヘブライ語　☐ Kurdish クルド語　❹☐ horizontally 横に　❺☐ vertical 縦の
☐ column (読み物の)縦の行、縦欄　☐ horizontal 横の　☐ line 列、線　❻☐ direction 方向
☐ determine …を決定する　☐ imprint …に判を押す　☐ clay 粘土、土　☐ slab 厚板、石板
☐ scroll 巻物　❼☐ in the end 結局は　☐ set 定められた、決まった　☐ principle 原理、原則
☐ logical 論理的な　☐ one way or another 何らかの方法で

筆記③

第2段落

❶ Researchers say the scripts of languages, including their symbols, alphabets, and writing patterns, are the results of thousands of years of social evolution.

❷ Even two states existing right next to one another can have very different languages and writing styles.

❸ Vietnam had used Chinese writing for many centuries, but in the 17th century—under European influence and later colonial control—began gradually switching to a modified Roman alphabet, making the change complete by the mid 20th century.

❹ Swahili, a language common to much of East and Southern Africa, originally used Arabic script but then, as Africa fell under European control, gradually switched to the Roman alphabet.

❺ However, Swahili has kept a very large number of Arabic words and concepts.

---

❹ Swahili, a language (common to much of East and Southern Africa),
S　　　　　同格

originally used Arabic script
V① 　　　O①

but then, (as Africa fell under European control),
　　　　　 S'　　V'　　　　O'

gradually switched to the Roman alphabet.
V②　　　　　　O②

❶ 研究者によれば、記号、文字体系、書き方など、言語の表記法は、何千年にもわたる社会の進化の結果である。

❷ 隣り合って存在する二つの国でさえ、言語や書き方が全く異なることがある。

❸ ベトナムは何世紀も前から漢字を使っていたが、17世紀のヨーロッパからの影響と植民地支配を受けて、変形させたローマ字の表記に移行し、20世紀半ばには完全に切り替えた。

❹ スワヒリ語は東アフリカと南アフリカに共通する言語で、もともとはアラビア文字を使っていたが、アフリカがヨーロッパの支配下に置かれるようになると、徐々にローマ字に切り替えていった。

❺ しかし、スワヒリ語には非常に多くのアラビア語の単語や概念が残されている。

❶□ script 表記法　□ symbol 記号、符合　□ evolution 進化、進展　❷□ right next to …のすぐ隣に
□ one another 互いに　❸□ switch 切り替える　□ modify …を少し変える　□ colonial 植民地の
❹□ Swahili スワヒリ語　□ common to …に共通の　□ fall under …の影響下に入る
❺□ concept 概念

第3段落

❶ The Roman alphabet is the same one used for English.

❷ Most European countries also use it, although Russia uses the Cyrillic alphabet, as do Serbia and Ukraine.

❸ Cyrillic, like the Korean alphabet "Hangeul," is unique in that its creator is known.

❹ While Hangeul was created in the mid 15th century by King Sejong the Great, Cyrillic dates further back to the 9th century and was named after St. Cyril, who is credited with its formation.

❺ Most other languages are so old that their alphabets or characters developed over time, instead of being the design of one person.

❹ (While Hangeul was created in the mid 15th century
        S'   V'
by King Sejong the Great),

Cyrillic dates further back to the 9th century
   S   V   O
and was named after St. Cyril, (who is credited with its formation).
     name A after Bの受身   S''   V'' credit 人 with 行為
                                        「…の功績があると思う」の受身
❺ Most other languages are so old (that
           S   V   C   └→ Cのoldの程度に関する説明が入る
their alphabets or characters developed over time,
          S'   V'
(instead of being the design of one person)).
  副詞句

❶ ローマ字は英語で使われているのと同じものだ。

❷ ほとんどのヨーロッパ諸国はローマ字を使っているが、ロシアはキリル文字を使っており、セルビアやウクライナも同様である。

❸ キリル文字は、韓国のアルファベット「ハングル」と同様に、その作成者が判明している点に特徴がある。

❹ ハングルは15世紀半ばに世宗によって創出されたが、キリル文字はさらに9世紀までさかのぼり、その成立に貢献したとされる聖キュリロスにちなんで名づけられた。

❺ その他の多くの言語はとても古く、それらの文字や記号は一人の人間がデザインしたものではなく、長い時間をかけて発展してきた。

❷□ Cyrillic キリル文字の　❸□ in that 節 …という点で　❹□ date back to …にさかのぼる
□ further さらに　□ credit A with B A に B の功績があると信じる　□ formation 形成、成立
❺□ character 文字、記号

問題英文の読み方 P.342　解説・正解 P.346　訳・語句 P.350

Birds and Climate Change

It is quite obvious that climate change is having a significant effect on specific regions, species, and habitats. Some of the largest effects of climate change—such as melting glaciers causing ocean levels to rise and threaten coastal cities—are fairly easy to understand. However, it is more difficult to assess climate change's effects on food webs, where the loss of one species could have damaging effects on others. Climate change may be affecting bee populations, for instance. The loss of bees could have a severely harmful impact on plants and animals, including humans. For this reason, scientists are working hard on ways to protect the surviving bee populations. Now, we may have a similar problem with birds. In 2020, birds began falling from the sky in large numbers in the Southwest United States. In some places, hundreds of thousands of the creatures have fallen dead.

Although the exact causes of the deaths are still being researched, some scientists are already identifying climate change as the reason. In this case, climate change may have been the indirect, rather than the direct, cause of these deaths. Researchers suspect that climate change caused both large wildfires and droughts in the American southwest. Migrating birds that would normally stop and rest in this area therefore could not find safe places to rest or get food. Eventually, they dropped from the sky exhausted. Likewise, extreme cold in the American Northwest—again possibly caused by climate change— may have prompted the birds to leave early on their migration trip, before they had eaten enough to survive the long journey across the desert. Experts point to the very small size and weight of the birds as evidence for both of these theories.

In any event, this trend will become a serious environmental problem if it continues. The birds migrate from North America to Central and South America and back each year, so their deaths affect ecosystems on both places. As with bees, birds have a critical place in food webs. They keep down insect populations, including those which attack farm crops. They also serve as food themselves for many types of predators, and, like bees, bring pollen to flowers. Without these birds, insect numbers could rise, bringing ecosystems in both regions out of balance. A population reduction or change in flight patterns would also affect many species along the birds' migratory route that depend on them seasonally.

(1) What is true of climate change?

1 The damage it causes to nature and the habitats of animals is mainly due to human failure to manage glaciers.

2 Some of its visible effects on the environment are easier to see compared to its less obvious effects on animal communities.

3 No one understands how its effect on glaciers is posing a risk to people and other animals living in coastal areas.

4 New research on bees shows that the impact of climate change on the environment is not as great as previously thought.

(2) One of the main causes of bird loss during their migration may be

1 flying creatures accidentally catching fire when they are passing over large areas of forests that are already in flames.

2 humans not allowing the birds to rest or eat wherever they stop on the way, since those areas are now heavily populated.

3 birds being pushed beyond their strength and flight capacity because they have insufficient food supply as a result of local weather conditions.

4 large farms in both North and South America forcing birds off of their properties and into early migration efforts.

(3) A change in migration routes could affect

1 the frequency of natural disasters such as droughts and wildfires occurring during the summer as well as their spread to new areas.

2 many species of animals which rely on the birds' passing through the area at specific times during the year.

3 the main food supply of people in rural North and South America who hunt the birds seasonally as they fly across the continents.

4 the health of predators who are forced to switch to consuming insect populations instead of their regular diet of small migratory birds.

第1段落

Birds and Climate Change

❶It is quite obvious that climate change is having a significant effect on specific regions, species, and habitats. ❷Some of the largest effects of climate change—such as melting glaciers causing ocean levels to rise and threaten coastal cities—are fairly easy to understand. ❸However, it is more difficult to assess climate change's effects on food webs, where the loss of one species could have damaging effects on others. ❹Climate change may be affecting bee populations, for instance. ❺The loss of bees could have a severely harmful impact on plants and animals, including humans. ❻For this reason, scientists are working hard on ways to protect the surviving bee populations. ❼Now, we may have a similar problem with birds. ❽In 2020, birds began falling from the sky in large numbers in the Southwest United States. ❾In some places, hundreds of thousands of the creatures have fallen dead.

この問題英文の長さは約400語です。

第1段落の❶は「気候変動が特定の地域、種、生息地に大きな影響を及ぼしていることは明白である」で、次の文からその具体的内容について述べています。❷では、影響を解明することが容易である例として、氷河の融解による海面上昇を挙げています。また、❸❹では、それと対照的に解明するのが困難な食物網に与える影響を、ミツバチの個体数に及ぼす影響を例に挙げて説明しようとしています。❺❻では「ミツバチがいなくなれば、動植物に深刻な影響を与える可能性があり、そのため、科学者はミツバチを保護する方法を研究している」とあります。この後、ようやくタイトルにある「鳥」の問題に触れています。❼から❾まで、「鳥についても同じような問題があると言われ、2020年にはアメリカ南西部で鳥が大量に空から降ってきて、場所によっては何十万羽も死んでいる」という衝撃的な例が挙げられています。

第2段落

❶Although the exact causes of the deaths are still being researched, some scientists are already identifying climate change as the reason. ❷In this case, climate change may have been the indirect, rather than the direct, cause of these deaths. ❸Researchers suspect that climate change caused both large wildfires and droughts in the American southwest. ❹Migrating birds that would normally stop and rest in this area therefore could not find safe places to rest or get food. ❺Eventually, they dropped from the sky exhausted. ❻Likewise, extreme cold in the American Northwest—again possibly caused by climate change—may have prompted the birds to leave early on their migration trip, before they had eaten enough to survive the long journey across the desert. ❼Experts point to the very small size and weight of the birds as evidence for both of these theories.

第3段落

❶In any event, this trend will become a serious environmental problem if it continues. ❷The birds migrate from North America to Central and South America and back each year, so their deaths affect ecosystems on both places. ❸As with bees, birds have a critical place in food webs. ❹They keep down insect populations, including those which attack farm crops. ❺They also serve as food themselves for many types of predators, and, like bees, bring pollen to flowers. ❻Without these birds, insect numbers could rise, bringing ecosystems in both regions out of balance. ❼A population reduction or change in flight patterns would also affect many species along the birds' migratory route that depend on them seasonally.

第1段落の鳥が落ちてきた原因について、第2段落❶❷で「気候変動を原因として見ている科学者もいるが、気候変動は直接的ではなく、間接的な原因であった可能性がある」とあります。❸から❺ではその間接的原因について、「気候変動がアメリカ南西部での山火事と干ばつの両方を引き起こしたので、ここで休息するはずの渡り鳥が、休憩場所や餌を得られなかった。だから鳥は疲れてしまい、落ちてきた」と説明しています。続く❻では「アメリカ北西部の極度の寒冷化が、鳥たちが砂漠を横断する長旅に耐えるだけの食料を得る前に移動させてしまったかもしれない」と言っています。❼では「この2つの説の根拠として、専門家が挙げているのは鳥が小さくて軽かったことだ」とあります。

第3段落❶の「この傾向が続けば深刻な環境問題に発展する」より、この段落でも環境に与える更なる影響について書かれていることが推測できます。❷❸では「鳥は、北米から中南米までを往復するため、鳥が死ぬと、どちらの場所の生態系にも影響を与える。なぜなら、ミツバチと同様、鳥は食物網の中で重要な位置を占めているからだ」とあります。具体的には、❹❺にあるように「鳥類は農作物に被害を及ぼす昆虫などの個体数を抑制していて、また、鳥類は捕食者の餌でもあり、ミツバチと同様に花粉を運んでもいる」と言っています。❻❼では、「これらの鳥がいなければ、生態系のバランスが崩れ、渡り鳥の移動ルート上に生息する多くの生物種に影響を与えるだろう」とまとめられています。

筆記③

(1) What is true of climate change?

1 The damage it causes to nature and the habitats of animals is mainly due to human failure to manage glaciers.

2 Some of its visible effects on the environment are easier to see compared to its less obvious effects on animal communities.

3 No one understands how its effect on glaciers is posing a risk to people and other animals living in coastal areas.

4 New research on bees shows that the impact of climate change on the environment is not as great as previously thought.

(2) One of the main causes of bird loss during their migration may be

1 flying creatures accidentally catching fire when they are passing over large areas of forests that are already in flames.

2 humans not allowing the birds to rest or eat wherever they stop on the way, since those areas are now heavily populated.

3 birds being pushed beyond their strength and flight capacity because they have insufficient food supply as a result of local weather conditions.

4 large farms in both North and South America forcing birds off of their properties and into early migration efforts.

(1) 🔲 気候変動について正しいのはどれですか。
1 気候変動が自然や動物の生息地に与える被害は、主に人間が氷河の管理をしなかったことに起因している。
2 気候変動が環境に与える目に見える影響の中には、動物群に与えるあまり明白ではない影響に比べれば、わかりやすいものもある。
3 気候変動が氷河に与える影響が、沿岸地域に住む人々や他の動物にどのようなリスクをもたらしているのか、誰も理解していない。
4 ミツバチに関する新しい研究により、気候変動が環境に与える影響は、これまで考えられていたほど大きくはないことが明らかになった。

🔍 第1段落❷❸に「氷河の融解によって海面が上昇し、沿岸の都市への脅威となるなど、気候変動による最大の影響を認識することはかなり容易だ。しかし、気候変動が食物網に与える影響を判定することはそれより困難で、食物網の中ではある生物種の消失が別の種に有害な影響を与える可能性がある」とあることから、問1はそれを簡潔に言い換えた選択肢2が正解だとわかります。

✏️ □ manage …を管理する、…を大切に扱う □ visible 目に見える □ community 群集
　 □ pose …を引き起こす □ previously 以前に

----

(2) 🔲 渡り鳥が移動中に減少する主な原因の一つかもしれないのは、
1 空を飛ぶ生物が燃え盛る森林の上空を通過する際に、誤って火に包まれてしまうこと。
2 人が多く住むようになったため、渡り鳥が移動中に休息し餌を取ることができなくなったこと。
3 地域の気象条件によって食料が不足しているために、鳥が自分の体力や飛行能力を超えた状況に追いやられること。
4 北米と南米にある大規模な農場が鳥を追い出し、早く移動させること。

🔍 第2段落❸❹に「研究者は気候変動がアメリカ南西部での大規模な山火事と干ばつの両方を引き起こしたのではないかと考えており、そのせいで、通常であればこの地域に立ち寄って休息するはずの渡り鳥が、安全な休憩場所や餌を得ることができなかった」とあり、❻にも「アメリカ北西部の極度の寒冷化（これも気候変動による可能性がある）も、砂漠を横断する長旅に耐えられるだけの食料を得る前に、鳥たちを早く移動させてしまったかもしれない」とあることから、問2の答えがわかります。❸の wildfires and droughts や❻の extreme cold が weather conditions で表され、❹の could not find safe places ... get food が insufficient food supply で表されています。

✏️ □ migration （鳥の）渡り □ creature 生き物 □ in flames 炎に包まれて □ populate …に居住する
　 □ insufficient 不十分な □ force …に強いる □ property 所有地

----

(3) A change in migration routes could affect

1 the frequency of natural disasters such as droughts and wildfires occurring during the summer as well as their spread to new areas.

2 many species of animals which rely on the birds' passing through the area at specific times during the year.

3 the main food supply of people in rural North and South America who hunt the birds seasonally as they fly across the continents.

4 the health of predators who are forced to switch to consuming insect populations instead of their regular diet of small migratory birds.

(3) 📷 渡り鳥の移動経路の変化が影響を与える可能性があるのは

1　夏季に発生する干ばつや山火事などの自然災害の頻度や、新たな地域への広がり。
2　渡り鳥が1年のうちの特定の時期にその地域を通過することに依存している多くの動物種。
3　鳥が大陸を横断する季節に鳥を狩る南北アメリカの農村部の人々の主な食料源。
4　小さな渡り鳥を通常の餌にできずに、昆虫群の摂取に切り替えざるを得なくなった捕食動物の健康状態。

🔍 第3段落❹から❻に「鳥類は、農作物に被害を及ぼす昆虫などの個体数を抑制している。また、鳥類は多種多様な捕食者の餌にもなり、ミツバチと同様に花粉を運んでくれる。これらの鳥がいなければ、昆虫の数が増え、両地域の生態系のバランスは崩れてしまうかもしれない」とあります。ここから問3の解答がわかります。

✒️ ☐ rely on …に依存する　☐ specific 特定の　☐ diet 食物　☐ migratory 移動性の

🏁 (3) 2　349

Birds and Climate Change

第1段落

❶ It is quite obvious that climate change is having a significant effect on specific regions, species, and habitats.

❷ Some of the largest effects of climate change—such as melting glaciers causing ocean levels to rise and threaten coastal cities—are fairly easy to understand.

❸ However, it is more difficult to assess climate change's effects on food webs, where the loss of one species could have damaging effects on others.

❹ Climate change may be affecting bee populations, for instance.

❺ The loss of bees could have a severely harmful impact on plants and animals, including humans.

❻ For this reason, scientists are working hard on ways to protect the surviving bee populations.

❼ Now, we may have a similar problem with birds.

❽ In 2020, birds began falling from the sky in large numbers in the Southwest United States.

❾ In some places, hundreds of thousands of the creatures have fallen dead.

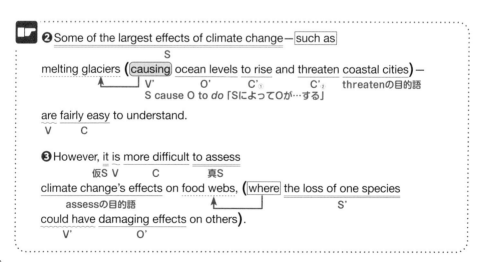

❷Some of the largest effects of climate change—such as
S
melting glaciers (causing ocean levels to rise and threaten coastal cities)—
V'   O'   C'①   C'②   threatenの目的語
S cause O to do 「SによってOが…する」

are fairly easy to understand.
V   C

❸However, it is more difficult to assess
仮S V   C   真S
climate change's effects on food webs, (where the loss of one species
assessの目的語   S'
could have damaging effects on others).
V'   O'

鳥類と気候変動

第1段落

❶ 気候変動が特定の地域、種、生息地に大きな影響を及ぼしていることは、極めて明白である。

❷ 氷河の融解によって海面が上昇し、沿岸の都市への脅威となるなど、気候変動による最大級の影響を認識することはかなり容易だ。

❸ しかし、気候変動が食物網に与える影響を判定することは困難で、食物網の中ではある生物種の消失が別の種に有害な影響を与える可能性がある。

❹ 例えば、気候変動はミツバチの個体数に影響を及ぼすかもしれない。

❺ ミツバチがいなくなれば、人間を含む動植物に深刻な影響を与える可能性があるのだ。

❻ そのため、科学者は、現存するミツバチの個体群を保護する方法を懸命に研究している。

❼ 最近では、鳥についても同じような問題があると言われている。

❽ 2020年、アメリカ南西部で鳥が大量に空から降ってくるようになった。

❾ 場所によっては、何十万羽も死んでいるという。

---

❶□ obvious 明白な　□ have an effect on …に影響を与える　□ significant 重大な
□ specific 特定の、具体的な　□ species (生物分類上の)種　□ habitat 生息地　**❷**□ melt 溶ける
□ glacier 氷河　□ coastal 沿岸の　□ fairly かなり　**❸**□ assess …を見積もる
□ food web 食物網(食物連鎖の関係を網目状に表したもの)　**❹**□ affect …に影響を及ぼす
□ population 個体数　□ for instance 例えば　**❺**□ harmful 有害な　□ impact 影響
❻□ protect …を守る　□ surviving 現存している　**❾**□ creature 生き物

筆記③

第2段落

❶ Although the exact causes of the deaths are still being researched, some scientists are already identifying climate change as the reason.

❷ In this case, climate change may have been the indirect, rather than the direct, cause of these deaths.

❸ Researchers suspect that climate change caused both large wildfires and droughts in the American southwest.

❹ Migrating birds that would normally stop and rest in this area therefore could not find safe places to rest or get food.

❺ Eventually, they dropped from the sky exhausted.

❻ Likewise, extreme cold in the American Northwest—again possibly caused by climate change—may have prompted the birds to leave early on their migration trip, before they had eaten enough to survive the long journey across the desert.

❼ Experts point to the very small size and weight of the birds as evidence for both of these theories.

---

❹ Migrating birds (that would normally stop and rest in this area)
　　　　S　　　　　S'　　　　V'①　　　　　　　V'②

therefore could not find safe places to rest or get food.
　　　　　　　V　　　　　　O

❻ Likewise, extreme cold in the American Northwest
　　　　　　　　　　S

—again possibly (caused by climate change)—

may have prompted the birds to leave early on their migration trip,
V (prompt X to do)　　　O

(before they had eaten enough to survive the long journey across the desert).
　　　　S'　　V'　　　O'　　　　　　　surviveの目的語

第2段落

❶ 正確な死因はまだ調査中だが、一部の科学者はすでに、気候変動が原因であると特定している。

❷ この場合、気候変動はこれらの死の直接的な原因ではなく、間接的な原因であった可能性がある。

❸ 研究者は気候変動がアメリカ南西部での大規模な山火事と干ばつの両方を引き起こしたのではないかと考えている。

❹ そのせいで、通常であればこの地域に立ち寄って休息するはずの渡り鳥が、安全な休憩場所や餌を得ることができなかった。

❺ その結果、鳥たちは疲れ果てて空から落ちてきたのだ。

❻ 同様に、アメリカ北西部の極度の寒冷化（これも気候変動による可能性がある）によって、砂漠を横断する長旅に耐えられるだけの食料を得る前に、鳥たちは早く移動させられてしまったかもしれない。

❼ 専門家は、この2つの説の根拠として、鳥が非常に小さくて軽かったことを挙げている。

❶□ exact 正確な　□ cause 根拠、原因、理由　□ identify A as B A が B であると確認する
❷□ indirect 間接的な　**❸**□ suspect that 節 …ではないかと推測する　□ wildfire 野火、森林火災
□ drought 干ばつ　**❹**□ migrating 移動する　**❺**□ exhausted 疲れ切った　**❻**□ likewise 同様に
□ extreme 極度の　□ prompt X to *do* X を促して…させる　□ migration（鳥の）移動
❼□ point to …を指摘する　□ evidence 証拠

第3段落

❶ In any event, this trend will become a serious environmental problem if it continues.

❷ The birds migrate from North America to Central and South America and back each year, so their deaths affect ecosystems on both places.

❸ As with bees, birds have a critical place in food webs.

❹ They keep down insect populations, including those which attack farm crops.

❺ They also serve as food themselves for many types of predators, and, like bees, bring pollen to flowers.

❻ Without these birds, insect numbers could rise, bringing ecosystems in both regions out of balance.

❼ A population reduction or change in flight patterns would also affect many species along the birds' migratory route that depend on them seasonally.

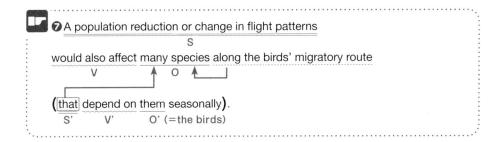

❶ いずれにせよ、この傾向が続けば、深刻な環境問題に発展する。

❷ 鳥は毎年、北米から中南米までを往復するため、その死はどちらの場所の生態系にも影響を与える。

❸ ミツバチと同様、鳥類は食物網の中で重要な位置を占めているからだ。

❹ 鳥類は、農作物に被害を及ぼす昆虫などの個体数を抑制している。

❺ また、鳥類は多種多様な捕食者の餌にもなり、ミツバチと同様に花粉を運んでくれる。

❻ これらの鳥がいなければ、昆虫の数が増え、両地域の生態系のバランスは崩れてしまうかもしれない。

❼ 個体数の減少や飛来パターンの変化は、渡り鳥の移動ルート上に生息し、季節によって渡り鳥に依存する多くの生物種に影響を与えるだろう。

❶□ in any event いずれにしても、とにかく　□ trend 傾向　❷□ migrate 移動する
□ ecosystem 生態系　❸□ as with …と同様に　□ critical 重要な　❹□ keep down …を抑える
□ farm crop 農作物　❺□ serve as …としての役目を果たす　□ predator 捕食者　□ pollen 花粉
❼□ reduction 減少　□ migratory route 移動の道筋　□ seasonally 季節的に、周期的に

筆記③

問題英文の読み方 P.358　解説・正解 P.362　訳・語句 P.364

Harlem Renaissance

The Harlem Renaissance was perhaps the first concentration of African American capital, culture, art, and politics. Spanning the 1920s, it brought together a varied group of high-profile Black Americans of the day, from writers such as Langston Hughes to entertainers such as Louis Armstrong and Josephine Baker. It also included intellectuals such as W.E.B. Du Bois and civil rights leaders such as Marcus Garvey. There had never been such a collaboration of African American talent in one neighborhood and there might never be again.

The Harlem Renaissance emerged for a number of reasons. Millions of Blacks had migrated to the North after the 1860s Civil War, in search of better pay and better lives—away from the racial violence of the South. This Great Migration accelerated after the 1880s, as American industrial power advanced and new factories—primarily in the North—were regularly short of workers. While the North did not have a legal code of racism as the South did, these newcomers could not live wherever they wanted. In fact, Northern property owners informally separated groups by neighborhood. Harlem then gradually became the "Black" part of New York City because Blacks were not really allowed to live anywhere else.

The Harlem Renaissance was impressive to many types of people. Jazz music, for instance, had originated in Black communities, but by the 1920s was popular nationally as well. Whites were attracted to the poetry readings of Zora Neale Hurston or orchestras led by Duke Ellington. Europeans were also drawn to the Renaissance, some coming in specifically to experience the art, writings, politics, and music of Harlem. Beyond being an African American cultural hub, it may have also been one of the first occasions where different races could mingle freely, outside the race rules that were common in most of the West.

However, the Renaissance was not all positive. As more Whites were drawn to the elite clubs of the neighborhood, some establishments, such as the famed Cotton Club, set out a Whites-only audience policy. Its top-class entertainers, though, were almost all Black, as were the service staff. The Great Depression of the 1930s ended the Renaissance, as widespread poverty made a night out on the town too much of a luxury for most Americans. Formal race division itself came to an end several decades later, in the 1960s.

(1) What do we learn about the Harlem Renaissance?

1 It was a training ground for the earliest Black intellectuals and entertainers from the Southern United States.
2 It was a New York City trend that began during the Civil War and then grew larger through the 1920s and 1930s.
3 It was a period when a large number of Black Americans who excelled in diverse fields gathered in a single place.
4 It was a section of New York City that had been slowly attracting both White and Black elites from other parts of the country.

(2) According to the author, why was Harlem the location of the renaissance?

1 Northern housing customs of the time forced most African Americans to live in certain neighborhoods of major cities.
2 The neighborhood had been the home of various high-performing talent even before the start of the American Civil War.
3 It was the last stop of the Great Migration that started in the American South and ended in the North.
4 It was ideal as a place where both customers and entertainers from the northern and southern states could mingle.

(3) How did establishments such as the Cotton Club operate?

1 They had both Black and White people as entertainers and serving staff, but only Blacks were allowed in as audience members.
2 They gave preference to Whites by allowing them in first, while forcing Black audience members to wait outside.
3 They showed top Black performers on stage and had Black staff serve an audience that was exclusively White.
4 They welcomed all types of American performers, but only allowed Black or White men as audience members or staff.

Harlem Renaissance

❶The Harlem Renaissance was perhaps the first concentration of African American capital, culture, art, and politics. ❷Spanning the 1920s, it brought together a varied group of high-profile Black Americans of the day, from writers such as Langston Hughes to entertainers such as Louis Armstrong and Josephine Baker. ❸It also included intellectuals such as W.E.B. Du Bois and civil rights leaders such as Marcus Garvey. ❹There had never been such a collaboration of African American talent in one neighborhood and there might never be again.

❶The Harlem Renaissance emerged for a number of reasons. ❷Millions of Blacks had migrated to the North after the 1860s Civil War, in search of better pay and better lives—away from the racial violence of the South. ❸This Great Migration accelerated after the 1880s, as American industrial power advanced and new factories—primarily in the North—were regularly short of workers. ❹While the North did not have a legal code of racism as the South did, these newcomers could not live wherever they wanted. ❺In fact, Northern property owners informally separated groups by neighborhood. ❻Harlem then gradually became the "Black" part of New York City because Blacks were not really allowed to live anywhere else.

この問題英文の長さは約400語です。

第1段落❶はタイトルでもある「ハーレム・ルネサンス」とは「初めての集中である」としていて、初めてアフリカ系アメリカ人の資本、文化、芸術、政治が結集した時代だと述べています。❷❸では、作家、エンターテイナー、知識人、指導者の人物名を紹介しています。❹では「このような人々が一つの地域に結集することは非常にまれだった」として、この段落を締めくくっています。

．．．

第2段落

第2段落では、ハーレム・ルネサンスの背景について説明していることが❶よりわかります。❷❸ではその理由として、南北戦争の後に、黒人が人種的暴力から逃れて北部に移住してきたこと、アメリカの工業力が向上し、北部の工場が頻繁に労働者不足に陥ったことを挙げています。❹から❻では、北部に人種差別の法規はなかったけれども、新参者が好きな場所に住めるわけではなかったため、土地所有者の振り分けによって次第にハーレムに「黒人」が居住することになったといういきさつについて述べています。

．．．

筆記③

第3段落

❶The Harlem Renaissance was impressive to many types of people. ❷Jazz music, for instance, had originated in Black communities, but by the 1920s was popular nationally as well. ❸Whites were attracted to the poetry readings of Zora Neale Hurston or orchestras led by Duke Ellington. ❹Europeans were also drawn to the Renaissance, some coming in specifically to experience the art, writings, politics, and music of Harlem. ❺Beyond being an African American cultural hub, it may have also been one of the first occasions where different races could mingle freely, outside the race rules that were common in most of the West.

第4段落

❶However, the Renaissance was not all positive. ❷As more Whites were drawn to the elite clubs of the neighborhood, some establishments, such as the famed Cotton Club, set out a Whites-only audience policy. ❸Its top-class entertainers, though, were almost all Black, as were the service staff. ❹The Great Depression of the 1930s ended the Renaissance, as widespread poverty made a night out on the town too much of a luxury for most Americans. ❺Formal race division itself came to an end several decades later, in the 1960s.

第3段落❶から、この段落ではハーレム・ルネサンスが人々に与えた強い印象について書かれているとわかります。❷❸で黒人のコミュニティで生まれたものの具体例としてジャズ音楽、白人を魅了した黒人の文化として詩の朗読や、あるオーケストラを挙げています。❹ではこのようなハーレムの芸術、著作、政治、音楽を体験するためにヨーロッパの人々が訪れたことを述べています。つまり、そこは、異なる人種が自由に交流できる場であったとまとめているのが❺です。

第4段落は、ルネサンスのネガティブな側面について述べていることが❶から推測できます。❷❸では「この地域に白人が増えてくると、白人客以外お断りという方針を打ち出した、コットンクラブのような店が出てきたが、そのクラブのトップクラスのエンターテイナーもスタッフも黒人だった」とあります。❹❺では、世界恐慌により、ルネサンスは幕を下ろし、1960年代に人種差別は終わりを告げたとまとめています。

筆記
③

(1) What do we learn about the Harlem Renaissance?

1 It was a training ground for the earliest Black intellectuals and entertainers from the Southern United States.

2 It was a New York City trend that began during the Civil War and then grew larger through the 1920s and 1930s.

3 It was a period when a large number of Black Americans who excelled in diverse fields gathered in a single place.

4 It was a section of New York City that had been slowly attracting both White and Black elites from other parts of the country.

---

(2) According to the author, why was Harlem the location of the renaissance?

1 Northern housing customs of the time forced most African Americans to live in certain neighborhoods of major cities.

2 The neighborhood had been the home of various high-performing talent even before the start of the American Civil War.

3 It was the last stop of the Great Migration that started in the American South and ended in the North.

4 It was ideal as a place where both customers and entertainers from the northern and southern states could mingle.

---

(3) How did establishments such as the Cotton Club operate?

1 They had both Black and White people as entertainers and serving staff, but only Blacks were allowed in as audience members.

2 They gave preference to Whites by allowing them in first, while forcing Black audience members to wait outside.

3 They showed top Black performers on stage and had Black staff serve an audience that was exclusively White.

4 They welcomed all types of American performers, but only allowed Black or White men as audience members or staff.

(1) 🔁 ハーレム・ルネサンスについて、何がわかりますか。
1 米国南部から来た初期の黒人の知識人や芸能人の訓練の場であった。
2 南北戦争中に始まり、1920年代から1930年代にかけて盛り上がったニューヨークの風潮である。
3 多様な分野に秀でた多くのアフリカ系アメリカ人が一堂に会した時代だった。
4 ニューヨーク市内で、白人と黒人のエリートが他の地域から徐々に引きつけられてきた一角だった。

🔍 第1段落**②③**に「ラングストン・ヒューズなどの作家から、ルイ・アームストロングやジョセフィン・ベイカーなどのエンターテイナーまで、多分野にわたり当時の著名なアメリカ黒人が集結した。また、ウィリアム・エドワード・バーグハード・デュボイスのような知識人やマーカス・ガーベイのような公民権運動の指導者も含まれていた」とあり、この情報から、問1に解答することができます。

✏️ ☐ trend 動向 ☐ excel 秀でている ☐ diverse 多様な

- -

(2) 🔁 筆者によると、なぜハーレムがルネサンスの舞台となったのでしょうか。
1 当時の北部の住宅供給の慣習により、ほとんどのアフリカ系アメリカ人は大都市の特定の地域に住むことを余儀なくされていた。
2 アメリカ南北戦争が始まる以前から、この地区にはさまざまな優秀な人材が集まっていた。
3 アメリカ南部から北部への大移動の終着点であった。
4 北部の州と南部の州から来た客と芸能人が交流する場所として理想的であった。

🔍 第2段落**④**から**⑥**に「新参者が好きな場所に住めるわけではなかった。北部の土地所有者たちは、非公式に地域ごとにグループを分け、ハーレムは次第にニューヨークの「黒人」地域となった。なぜなら、黒人は他の場所に住むことが許されなかったからである」とあります。ここから問2の解答がわかります。

✏️ ☐ mingle 混ざる

- -

(3) 🔁 コットンクラブのような施設はどのように運営されていたのでしょうか。
1 芸能人や接客係には黒人と白人の両方がいたが、観客として入れるのは黒人だけであった。
2 白人を優先して先に入場させ、黒人の観客は外で待たせていた。
3 黒人のトップスターをステージに立たせ、もっぱら白人だけの観客のサービスを黒人スタッフにさせた。
4 あらゆるタイプのアメリカ人の出演者を歓迎したが、観客やスタッフは黒人か白人の男性しか入場を許されなかった。

🔍 第4段落**②③**に「この地域にある上流階級向けの娯楽の場に引き寄せられる白人が増えてくると、有名な「コットンクラブ」のように、白人以外お断りという方針を打ち出した店もあった。そのクラブのトップクラスのエンターテイナーのほとんどが黒人で、接客スタッフも黒人であった」とあります。ここから問3の答えがわかります。

✏️ ☐ give preference 優遇する ☐ exclusively もっぱら

Harlem Renaissance

第1段落

❶ The Harlem Renaissance was perhaps the first concentration of African American capital, culture, art, and politics.

❷ Spanning the 1920s, it brought together a varied group of high-profile Black Americans of the day, from writers such as Langston Hughes to entertainers such as Louis Armstrong and Josephine Baker.

❸ It also included intellectuals such as W.E.B. Du Bois and civil rights leaders such as Marcus Garvey.

❹ There had never been such a collaboration of African American talent in one neighborhood and there might never be again.

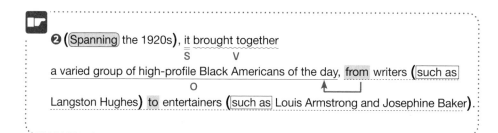

❷ (Spanning the 1920s), it brought together
                S   V

a varied group of high-profile Black Americans of the day, from writers (such as
                      O

Langston Hughes) to entertainers (such as Louis Armstrong and Josephine Baker).

ハーレム・ルネサンス

第1段落

❶ ハーレム・ルネサンスは、アフリカ系アメリカ人の資本、文化、芸術、政治が初めて結集した時代といえる。

❷ 1920年代には、ラングストン・ヒューズなどの作家から、ルイ・アームストロングやジョセフィン・ベイカーなどのエンターテイナーまで、多分野にわたり当時の著名なアメリカ黒人が集結した。

❸ また、ウィリアム・エドワード・バーグハード・デュボイスのような知識人やマーカス・ガーベイのような公民権運動の指導者も含まれていた。

❹ このような才能のあるアフリカ系アメリカ人が一つの地域に結集することは、かつてなかったことであり、今後もありえないことかもしれない。

☐ renaissance 復興、再生　❶☐ concentration 集中、集結　☐ capital 資本
❷☐ span (時間)にわたる　☐ brought together …を集める　☐ varied さまざまな
☐ high-profile 注目を集める　☐ of the day 当時の、現代の　❸☐ intellectual 知識人
❹☐ collaboration 共同

筆記③

第2段落

❶ The Harlem Renaissance emerged for a number of reasons.

❷ Millions of Blacks had migrated to the North after the 1860s Civil War, in search of better pay and better lives—away from the racial violence of the South.

❸ This Great Migration accelerated after the 1880s, as American industrial power advanced and new factories—primarily in the North—were regularly short of workers.

❹ While the North did not have a legal code of racism as the South did, these newcomers could not live wherever they wanted.

❺ In fact, Northern property owners informally separated groups by neighborhood.

❻ Harlem then gradually became the "Black" part of New York City because Blacks were not really allowed to live anywhere else.

❷ Millions of Blacks had migrated to the North
　　　　S　　　　　　　　　V
after the 1860s Civil War, (☐ in search of better pay and better lives
　　　　　　　　　　　　　　┗→beingを省略した分詞構文
—away from the racial violence of the South).
┗→ダーシ(—)で直前の内容を具体的に説明

❸ This Great Migration accelerated after the 1880s,
　　　　　S　　　　　　　　　V
(as American industrial power advanced and
理由を表す副詞節　　S'①　　　　　　V'①
new factories (—primarily in the North—) were regularly short of workers).
　　S'②　　　　　　　　　　　　　　　　　V'②　　　　　　C'

❶ ハーレム・ルネサンスが起こった背景には、さまざまな理由がある。

❷ 1860年代の南北戦争の後、何百万人もの黒人が、南部の人種的暴力から逃れ、より良い賃金と生活を求めて北部に移住してきた。

❸ この大移動が1880年代以降に加速したのは、アメリカの工業力が向上し、主に北部の新しい工場が恒常的に労働者不足に陥ったからである。

❹ 北部には南部のような人種差別の法規はなかったが、新参者が好きな場所に住めるわけではなかった。

❺ 実際、北部の土地所有者たちは、非公式に地域ごとにグループを分けていた。

❻ そして、ハーレムは次第にニューヨークの「黒人」地域となった。なぜなら、黒人は他の場所に住むことが許されなかったからである。

---

❶ ☐ emerge 出現する、発生する **❷** ☐ migrate 移住する、移動する ☐ in search of …を探し求めて
☐ pay 賃金 ☐ racial 人種の **❸** ☐ migration 移住、移動 ☐ accelerate 加速する
☐ industrial 工業の ☐ advance 進歩する、向上する ☐ primarily 主に、最初に
☐ short of …が不足して **❹** ☐ legal code 法規 ☐ racism 人種差別 ☐ newcomer 新参者
❺ ☐ property 所有地、財産 ☐ informally 非公式に **❻** ☐ gradually 徐々に、次第に
☐ allow X to *do* X が…するのを許可する、X に…させておく

筆記 ③

第3段落

❶ The Harlem Renaissance was impressive to many types of people.

❷ Jazz music, for instance, had originated in Black communities, but by the 1920s was popular nationally as well.

❸ Whites were attracted to the poetry readings of Zora Neale Hurston or orchestras led by Duke Ellington.

❹ Europeans were also drawn to the Renaissance, some coming in specifically to experience the art, writings, politics, and music of Harlem.

❺ Beyond being an African American cultural hub, it may have also been one of the first occasions where different races could mingle freely, outside the race rules that were common in most of the West.

---

❺ (Beyond being an African American cultural hub),

it may have also been one of the first occasions (where different races
S   V   C   S'

could mingle freely,
     V'

(outside the race rules (that were common in most of the West))).
  → beingを省略した   S''   V''   C''
    分詞構文

❶ ハーレム・ルネサンスは、さまざまな人々に強い印象を与えた。

❷ 例えば、ジャズ音楽は黒人のコミュニティで生まれたものだが、1920年代には全米でも人気を博した。

❸ 白人は、ゾラ・ニール・ハーストンの詩の朗読やデューク・エリントン率いるオーケストラに魅了された。

❹ ヨーロッパの人々もルネサンスに惹かれ、ハーレムの芸術、著作、政治、音楽を体験するという明確な目的で訪れる者もいた。

❺ そこはアフリカ系アメリカ人の文化の拠点であったということにとどまらず、西洋で一般的だった人種間のルールにとらわれず、異なる人種が自由に交流できる最初の場でもあったのだろう。

❶ □ impressive 強い印象を与える　❷ □ for instance 例えば　□ originate 源を発する
□ nationally 全国的に　□ as well そのうえ…も　❸ □ White 白人
□ be attracted to …に引き付けられる　❹ □ draw …を引き付ける
□ come in …に入って来る、…に入場する　□ specifically 特に、明確に　□ experience …を経験する
❺ □ beyond …を越えて　□ hub (活動の)中心　□ occasion (特定の)時、場合　□ mingle つき合う

第4段落

❶ However, the Renaissance was not all positive.

❷ As more Whites were drawn to the elite clubs of the neighborhood, some establishments, such as the famed Cotton Club, set out a Whites-only audience policy.

❸ Its top-class entertainers, though, were almost all Black, as were the service staff.

❹ The Great Depression of the 1930s ended the Renaissance, as widespread poverty made a night out on the town too much of a luxury for most Americans.

❺ Formal race division itself came to an end several decades later, in the 1960s.

---

❹ The Great Depression of the 1930s ended the Renaissance,
　　　　　　　　S　　　　　　　　　　　　V　　　　　O

主節の後につける補足的なas節
(as widespread poverty made a night out on the town
　　　　　　S'　　　　　　　V'　　　　　　O'
too much of a luxury for most Americans).
　　　　C'

❶ しかし、ルネサンスは決してポジティブなものばかりではなかった。

❷ この地域にある上流階級向けの娯楽の場に引き寄せられる白人が増えてくると、有名な「コットンクラブ」のように、白人以外お断りという方針を打ち出した店もあった。

❸ ただ、そのクラブのトップクラスのエンターテイナーのほとんどが黒人であり、接客担当のスタッフも黒人であった。

❹ 1930年代の世界恐慌により、ルネサンスは終わりを告げ、貧困が蔓延し、アメリカ人にとって街で一夜を過ごすことはあまりにも贅沢なものとなってしまった。

❺ そして、その数十年後の1960年代に、人種差別は終わりを告げたのである。

❷□ elite エリート、選ばれた者　□ establishment 設立物　□ famed 名高い　□ set out …を述べる
❹□ the Great Depression（1929年10月にアメリカに始まった）大恐慌
　□ widespread 広く行き渡った　□ poverty 貧困　□ night out 外で楽しく過ごす夜
　□ luxury ぜいたくな　❺□ division 分割　□ come to an end 終わる　□ decade 10年間

問題英文の読み方 P.374　解説・正解 P.378　訳・語句 P.380

Poster Art of Poland

　Lithography, or more simply poster-making, dates back to at least 1798. In an era of low literacy, posters were easier for common people to understand. In addition, they were attractive, with bright colors and impressive lines. Unlike pamphlets, they could be pasted on the interior or exterior of buildings, and could often endure a few days in the rain or snow. In the United States, posters were usually for business: early 19th century American posters promoted various medicines, tools, travel, and foods because they easily and directly caught the attention of consumers and were not expensive. In France, however, posters were being transformed into real art. French poster makers experimented with unique colors and themes, and created characters that were lifelike.

　Surprisingly, 19th century Poland became a hub of poster design and its broader field, graphic design. Polish designs became known for their complex images and began to win various European awards. This was despite Moscow's intensifying "Russification" efforts against Poles from the 1860s. Poland had been absorbed by Russia in the 18th century, and Poles were too politically and militarily weak to challenge Moscow. However, they could fight back through posters with hidden anti-government sentiments or ideas of independence. Posters of King Sobieski, the Polish king who had defeated invading Turks at Vienna, for instance, conveyed a second meaning: freedom from Imperial Russia. Moscow authorities were not blind to the hidden meanings in Polish graphic art, but did not feel confident enough to use mass arrests or other tools to stop the artists.

　When Poland regained its independence at the end of World War I, its poster art continued to develop in new ways. This period saw the strong growth of poster art under Tadeusz Gronowski, perhaps Poland's greatest graphic artist. A graduate of both the Warsaw University of Technology and the famed art school École Supérieure des Beaux-Arts of Paris, Gronowski eventually elevated poster art to its highest form. His work was featured in international fairs and chosen to be the logo for the national Polish airlines, LOT, in the 1920s. When Poland fell under Russian control again after World War II, Polish poster art lost the freedom of expression it had enjoyed in the 1920s and 1930s. Only after Poland finally escaped Russian control in 1991 could its graphic art become free again.

(1) What is said about the significance of poster art?

1 It has been used by national leaders at times to reach out and influence the populations of other nations.

2 It enjoys the freedom to be displayed on the inside and outside of buildings regardless of how the property owners feel about it.

3 It helps businesses advertise products and services in a more direct and cheaper way to a large number of people.

4 It differs from other types of printed materials in that it carries images and texts that politically challenge foreign governments.

(2) The example of King Sobieski illustrates how

1 strong leadership is needed in times of crisis to decide on what print messages are to be sent to people.

2 the freedom of a nation can only be won through art when it has been under centuries of foreign control.

3 Polish people could always prevent their enemies such as Turks and Russians from taking over their nation because their leaders were strong.

4 images in posters can communicate a second meaning to people when it is not possible to directly convey ideas.

(3) How did Polish independence affect graphic design?

1 It allowed local artists such as Tadeusz Gronowski to raise this art to an internationally award-winning level while its absence took that away.

2 Constant efforts at using anti-government images in local posters finally resulted in the collapse of communism in Poland.

3 Poster projects in Paris showed the Polish artists there how they could learn and bring the spirit of artistic freedom to Warsaw.

4 Russian control forced Polish people to work on more ordinary artistic topics, such as graphic designs for airline logos.

筆記③

Poster Art of Poland

❶Lithography, or more simply poster-making, dates back to at least 1798. ❷In an era of low literacy, posters were easier for common people to understand. ❸In addition, they were attractive, with bright colors and impressive lines. ❹Unlike pamphlets, they could be pasted on the interior or exterior of buildings, and could often endure a few days in the rain or snow. ❺In the United States, posters were usually for business: early 19th century American posters promoted various medicines, tools, travel, and foods because they easily and directly caught the attention of consumers and were not expensive. ❻In France, however, posters were being transformed into real art. ❼French poster makers experimented with unique colors and themes, and created characters that were lifelike.

❶Surprisingly, 19th century Poland became a hub of poster design and its broader field, graphic design. ❷Polish designs became known for their complex images and began to win various European awards. ❸This was despite Moscow's intensifying "Russification" efforts against Poles from the 1860s. ❹Poland had been absorbed by Russia in the 18th century, and Poles were too politically and militarily weak to challenge Moscow. ❺However, they could fight back through posters with hidden anti-government sentiments or ideas of independence. ❻Posters of King Sobieski, the Polish king who had defeated invading Turks at Vienna, for instance, conveyed a second meaning: freedom from Imperial Russia. ❼Moscow authorities were not blind to the hidden meanings in Polish graphic art, but did not feel confident enough to use mass arrests or other tools to stop the artists.

この問題英文の長さは約400語です。

タイトルに「ポーランドのポスター芸術」とあり、❶の「ポスター作りの歴史は1798年にさかのぼる」で始まっています。❷から❹ではポスターが流行った背景として「識字率が低かった当時は、ポスターの方が理解されやすく、鮮やかで魅力的で、雨や雪にも耐えられるものだった」と述べています。ポーランド以外の国でのポスターについて、❺では「アメリカではポスターはビジネスに使われ、19世紀初頭ではさまざまな宣伝に役立った」と述べ、続く❻❼では「フランスではポスターは芸術へと変化し、独自の色彩やテーマで、実物そっくりのキャラクターをつくった」と紹介しています。

第2段落でようやく19世紀のポーランドのポスターデザインの話になり、❶から「グラフィックデザインの拠点となった」で始まっています。❷から❺では「ポーランドのデザインはヨーロッパのさまざまな賞を獲得したが、それはロシアがポーランドに対してロシア化工作を強める中でのことであった。ポーランドは18世紀にロシアに併合され、ポーランド人は政治的にも軍事的にも弱かったが、ポスターでなら抵抗ができた」と、ポーランドでポスターのデザインが発展した背景が書かれています。その具体例を❻で「ポーランド王、ソビエスキーのポスターはロシアからの解放という意味を含んでいた」と挙げ、続く❼では「ロシア当局はポーランドのアートに隠された意味についてわかっていたが、それを止めるに至らなかった」とあることから、その表現方法が発展していった様子がうかがえます。

筆記③

❶When Poland regained its independence at the end of World War I, its poster art continued to develop in new ways. ❷This period saw the strong growth of poster art under Tadeusz Gronowski, perhaps Poland's greatest graphic artist. ❸A graduate of both the Warsaw University of Technology and the famed art school École Supérieure des Beaux-Arts of Paris, Gronowski eventually elevated poster art to its highest form. ❹His work was featured in international fairs and chosen to be the logo for the national Polish airlines, LOT, in the 1920s. ❺When Poland fell under Russian control again after World War II, Polish poster art lost the freedom of expression it had enjoyed in the 1920s and 1930s. ❻Only after Poland finally escaped Russian control in 1991 could its graphic art become free again.

前の段落ではロシアに併合されていた時代について述べていましたが、❶では「第一次世界大戦の終わりにポーランドが独立を取り戻すと、ポスター芸術は新たな発展を遂げた」とあり、独立後の発展について述べていくと予測できます。❷から❹で、「ポスター芸術はポーランド最大のアーティスト、タデウシュ・グロノフスキの下で発展したのだが、彼はポスター芸術を最高の形に高め、彼の作品は1920年代には航空会社のロゴに採用された」と、具体例について書かれています。その後は❺❻にあるように、「第二次世界大戦後、ポーランドが再びロシアの支配下に入ると、ポーランドのポスター芸術も表現の自由を失い、1991年にロシアの支配から抜けるとポーランドのグラフィックアートは再び自由になった」とポスターの表現の自由度から見た社会の動乱との関係について述べて、文章を締めくくっています。

筆記③

(1) What is said about the significance of poster art?

1 It has been used by national leaders at times to reach out and influence the populations of other nations.

2 It enjoys the freedom to be displayed on the inside and outside of buildings regardless of how the property owners feel about it.

3 It helps businesses advertise products and services in a more direct and cheaper way to a large number of people.

4 It differs from other types of printed materials in that it carries images and texts that politically challenge foreign governments.

(2) The example of King Sobieski illustrates how

1 strong leadership is needed in times of crisis to decide on what print messages are to be sent to people.

2 the freedom of a nation can only be won through art when it has been under centuries of foreign control.

3 Polish people could always prevent their enemies such as Turks and Russians from taking over their nation because their leaders were strong.

4 images in posters can communicate a second meaning to people when it is not possible to directly convey ideas.

(3) How did Polish independence affect graphic design?

1 It allowed local artists such as Tadeusz Gronowski to raise this art to an internationally award-winning level while its absence took that away.

2 Constant efforts at using anti-government images in local posters finally resulted in the collapse of communism in Poland.

3 Poster projects in Paris showed the Polish artists there how they could learn and bring the spirit of artistic freedom to Warsaw.

4 Russian control forced Polish people to work on more ordinary artistic topics, such as graphic designs for airline logos.

(1) 🔲 ポスター芸術の意義について、どのようなことが言われていますか。

1 諸国の指導者が他国の人々に働きかけ、影響を与えるために使うことがあった。

2 所有者の意向に関係なく、建物の内外に自由に掲示することができる。

3 企業が商品やサービスをより直接的かつ安価に、多くの人々に宣伝できるようにする。

4 他の印刷物とは、外国政府に対して政治的な戦いを挑むような画像や文章が掲載されている点で異なる。

🔍 第1段落❷❸の「識字率の低かった時代、ポスターは庶民にとって理解しやすいものだった。また、鮮やかな色彩と印象的な線で構成された魅力的なものであった」と❺の「アメリカではポスターはビジネスに使われることが多かった。19世紀初頭のアメリカのポスターは消費者の目に留まりやすく、高価でなかったため、さまざまな薬や道具、旅行、食品などを宣伝した」がポスターの意義を述べているものとして問1を解くヒントとなります。

✏️ ☐ reach out 手を伸ばす ☐ regardless of …にかかわらず ☐ help X do X が…するのに役立つ
☐ in that 節 …という点で

- -

(2) 🔲 ソビエスキ王の例が物語っているのは

1 危機に際して、国民に送る印刷物に書くメッセージを決定するためには、強力なリーダーシップが必要であることだ。

2 何世紀にもわたって外国の支配下にあるとき、国の自由は芸術によってしか勝ち取れないことだ。

3 指導者が強かったからポーランド人はトルコ人やロシア人などの敵に国を乗っ取られるのを常に防ぐことができたことだ。

4 ある概念を直接伝えることができない場合でも、ポスターの画像は人々に別の意味を伝えることができることだ。

🔍 King Sobieski のポスターは第2段落❺の内容の具体例として挙げられています。それを手掛かりに、もとの文を見ると❹❺「ポーランド人は政治的にも軍事的にも弱くモスクワに抗うことはできなかったが、反政府的な感情や独立の思想を秘めたポスターで抵抗することができた」とあることから、問2の答えがわかります。

✏️ ☐ take over …を乗っ取る ☐ convey …を伝達する

- -

(3) 🔲 ポーランドの独立はグラフィックデザインにどのような影響を与えましたか。

1 独立していた時期は、タデウシュ・グロノフスキのような地元のアーティストはこの芸術を国際的な賞を受けるレベルまで引き上げられたが、独立が失われるとそれができなくなってしまった。

2 反政府的なイメージを地元のポスターに使用する絶え間ない努力は、最終的にポーランドの共産主義を崩壊させることになった。

3 パリでのポスタープロジェクトは、現地のポーランド人アーティストに、いかにして芸術的自由の精神を学び、ワルシャワに持ち込むことができるかを示した。

4 ロシアの支配により、ポーランド人は航空会社のロゴのグラフィックデザインなど、より一般的な芸術的テーマに取り組むことを余儀なくされた。

🔍 第3段落全体が問3の答えを導く手がかりになります。❶から❹の「ポーランド独立時のポスターデザインがタデウシュ・グロノフスキによって国際的な舞台を得るまでに高められた」こと、❺の「再び支配されるとその表現の自由が失われた」こと、❻の「支配から抜け出し自由になった」ことを関連づけることで正解の選択肢が選べます。

🚩 **(1) 3 (2) 4 (3) 1**

Poster Art of Poland

第1段落

❶ Lithography, or more simply poster-making, dates back to at least 1798.

❷ In an era of low literacy, posters were easier for common people to understand.

❸ In addition, they were attractive, with bright colors and impressive lines.

❹ Unlike pamphlets, they could be pasted on the interior or exterior of buildings, and could often endure a few days in the rain or snow.

❺ In the United States, posters were usually for business: early 19th century American posters promoted various medicines, tools, travel, and foods because they easily and directly caught the attention of consumers and were not expensive.

❻ In France, however, posters were being transformed into real art.

❼ French poster makers experimented with unique colors and themes, and created characters that were lifelike.

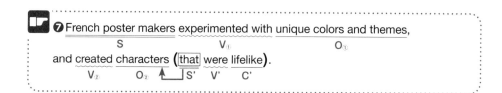

ポーランドのポスター芸術

第1段落

❶ リトグラフ、あるいはもっと簡単に言えばポスター作りの歴史は、少なくとも1798年にまでさかのぼる。

❷ 識字率の低かった時代、ポスターは庶民にとって理解しやすいものだった。

❸ また、鮮やかな色彩と印象的な線で構成された魅力的なものであった。

❹ パンフレットと違って、建物の内外に貼ることができ、たいてい雨や雪に数日間耐えられる。

❺ アメリカではポスターはビジネスに使われることが多かった。19世紀初頭のアメリカのポスターは消費者の目に留まりやすく高価でなかったため、さまざまな薬や道具、旅行、食品などを宣伝した。

❻ しかし、フランスでは、ポスターは芸術へと変貌を遂げつつあった。

❼ フランスのポスター職人たちは、独自の色彩やテーマで試行錯誤し、実物そっくりのキャラクターを作り上げた。

❶□ lithography 石版印刷 □ date back to …にさかのぼる **❷**□ era 時代、年代
□ literacy 読み書きの能力 **❸**□ in addition それに加えて **❹**□ unlike …と異なって
□ paste on …に貼る □ exterior 外側 □ endure …に耐える **❺**□ promote …を売り込む
❻□ transform A into B A を B に変化させる **❼**□ experiment with …で実験をする
□ lifelike 生きているような

筆記③

第2段落

❶ Surprisingly, 19th century Poland became a hub of poster design and its broader field, graphic design.

❷ Polish designs became known for their complex images and began to win various European awards.

❸ This was despite Moscow's intensifying "Russification" efforts against Poles from the 1860s.

❹ Poland had been absorbed by Russia in the 18th century, and Poles were too politically and militarily weak to challenge Moscow.

❺ However, they could fight back through posters with hidden anti-government sentiments or ideas of independence.

❻ Posters of King Sobieski, the Polish king who had defeated invading Turks at Vienna, for instance, conveyed a second meaning: freedom from Imperial Russia.

❼ Moscow authorities were not blind to the hidden meanings in Polish graphic art, but did not feel confident enough to use mass arrests or other tools to stop the artists.

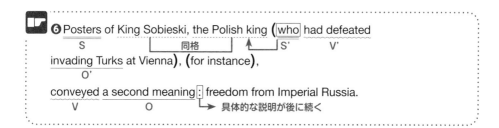

❻Posters of King Sobieski, the Polish king (who had defeated
　　S　　　　　　　同格　　　　　　S'　　V'
invading Turks at Vienna), (for instance),
　　　　O'
conveyed a second meaning: freedom from Imperial Russia.
　　V　　　　　O　　　　→ 具体的な説明が後に続く

❶ 意外なことに、19世紀のポーランドは、ポスターデザイン、そしてより広い分野となるグラフィックデザインの拠点となった。

❷ ポーランドのデザインは複雑なイメージで知られるようになり、ヨーロッパのさまざまな賞を獲得するようになった。

❸ それはモスクワ（＝ロシア政府）が1860年代からポーランドに対してロシア化工作を強める中でのことであった。

❹ ポーランドは18世紀にロシアに併合されており、ポーランド人がモスクワに抗うには政治的にも軍事的にも弱かった。

❺ しかし、反政府的な感情や独立の思想を秘めたポスターで抵抗することができた。

❻ 例えば、ウィーンでトルコ軍の侵略を破ったポーランド王ソビエスキのポスターは、帝政ロシアからの解放という第二の意味を含んでいた。

❼ ロシア当局は、ポーランドのグラフィックアートに隠された意味に気がついていないわけではなかったが、アーティストたちを止めるために集団検挙などの手段を取るほどの確信はなかった。

❶□ hub 中心　❷□ Polish ポーランド（語・人）の　□ award 賞　❸□ intensify 強まる、激化する　□ russification ロシア化　□ effort 活動　❹□ militarily 軍事的に　□ challenge …を疑う、挑戦する　❺□ fight back 抵抗する　□ hidden 隠された、秘密の　□ sentiment 感情　❻□ defeat …を負かす　□ invade 侵略する　□ Turk トルコ人　□ convey …を伝える　❼□ authorities 当局、官庁　□ be blind to …に気がつかない　□ confident 自信がある　□ arrest 逮捕

筆記 ③

第3段落

❶ When Poland regained its independence at the end of World War I, its poster art continued to develop in new ways.

❷ This period saw the strong growth of poster art under Tadeusz Gronowski, perhaps Poland's greatest graphic artist.

❸ A graduate of both the Warsaw University of Technology and the famed art school École Supérieure des Beaux-Arts of Paris, Gronowski eventually elevated poster art to its highest form.

❹ His work was featured in international fairs and chosen to be the logo for the national Polish airlines, LOT, in the 1920s.

❺ When Poland fell under Russian control again after World War II, Polish poster art lost the freedom of expression it had enjoyed in the 1920s and 1930s.

❻ Only after Poland finally escaped Russian control in 1991 could its graphic art become free again.

---

❸ A graduate of both the Warsaw University of Technology
S_1～

and the famed art school École Supérieure des Beaux-Arts of Paris,
～S_1

Gronowski eventually elevated poster art to its highest form.
S_2（S_1と同格）　　　V　　　O

❻ (Only after Poland finally escaped Russian control in 1991)
　　　　　　　S'　　　　V'　　　O'

could its graphic art become free again.
V～　　S　　　～V　C
倒置

第3段落

❶ 第一次世界大戦の終わりにポーランドが独立を取り戻すと、ポーランドのポスター芸術は新たな発展を遂げることになる。

❷ この時期、ポスター芸術は、おそらくポーランド最大のグラフィックアーティストであるタデウシュ・グロノフスキの下で力強く発展した。

❸ ワルシャワ工科大学とパリ国立高等美術学校を卒業したグロノフスキは、やがてポスター芸術を最高の形にまで高めていく。

❹ 彼の作品は国際的な見本市で紹介され、1920年代にはポーランド国営航空会社 LOT のロゴに採用された。

❺ 第二次世界大戦後、ポーランドが再びロシアの支配下に入ると、ポーランドのポスター芸術は1920年代から30年代にかけて享受していた表現の自由を失ってしまった。

❻ 1991年にロシアの支配を脱して、ようやくポーランドのグラフィックアートは再び自由になったのである。

❶☐ regain …を取り戻す・奪還する ☐ independence 独立 **❸**☐ graduate 卒業生
☐ eventually ついに ☐ elevate …を高める **❹**☐ feature …を大々的に紹介する
❺☐ freedom of expression 表現の自由 ☐ enjoy …を享受する・もっている

問題英文の読み方 P.390　解説・正解 P.394　訳・語句 P.398

How Should We Teach Reading?

Reading ability forms the basis of a child's education. For many decades, researchers have debated the best way to teach this critical subject. Studies show that children who fall behind in reading have great difficulty in catching up on it later, and this reduces their chances of achieving their life goals. Even knowing this, scholars have differed as to how children should learn to read. Some scholars have suggested that reading is a free and natural process, so children should be surrounded with books, and they will use these to figure out how to read on their own.

However, experiments show that only 1-7% of children can actually do this. For the vast majority of children, simply setting up printed text around them will not help them learn to read. Other scholars suggest memorization of basic, high-frequency words, perhaps with pictures. This word memorization helps, but research shows that this is often a stressful approach for children, who struggle to remember so many words. This approach also fails to teach the underlying language system, which children then have to master on their own. Other scholars have focused on phonics: having kids master the letters and the sounds that they make, and then learn how to combine these into words and sentences. Phonics has been proven useful because it helps associate letters of an alphabet and letter combinations with specific sounds. Children can also experiment with phonics, trying to create words of their own. When they don't know what a word means, they can still make reasonable estimates, based on the context in which a word is placed. In all these ways, phonics makes a great bridge from learning the alphabet to full reading, writing, and spelling. Yet, phonics still requires the child to remember a large amount of letter combinations.

The newest approach is that of phonemes. In this approach, children learn the sounds of a language and how these sounds are arranged and rearranged to create words. Research has shown that children can master this system much easier than trying to remember entire words or letter combinations. Phonemes are similar to phonics, but are much easier because children have already been exposed to these sounds in their everyday speech. Phoneme study just helps them organize these sounds into a system. Later, the child can move on to phonics—and phonics will make much more sense at that point, since the child will be able to match letter combinations to sounds that he or she already knows and practices.

(1) What is true of the natural process of learning reading?

    1 Children are guided slowly through a variety of texts until they memorize them and then start to read on their own.

    2 Only about 1-7% of children who use this method fail to achieve a high reading level by the time they finish schooling.

    3 Children can pick the printed books that are presented to them and then eventually teach themselves to read them.

    4 It suits children's emotions, since they do not feel as stressed as they usually do when they try to memorize words.

(2) One of the main advantages of phonics is that

    1 children can learn to understand the basics of reading by coming to understand how letters combine to form certain sounds.

    2 students immediately come to find that some letter combinations create the exact same sounds as other combinations.

    3 learners see that the words formed by letters of an alphabet sometimes hold the same meaning across languages.

    4 experts have proved that certain phonetic sounds appear across every language and reading is made easier when these sounds appear.

(3) According to the author, what is a risk of studying phonics without phonemes?

1 Children could mistake the letter or sound combination of the phonic system with the sounds introduced in the phonemic system.

2 Students may lose interest in reading from having to memorize strange sounds that they do not hear in day-to-day spoken language.

3 Learners must form words from letter combinations, without knowing the sound each of the letters make.

4 Children must learn a large number of letter combinations, without a clear understanding of the major sounds of the language.

How Should We Teach Reading?

❶Reading ability forms the basis of a child's education. ❷For many decades, researchers have debated the best way to teach this critical subject. ❸Studies show that children who fall behind in reading have great difficulty in catching up on it later, and this reduces their chances of achieving their life goals. ❹Even knowing this, scholars have differed as to how children should learn to read. ❺Some scholars have suggested that reading is a free and natural process, so children should be surrounded with books, and they will use these to figure out how to read on their own.

❶However, experiments show that only 1-7% of children can actually do this. ❷For the vast majority of children, simply setting up printed text around them will not help them learn to read. ❸Other scholars suggest memorization of basic, high-frequency words, perhaps with pictures. ❹This word memorization helps, but research shows that this is often a stressful approach for children, who struggle to remember so many words. ❺This approach also fails to teach the underlying language system, which children then have to master on their own. ❻Other scholars have focused on phonics: having kids master the letters and the sounds that they make, and then learn how to combine these into words and sentences. ❼Phonics has been proven useful because it helps associate letters of an alphabet and letter combinations with specific sounds. ❽Children can also experiment with phonics, trying to create words of their own. ❾When they don't know what a word means, they can still make reasonable estimates, based on the context in which a word is placed. ❿In all these ways, phonics makes a great bridge from learning the alphabet to full reading, writing, and spelling. ⓫Yet, phonics still requires the child to remember a large amount of letter combinations.

第1段落

この問題英文の長さは約400語です。

タイトルは「読み方をどう教えるべきか」で、❶❷では「読む能力は子どもの教育の基礎を形成するもので、研究者はこれを教えるための最良の方法について議論してきた」と言っています。❸では、読むのが苦手な子どもについて、「その遅れを取り戻すのが非常に難しい」とあり、❹で「それでも、どのように読み方を学ぶべきかについては意見が分かれている」と述べています。❺では「読むということは自然なプロセスなのだから、子どもを本に囲まれた環境に置けば、読み方がわかるようになる」というある学者の見解を紹介しています。

第2段落

第2段落は However で始まるので、前の段落の最後に出てきた見解に対する反対の意見が展開されると予想できます。❶❷で「実際に本に囲まれただけで読み方がわかる子どもは少なく、大多数の子どもは周りに活字を並べられただけでは読み方を覚えることはできない」と言っています。❸から❺では、別の学者の見解が紹介され、「絵を見ながら頻出単語を暗記することは効果があるが、子どもたちにとってはストレスになることが多く、この方法では基本的な言語体系を教えることはできないため、子どもたちは自分で習得しなければならない」と述べています。❻から❽では、さらに別の学者が「フォニックス」に焦点を当て、「文字とその音を覚えて単語や文を作ることにより、文字と音を結び付けやすくすることができ、子どもたちが、フォニックスを使って、自分で言葉を作ることもできる」と紹介しています。❾❿では、フォニックスの長所を「言葉の意味がわからなくても、文脈から推測できることもあり、フォニックスがアルファベットの学習から読み、書き、綴りの学習への橋渡しとなる」とまとめていますが、この段落の最終文の⓫では、フォニックスを学ぶ場合の注意点として「子どもは大量の文字の組み合わせを覚えなければならない」と述べ、次の段落への問題提起をしています。

❶The newest approach is that of phonemes. ❷In this approach, children learn the sounds of a language and how these sounds are arranged and rearranged to create words. ❸Research has shown that children can master this system much easier than trying to remember entire words or letter combinations. ❹Phonemes are similar to phonics, but are much easier because children have already been exposed to these sounds in their everyday speech. ❺Phoneme study just helps them organize these sounds into a system. ❻Later, the child can move on to phonics—and phonics will make much more sense at that point, since the child will be able to match letter combinations to sounds that he or she already knows and practices.

前の段落のフォニックスで学ぶ際の注意点を踏まえて、❶で最新のアプローチは「音素によるものだ」と紹介し、❷でそれについての説明として「子どもたちは言語の音と、その音がどのように配置され、並べ替えられて単語が作られるのか学ぶ」と述べています。❸では、音素学習の長所として「単語全体や文字の組み合わせを覚えるよりも、はるかに簡単に習得できる」と述べ、❹ではその理由を「音素はフォニックスと似ているが、子どもたちはすでに日常会話でこれらの音に触れているため」と、フォニックスとの対比を交えて説明しています。さらに、❺❻でも「音素の学習は音を体系的に整理するのに役立ち、その後でフォニックスの学習に移行してもよい。子どもは文字の組み合わせと知っている音とを一致させることができるので、その時点でフォニックスを学習した方が理解できるのだ」と、音素学習の利点をさらに挙げて文を締めくくっています。

筆記③

(1) What is true of the natural process of learning reading?

1 Children are guided slowly through a variety of texts until they memorize them and then start to read on their own.

2 Only about 1-7% of children who use this method fail to achieve a high reading level by the time they finish schooling.

3 Children can pick the printed books that are presented to them and then eventually teach themselves to read them.

4 It suits children's emotions, since they do not feel as stressed as they usually do when they try to memorize words.

(2) One of the main advantages of phonics is that

1 children can learn to understand the basics of reading by coming to understand how letters combine to form certain sounds.

2 students immediately come to find that some letter combinations create the exact same sounds as other combinations.

3 learners see that the words formed by letters of an alphabet sometimes hold the same meaning across languages.

4 experts have proved that certain phonetic sounds appear across every language and reading is made easier when these sounds appear.

(1) 📝 自然に読み方を学習していくというプロセスについて、正しいものはどれですか。

 1 子どもたちは、さまざまな文章を記憶するまでゆっくりと指導され、その後、自分で読み始める。

 2 この学習法だと、学校教育を終えるまでに高い読書レベルに到達できない子どもは、1～7%程度しかいない。

 3 子どもたちは、与えられた書籍を選び、やがて自分で読むことを学んでいく。

 4 単語を覚えようとするときほどストレスを感じないため、子どもの情緒に合っている。

🔍 まず問題文の the natural process of learning reading が指すものを特定しましょう。第1段落❺の学者の見解の中に reading is a free and natural process という表現がありますが、これ以降の内容が当てはまります。この部分を含む文を読むと、「読むということは自然なプロセスなのだから、子どもを本に囲まれた環境に置けば読み方がわかるようになる」という考え方が問1の選択肢の内容と合致することがわかります。本文では反対の見解なども展開しますが、あくまでここで問われているものに焦点をしぼって迷わないようにしましょう。

✎ □ schooling 学校教育　□ eventually やがて

. . . .

(2) 📝 フォニックスの主な長所の一つは、

 1 文字がどのように組み合わさって特定の音になるのかを理解することで、子どもたちが読み方の基本を身に付けることができることだ。

 2 ある文字の組み合わせが、他の組み合わせと全く同じ音になる場合があることを、生徒たちがすぐにわかるようになることだ。

 3 アルファベットの文字によって形成される単語が、ときに言語を超えて同じ意味を持つことを、学習者が理解することだ。

 4 特定の発音がどの言語にも現れ、これらの音が現れると読むのが容易になることを、専門家が証明していることだ。

🔍 第2段落の❻から❼に「フォニックスでは、文字とその音を覚えさせ、それらを組み合わせて単語や文を作る方法を学ばせる。アルファベットの個々の文字や文字の組み合わせと特定の音を結び付けやすくなることが証明されている」とあります。ここから、問2の答えがわかります。

✎ □ hold …を保持する　□ phonetic sound 音声

. . . .

(3) According to the author, what is a risk of studying phonics without phonemes?

1 Children could mistake the letter or sound combination of the phonic system with the sounds introduced in the phonemic system.

2 Students may lose interest in reading from having to memorize strange sounds that they do not hear in day-to-day spoken language.

3 Learners must form words from letter combinations, without knowing the sound each of the letters make.

4 Children must learn a large number of letter combinations, without a clear understanding of the major sounds of the language.

(3) 著者によると、音素を使わずにフォニックスを勉強することのリスクは何ですか。

1　子どもたちは、音声体系の文字や音の組み合わせを、音素体系に取り入れられた音と勘違いしてしまう可能性がある。

2　日常の話し言葉では聞かないような不思議な音を覚えなければならないため、生徒たちが読むことへの興味を失う可能性がある。

3　学習者はそれぞれの文字が作る音を知らない状態で、文字の組み合わせから単語を作らなければならない。

4　子どもたちは言語の主要な音を明確に理解することなく、多数の文字の組み合わせを学ばなければならない。

第2段落の⓫にフォニックスで学ぶ場合の注意点について「子どもは大量の文字の組み合わせを覚えなければならない」とあります。また、第3段落の❹ではフォニックスと対比させた場合の音素の利点として「音素はフォニックスと似ているが、子どもたちはすでに日常会話でこれらの音に触れているため、はるかに簡単だ」と説明しているので、フォニックスは「日常会話で触れているものを活用していない」と捉えると問3の答えを導くヒントになります。2もほとんどの点で一致しますが、読むことに対する興味を失うとまでは述べられていないので不正解となります。

□ phonemic 音素の　□ day-to-day 日々の

How Should We Teach Reading?

第1段落

❶ Reading ability forms the basis of a child's education.

❷ For many decades, researchers have debated the best way to teach this critical subject.

❸ Studies show that children who fall behind in reading have great difficulty in catching up on it later, and this reduces their chances of achieving their life goals.

❹ Even knowing this, scholars have differed as to how children should learn to read.

❺ Some scholars have suggested that reading is a free and natural process, so children should be surrounded with books, and they will use these to figure out how to read on their own.

---

❸ Studies show ([that] children ([who] fall behind in reading)
  S   V   O   S'₁ ∧ S''   V''

have great difficulty in catching up on it later,
V'₁   O'₁

and this reduces their chances of achieving their life goals).
   S'₂   V'₂   O'₂

読み方をどう教えるべきか

第1段落

❶ 読む能力は子どもの教育の基礎を形成するものだ。

❷ 何十年もの間、研究者たちはこの重要項目をどのように教えるのがベストなのか、議論してきた。

❸ 研究によると、読むのが苦手な子どもには、その遅れを取り戻すのが非常に難しく、人生の目標を達成する可能性も低くなるという。

❹ しかし、このような事実がわかっていても、子どもたちがどのように読み方を学ぶべきかについては、学者たちの間で意見が分かれている。

❺ ある学者は、読むということは自由で自然なプロセスだから、子どもを本に囲まれた環境に置けば、その本を頼りに自力で読み方がわかるようになるはずだという考えを提唱している。

❶□ form …を形作る　□ basis 基礎　❷□ decade 10年間　□ critical 重大な
□ subject 主題、テーマ、科目　❸□ fall behind 後に取り残される
□ have difficulty in *doing* …するのが困難である　□ catch up on …の遅れを取り戻す
□ reduce …を小さくする　□ achieve …を達成する　❹□ differ 意見を異にする
□ as to …に関して　❺□ suggest that 節 …だと示唆する
□ be surrounded with …に囲まれている　□ figure out …を理解する

筆記3

第2段落

❶ However, experiments show that only 1-7% of children can actually do this.

❷ For the vast majority of children, simply setting up printed text around them will not help them learn to read.

❸ Other scholars suggest memorization of basic, high-frequency words, perhaps with pictures.

❹ This word memorization helps, but research shows that this is often a stressful approach for children, who struggle to remember so many words.

❺ This approach also fails to teach the underlying language system, which children then have to master on their own.

❻ Other scholars have focused on phonics: having kids master the letters and the sounds that they make, and then learn how to combine these into words and sentences.

❼ Phonics has been proven useful because it helps associate letters of an alphabet and letter combinations with specific sounds.

❽ Children can also experiment with phonics, trying to create words of their own.

❾ When they don't know what a word means, they can still make reasonable estimates, based on the context in which a word is placed.

❿ In all these ways, phonics makes a great bridge from learning the alphabet to full reading, writing, and spelling.

⓫ Yet, phonics still requires the child to remember a large amount of letter combinations.

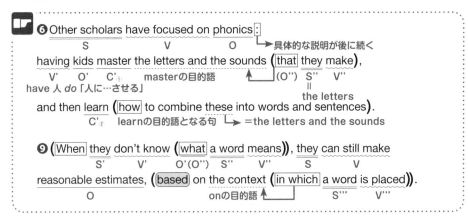

❶ しかし、実験の結果によると、実際にそれができる子どもは1 ～ 7%に過ぎない。

❷ 大多数の子どもは、周りに活字を並べられただけでは、読み方を覚えることはできないのだ。

❸ 基本となる使用頻度の高い単語を、できれば絵を見ながら暗記することを勧める学者もいる。

❹ 単語のこうした暗記は効果があるが、調査によると、多くの単語を覚えるのに苦労している子どもたちにとって、この方法はストレスになることが多いようだ。

❺ また、この方法では、基本的な言語体系を教えることができないため、子どもたちは自分で習得しなければならない。

❻ 別の学者はフォニックスに焦点を当てた。フォニックスでは、文字とその音を子どもたちに覚えさせ、それらを単語や文に結びつける方法を学ばせる。

❼ フォニックスによって、アルファベットの個々の文字や文字の組み合わせと特定の音を結び付けやすくなることが証明されている。

❽ また、子どもたちはフォニックスを使って、自分で言葉を作ってみることもできる。

❾ 言葉の意味がわからなくても、その言葉が置かれた文脈から推測することができる。

❿ このように、フォニックスは、アルファベットの学習から、読み、書き、綴りの学習への大きな橋渡しをする。

⓫ しかし、フォニックスで学ぶ場合も、子どもは大量の文字の組み合わせを覚えなければならない。

❷□ vast 非常に大きな □ majority 大多数 □ set up …を準備する ❸□ memorization 記憶、暗記
□ frequency 頻度 ❹□ struggle 苦心する ❺□ fail to *do* …しそこなう、…しない
□ underlying 基礎を成す
❻□ phonics フォニックス（初心者を対象に英語のつづり字と発音の関係を教える教授法）
□ combine A into B A を合わせて B にする ❼□ prove A B A が B であることを証明する
□ associate A with B A を B と関連づけて考える □ combination 組み合わせ
❾□ reasonable 理にかなった □ estimate 推定、見積り □ context 文脈、文の前後関係
⓫□ require X to *do* X に…するよう求める

筆記③

第3段落

❶ The newest approach is that of phonemes.

❷ In this approach, children learn the sounds of a language and how these sounds are arranged and rearranged to create words.

❸ Research has shown that children can master this system much easier than trying to remember entire words or letter combinations.

❹ Phonemes are similar to phonics, but are much easier because children have already been exposed to these sounds in their everyday speech.

❺ Phoneme study just helps them organize these sounds into a system.

❻ Later, the child can move on to phonics—and phonics will make much more sense at that point, since the child will be able to match letter combinations to sounds that he or she already knows and practices.

---

❷ In this approach, children learn the sounds of a language
S V O₁

and (how these sounds are arranged and rearranged to create words).
O₂ S' V'₁ V'₂

❻ Later, the child can move on to phonics
S V O

—and phonics will make much more sense at that point,
S' V' O'

(since the child will be able to match letter combinations to sounds (that
S'' V'' O'' (O''')

                              match A to B

he or she already knows and practices)).
S''' V'''₁ V'''₂

❶ 最新のアプローチは、音素によるものだ。

❷ このアプローチでは、子どもたちは言語の音と、その音がどのように配置され、そして並べ替えられて単語が作られるのかを学ぶ。

❸ この方式は、単語全体や文字の組み合わせを覚えるよりも、はるかに簡単に習得できることが研究により明らかにされている。

❹ 音素はフォニックスと似ているが、子どもたちはすでに日常会話でこれらの音に触れているため、はるかに簡単だ。

❺ 音素の学習は、これらの音を体系的に整理するのに役立つ。

❻ その後でフォニックスの学習に移行してもよい。子どもは、文字の組み合わせとすでに知っていて使いこなしている音とを一致させることができるので、この時点でフォニックスを学習した方が理解できるのだ。

❶□ phoneme 音素　❷□ rearrange …を再び配列する　❸□ entire 全体の
❹□ be similar to …に似ている　□ expose A to B A に B を経験させる
□ everyday speech ふだんの談話　❺□ organize A into B A を B にまとめる・整理する
❻□ move on to (新たな課題・仕事)に移る　□ make sense 意味を成す、理解できる
□ match A to B A を B に合わせる、A を B と調和させる

問題英文の読み方 P.408　解説・正解 P.412　訳・語句 P.416

Dinosaur Parenting Styles

When we see the term "good parent," we typically think of parents (human or animal) who raise a child for months or years after birth. Lions, for instance, raise their babies until about two years of age, while panda babies remain with their mothers for about 18 months. However, this type of parenting is not standard. Sea turtles, for instance, lay eggs at night on sandy beaches, and then return to the water, never to see them again. Neither type of parenting style is superior to the other. Rather, both are suitable to the species and the habitat in which they live. And in all cases, only a small percentage of these babies survive into adulthood themselves.

Since they are long extinct, dinosaurs can only be studied through fossils. More specifically, to get any idea of dinosaur parenting styles, researchers have compared dinosaur egg fossils and developed dinosaur parent theories based on them. Specifically, dinosaur egg types can indicate the length and style of parenting. For example, hard-shelled eggs are strong enough for a mother to sit on and keep warm, while soft-shelled ones are not. Babies who emerge from soft shells are usually on their own from the beginning, with the parent long gone away and unable to help. Therefore, hard shell fossils suggest that a creature was a long-term parent who spent time guarding and raising its young—like a bird. A soft shell would indicate little or no parenting—like a turtle.

Initially, scientists found only hard-shelled dinosaur eggs. This led them to believe that dinosaurs were "good parents" and stayed with their eggs to keep them warm. Yet, in contradiction to this theory, some soft-shelled dinosaur eggs have been discovered, although not nearly at the scale of hard shells. Scientists are now suggesting that the lack of soft-shelled egg fossils is because, while hard shells more easily absorb minerals, soft shells rapidly decay and disappear after the baby emerges. Broad scientific opinion now suggests that different types of dinosaurs had different parenting styles. Oviraptorosaurs, for example, seemed to have sat on their eggs like modern birds, and protected their babies. Protoceratops and Mussaurus dinosaurs, on the other hand, appear to have simply laid soft-shelled eggs and then left.

New research seems to support the theory that the oldest dinosaur eggs, dating back some 150 million years, were actually like leather, similar to snake or lizard eggs. From there, some dinosaur species slowly developed over the centuries to lay hard-shelled eggs while others laid soft-shelled eggs, reflecting the distinct parenting methods of the respective species. In sum, it may not be correct to claim that dinosaurs had a typical parenting style. Instead, parenting styles may have varied based on the species and the types of eggs they laid. As more egg fossils are discovered, there will be more opportunities to test this emerging theory.

筆記 ③

(1) What is one thing the passage says about animal births?

  1 The newborn babies of some animals must live completely on their own from their first moments of life.

  2 Animal babies which are protected by their parents after birth have a much higher rate of survival into adulthood.

  3 Parenting is a special skill that all animal babies learn from their parents when they are old enough to live on their own.

  4 Only a small fraction of animal babies ever leave their parents when they are mature enough to start their own families.

(2) Scientists rely on the egg fossil records because they may give indications as to

  1 where the fossils of adult animals may be found and what condition they may be found in.

  2 when an animal finally died and what predator or force of nature had actually caused its death.

  3 why some types of animals were so much more successful at reproducing and parenting than other types.

  4 how animal species that lived and died out long ago might have raised their young when they were alive.

(3) The passage suggests that one reason few soft-shelled dinosaur eggs have been found is that

1 dinosaurs that had soft-shelled eggs were smaller in size, so they could not protect their eggs from bigger dinosaurs.

2 as soon as the dinosaur babies came out of their soft-shelled eggs, their mothers ate the remains of the eggs.

3 they broke down quickly and completely fairly soon after babies emerged from them.

4 dinosaurs that had soft-shelled eggs lived at an earlier period and the fossils of that period are too deeply buried.

(4) What does the author of the passage say about leather-like dinosaur eggs?

1 They were protected from other reptiles of the time, such as snakes and lizards, which also laid similar eggs.

2 They may have been the initial dinosaur egg types from which both soft-shelled and hard-shelled eggs later developed.

3 They were thought to be hard-shelled eggs when their fossils were first discovered, because mineral deposits had made them hard.

4 They were ideal for the lifestyle of dinosaurs because they were easy to carry, while being tough enough to sit on.

第1段落

Dinosaur Parenting Styles

❶When we see the term "good parent," we typically think of parents (human or animal) who raise a child for months or years after birth. ❷Lions, for instance, raise their babies until about two years of age, while panda babies remain with their mothers for about 18 months. ❸However, this type of parenting is not standard. ❹Sea turtles, for instance, lay eggs at night on sandy beaches, and then return to the water, never to see them again. ❺Neither type of parenting style is superior to the other. ❻Rather, both are suitable to the species and the habitat in which they live. ❼And in all cases, only a small percentage of these babies survive into adulthood themselves.

第2段落

❶Since they are long extinct, dinosaurs can only be studied through fossils. ❷More specifically, to get any idea of dinosaur parenting styles, researchers have compared dinosaur egg fossils and developed dinosaur parent theories based on them. ❸Specifically, dinosaur egg types can indicate the length and style of parenting. ❹For example, hard-shelled eggs are strong enough for a mother to sit on and keep warm, while soft-shelled ones are not. ❺Babies who emerge from soft shells are usually on their own from the beginning, with the parent long gone away and unable to help. ❻Therefore, hard shell fossils suggest that a creature was a long-term parent who spent time guarding and raising its young—like a bird. ❼A soft shell would indicate little or no parenting—like a turtle.

この問題英文の長さは約500語です。

❶は「『良い親』という言葉を見ると、子どもが生まれてしばらくの間、子育てをするような親を思い浮かべるのが普通だ」と、読者に想像させるような書き出しになっています。❷では例として、ライオンやパンダの親がそれに当てはまると述べていますが、❸❹では「そのような育児は普通ではなく、ウミガメなどは卵を産んだまま二度と卵を見に戻ることがない」と展開しています。❺から❼では、「どちらの子育てタイプが優れているというわけではなく、どちらもその種や生息環境に適していて、いずれの場合も、大人になるまで生き残るのは赤ちゃんのうちのごく一部に過ぎない」と、子育てをする親と卵を産むだけの親の共通点を述べて第1段落を終えています。

タイトルにある「恐竜」が1文目（❶）から出てくることから、第2段落は恐竜の子育てについて書かれていると推測できます。❶から❸で「恐竜が絶滅してから時間が経っているので、研究者は卵の化石を比較して、それらが示唆する恐竜の子育ての期間やスタイルを解明した」と言っています。❹では、「殻が硬い卵は母親が座って温めるのに十分強度があるが、軟らかい殻はそうではない」と述べ、❺から❼で「軟らかい殻から出てきた赤ちゃんは、最初から自力で生きているが、硬い殻の化石は、親が長い期間にわたって子どもを守りながら育てたことを示唆している」と、硬い殻と軟らかい殻の強度の違いからそれぞれの生物の子育ての違いについて考えられることを説明しています。

第3段落

❶Initially, scientists found only hard-shelled dinosaur eggs. ❷This led them to believe that dinosaurs were "good parents" and stayed with their eggs to keep them warm. ❸Yet, in contradiction to this theory, some soft-shelled dinosaur eggs have been discovered, although not nearly at the scale of hard shells. ❹Scientists are now suggesting that the lack of soft-shelled egg fossils is because, while hard shells more easily absorb minerals, soft shells rapidly decay and disappear after the baby emerges. ❺Broad scientific opinion now suggests that different types of dinosaurs had different parenting styles. ❻Oviraptorosaurs, for example, seemed to have sat on their eggs like modern birds, and protected their babies. ❼Protoceratops and Mussaurus dinosaurs, on the other hand, appear to have simply laid soft-shelled eggs and then left.

第4段落

❶New research seems to support the theory that the oldest dinosaur eggs, dating back some 150 million years, were actually like leather, similar to snake or lizard eggs. ❷From there, some dinosaur species slowly developed over the centuries to lay hard-shelled eggs while others laid soft-shelled eggs, reflecting the distinct parenting methods of the respective species. ❸In sum, it may not be correct to claim that dinosaurs had a typical parenting style. ❹Instead, parenting styles may have varied based on the species and the types of eggs they laid. ❺As more egg fossils are discovered, there will be more opportunities to test this emerging theory.

前の段落での「硬い殻」と「軟らかい殻」に関する研究について、第3段落❶❷で「当初は、殻が硬い恐竜の卵しか発見されなかったので、恐竜は卵のそばにいる『良い親』であったと考えられた」と述べています。これに反する説について、❸❹で「殻が軟らかい恐竜の卵もいくつか発見されている。軟らかい殻は赤ちゃんが生まれると急速に腐敗して消えてしまうから、軟らかい殻の卵は少ない」と書かれています。❺では恐竜の子育てに関する現在の見解として「恐竜の種類によって、子育てのスタイルは異なる」とあり、その例として、❻❼で赤ちゃんを守ったオヴィラプトロサウルスや、軟らかい卵を産んだまま去ったプロトケラトプス、ムスサウルスが挙げられています。

最後の段落では、❶で「約1億5千万年前の最古の恐竜の卵が、蛇やトカゲの卵と同様に革のようなものだった」という新しい説について述べています。その説について、❷で「何世紀もかけてゆっくり進化した結果、硬い殻の卵と軟らかい殻の卵の種がいたということで、それぞれの種が異なる子育てをしていたことを示している」と説明しています。❸は In sum, で始まっているので、この文章をまとめようとしていることがわかります。「つまり、恐竜の子育てスタイルは一様であったとは言えない」とあり、続く❹❺で「子育ての方法は種や生んだ卵のタイプによって異なっていたと考えられ、今後、卵の化石の発見が増えれば、この説を検証する機会も増えていくだろう」と、今後の研究の展望を述べて、文を締めくくっています。

筆記③

(1) What is one thing the passage says about animal births?

1 The newborn babies of some animals must live completely on their own from their first moments of life.

2 Animal babies which are protected by their parents after birth have a much higher rate of survival into adulthood.

3 Parenting is a special skill that all animal babies learn from their parents when they are old enough to live on their own.

4 Only a small fraction of animal babies ever leave their parents when they are mature enough to start their own families.

(2) Scientists rely on the egg fossil records because they may give indications as to

1 where the fossils of adult animals may be found and what condition they may be found in.

2 when an animal finally died and what predator or force of nature had actually caused its death.

3 why some types of animals were so much more successful at reproducing and parenting than other types.

4 how animal species that lived and died out long ago might have raised their young when they were alive.

(1) 📝 動物の誕生について、この文章で言われていることは何ですか。

   1 ある種の動物の赤ちゃんは、生まれた瞬間から完全に自分の力で生きていかなければならない。

   2 生まれた後に親に保護される動物の赤ちゃんの方が、大人になるまで生き残る確率がはるかに高い。

   3 子育ては、すべての動物の赤ちゃんが、自力で生きられるようになったときに親から学ぶ特別な技術である。

   4 動物の赤ちゃんのうち、自分の家族を持てるほど成長したときに親元を離れるのはごく一部である。

🔍 第1段落の❹で「ウミガメは卵を産んだまま二度と卵を見に戻ることがない」と子育てのスタイルの一例を挙げています。このウミガメの例を読むと、1と解答することができます。

✏️ ☐ newborn 生まれたての　☐ fraction 小部分、断片　☐ mature 成長しきった

---

(2) 📝 科学者が卵の化石の記録を当てにするのは、それによって次のことがわかるかもしれないからです。

   1 動物の成体の化石がどこで、どのような状態で発見されるか。

   2 ある動物がいつ死んだのか、また、どんな捕食者や自然の力がその死を引き起こしたのか。

   3 ある種の動物が他の種より繁殖や子育てに成功したのはなぜか。

   4 大昔に絶滅した動物が、生きているときにどのように子どもを育てていたのか。

🔍 第2段落の❶から❸で「恐竜が絶滅してから時間が経っているので、研究者は恐竜の子育てについて、卵の化石を比較して、それらが示唆する恐竜の子育ての期間やスタイルを解明した」とあります。これにより正解は4と解答することができます。

✏️ ☐ as to …に関して　☐ predator 捕食者　☐ reproduce 繁殖する　☐ die out 絶滅する

(3) The passage suggests that one reason few soft-shelled dinosaur eggs have been found is that

1　dinosaurs that had soft-shelled eggs were smaller in size, so they could not protect their eggs from bigger dinosaurs.

2　as soon as the dinosaur babies came out of their soft-shelled eggs, their mothers ate the remains of the eggs.

3　they broke down quickly and completely fairly soon after babies emerged from them.

4　dinosaurs that had soft-shelled eggs lived at an earlier period and the fossils of that period are too deeply buried.

(4) What does the author of the passage say about leather-like dinosaur eggs?

1　They were protected from other reptiles of the time, such as snakes and lizards, which also laid similar eggs.

2　They may have been the initial dinosaur egg types from which both soft-shelled and hard-shelled eggs later developed.

3　They were thought to be hard-shelled eggs when their fossils were first discovered, because mineral deposits had made them hard.

4　They were ideal for the lifestyle of dinosaurs because they were easy to carry, while being tough enough to sit on.

(3) 🚩 殻が軟らかい恐竜の卵がほとんど見つかっていない理由の一つとして、この文章が示唆しているのは、

1　卵の殻が軟らかい恐竜は体が小さかったので、大きな恐竜から卵を守ることができなかったということだ。
2　軟らかい殻の卵から赤ちゃんが出てくると、すぐに母親が卵の残骸を食べたということだ。
3　卵から赤ちゃんが出てきた後、卵はすぐに完全に壊れてしまったということだ。
4　卵の殻が軟らかい恐竜は、もっと前に生きており、その時期の化石は深く埋もれてしまっているということだ。

🔍 第3段落の❹で「軟らかい殻は赤ちゃんが生まれると急速に腐敗して消えてしまうから、軟らかい殻の卵は少ない」と述べています。ここから問3の答えがわかります。

🖋 ☐ break down 分解される、壊れる　☐ fairly 全く

- -

(4) 🚩 この文章の著者は、革のような恐竜の卵について、どのように述べていますか。

1　同じような卵を産むヘビやトカゲなど、当時の他の爬虫類からは守られていた。
2　恐竜の卵の初期の型であった可能性があり、そこから軟らかい殻の卵と硬い殻の卵の両方が発生した。
3　鉱物の堆積によって硬くなったため、化石が発見された当初は、硬い殻の卵だと考えられていた。
4　持ち運びに便利で、その上に座ることもできるほど丈夫なため、恐竜の生活様式に適していた。

🔍 第4段落の❶で「約1億5千万年前の最古の恐竜の卵が、蛇やトカゲの卵と同様に革のようなものだった」と述べています。そして、❷で「そこから、何世紀もかけてゆっくり進化した結果、硬い殻の卵と軟らかい殻の卵の種がいたということで、それぞれの種が異なる子育てをしていたことを示している」と説明しています。ここから、問4を解答することができます。

🖋 ☐ reptile 爬虫類の動物　☐ deposit 堆積、沈着

Dinosaur Parenting Styles

第1段落

❶ When we see the term "good parent," we typically think of parents (human or animal) who raise a child for months or years after birth.

❷ Lions, for instance, raise their babies until about two years of age, while panda babies remain with their mothers for about 18 months.

❸ However, this type of parenting is not standard.

❹ Sea turtles, for instance, lay eggs at night on sandy beaches, and then return to the water, never to see them again.

❺ Neither type of parenting style is superior to the other.

❻ Rather, both are suitable to the species and the habitat in which they live.

❼ And in all cases, only a small percentage of these babies survive into adulthood themselves.

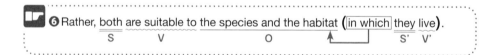

❻ Rather, both are suitable to the species and the habitat (in which they live).
　　　　S　　　V　　　　　　　　O　　　　　　　　　　　　S'　V'

恐竜の子育てスタイル

第1段落

❶ 「良い親」という言葉を目にすると、子どもが生まれて数か月から数年間は子育てをする（人間や動物の）親を、思い浮かべるのが普通だ。

❷ 例えば、ライオンは2歳くらいまで母親が赤ちゃんを育て、パンダの赤ちゃんは1歳半くらいまで母親と一緒にいる。

❸ しかし、このような類の育児が普通のことというわけではない。

❹ 例えばウミガメは、夜、砂浜に卵を産み、その後、海に戻り、二度と卵を見に戻ることはない。

❺ 一方のタイプの子育てだけが優れているというわけではない。

❻ どちらもその種や生息環境に適しているのだ。

❼ そして、いずれの場合も、大人になるまで生き残るのは、赤ちゃんのうちのごく一部に過ぎない。

□ dinosaur 恐竜　□ parenting 子育て　❶□ raise (子ども)を育てる・養う　❹□ sea turtle ウミガメ
□ lay (卵)を産む　□ sandy 砂地の　❺□ superior to …より優れた
❻□ be suitable to …に適している　□ species 種　□ habitat 生息地
❼□ survive into …まで生き延びる　□ adulthood 成熟、成体

筆記③

417

第2段落

❶ Since they are long extinct, dinosaurs can only be studied through fossils.

❷ More specifically, to get any idea of dinosaur parenting styles, researchers have compared dinosaur egg fossils and developed dinosaur parent theories based on them.

❸ Specifically, dinosaur egg types can indicate the length and style of parenting.

❹ For example, hard-shelled eggs are strong enough for a mother to sit on and keep warm, while soft-shelled ones are not.

❺ Babies who emerge from soft shells are usually on their own from the beginning, with the parent long gone away and unable to help.

❻ Therefore, hard shell fossils suggest that a creature was a long-term parent who spent time guarding and raising its young—like a bird.

❼ A soft shell would indicate little or no parenting—like a turtle.

---

❺ Babies (who emerge from soft shells)
　　S 　　S'　　V'　　　　O'

are usually on their own from the beginning,
　V　　　　　C

(with the parent long gone away and unable to help).
付帯状況を
表すwithの　　　　　　　　　　(helpの目的語はBabies)
独立分詞構文

❻ Therefore, hard shell fossils suggest (that a creature was
　　　　　　　　　S　　　　　V　　O　　S'　　V'

a long-term parent (who spent time guarding and raising its young
　　　C'　　　　　S''　V''　O''　spend O *doing*　guardingと
　　　　　　　　　　　　　　　　「…してOを費やす」　raisingの目的語

—like a bird)).

❶ 恐竜は絶滅して長い時間が経っているので、化石を通してしか研究することができない。

❷ 具体的に言うと、恐竜がどんな子育てをしていたか理解するために、研究者は恐竜の卵の化石を比較し、それをもとに恐竜の子育てを解明した。

❸ 具体的には、恐竜の卵のタイプによって、子育ての期間やスタイルがわかるのだ。

❹ 例えば、殻が硬い卵は母親が座って温めるのに十分な強度があるが、軟らかい殻の卵はそうではない。

❺ 軟らかい殻から出てきた赤ちゃんは、たいてい最初から自力で生きており、親はとっくにいなくなっていて助けることができない。

❻ そのため、硬い殻の化石は、その生物の親が鳥のように子どもを守りながら長い時間をかけて育てたことを示唆している。

❼ 殻が軟らかいのは、亀のように子育てをほとんどしていないことを意味する。

❶☐ extinct 絶滅した ☐ fossil 化石 ❷☐ specifically 具体的に言うと
☐ get an idea of …を理解する ☐ compare …を比較する ☐ develop …を明らかにする
❸☐ indicate …を示す ❹☐ hard-shelled 殻の堅い ☐ soft-shelled 殻の軟らかい
❺☐ emerge 出てくる ❻☐ spend X *doing* …してX(時間)を過ごす ☐ guard …を守る

筆記③

第3段落

❶ Initially, scientists found only hard-shelled dinosaur eggs.

❷ This led them to believe that dinosaurs were "good parents" and stayed with their eggs to keep them warm.

❸ Yet, in contradiction to this theory, some soft-shelled dinosaur eggs have been discovered, although not nearly at the scale of hard shells.

❹ Scientists are now suggesting that the lack of soft-shelled egg fossils is because, while hard shells more easily absorb minerals, soft shells rapidly decay and disappear after the baby emerges.

❺ Broad scientific opinion now suggests that different types of dinosaurs had different parenting styles.

❻ The Oviraptorosaurs, for example, seemed to have sat on their eggs like modern birds, and protected their babies.

❼ Protoceratops and Mussaurus dinosaurs, on the other hand, appear to have simply laid soft-shelled eggs and then left.

---

❷ This led them to believe (that dinosaurs were "good parents"
　 S　　V　　O　　　　　　　　　　　　　S'　　 V'① 　　　C'①
　　　　 lead O to do「(Sを理由として)Oに…する気にさせる」

and stayed with their eggs to keep them warm).
　　 V'②

❹ Scientists are now suggesting (that the lack of soft-shelled egg fossils
　 S　　　　　 V　　　　　　　　　 O　　　　　　　　　　 S'

is (because, (while hard shells more easily absorb minerals),
V'　　　　　　　　　　　 S'''　　　　　　　　 V'''　　 O'''
　 └ C'　　 譲歩を表す
　　　　　　 副詞節

soft shells rapidly decay and disappear (after the baby emerges))).
　 S''　　　　 V''①　　　 V''②　　　　　　　　 S''''　　 V''''

---

❶ 当初、科学者たちは殻が硬い恐竜の卵しか発見しなかった。

❷ このため、恐竜は卵のそばにいて温める「良い親」であったと考えた。

❸ しかし、この説を覆すように、硬い殻の数には到底及ばないものの、殻が軟らかい恐竜の卵もいくつか発見されている。

❹ 現在の科学者の見解では、硬い殻はミネラルを吸収しやすいのに対し、軟らかい殻は赤ちゃんが生まれると、急速に腐敗して消えてしまうから、軟らかい殻の卵は少ないのだ。

❺ 現在では、恐竜の種類によって子育てのスタイルが異なるというのが、一般的な科学的見解となっている。

❻ 例えば、オヴィラプトロサウルスは今の鳥のように卵の上に座り、赤ちゃんを守っていたようだ。

❼ 一方、プロトケラトプスやムスサウルスは、殻の軟らかい卵を産んで、そのまま去っていったようだ。

❶□ initially 当初、最初は　❷□ lead X to *do* X に…させる、X に…する気にさせる
❸□ in contradiction to …と正反対に　□ scale 規模　❹□ absorb …を吸収する
□ decay 腐敗する　□ disappear 消失する

筆記③

第4段落

❶ New research seems to support the theory that the oldest dinosaur eggs, dating back some 150 million years, were actually like leather, similar to snake or lizard eggs.

❷ From there, some dinosaur species slowly developed over the centuries to lay hard-shelled eggs while others laid soft-shelled eggs, reflecting the distinct parenting methods of the respective species.

❸ In sum, it may not be correct to claim that dinosaurs had a typical parenting style.

❹ Instead, parenting styles may have varied based on the species and the types of eggs they laid.

❺ As more egg fossils are discovered, there will be more opportunities to test this emerging theory.

---

❶ New research seems to support the theory (that
　　S　　　　　　V　　　　　　O　　同格

the oldest dinosaur eggs, (dating back some 150 million years),
　　　　　　S'

were actually like leather, similar to snake or lizard eggs).
　V'　　　　　　C'

❷ From there, some dinosaur species slowly developed
　　　　　　　　　S　　　　　　　　V

over the centuries / to lay hard-shelled eggs

(while others laid soft-shelled eggs),
　　　S'　　V'　　　O'

(reflecting the distinct parenting methods of the respective species).

❶ 新しい研究の結果、約1億5千万年前の最古の恐竜の卵が、実は蛇やトカゲの卵と同様に革の ようなものだったという説が支持されているようだ。

❷ その説では、何世紀もかけてゆっくり進化した結果、硬い殻の卵を産んだ種類もいれば、軟ら かい卵を産んだ種類もいたということで、それぞれの種が異なる子育てをしていたことを示 している。

❸ つまり、恐竜の子育てスタイルは一様であったとは言い切れないのだろう。

❹ というよりは、子育ての方法は種や産んだ卵のタイプによって異なっていたのかもしれない。

❺ 今後、卵の化石の発見が増えれば、この新たな説を検証する機会も増えていくことだろう。

❶□ date back さかのぼる　□ leather 革　□ lizard トカゲ　❷□ reflect …を映し出す
□ distinct 異なった　□ respective それぞれの　❸□ in sum 要するに
□ claim that 節 …だと主張する　❹□ vary 異なる　❺□ test …の検査をする
□ emerging 発展中の、新生の

問題英文の読み方 P.428　解説・正解 P.432　訳・語句 P.436

The Importance of Keystone Species

Every species lives in an ecosystem. The ecosystem sustains itself through the activities of each plant or animal species within it. More specifically, the activities of each species impact others, and the ecosystem itself. Wildebeest herds on the plains of Africa, for example, leave large amounts of animal waste as they migrate. African dung beetles use this waste as a food source and even a way to attract partners. The beetles carry it away, and thereby prevent excessive animal waste from killing off plant life. Just enough waste remains on the grasses, however, to fertilize those same plants. All three species: plants, beetles, and wildebeest, interact to preserve their ecosystem in a delicate balance.

A keystone species is one that—similar to its counterpart in architecture—keeps an ecosystem intact. Removal of a keystone—the most important section to offset gravity, weight and structural stress—in a bridge or arch can cause the entire structure to fall. Similarly, removal or reduction of a keystone species can cause an entire ecosystem to fall apart. Not all scientists agree on the concept of this species, or which species might qualify as this type within an ecosystem, but ecologists have identified three types: mutualists, predators, and engineers. Within any ecosystem, predators control the number of herbivores, or grass-eaters, and the number of herbivores, in turn, affects the amount of both plant life and predators. Each species is important in this system, although some species are more central than others.

One good example of a predator keystone species is the gray wolves of Yellowstone Park. After they were nearly killed off by humans in the last century, the populations of herbivores such as elk and deer began to grow too large, over-eating plants, including plants that were crucial to preventing soil loss near river banks. This soil loss harmed riverbanks and threatened species that rely on them, such as insects that fish and other creatures consume. Only through the reintroduction of wolves into Yellowstone in the 1990s could the number of elk be reduced and the ecosystem returned to balance. The wolves usually picked off the youngest, oldest or sickest of a herd, allowing only the quickest and strongest members to survive. As a result, overall herd health also improved.

Wolves may be a keystone species in Yellowstone, but that raises the question as to why elk are not. Scientists answer that by defining a keystone species as one that cannot easily be replaced. Yellowstone, for instance, has a wide range of herbivores, from bison to moose. There is only one top predator, though, so taking it away caused severe and unique damage to the entire ecosystem. The experience with the Yellowstone wolves indicates how balance may be restored to ecosystems whose top predators are declining or endangered. Certain species of tigers, lions, and cougars are already at risk, and if they disappear altogether other ecosystem failures could occur. While some nations or territories have sanctioned licensed hunting to make up for a lack of predators, random shooting of animals cannot create the herd health benefits that predators can.

筆記③

(1) What is one thing we learn about African dung beetles?

1 They occur in large populations and are one of the most common food sources of other members of their ecosystem.

2 They use the waste product of another member of their ecosystem, which helps maintain the overall balance of the habitat.

3 They kill off crucial plant types when they grow into large numbers, thereby causing wildebeest to go without food.

4 They are eaten by wildebeest and then become a part of animal waste that fertilizes the plants and keeps them healthy.

(2) The passage suggests that one reason the keystone species are similar to particular sections of architecture is that

1 every natural or human-made system has a weak point whose removal always results in system-wide failure.

2 ecosystems are complex structures similar to some of the oldest forms of stone architecture in the world.

3 removing certain parts of either a natural or an artificial system can result in widespread and severely negative effects.

4 natural ecosystems have to be built step by step, similar to how stone buildings such as bridges are constructed.

(3) What is true of animal herds?

1 When some of their weakest members are removed by predators in an ecosystem, the group itself becomes healthier.

2 When their aggressive enemies like wolves are removed from an ecosystem, the general health of the animals in that group significantly increases.

3 When they become healthy enough, they can be hunted like any other herbivore that is at risk of becoming too numerous in a location.

4 When they become completely dependent on grass in an area, they become easy targets for animals such as the grey wolves of Yellowstone.

(4) What is one reason that elk may be less vital to Yellowstone than wolves?

1 Several keystone species of herbivores in the area were killed off by wolves, but it had little effect on the entire ecosystem.

2 Other herbivores could play the same role as elk but no animal in that ecosystem performs the function of wolves.

3 Herbivores such as elk, bison and moose are very numerous, so they could never be as important to an ecosystem as the less numerous predators.

4 Elk and other herbivores can only control the plant population, which is not as important as wolves that can control the herbivore population.

第1段落

The Importance of Keystone Species

❶Every species lives in an ecosystem. ❷The ecosystem sustains itself through the activities of each plant or animal species within it. ❸More specifically, the activities of each species impact others, and the ecosystem itself. ❹Wildebeest herds on the plains of Africa, for example, leave large amounts of animal waste as they migrate. ❺African dung beetles use this waste as a food source and even a way to attract partners. ❻The beetles carry it away, and thereby prevent excessive animal waste from killing off plant life. ❼Just enough waste remains on the grasses, however, to fertilize those same plants. ❽All three species: plants, beetles, and wildebeest, interact to preserve their ecosystem in a delicate balance.

第2段落

❶A keystone species is one that—similar to its counterpart in architecture—keeps an ecosystem intact. ❷Removal of a keystone—the most important section to offset gravity, weight and structural stress—in a bridge or arch can cause the entire structure to fall. ❸Similarly, removal or reduction of a keystone species can cause an entire ecosystem to fall apart. ❹Not all scientists agree on the concept of this species, or which species might qualify as this type within an ecosystem, but ecologists have identified three types: mutualists, predators, and engineers. ❺Within any ecosystem, predators control the number of herbivores, or grass-eaters, and the number of herbivores, in turn, affects the amount of both plant life and predators. ❻Each species is important in this system, although some species are more central than others.

428

この問題英文の長さは約500語です。

タイトルの Keystone Species とはどのようなものか、気になるところですが、初めには出てきません。一体どんな話か、何が先につながるか注意しながら読み進めてみましょう。第1段落❶❷は、「すべての生物種はある生態系の中で生きていて、生態系はその中の種の活動によって維持されている」と、生態系についての説明で始まります。❸では「具体的には、それぞれの種の活動が他の種や生態系に影響を与えている」と言って、続く❹から❻で実際の具体例を示しています。「アフリカに生息するヌーの群れが移動の際に残していく排泄物をフンコロガシが食料として利用し、そのフンコロガシが糞を取り除くことで、動物の過剰な排泄物による植物の枯死を防いでいる」とあり、❼で、草の上に残った排泄物が植物の肥料になると付け加えています。この段落の最終文の❽では、「植物、フンコロガシ、ヌーの3種がそれらの間での生態系を維持している」と、この具体例をまとめています。

第2段落

第2段落の❶でようやくタイトルの keystone species が出てきます。「キーストーン種は、建築物のキーストーンと同様に生態系を維持する」とあり、❷❸では、建築物のキーストーンを例にして「重力や重量や圧力を相殺するキーストーンを橋やアーチから取り除くと、構造物全体が倒壊する可能性があるのと同じく、要となる種がなくなると、生態系全体が崩壊する」とキーストーン種について説明しています。❹では「すべての科学者がこの概念に賛同しているわけではなく、生態系の中でどの種がこれに相当するのかについても意見が分かれているが、共生者、捕食者、技術者の3つのタイプを特定している」と紹介し、❺では、この3つのタイプの役割について「生態系において、捕食者が草食動物の数をコントロールし、草食動物の数は植物と捕食者の両方の数に影響を与える」と説明しています。❻で、「このシステム（生態系）では、それぞれの種が重要な役割を担っているが、他の種よりも中心的な役割を果たす種もある」と、他よりも影響力を持つ種がいることを示唆して、次の段落につなげています。

筆記③

第3段落

❶One good example of a predator keystone species is the gray wolves of Yellowstone Park. ❷After they were nearly killed off by humans in the last century, the populations of herbivores such as elk and deer began to grow too large, over-eating plants, including plants that were crucial to preventing soil loss near river banks. ❸This soil loss harmed riverbanks and threatened species that rely on them, such as insects that fish and other creatures consume. ❹Only through the reintroduction of wolves into Yellowstone in the 1990s could the number of elk be reduced and the ecosystem returned to balance. ❺The wolves usually picked off the youngest, oldest or sickest of a herd, allowing only the quickest and strongest members to survive. ❻As a result, overall herd health also improved.

第4段落

❶Wolves may be a keystone species in Yellowstone, but that raises the question as to why elk are not. ❷Scientists answer that by defining a keystone species as one that cannot easily be replaced. ❸Yellowstone, for instance, has a wide range of herbivores, from bison to moose. ❹There is only one top predator, though, so taking it away caused severe and unique damage to the entire ecosystem. ❺The experience with the Yellowstone wolves indicates how balance may be restored to ecosystems whose top predators are declining or endangered. ❻Certain species of tigers, lions, and cougars are already at risk, and if they disappear altogether other ecosystem failures could occur. ❼While some nations or territories have sanctioned licensed hunting to make up for a lack of predators, random shooting of animals cannot create the herd health benefits that predators can.

第3段落

第3段落❶は「ハイイロオオカミが捕食者のキーストーンの代表例」とあるので、いよいよ、キーストーン種の具体例が説明されるとわかります。❷❸で「オオカミが前世紀に絶滅しかけてから、草食動物の数が増えすぎて、植物を過剰に食べてしまった。その植物の中には、土壌の流出を防ぐのに重要なものも含まれていたため、この土壌の消失により、川岸が傷つき、そこで生きる昆虫などの種が絶滅の危機に瀕した」とハイイロオオカミを失いかけたことで及ぼされた影響について述べ、❹では「1990年代にイエローストーンにオオカミを復活させると、生態系のバランスが回復した」と説明しています。❺❻では、生態系のバランスを保つのとは別の側面として「オオカミがエルクの群れの中で、一番若いもの、年をとったもの、病弱なものを追い出し、最も素早く強いものだけが生き残れるようにした結果、群れ全体の健康状態も改善された」と述べています。捕食者が餌とする種の良好な状態の維持にも影響を与えていることがわかります。

第4段落

最後の段落は❶の「オオカミはイエローストーンのキーストーン種かもしれないが、なぜエルクはそうでないのかという疑問も生じる」という問題提起で始まり、キーストーン種の定義を詳しく掘り下げようとしています。❷の科学者による定義では「簡単に代替できない種がキーストーン種だ」とあり、その例として、❸❹で「イエローストーンにはバイソンからヘラジカまで、草食動物が生息しているが、頂点に立つ捕食者は1種類で、その捕食者がいなくなると生態系全体に深刻なダメージを与える」と説明しています。❺はこのハイイロオオカミの例から「頂点にいる捕食者が危機に瀕している場合、生態系のバランスがどのように回復されるかわかる」と述べ、❻では「トラやライオン、クーガーが完全にいなくなると他の生態系も破綻してしまう」という同様のことが起こりかねない他の捕食者の例を挙げています。❼では「捕食者の不足を補うために狩猟を許可している国や地域があるけれども、無差別に動物を撃ち殺すと、群れの健全性を保つことはできない」と、個体の数が減るという点は同じでも、それが捕食者による生態系の維持とは異なることを示して、文章を終えています。

筆記③

431

(1) What is one thing we learn about African dung beetles?

1 They occur in large populations and are one of the most common food sources of other members of their ecosystem.

2 They use the waste product of another member of their ecosystem, which helps maintain the overall balance of the habitat.

3 They kill off crucial plant types when they grow into large numbers, thereby causing wildebeest to go without food.

4 They are eaten by wildebeest and then become a part of animal waste that fertilizes the plants and keeps them healthy.

(2) The passage suggests that one reason the keystone species are similar to particular sections of architecture is that

1 every natural or human-made system has a weak point whose removal always results in system-wide failure.

2 ecosystems are complex structures similar to some of the oldest forms of stone architecture in the world.

3 removing certain parts of either a natural or an artificial system can result in widespread and severely negative effects.

4 natural ecosystems have to be built step by step, similar to how stone buildings such as bridges are constructed.

(1) 🔲 アフリカのフンコロガシについてわかることは何ですか。

1 大量に発生し、その生態系の他の種にとって最も一般的な食料源の一つだ。
2 生態系の他の種の排泄物を利用し、生息地の全体的なバランスを維持するのに役立っている。
3 大量に発生すると重要な植物を枯らしてしまうため、ヌーの餌不足の原因になる。
4 ヌーに食べられてその排泄物の一部となり、肥料となって植物の健康を保つ。

🔍 第1段落の❹から❻に「アフリカに生息するヌーの群れが移動の際に残していく排泄物を、フンコロガシが食料として利用し、そのフンコロガシが糞を取り除くことで、動物の過剰な排泄物による植物の枯死を防いでいる」と書いてあります。これを抽象的に言い換えた選択肢2が正解です。

✎ □ habitat 生息地

....

(2) 🔲 キーストーン種が建築物の特定の部分に似ている理由としてこの文章が示唆しているのは

1 自然や人間が作ったあらゆるシステムには弱点があり、それを取り除くと必ずシステム全体に支障をきたす、ということだ。
2 生態系は、世界最古の石造建築の一部に似た複雑な構造をしている、ということだ。
3 自然のシステムでも人工のシステムでも、ある部分を取り除くと、広範囲にわたって深刻な悪影響が生じる可能性がある、ということだ。
4 自然の生態系は、橋のような石造りの建築物が建設されるのと同じように、段階を踏んで構築されなければならない、ということだ。

🔍 第2段落の❷❸の「重力や重量や圧力を相殺するキーストーンを橋やアーチから取り除くと構造物全体が倒壊する可能性があるのと同じく、要となる種がなくなると生態系全体が崩壊する」という説明から答えがわかります。

✎ □ removal 除去 □ remove …を除去する □ artificial 人工の □ widespread 広範囲にわたる

....

筆記③

(3) What is true of animal herds?

    1 When some of their weakest members are removed by predators in an ecosystem, the group itself becomes healthier.

    2 When their aggressive enemies like wolves are removed from an ecosystem, the general health of the animals in that group significantly increases.

    3 When they become healthy enough, they can be hunted like any other herbivore that is at risk of becoming too numerous in a location.

    4 When they become completely dependent on grass in an area, they become easy targets for animals such as the grey wolves of Yellowstone.

(4) What is one reason that elk may be less vital to Yellowstone than wolves?

    1 Several keystone species of herbivores in the area were killed off by wolves, but it had little effect on the entire ecosystem.

    2 Other herbivores could play the same role as elk but no animal in that ecosystem performs the function of wolves.

    3 Herbivores such as elk, bison and moose are very numerous, so they could never be as important to an ecosystem as the less numerous predators.

    4 Elk and other herbivores can only control the plant population, which is not as important as wolves that can control the herbivore population.

(3) 📝 動物の群れについて言えることはどれですか。

1 生態系の中で最も弱い個体が捕食者に駆逐されると、その群れ自体は健全になる。

2 オオカミのような強力な天敵が生態系からいなくなると、その群れの動物たちの健康状態が大きく向上する。

3 十分に健全な状態になれば、その場所で増えすぎてしまう危険性のある他の草食動物と同様に、駆逐される可能性がある。

4 ある地域の草に完全に依存するようになると、イエローストーンのハイイロオオカミのような動物の格好の餌食になる。

🔍 第3段落の❺❻で「オオカミはエルクの群れの中で、一番若いもの、年をとったもの、病弱なものを追い出し、最も素早く強いものだけが生き残れるようにした結果、群れ全体の健康状態も改善された」と述べています。ここから答えがわかります。

✒️ ☐ aggressive 強力な、攻撃的な　☐ general health 身体全体の健康　☐ numerous 非常に多くの
☐ dependent on …に依存している

....

(4) 📝 オオカミよりもエルクの方がイエローストーンにとっての重要度が低いかもしれない理由の一つは何ですか。

1 この地域の草食動物のキーストーン種が数種類、オオカミによって絶滅させられたが、生態系全体にはほとんど影響がなかった。

2 他の草食動物がエルクと同じ役割を果たす可能性はあるが、その生態系にはオオカミの機能を果たす動物はいない。

3 エルク、バイソン、ヘラジカなどの草食動物は非常に数が多いので、少ない捕食動物と同程度に生態系にとって重要であるということはありえない。

4 エルクなどの草食動物は植物の個体数をコントロールすることしかできないので、草食動物の個体数をコントロールできるオオカミほどには重要ではない。

🔍 第4段落の❷で「簡単に代替できない種がキーストーン種だ」と定義づけをして、❸❹で「イエローストーンにはバイソンからヘラジカまで、草食動物が生息しているが、頂点に立つ捕食者は1種類で、その捕食者がいなくなると生態系全体に深刻なダメージを与える」と説明していることから答えがわかります。

✒️ ☐ vital きわめて重要な

筆記③

The Importance of Keystone Species

❶ Every species lives in an ecosystem.

❷ The ecosystem sustains itself through the activities of each plant or animal species within it.

❸ More specifically, the activities of each species impact others, and the ecosystem itself.

❹ Wildebeest herds on the plains of Africa, for example, leave large amounts of animal waste as they migrate.

❺ African dung beetles use this waste as a food source and even a way to attract partners.

❻ The beetles carry it away, and thereby prevent excessive animal waste from killing off plant life.

❼ Just enough waste remains on the grasses, however, to fertilize those same plants.

❽ All three species: plants, beetles, and wildebeest, interact to preserve their ecosystem in a delicate balance.

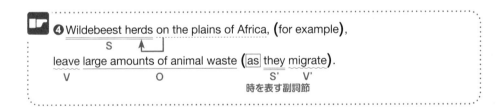

❹ Wildebeest herds on the plains of Africa, (for example),
         S

leave large amounts of animal waste (as they migrate).
  V   O   S'   V'
                                     時を表す副詞節

キーストーン種の重要性

❶ すべての生物種は、ある生態系の中で生きている。

❷ 生態系そのものは、その中で生きている植物や動物の一つ一つの種の活動によって維持されている。

❸ 具体的には、それぞれの種の活動が他の種や生態系に影響を与えているのである。

❹ 例えば、アフリカの平原に生息するヌーの群れは、移動の際に大量の排泄物を残していく。

❺ アフリカのフンコロガシは、この糞を食料として、さらにパートナーを引き寄せる手段としても利用している。

❻ フンコロガシが糞を取り除き、それによって動物の過剰な排泄物による植物の枯死を防いでいる。

❼ それでも、草の上には肥料となるのに十分な量の排泄物が残る。

❽ 植物、フンコロガシ、ヌーの3種が互いに影響しあって、微妙なバランスを保ちながら生態系を維持しているのだ。

☐ keystone species キーストーン種、中枢種　❶☐ ecosystem 生態系
❷☐ sustain …を維持する・持続させる　❸☐ specifically 具体的に言うと
☐ impact …に影響を与える　❹☐ wildebeest ヌー　☐ herd 動物の群れ　☐ plain 平地
☐ migrate 移動する　❺☐ dung beetle フンコロガシ　☐ food source 食料源
☐ attract …を引き付ける　❻☐ carry away …を取り除く・持ち去る
☐ prevent X from *doing* X が…するのを防ぐ　☐ excessive 過度の
☐ kill off …を殺す、…を絶滅させる　❼☐ fertilize …を肥沃にする　❽☐ interact 相互に影響し合う
☐ preserve (自然環境など)を保護する　☐ delicate 微妙な

筆記③

第2段落

❶ A keystone species is one that―similar to its counterpart in architecture―keeps an ecosystem intact.

❷ Removal of a keystone―the most important section to offset gravity, weight and structural stress―in a bridge or arch can cause the entire structure to fall.

❸ Similarly, removal or reduction of a keystone species can cause an entire ecosystem to fall apart.

❹ Not all scientists agree on the concept of this species, or which species might qualify as this type within an ecosystem, but ecologists have identified three types: mutualists, predators, and engineers.

❺ Within any ecosystem, predators control the number of herbivores, or grass-eaters, and the number of herbivores, in turn, affects the amount of both plant life and predators.

❻ Each species is important in this system, although some species are more central than others.

---

❹ Not all scientists agree on the concept of this species,
　部分否定　S₁　　V₁　　　　　　　　　O₁・₁

or (which species might qualify as this type within an ecosystem),
　　　　S'　　　　V'
　　　　　　　　　　　O₁・₂

but ecologists have identified three types:
　　S₂　　　V₂　　　　　　O₂　　→具体的な例が続く

mutualists, predators, and engineers.

❺ Within any ecosystem, predators control
　　　　　　　　　　　S₁　　V₁

the number of herbivores, or grass-eaters,
　　　O₁　　　　　↑　言い換え

and the number of herbivores, (in turn),
　　　　S₂

affects the amount of both plant life and predators.
　V₂　　　　　　O₂

第2段落

❶ キーストーン種とは、建築物のキーストーンと同様に、生態系が損なわれないように維持する種のことである。

❷ 橋やアーチから、重力や重さ、構造的な圧力を相殺する最も重要な部分であるキーストーンを取り除くと、構造物全体が倒壊する可能性がある。

❸ 同様に、要となる種がなくなったり減少したりすると、生態系全体が崩壊してしまう可能性があるのだ。

❹ すべての科学者がキーストーン種という概念に賛同しているわけではなく、また生態系の中でどの種がこれに相当するのかについても意見は一致していないが、生態学者は、共生者、捕食者、技術者の3つのタイプを特定している。

❺ どのような生態系においても、草食動物の数は捕食者によってコントロールされ、それによって草食動物の数は植物と捕食者の両方の数に影響を与える。

❻ このシステムではそれぞれの種が重要な役割を担っているが、他の種と比べて中心的な役割を果たす種もある。

❶□ counterpart 対応するもの　□ architecture 建物全体、建築学　□ intact 損なわれていない
❷□ removal 除去、撤退　□ offset …を相殺する　□ gravity 重力　□ arch (橋や窓を支える)アーチ
❸□ fall apart (関係・組織などが)崩壊する　❹□ agree on …の意見がまとまる
□ concept 考え、概念　□ qualify as …の資格を得る　□ ecologist 生態学者
□ identify …を究明する、…を見分ける　□ mutualist 共生動物　□ predator 捕食動物
❺□ herbivore 草食動物　□ in turn 相互に　□ affect …に影響を与える
❻□ central 主要な、中心となる

第3段落

❶ One good example of a predator keystone species is the gray wolves of Yellowstone Park.

❷ After they were nearly killed off by humans in the last century, the populations of herbivores such as elk and deer began to grow too large, over-eating plants, including plants that were crucial to preventing soil loss near river banks.

❸ This soil loss harmed riverbanks and threatened species that rely on them, such as insects that fish and other creatures consume.

❹ Only through the reintroduction of wolves into Yellowstone in the 1990s could the number of elk be reduced and the ecosystem returned to balance.

❺ The wolves usually picked off the youngest, oldest or sickest of a herd, allowing only the quickest and strongest members to survive.

❻ As a result, overall herd health also improved.

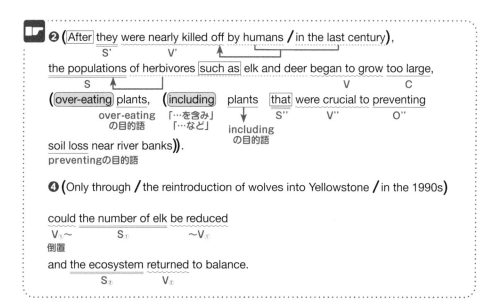

❶ イエローストーン公園のハイイロオオカミは、捕食者のキーストーンとなる種の代表例だ。

❷ オオカミが前世紀に人間によってほぼ絶滅させられた後、エルクやシカなどの草食動物の個体数が増え過ぎて、植物を過剰に食べてしまった。その植物の中には、川岸付近の土壌の流出を防ぐのに重要な植物も含まれていた。

❸ この土壌の消失は川岸を傷つけ、魚などの生物が食べる昆虫など、川岸の恩恵を受けている生物種が絶滅の危機に瀕した。

❹ 1990年代、イエローストーンにオオカミを復活させて初めて、エルクの数が減り、生態系のバランスが回復した。

❺ オオカミは大抵、エルクの群れの中で一番若いもの、一番年をとったもの、一番病弱なものを追い出し、最も素早く強いものだけが生き残るようにした。

❻ その結果、エルクの群れ全体の健康状態も改善された。

❷□ population 個体数　□ elk ヘラジカ　□ deer 鹿　□ crucial 重大な、決定的な
　□ river bank 川岸　❸□ harm …を害する　□ threaten …に脅威を与える　□ rely on …に頼っている
　□ creature 生き物　□ consume …を（大量に）食べる
❹□ reintroduction （生物を）元の生息地に戻すこと　□ reduce …を減少させる
❺□ pick off …を抜き取る　□ herd 動物の群れ　□ allow X to do X に…させておく
❻□ overall 全体にわたる　□ improve 良くなる、好転する

筆記③

441

第4段落

❶ Wolves may be a keystone species in Yellowstone, but that raises the question as to why elk are not.

❷ Scientists answer that by defining a keystone species as one that cannot easily be replaced.

❸ Yellowstone, for instance, has a wide range of herbivores, from bison to moose.

❹ There is only one top predator, though, so taking it away caused severe and unique damage to the entire ecosystem.

❺ The experience with the Yellowstone wolves indicates how balance may be restored to ecosystems whose top predators are declining or endangered.

❻ Certain species of tigers, lions, and cougars are already at risk, and if they disappear altogether other ecosystem failures could occur.

❼ While some nations or territories have sanctioned licensed hunting to make up for a lack of predators, random shooting of animals cannot create the herd health benefits that predators can.

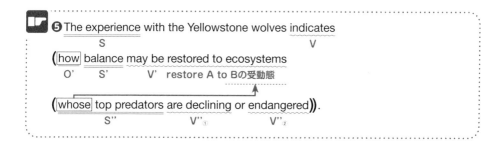

第4段落

❶ オオカミはイエローストーンのキーストーン種かもしれないが、するとなぜエルクはそうではないのかという疑問が生じる。

❷ 科学者は、「簡単に代替できない種」を「キーストーン種」と定義し、それに答えている。

❸ 例えば、イエローストーンにはバイソンからヘラジカまで、さまざまな草食動物が生息している。

❹ しかし、頂点に立つ捕食者はたった一種類しかいないため、その捕食者がいなくなると生態系全体に深刻かつ他では見られないダメージを与えることになる。

❺ このイエローストーンのオオカミを巡る経験から学べるのは、頂点にいる捕食者が減少したり絶滅の危機に瀕したりしている生態系のバランスをどのように回復させればいいかということだ。

❻ トラやライオン、クーガーなど一部の種はすでに危機に瀕しており、それらが完全にいなくなれば、他の生態系の破綻も起こりかねない。

❼ 捕食者の不足を補うために狩猟を許可している国や地域もあるが、無差別に動物を撃ち殺せば、捕食者がもたらすことができるような群れの健全性を保つ利点は得られない。

❶☐ raise …を生じさせる ☐ as to …に関して ❷☐ define A as B A を B と定義する
☐ replace …に取って代わる ❸☐ bison バイソン ☐ moose ヘラジカ ❹☐ predator 捕食者
☐ take away …を取り除く ❺☐ restore A to B A を B に回復させる・修復する
☐ decline 減少する、低下する ☐ endangered 絶滅の危機にさらされた ❻☐ cougar クーガー
☐ be at risk 危険にさらされている ☐ failure 衰退、障害 ❼☐ sanction …を認可する
☐ licensed 認可された、免許を受けた ☐ hunting 狩猟 ☐ make up for (不足など) を埋め合わせる
☐ random 手あたり次第の ☐ shooting 狩猟、銃撃 ☐ health benefits 健康上の利益

筆記③

問題英文の読み方 P.448　解説・正解 P.452　訳・語句 P.456

Updating Maslow's Hierarchy of Needs

Abraham Maslow was one of the pioneers of psychology. In the 1940s he developed a model called the Hierarchy of Needs. It was a pyramid—a geometric structure with a wide bottom and triangular sides coming to a point at the top—that classified human physical and psychological needs based on their priority. At the bottom of this pyramid came the basic requirements necessary for survival: food, shelter, and clothing. Maslow labeled these Basic Physiological Needs. Once these are satisfied, humans move up to satisfy their various psychological needs, which are, in order of importance, safety, love and belonging, esteem, and self-actualization (or reaching your full potential). Maslow's model was supposed to be true across all cultures and time periods. However, more recent inquiries have challenged Maslow's work, and questioned whether it really was supported by real-world information—especially with the advance of more complex data modeling tools.

An Arizona State University research team has taken a fresh look at Maslow's work, using modern survey techniques and computers that could process large data sets. Douglas Kenrick, one of the ASU researchers, said that an update of Maslow's hierarchy "should include findings from neuroscience, developmental psychology, and evolutionary psychology." Only when lines of research from these important fields related to Maslow's model were combined could Maslow's work be truly verified. The ASU team, which was made up of experts from these various areas, set that verification as their main goal. In the end, they came up with a model that was indeed similar to Maslow's in important ways, but also significantly different.

The ASU research model created what they felt were important updates to Maslow's famous pyramid. In their new Maslow model, the base of the pyramid mainly continues with its focus on survival, but the ASU team repositioned the psychological needs. Starting with self-protection, they arranged affiliation, status/esteem, and finding mates above it. Removing self-actualization altogether, they placed parenting at the very top of the pyramid. In other words, parenting is the ultimate human goal or the highest need to be met. People generally seek to become parents only when they have enough self-sufficiency and social status, because these characteristics may be necessary to find and keep a mate, especially in a competitive environment where people can choose from several mate options.

The ASU work may not be the final word on Maslow, though. Other researchers, such as Landon T. Smith, feel that new social and technology trends need to be accounted for. For example, Internet communities may be replacing long-term, in-person social groups. This means that more people are spending years of their lives in online groups where people easily come and go, with very little sense of belonging. Also, people today are more mobile. Status and esteem may not matter as much to them as they often relocate from one place to another. Other researchers question whether human needs exist in a fixed hierarchy at all. Rather, they may change and take on different levels of importance throughout one's life. As these questions are researched, we can expect more updates to Maslow's work in the future.

筆記③

(1) What do we learn about Abraham Maslow in the first paragraph?

    1 He was able to discover and correct many errors in our prior understanding of psychology.

    2 He developed a model that organized human needs into different levels according to the order in which they should be fulfilled.

    3 Scholars later came to depend on the big sets of data in his research in order to test other theories on human needs.

    4 Most of his theories on human needs were popular in the late 1940s, but did not last much longer than that.

(2) According to Douglas Kenrick, what may Maslow have overlooked in his original work?

    1 The necessity of getting his claims verified by researchers from a broad group of international experts.

    2 The fact that the early computer models that Maslow used did not create reliable surveys most of the time.

    3 The large amount of scientific data that had gone against most of the claims that he had developed over time.

    4 The scientific necessity to include research and information from a wide variety of fields.

(3) The ASU research that has been done since Maslow's time suggests that

1 the highest life goal of humans may be tied to their ability to successfully form and maintain stable family units.

2 meeting basic physiological requirements may not be as important for ordinary human beings as fulfilling their psychological and social needs.

3 scientific data that later researchers were able to collect and present prove that nearly all of Maslow's original insights were entirely wrong.

4 virtually all human physiological and psychological needs are much easier to meet by those who can compete well in modern societies.

(4) According to the author of the passage, how may Internet technology affect Maslow's pyramid?

1 It makes it easier for people to find suitable mates with whom they could form long-lasting relationships and have children.

2 It may keep many people from being involved for long in social groups that are permanent, unlike how it was in the past.

3 It may lead people to use technology for protection against outsiders who threaten to break up their group or harm their family units.

4 It makes it necessary to re-shape one's life into a non-pyramid structure where psychological needs are as important as physiological ones.

第1段落

Updating Maslow's Hierarchy of Needs

❶Abraham Maslow was one of the pioneers of psychology. ❷In the 1940s he developed a model called the Hierarchy of Needs. ❸It was a pyramid—a geometric structure with a wide bottom and triangular sides coming to a point at the top—that classified human physical and psychological needs based on their priority. ❹At the bottom of this pyramid came the basic requirements necessary for survival: food, shelter, and clothing. ❺Maslow labeled these Basic Physiological Needs. ❻Once these are satisfied, humans move up to satisfy their various psychological needs, which are, in order of importance, safety, love and belonging, esteem, and self-actualization (or reaching your full potential). ❼Maslow's model was supposed to be true across all cultures and time periods. ❽However, more recent inquiries have challenged Maslow's work, and questioned whether it really was supported by real-world information—especially with the advance of more complex data modeling tools.

第2段落

❶An Arizona State University research team has taken a fresh look at Maslow's work, using modern survey techniques and computers that could process large data sets. ❷Douglas Kenrick, one of the ASU researchers, said that an update of Maslow's hierarchy "should include findings from neuroscience, developmental psychology, and evolutionary psychology." ❸Only when lines of research from these important fields related to Maslow's model were combined could Maslow's work be truly verified. ❹The ASU team, which was made up of experts from these various areas, set that verification as their main goal. ❺In the end, they came up with a model that was indeed similar to Maslow's in important ways, but also significantly different.

この問題英文の長さは約500語です。

第1段落では、タイトルと❶❷から1940年にマズローが提唱した「欲求段階説」モデルについて説明をすると予想できます。❸で「これはピラミッド構造で、人間の身体的ならびに心理的欲求を優先順位によって分類したものだ」と簡潔に説明しています。❹から❻には詳しい説明があり、「ピラミッドの底辺は基本的な欲求である、食・住・衣で、基本的生理的欲求と名付けられ、これらが満たされれば、『安全』『愛情と所属』『承認』『自己実現』という重要度の順に欲求が高まる」と述べています。❼❽では「マズローのモデルはあらゆる文化や時代に通用するものとされていたが、データモデリングツールの進化により、実際の情報データに裏付けられるかどうかを疑問視する声が上がっている」と、研究の新たな局面を示して次の段落への展開につなげています。

❶から「アリゾナ州立大学（ASU）のチームは最新の技術とコンピュータを駆使して、マズローの研究を見直すことにした」とあり、第1段落と対比して、第2段落は新たな研究について紹介していくと推測できます。❷の「ASU のダグラス・ケンリック氏によると、マズローの段階説には神経科学、発達心理学、進化心理学からの知見を含めるべきだ」で新たな研究の方針が示されており、❸から❺で「これらの重要な分野の研究が組み合わされて初めてマズローの業績は検証されるので、ASU チームはその検証を目的として取り組み、マズローのモデルと異なるモデルを提案した」と、その方針に沿って研究を行ったと述べています。

第3段落

❶The ASU research model created what they felt were important updates to Maslow's famous pyramid. ❷In their new Maslow model, the base of the pyramid mainly continues with its focus on survival, but the ASU team repositioned the psychological needs. ❸Starting with self-protection, they arranged affiliation, status/esteem, and finding mates above it. ❹Removing self-actualization altogether, they placed parenting at the very top of the pyramid. ❺In other words, parenting is the ultimate human goal or the highest need to be met. ❻People generally seek to become parents only when they have enough self-sufficiency and social status, because these characteristics may be necessary to find and keep a mate, especially in a competitive environment where people can choose from several mate options.

第4段落

❶The ASU work may not be the final word on Maslow, though. ❷Other researchers, such as Landon T. Smith, feel that new social and technology trends need to be accounted for. ❸For example, Internet communities may be replacing long-term, in-person social groups. ❹This means that more people are spending years of their lives in online groups where people easily come and go, with very little sense of belonging. ❺Also, people today are more mobile. ❻Status and esteem may not matter as much to them as they often relocate from one place to another. ❼Other researchers question whether human needs exist in a fixed hierarchy at all. ❽Rather, they may change and take on different levels of importance throughout one's life. ❾As these questions are researched, we can expect more updates to Maslow's work in the future.

❶は前のパラグラフの最後で紹介された研究モデルを再度取り上げ、「ASU の研究モデルはマズローのピラミッドにアップデートを施している」と述べ、この段落では新たな研究モデルについて説明するとわかります。❷は新旧モデルの共通点と相違点として「新しいモデルでもピラミッドの底辺では生存に焦点を当てているが、心理的欲求を再配置している」と述べ、❸❹では新たな項目として「『自己防衛』、『親和関係』、『地位・自尊心』、『配偶者探し』を置き、そして『自己実現』は排除して、『子育て』を頂点に置いた」とあります。このピラミッドについて❺で「つまり、『子育て』は人間の最高の欲求なのだ」と言っています。その理由として、❻で「一般に人は十分な自給自足と社会的地位が得られて初めて親になろうとする。なぜなら、競争的な環境において伴侶を見つけ維持するためにこういった条件（＝十分な自給自足と社会的地位）が必要だからだ」と説明しています。

最後の段落は「しかし、ASU の研究でさえも、最終的な結論ではないかもしれない」とする❶で始まっています。その根拠として、❷で「他の研究者らは社会や技術の新しい傾向を考慮する必要があると感じている」と述べています。❸❹では具体例として、「インターネット・コミュニティなどが対面式の社会集団の代わりをし、帰属意識がないグループで人生の何年かを過ごすようになる」と述べ、さらに❺❻では「現代人は移動が多いので、頻繁に移動すると、地位や名声は重要ではないかもしれない」と述べています。締めくくりの❼から❾では「そもそも人間の欲求が固定的な段階構造に組み込まれるのか疑問視する研究者もいる。欲求は個人の生涯を通じて変化し、重要性のレベルも変わり得るので、これらの疑問が追究されることでマズローの研究はさらにアップデートされていくことだろう」と、今後の研究の可能性を示唆しています。

筆記③

(1) What do we learn about Abraham Maslow in the first paragraph?

1 He was able to discover and correct many errors in our prior understanding of psychology.

2 He developed a model that organized human needs into different levels according to the order in which they should be fulfilled.

3 Scholars later came to depend on the big sets of data in his research in order to test other theories on human needs.

4 Most of his theories on human needs were popular in the late 1940s, but did not last much longer than that.

(2) According to Douglas Kenrick, what may Maslow have overlooked in his original work?

1 The necessity of getting his claims verified by researchers from a broad group of international experts.

2 The fact that the early computer models that Maslow used did not create reliable surveys most of the time.

3 The large amount of scientific data that had gone against most of the claims that he had developed over time.

4 The scientific necessity to include research and information from a wide variety of fields.

(1) 🔲 第1段落でアブラハム・マズローについてわかることは何ですか。

    1 彼は、それまでの我々の心理学に対する理解における多くの誤りを発見し、修正することができた。

    2 人間の欲求を、満たすべき順序に従ってさまざまなレベルに整理したモデルを開発した。

    3 後世の学者は、人間の欲求に関する他の理論を証明するために、彼の研究の膨大なデータに頼るようになった。

    4 人間の欲求に関する彼の理論の多くは、1940年代後半に流行したが、それ以上長くは続かなかった。

🔍 第1段落の❷❸に「彼 (マズロー) は『欲求段階説』というモデルを提唱した。これはピラミッド構造で、人間の物理的ならびに心理的欲求を優先順位によって分類した」とあるので、ここで問1に解答することができます。

----

(2) 🔲 ダグラス・ケンリックによれば、マズローは自身の独自の業績の中で何を見落としていたでしょうか。

    1 自分の主張が、さまざまな国の専門の研究者によって検証される必要性があること。

    2 マズローが使用した初期のコンピュータ・モデルは、ほとんどの場合、信頼できる調査を設計することができなかったという事実。

    3 彼が時間をかけて構築した主張のほとんどに反する大量の科学的データ。

    4 幅広い分野の調査や情報を盛り込むという科学的な必要性。

🔍 第2段落の❷で「ASU のダグラス・ケンリック氏によると、マズローの段階説をアップデートするには神経科学、発達心理学、進化心理学からの知見を含めるべきだ」と述べているため、ここで問2の答えがわかります。

🖊 ☐ overlook …を見落とす　☐ get X *done* X を…させる・してもらう　☐ most of the time たいていの場合は
☐ necessity 必要性

筆記 ③

(3) The ASU research that has been done since Maslow's time suggests that

1 the highest life goal of humans may be tied to their ability to successfully form and maintain stable family units.

2 meeting basic physiological requirements may not be as important for ordinary human beings as fulfilling their psychological and social needs.

3 scientific data that later researchers were able to collect and present prove that nearly all of Maslow's original insights were entirely wrong.

4 virtually all human physiological and psychological needs are much easier to meet by those who can compete well in modern societies.

(4) According to the author of the passage, how may Internet technology affect Maslow's pyramid?

1 It makes it easier for people to find suitable mates with whom they could form long-lasting relationships and have children.

2 It may keep many people from being involved for long in social groups that are permanent, unlike how it was in the past.

3 It may lead people to use technology for protection against outsiders who threaten to break up their group or harm their family units.

4 It makes it necessary to re-shape one's life into a non-pyramid structure where psychological needs are as important as physiological ones.

(3) 📝 マズローの時代以降に行われた ASU の研究が示唆しているのは

1 人生の最高の目標は、安定した家族というまとまりをうまく形成し維持する能力と結びついている可能性があることだ。

2 一般の人間にとって、基本的な生理的欲求を満たすことは、心理的・社会的欲求を満たすことほど重要ではないかもしれないことだ。

3 マズロー独自の洞察は、後世の研究者が収集し発表した科学的データにより、ほぼすべてが全くの間違いだったことが証明されていることだ。

4 人間の生理的・心理的欲求は、現代社会でうまく競争できる人なら、ほとんどすべて容易に満たすことができることだ。

🔍 第3段落の❺で「『子育て』は人間の最高の欲求だ」と述べ、その理由を❻で「一般に人は十分な自給自足と社会的地位が得られて初めて親になろうとする。それは、競争的な環境において伴侶を見つけ維持するためにこういった条件（＝十分な自給自足と社会的地位）が必要だからだ」と説明しているところから、問3の答えがわかります。

✏️ ☐ be tied to …に関係している　☐ physiological 生理学上の　☐ requirement 要求するもの
☐ insight 洞察、識見　☐ virtually ほとんど

・・・

(4) 📝 この文章の著者によると、インターネット技術はマズローのピラミッドにどのような影響を与えるでしょうか。

1 長期的な関係を築き、子どもを作ることができる適切な相手を人々が見つけることが容易になる。

2 以前とは異なり、多くの人々が、永続的な社会集団に長く属し続けることを阻むかもしれない。

3 集団を崩壊させたり、家族に危害を加えたりする恐れのある部外者から、人々が自己防衛を図って技術を用いる可能性がある。

4 生理的な欲求と同じくらい心理的な欲求が重要になる非ピラミッド型の構造に、自分の人生を作り替える必要が出てくる。

🔍 第4段落の❶❷で「ASU の研究でさえも、最終的な結論ではないかもしれず、他の研究者らは社会や技術の新しい傾向を考慮する必要があると感じている」と述べ、続く❸で「インターネット・コミュニティなどが長期にわたる対面式の社会集団にとって代わる」と例を述べているところから、2が正解であると考えることができます。

✏️ ☐ involved 関係している　☐ unlike …と違って　☐ harm …を害する

🚩 **(3) 1　(4) 2**　455

Updating Maslow's Hierarchy of Needs

第1段落

❶ Abraham Maslow was one of the pioneers of psychology.

❷ In the 1940s he developed a model called the Hierarchy of Needs.

❸ It was a pyramid—a geometric structure with a wide bottom and triangular sides coming to a point at the top—that classified human physical and psychological needs based on their priority.

❹ At the bottom of this pyramid came the basic requirements necessary for survival: food, shelter, and clothing.

❺ Maslow labeled these Basic Physiological Needs.

❻ Once these are satisfied, humans move up to satisfy their various psychological needs, which are, in order of importance, safety, love and belonging, esteem, and self-actualization (or reaching your full potential).

❼ Maslow's model was supposed to be true across all cultures and time periods.

❽ However, more recent inquiries have challenged Maslow's work, and questioned whether it really was supported by real-world information—especially with the advance of more complex data modeling tools.

---

❻ (Once these are satisfied), 条件を表す副詞節
　　　　　　S'　　V'

humans move up to satisfy their various psychological needs, (which are,
　S　　　V　　　　　　　　　　　　　　O　　　　　　　　　　　S''　V''

(in order of importance), safety, love and belonging, esteem,
　　　　　　　　　　　　　C''①　　　C''②　　　　　C''③

and self-actualization (or reaching your full potential)).
　　C''④　　　　　self-actualizationの言い換え

❽ However, more recent inquiries have challenged Maslow's work, and
　　　　　　　　　　S　　　　　　　　V①　　　　　　O①

questioned (whether it really was supported by real-world information
　V②　　　　O②　　S'　　　　V'

(—especially with the advance of more complex data modeling tools)).

マズローの欲求段階説のアップデート

❶ アブラハム・マズローは心理学のパイオニアの一人だった。

❷ 彼は、1940年代に「欲求段階説」というモデルを提唱した。

❸ これは、底辺が広く、三角形の辺が頂点に達する幾何学的なピラミッド構造で、人間の身体的・心理的欲求を優先順位によって分類したものである。

❹ このピラミッドの底辺に位置するのが、生存に必要な基本的な欲求である「食・住・衣」だ。

❺ マズローはこれを「基本的生理的欲求」と名付けた。

❻ これらが満たされれば、人間はさまざまな心理的な欲求を満たそうとする。それは重要な順に、安全欲求、愛情と所属欲求、承認欲求、自己実現欲求（あるいは自分の可能性を大いに発揮すること）である。

❼ マズローのモデルは、あらゆる文化や時代に通用するものとされていた。

❽ しかし、最近の議論ではマズローの見解には異議が唱えられていて、特にデータモデリングツールが複雑に進化したこともあり、本当に実際の情報によって裏付けられているのかどうか疑問視されている。

□ hierarchy 階層制　❶□ psychology 心理学　❸□ geometric 幾何学的な　□ triangular 三角形の
□ classify …を分類する　□ physical 身体の　□ psychological needs 心理的な欲求
□ priority 優先　❹□ requirement 必要とするもの　❺□ label A B AをBと分類する
❻□ move up to *do* …しようとする、…することを目指す　□ in order of …の順に
□ belonging 所属　□ esteem 尊敬、名声　□ self-actualization 自己実現
❼□ be supposed to be 世間では…だと考えられている　❽□ inquiry 調査、研究
□ challenge …に異議を唱える　□ question whether 節 …かどうか疑わしい　□ advance 進化、向上

筆記③

第2段落

❶ An Arizona State University research team has taken a fresh look at Maslow's work, using modern survey techniques and computers that could process large data sets.

❷ Douglas Kenrick, one of the ASU researchers, said that an update of Maslow's hierarchy "should include findings from neuroscience, developmental psychology, and evolutionary psychology."

❸ Only when lines of research from these important fields related to Maslow's model were combined could Maslow's work be truly verified.

❹ The ASU team, which was made up of experts from these various areas, set that verification as their main goal.

❺ In the end, they came up with a model that was indeed similar to Maslow's in important ways, but also significantly different.

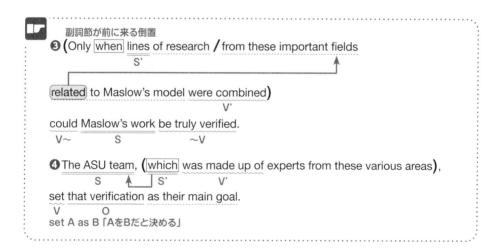

副詞節が前に来る倒置
❸(Only when lines of research / from these important fields
　　　　　　　S'
related to Maslow's model were combined)
　　　　　　　　　　　　　　V'
could Maslow's work be truly verified.
V～　　　　S　　　　　～V

❹The ASU team, (which was made up of experts from these various areas),
　　　S　　　　　S'　　　V'
set that verification as their main goal.
V　　　O
set A as B「AをBだと決める」

❶ アリゾナ州立大学 (ASU) の研究チームは、最新の調査技術と大規模なデータの集合を処理できるコンピュータを駆使して、マズローの研究を見直すことにした。

❷ ASU の研究者の一人であるダグラス・ケンリック氏は、マズローの段階説をアップデートするには、「神経科学、発達心理学、進化心理学からの知見を含めるべきだ」と述べている。

❸ マズローのモデルに関連するこれらの重要な分野の研究が組み合わされて初めて、マズローの業績は真に検証されることになるのである。

❹ そこで、これらの分野の専門家で構成された ASU のチームが、その検証を最大の目標とした。

❺ その結果、マズローのモデルと重要な点でかなり似ているようでいて、大きく異なるモデルを導き出した。

❶ ☐ take a fresh look at …を見直す　☐ survey 調査
☐ data set データセット（ひとまとまりのデータ）　❷ ☐ findings 研究結果
☐ neuroscience 神経科学　☐ developmental psychology 発達心理学
☐ evolutionary psychology 進化心理学　❸ ☐ relate A to B A を B と関連させる
☐ combine …を結びつける　☐ verify …を確かめる、…を検証する　❹ ☐ be made up of …から成る
☐ set X as one's goal X を目標とする　☐ verification 検証　❺ ☐ in the end 結局
☐ come up with …を考え出す・提案する　☐ significantly 相当に、著しく

第3段落

❶ The ASU research model created what they felt were important updates to Maslow's famous pyramid.

❷ In their new Maslow model, the base of the pyramid mainly continues with its focus on survival, but the ASU team repositioned the psychological needs.

❸ Starting with self-protection, they arranged affiliation, status/esteem, and finding mates above it.

❹ Removing self-actualization altogether, they placed parenting at the very top of the pyramid.

❺ In other words, parenting is the ultimate human goal or the highest need to be met.

❻ People generally seek to become parents only when they have enough self-sufficiency and social status, because these characteristics may be necessary to find and keep a mate, especially in a competitive environment where people can choose from several mate options.

---

❶The ASU research model created
　　　　　　S　　　　　　　 V

(what (they felt) were important updates to Maslow's famous pyramid).
 O(S')　S'' V''　　V'　　　　 O'

❻People generally seek to become parents
　　S　　　　　　　 V　　　　　 O

(only when they have enough self-sufficiency and social status),
　　　　 S'　V'　　　　　　　　　　O'

(because these characteristics may be necessary to find and keep a mate,
　　　　 S''　　　　　　 V''　　 C''　　　　　　　　　findとkeep
　　　　　　　　　　　　　　　　　　　　　　　　　　　　　の目的語
especially in a competitive environment

(where people can choose from several mate options)).
　　　　 S'''　　V'''

第3段落

❶ ASU の研究モデルは、マズローの有名なピラミッドに重要だと考えたアップデートを施したものである。

❷ ASU の新しいマズローモデルでも、ピラミッドの底辺では主に生存に焦点を当てているが、ASU チームは心理的欲求を再配置している。

❸ 自己防衛から始め、その上に親和関係、地位・自尊心、配偶者探しを配置した。

❹ そして、自己実現を完全に排除し、子育てをピラミッドの頂点に据えた。

❺ つまり、子育ては人間の究極の目標であり、満たされるべき最高の欲求なのだ。

❻ 一般に人は、自分で十分に生活に必要なものを調達でき、社会的な地位が得られるようになって初めて親になろうとする。なぜなら、こういった性質は、特に、人が何人かの候補から配偶者を選ぶ競争的な環境において、配偶者を見つけ関係を維持していくために必要だと考えられるからである。

❷□ continue with …を続ける　□ survival 生き残り、生存　□ reposition …の位置を変える
❸□ affiliation 親和関係　□ mate 配偶者、仲間　**❹**□ remove …を取り除く　□ altogether 完全に
□ place …を配置する　**❺**□ ultimate (順序が) 最後の　**❻**□ seek to *do* …しようと努める
□ self-sufficiency 自給自足　□ characteristics 特徴、特性、特色　□ competitive 競争的な

第4段落

❶ The ASU work may not be the final word on Maslow, though.

❷ Other researchers, such as Landon T. Smith, feel that new social and technology trends need to be accounted for.

❸ For example, Internet communities may be replacing long-term, in-person social groups.

❹ This means that more people are spending years of their lives in online groups where people easily come and go, with very little sense of belonging.

❺ Also, people today are more mobile.

❻ Status and esteem may not matter as much to them as they often relocate from one place to another.

❼ Other researchers question whether human needs exist in a fixed hierarchy at all.

❽ Rather, they may change and take on different levels of importance throughout one's life.

❾ As these questions are researched, we can expect more updates to Maslow's work in the future.

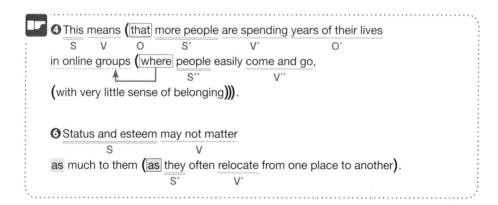

❶ しかし、ASU の研究は、マズローに関する最終的な結論ではないかもしれない。

❷ ランドン・T・スミスなど他の研究者は、社会や技術の新しい傾向を考慮する必要があると感じている。

❸ 例えば、インターネット・コミュニティは、長期にわたる対面式の社会集団に取って代わるかもしれない。

❹ つまり、より多くの人々が簡単に行き来でき、帰属意識がほとんどないオンライングループで人生の何年かを過ごすようになる。

❺ また、現代人は移動が多い。

❻ ある場所から別の場所への移動が頻繁にあるのと比べると、地位や名声はそれほど重要ではないかもしれない。

❼ 人間の欲求が固定的な段階構造に組み込まれるのかどうか、疑問視する研究者もいる。

❽ むしろ、欲求は生涯を通じて変化し、異なるレベルの重要性を帯びるかもしれない。

❾ これらの疑問が研究されることで、マズローの研究が今後さらにアップデートされることが期待される。

❷□ account for …の理由を説明する　❸□ replace …に取って代わる　□ in-person 人が直接会う…
❹□ belonging 帰属　❺□ mobile 移動する…、流動性のある　❻□ matter 問題となる、重要である
□ relocate 移転する　❼□ question whether 節 …かどうか疑問である　□ exist 存在する
□ fixed 固定した　❽□ rather むしろ　□ take on (ある性質など)を帯びる・持つようになる
□ expect …を期待する

筆記 ③

問題英文の読み方 P.468　解説・正解 P.472　訳・語句 P.476

Tower of Pisa: Amazing History

The Tower of Pisa is one of the most well-known tourist attractions in the world. Most ordinary people marvel at how any building, especially one so old, can lean downwards without collapsing. The Romanesque structure can actually remain at this unusual angle because of a continual investment of time, money, and engineering techniques over many centuries. The building itself was planned to be an ordinary bell tower in a large plaza of greater attractions in Pisa's "Square of Miracles," which included a church, statues, and domes. Pisa was an independent city-state, and its fleets fought and traded throughout the Mediterranean Sea. It was this wealth that enabled it to build the Square. Work began in 1172, during the height of Pisa's economic prosperity and military power. The actual architects of the tower remain a mystery, perhaps, as many suggest, because no one wanted to take responsibility for the design flaws that appeared later.

It was in 1178, after about two floors had been created, that engineers realized the tower was "leaning south." The planners were initially puzzled, since they had used Roman design principles that had proved effective across a range of Mediterranean buildings over many centuries. The builders only realized later that these designs would not necessarily work in Pisa. A strong, firm, and deep foundation—the part of the structure that is underground—is necessary for tall buildings, but the Tower of Pisa had a shallow foundation of just 3 meters. Worse, the soil underneath the tower was made of many layers, including wet clay. The tower sank into this clay and then one side began to sink deeper than the other, causing the lean.

From that point on, across several centuries, engineers tried many approaches to correct this structural problem. At first, they tried to balance the southern lean by designing the higher floors with a slightly northern one. This is why, if one looks carefully, one can see that the tower is actually curved, not straight. This did not counter the tower's southern lean, however. Other strategies were tried, but the tower continued its gradual southerly slide toward earth. By the 19th and 20th centuries, other Italian towers with similar problems were collapsing, including the bell tower of St. Mark's Basilica in 1902 and the Civic Tower of Pavia in 1989. Since tourists also added to the lean, the Tower of Pisa was closed to the public in 1990 for the first time. International groups of scientists conferenced to deal with the engineering challenge and save the tower, but none could solve the problem that had lasted about 900 years.

Finally, Professor John Burland of Imperial College London found a solution: simply remove and replace the soil, especially the wet clay. About US$30 million was spent to remove 77 tons of soil, and correct the tower's lean to only about 3.99 degrees. It may have been possible to straighten the tower completely, but the recovery team did not: by this time, the Tower of Pisa was bringing in millions of euros in tourist revenue yearly, and it seemed unlikely that a "straight" tower could do the same.

(1) What do we learn about the Tower of Pisa from the passage?

    1 It is a big design and engineering mistake that is impossible to fix, despite spending millions of dollars over many years.

    2 It is a typical example of how clever architects designed and built unusual and exciting towers to attract tourists.

    3 It is a unique structure whose initial defect required many centuries of analysis and engineering efforts to prevent a collapse.

    4 It is a clear example of the failure of Roman architecture whenever it was adopted by other cities.

(2) Early engineers were baffled by the first leaning of the Tower of Pisa because

    1 they had used a building method that worked well in many other locations where it had been previously used.

    2 they had never imagined that the bell tower could lean so far over without actually collapsing into the earth.

    3 their research on soil types had suggested the ground was strong enough to support the type of structure that they were developing.

    4 the architects they had worked with had been experts in this field for many years across Pisa and other Italian city-states.

(3)   What role were the higher levels of the Tower of Pisa expected to play?

1   They would prevent the tower from sliding northward into an unstable curve that could never be maintained for long.

2   They would be constructed of lighter materials and thereby balance the heavier weight of the lower floors.

3   They would offer unique views of the Square of Miracles and its churches, domes, and other bell towers.

4   They would straighten the tower by pulling it in the opposite direction that it was leaning toward.

(4)   How have the engineering problems of the Tower of Pisa been resolved?

1   The government closes the tower to the public during the tourist season every year, preventing the collapse of the structure.

2   More layers of soil have been added around the tower, making the ground stable enough for a somewhat bigger lean now.

3   Experts removed parts of the sinking ground, but kept the tower at a slight lean to retain its tourist value.

4   British colleges spent $30 million to replace some of the building foundations, ensuring a permanent 3.99 degree lean.

第1段落

Tower of Pisa: Amazing History

❶The Tower of Pisa is one of the most well-known tourist attractions in the world. ❷Most ordinary people marvel at how any building, especially one so old, can lean downwards without collapsing. ❸The Romanesque structure can actually remain at this unusual angle because of a continual investment of time, money, and engineering techniques over many centuries. ❹The building itself was planned to be an ordinary bell tower in a large plaza of greater attractions in Pisa's "Square of Miracles," which included a church, statues, and domes. ❺Pisa was an independent city-state, and its fleets fought and traded throughout the Mediterranean Sea. ❻It was this wealth that enabled it to build the Square. ❼Work began in 1172, during the height of Pisa's economic prosperity and military power. ❽The actual architects of the tower remain a mystery, perhaps, as many suggest, because no one wanted to take responsibility for the design flaws that appeared later.

第2段落

❶It was in 1178, after about two floors had been created, that engineers realized the tower was "leaning south." ❷The planners were initially puzzled, since they had used Roman design principles that had proved effective across a range of Mediterranean buildings over many centuries. ❸The builders only realized later that these designs would not necessarily work in Pisa. ❹A strong, firm, and deep foundation—the part of the structure that is underground—is necessary for tall buildings, but the Tower of Pisa had a shallow foundation of just 3 meters. ❺Worse, the soil underneath the tower was made of many layers, including wet clay. ❻The tower sank into this clay and then one side began to sink deeper than the other, causing the lean.

この問題英文の長さは約500語です。

タイトルと、❶の「ピサの斜塔は世界で最も有名な観光名所の一つだ」から、この文章がピサの斜塔に関するものだと確認できます。❷は、「普通の人なら、建物が傾いたまま壊れないでいることにびっくりするだろう」と、ピサの斜塔に関する一般的な視点を示しています。❸ではピサの斜塔を「このロマネスク様式の建築物」と言い換えて、「この建築物が保たれたのは時間と資金と技術力が投入され続けたからである」と、人々がピサの斜塔を保つために労力を費やしたことについて説明しています。❹から❻にはこの建物が計画された経緯と、ピサ艦隊が貿易活動をしていたこともあって都市国家ピサが豊かだったことについて書かれていて、❼には「ピサの繁栄が絶頂期だった1172年にピサの斜塔の工事が始まった」とあります。この段落の最終文である❽は、「実際、誰が設計したのかは謎に包まれていて、それは設計上の欠陥の責任を誰も取りたくなかったからだろう」という興味深い文で次の段落につなげています。

第2段落

❶は「塔が南に傾いていることに技術者が気づいたのは、2階部分まで建築された後の1178年のことだった」で始まり、第2段落では塔が傾いていることがわかったときの状況について書かれていると予測できます。❷❸で「設計者たちは、何世紀にもわたって、さまざまな建物で有効だった設計原理を使っていたが、この設計がピサで通用するとは限らないことが後になってわかった」とあります。❹から❻では、その理由について、「高層建築にはしっかりとした基礎が必要だが、ピサの塔の基礎はわずか3メートルだった。しかも土壌は粘土を含んでいて、その粘土に塔が沈み込み、片側がより深く沈み込んで傾いた」と言っています。

筆記③

第3段落

❶From that point on, across several centuries, engineers tried many approaches to correct this structural problem. ❷At first, they tried to balance the southern lean by designing the higher floors with a slightly northern one. ❸This is why, if one looks carefully, one can see that the tower is actually curved, not straight. ❹This did not counter the tower's southern lean, however. ❺Other strategies were tried, but the tower continued its gradual southerly slide toward earth. ❻By the 19th and 20th centuries, other Italian towers with similar problems were collapsing, including the bell tower of St. Mark's Basilica in 1902 and the Civic Tower of Pavia in 1989. ❼Since tourists also added to the lean, the Tower of Pisa was closed to the public in 1990 for the first time. ❽International groups of scientists conferenced to deal with the engineering challenge and save the tower, but none could solve the problem that had lasted about 900 years.

第4段落

❶Finally, Professor John Burland of Imperial College London found a solution: simply remove and replace the soil, especially the wet clay. ❷About US$30 million was spent to remove 77 tons of soil, and correct the tower's lean to only about 3.99 degrees. ❸It may have been possible to straighten the tower completely, but the recovery team did not: by this time, the Tower of Pisa was bringing in millions of euros in tourist revenue yearly, and it seemed unlikely that a "straight" tower could do the same.

第3段落では、**❶**に「それ以来、何世紀にもわたって技術者たちはこの問題を解決するために、さまざまなアプローチを試みた」とあることから、この問題についての技術者の取り組みが書かれているとわかります。**❷**から**❺**ではその取り組みについて、「最初は、高層階を北寄りに設計したため、塔は曲がっていることがわかる。結局傾きは解消されず、他の方法を試しても塔は南に傾いていった」と言っています。**❻**では、同じような問題を抱えていたイタリアの塔について「サン・マルコ寺院の鐘楼や、パヴィアの市民塔なども崩壊していった」とあり、**❼**では「1990年にはピサの斜塔は公開を中止した」と、傾斜に拍車がかかったことが書かれています。**❽**で「国際的な科学者グループが対処しても問題を解決することはできなかった」と、さまざまなアプローチをしても解決できなかったと述べて、この段落を終えています。

第4段落

❶の「ついに、ジョン・バーランド教授が解決策を発見した。土壌を入れ替えるだけでよいのだ」より、最後の段落で新たな展開に入ると期待できます。**❷**で「約3,000万ドルをかけて塔の傾きを修正した」とあり、塔の傾きを修正することができるようになったとわかります。**❸**から終わりまでで、「塔をまっすぐにすることは可能だったかもしれないが、このとき既にピサの斜塔は年間数百万ユーロの観光収入を得ていたので、修復チームはあえてまっすぐにしなかった」と述べていることから、塔をわざと傾いた状態にすることで観光地として存続させていることがわかります。

筆記③

(1) What do we learn about the Tower of Pisa from the passage?

1 It is a big design and engineering mistake that is impossible to fix, despite spending millions of dollars over many years.

2 It is a typical example of how clever architects designed and built unusual and exciting towers to attract tourists.

3 It is a unique structure whose initial defect required many centuries of analysis and engineering efforts to prevent a collapse.

4 It is a clear example of the failure of Roman architecture whenever it was adopted by other cities.

(2) Early engineers were baffled by the first leaning of the Tower of Pisa because

1 they had used a building method that worked well in many other locations where it had been previously used.

2 they had never imagined that the bell tower could lean so far over without actually collapsing into the earth.

3 their research on soil types had suggested the ground was strong enough to support the type of structure that they were developing.

4 the architects they had worked with had been experts in this field for many years across Pisa and other Italian city-states.

(1) 🔀 ピサの斜塔について、この文章からは何がわかりますか。

1 何年もかけて何百万ドルも費やしても、修復することが不可能な、設計と土木工事の大きな失敗である。

2 観光客を引きつけるために、賢い建築家が普通ではない刺激的な塔を設計・建設した典型的な事例である。

3 初期欠陥のため、崩壊を防ぐために何世紀もの分析と工学を駆使した努力を必要とした珍しい建築物である。

4 ローマの建築技法が他の都市で採用されたときはいつも失敗する明確な例である。

🔍 第1段落❽の「設計上の欠陥の責任を誰も取りたくなかった」から初期欠陥があったことが確認できます。そして、第3段落❶の「それ以来、何世紀にもわたって技術者たちはこの問題を解決するために、さまざまなアプローチを試みた」と、第4段落❷で述べられている事例が何世紀にも及ぶ分析と技術者の努力に当てはまることから問1の答えは3であるとわかります。

✏️ □ attract（関心など）を引く □ initial defect 初期不良 □ require …を必要とする □ prevent …を防ぐ
□ collapse 崩壊 □ adopt …を採用する

．．．

(2) 🔀 初期の技術者がピサの塔の最初の傾きに困惑したのは、

1 以前使用されていた他の多くの場所でうまく機能していた建築方法を使用していたから。

2 鐘楼が実際に地面にくずれ落ちることなく、これほどまでに傾くとは想像もしていなかったから。

3 土壌の種類を調査した結果、その地盤は自分たちが建設するタイプの構造を支えるのに十分な強度があることがわかったから。

4 一緒に仕事をした建築家は、ピサや他のイタリアの都市国家で長年にわたってこの分野の専門家だったから。

🔍 第2段落の❷から❸で「設計者たちは、何世紀にもわたって、さまざまな建物で有効だった設計原理を使っていたのだが、この設計がピサで通用するとは限らないことが後になってわかった」とあります。ここで問2に答えることができます。

✏️ □ baffle …を困惑させる □ previously 以前 □ so far ここまでは

．．．

筆記 ③

(3) What role were the higher levels of the Tower of Pisa expected to play?

1 They would prevent the tower from sliding northward into an unstable curve that could never be maintained for long.

2 They would be constructed of lighter materials and thereby balance the heavier weight of the lower floors.

3 They would offer unique views of the Square of Miracles and its churches, domes, and other bell towers.

4 They would straighten the tower by pulling it in the opposite direction that it was leaning toward.

(4) How have the engineering problems of the Tower of Pisa been resolved?

1 The government closes the tower to the public during the tourist season every year, preventing the collapse of the structure.

2 More layers of soil have been added around the tower, making the ground stable enough for a somewhat bigger lean now.

3 Experts removed parts of the sinking ground, but kept the tower at a slight lean to retain its tourist value.

4 British colleges spent $30 million to replace some of the building foundations, ensuring a permanent 3.99 degree lean.

(3) 📄 ピサの塔の高層部はどのような役割を果たすことを期待されていましたか。

1 塔が北側に傾いていき、長くは持たない不安定な曲線の形になるのを防ぐ。

2 軽めの材料で作られ、それによって低層部の重さとバランスを取る。

3 奇跡の広場やそこにある教会、ドーム、他の鐘楼のユニークな眺めを見られるようにする。

4 塔が傾いている方向と逆に引っ張ることで、塔をまっすぐにする。

🔍 第3段落の❷に「高層階をやや北寄りに設計することで、南側の傾きのバランスを取ろうとした」とあります。ここで問3に答えることができます。

✏️ ☐ be expected to *do* …すると期待されている ☐ slide そっと動く ☐ northward 北に向かって
☐ unstable 不安定な ☐ straighten …をまっすぐにする

....

(4) 📄 ピサの塔の工学上の問題はどのように解決されましたか。

1 毎年、観光シーズンには政府が塔の公開を中止し、建築物の倒壊を防いでいる。

2 塔の周囲に土の層を増やし、現在では多少大きく傾いても大丈夫なように地盤を安定させている。

3 専門家が沈下した地盤の一部を取り除いたが、観光価値を保つために塔を少し傾けたままにしている。

4 イギリスのカレッジが3,000万ドルをかけて建物の基礎の一部を交換し、永久的な3.99度の傾きを確保した。

🔍 第4段落の❶に「土壌を入れ替える」とあります。そして、❸に「塔をまっすぐにすることは可能だったかもしれないが、ピサの斜塔がこれまでに年間数百万ユーロの観光収入を得ていたので、修復チームはあえてそうしなかった」とあります。ここから問4の答えがわかります。

✏️ ☐ resolve …を解決する ☐ stable 安定した ☐ somewhat 多少 ☐ retain …を保持する ☐ value 価値
☐ replace …を取り換える ☐ foundation 建物の土台・基礎 ☐ ensure …を確保する

Tower of Pisa: Amazing History

第1段落

❶ The Tower of Pisa is one of the most well-known tourist attractions in the world.

❷ Most ordinary people marvel at how any building, especially one so old, can lean downwards without collapsing.

❸ The Romanesque structure can actually remain at this unusual angle because of a continual investment of time, money, and engineering techniques over many centuries.

❹ The building itself was planned to be an ordinary bell tower in a large plaza of greater attractions in Pisa's "Square of Miracles," which included a church, statues, and domes.

❺ Pisa was an independent city-state, and its fleets fought and traded throughout the Mediterranean Sea.

❻ It was this wealth that enabled it to build the Square.

❼ Work began in 1172, during the height of Pisa's economic prosperity and military power.

❽ The actual architects of the tower remain a mystery, perhaps, as many suggest, because no one wanted to take responsibility for the design flaws that appeared later.

---

❷ Most ordinary people marvel at (how any building, (especially one so old),
　　　　　　S　　　　　　　　V　　　O　　　　　S'
can lean downwards without collapsing).
　　　V'

❻ It was this wealth that enabled it to build the Square.
　強調構文　　S　　　　V　　O=Pisa　　C
　　　　　S enable O to do「SのおかげでOが…できるようになる」

❽ The actual architects of the tower remain a mystery,
　　　　　　　S　　　　　　　　　V　　　C
perhaps, (as many suggest), (because no one wanted to take responsibility
　　　　　　S'　　V'　　　　　　　　　S''　　　V''　　　　　O''
for the design flaws (that appeared later)).
　　　　　　　　　　　　　S'''　V'''

ピサの斜塔：驚きの歴史

第1段落

❶ ピサの斜塔は、世界で最も有名な観光名所の一つだ。

❷ どのような建物であっても、これほど古い建物であればなおさら、倒壊することなく傾いた状態のままでいられることに普通の人は驚嘆する。

❸ このロマネスク様式の建築物が、このような普通ではない角度を保つことができたのは、何世紀にもわたって時間と資金と技術力が投入され続けたからである。

❹ この建物自体は、ピサの「奇跡の広場」と呼ばれる、教会や彫像、ドームなどの見どころの多い大きな広場の中に、普通の鐘楼として計画されたものであった。

❺ ピサは独立した都市国家であり、ピサ艦隊は地中海全域で戦いを繰り広げながら貿易活動もしていた。

❻ この豊かさが、広場の建設を可能にしたのである。

❼ 工事が始まったのは1172年、ピサの経済的繁栄と軍事力の絶頂期であった。

❽ この塔の設計者は謎に包まれている。多くの人が指摘するように、おそらく、後に判明した設計上の欠陥の責任を誰も取ろうとしなかったからだろう。

❷ ☐ ordinary 普通の、平凡な ☐ marvel at …に驚く ☐ lean 傾く ☐ downward 下向きに ☐ collapse 崩壊する ❸ ☐ unusual 普通ではない、異常な ☐ angle 角度 ☐ continual 継続的な ☐ investment 投資、出資 ❹ ☐ plaza (都市の)広場 ☐ attraction 人を引き付けるもの ☐ square (四角い)広場 ❺ ☐ fleet 艦隊 ☐ Mediterranean Sea 地中海 ❻ ☐ wealth 富、大きな財産 ☐ enable X to *do* X に…できるようにする ❼ ☐ prosperity 繁栄 ❽ ☐ architect 建築家 ☐ take responsibility for …に責任を持つ ☐ flaw 欠陥

筆記3

第2段落

❶ It was in 1178, after about two floors had been created, that engineers realized the tower was "leaning south."

❷ The planners were initially puzzled, since they had used Roman design principles that had proved effective across a range of Mediterranean buildings over many centuries.

❸ The builders only realized later that these designs would not necessarily work in Pisa.

❹ A strong, firm, and deep foundation—the part of the structure that is underground—is necessary for tall buildings, but the Tower of Pisa had a shallow foundation of just 3 meters.

❺ Worse, the soil underneath the tower was made of many layers, including wet clay.

❻ The tower sank into this clay and then one side began to sink deeper than the other, causing the lean.

---

❶ It was in 1178, (after about two floors had been created),
強調構文　　　　　　　　　　　S'　　　　　　　V'

that engineers realized (☐ the tower was "leaning south.")
　　　S　　　　V　　　　　that　S''　　　　　V''
　　　　　　　　　　　　　　　　O

❹ A strong, firm, and deep foundation
　　　　　　　　　　S①

└(—the part of the structure (that is underground)—)
　　　　　　　　　　　　　　　S' V'　　C'

is necessary for tall buildings,
V①　　C①

but the Tower of Pisa had a shallow foundation of just 3 meters.
　　　　S②　　　　　　V②　　　　　O②

❶ 塔が「南に傾いている」ことに技術者が気づいたのは、大体2階部分まで建築された後の1178年のことだった。

❷ 設計した人たちは最初戸惑った。というのも、彼らは何世紀にもわたって地中海沿岸のさまざまな建物で効果を発揮してきたローマの設計原理を使っていたからだ。

❸ しかし、この設計がピサで通用するとは限らないことが後になってわかった。

❹ 高層建築には、地下に深くしっかりとした基礎が必要だが、ピサの塔の基礎はわずか3メートルという浅さだったのだ。

❺ しかも、塔の下の土壌は湿った粘土を含む何層もの土でできていた。

❻ その粘土の中に塔が沈み込み、片側がより深く沈み込んで傾いたのである。

❶☐ realize（that 節）…だと気づく　❷☐ initially 当初は　☐ puzzle …を困らせる
☐ principle 原理、法則　☐ prove …であることがわかる　☐ effective 効力のある、有効な
☐ a range of さまざまな…　❸☐ work 正常に機能する、うまくいく　❹☐ foundation 基礎、土台
☐ shallow 浅い　❺☐ underneath …のすぐ下に　☐ layer 層、重なり　☐ clay 粘土
❻☐ sink into …に沈む　☐ cause …の原因となる

筆記③

479

第3段落

❶ From that point on, across several centuries, engineers tried many approaches to correct this structural problem.

❷ At first, they tried to balance the southern lean by designing the higher floors with a slightly northern one.

❸ This is why, if one looks carefully, one can see that the tower is actually curved, not straight.

❹ This did not counter the tower's southern lean, however.

❺ Other strategies were tried, but the tower continued its gradual southerly slide toward earth.

❻ By the 19th and 20th centuries, other Italian towers with similar problems were collapsing, including the bell tower of St. Mark's Basilica in 1902 and the Civic Tower of Pavia in 1989.

❼ Since tourists also added to the lean, the Tower of Pisa was closed to the public in 1990 for the first time.

❽ International groups of scientists conferenced to deal with the engineering challenge and save the tower, but none could solve the problem that had lasted about 900 years.

---

❽ International groups of scientists conferenced
              S_1 V_1

to deal with the engineering challenge and save the tower,
  V'_1 deal withの目的語 V'_2 saveの目的語
不定詞の副詞的用法

but none could solve the problem (that had lasted about 900 years).
    S_2 V_2 O_2 S''   V''

第3段落

❶ それ以来、何世紀にもわたって、技術者たちはこの構造的な問題を解決するために、さまざまなアプローチを試みた。

❷ 最初は、高層階をやや北寄りに設計することで、南側の傾きのバランスを取ろうとした。

❸ そのため、よく見ると塔はまっすぐではなく、曲がっていることがわかる。

❹ しかし、これでは塔の南側への傾きは解消されなかった。

❺ 他の方法も試されたが、塔は徐々に南へ傾き、地面に向かっていった。

❻ 19世紀から20世紀にかけて、1902年のサン・マルコ寺院の鐘楼、1989年のパヴィアの市民塔など、同じような問題を抱えたイタリアの塔が倒壊していった。

❼ 観光客がその傾斜に拍車をかけたこともあり、1990年にはピサの斜塔は初めて公開を中止した。

❽ 国際的な科学者グループが、この工学上の問題に対処し、塔を保存するために会議を開いたが、900年続いた問題を解決することはできなかった。

❶□ from ... on …からずっと　□ approach 手法、取り上げ方、接近　□ correct …を正す
□ structural 構造上の　❷□ balance …の釣り合いを保つ　□ slightly わずかに
❸□ this is why 節 こういうわけで…する　□ curved 曲がっている
❹□ counter …を阻止する・無効にする・打ち消す　❺□ strategy 方法、手順
□ gradual 徐々に進む、ゆるやかな　□ southerly 南寄りの　□ slide 崩れ　□ earth 地面
❻□ basilica バシリカ、会堂　❼□ add to …を増す　□ be closed to …は立ち入り禁止である
❽□ conference 会議を開く　□ deal with …に対処する　□ last 続く

筆記③

第4段落

❶ Finally, Professor John Burland of Imperial College London found a solution: simply remove and replace the soil, especially the wet clay.

❷ About US$30 million was spent to remove 77 tons of soil, and correct the tower's lean to only about 3.99 degrees.

❸ It may have been possible to straighten the tower completely, but the recovery team did not: by this time, the Tower of Pisa was bringing in millions of euros in tourist revenue yearly, and it seemed unlikely that a "straight" tower could do the same.

---

❸ It may have been possible to straighten the tower completely,
　　　仮S₁　　V₁　　　　C₁　　　　真S₁　　　straightenの目的語

but the recovery team did not ☐ :──▶コロンの後に補足説明が続く
　　　　S₂　　　　　V₂　　│
(by this time),　　　　　　　(straighten the tower completely)

the Tower of Pisa was bringing in millions of euros in tourist revenue yearly,
　　　S'₁　　　　　V'₁　　　　O'₁

and it seemed unlikely (that a "straight" tower could do the same).
　　　仮S'₂ V'₂　　C'₂　　　真S'₂　　S''　　　V''　　O''
　　　it seems unlikely that ...「(that以下のこと)はありそうではない」

❶ そして、インペリアルカレッジロンドンのジョン・バーランド教授が、土壌、特に湿った粘土を取り除き、入れ替えるだけでよいという解決策を発見したのである。

❷ 約3,000万ドルをかけて77トンの土を取り除き、塔の傾きを約3.99度まで修正することができた。

❸ 塔を完全にまっすぐにすることは可能だったかもしれないが、修復チームはそうしなかった。このとき既に、ピサの斜塔は年間数百万ユーロの観光収入を得ており、「まっすぐ」な塔に同じことができるとは思えなかったのだ。

❶□ solution 解決　❷□ degree（角度）度　❸□ straighten …をまっすぐにする
□ bring in （利益など）をもたらす　□ revenue 収入、歳入
□ it seems unlikely that 節 …とは考えられない

筆記③

483

著者:

松本恵美子 Emiko Matsumoto

順天堂大学講師。明治大学兼任講師。東京理科大学非常勤講師。上智大学大学院博士前期課程
修了（TESOL ／英語教授法）。言語テスティング専攻。全国の大学生向けテキストの執筆。
TOEIC、TOEFL、IELTS、英検などの資格試験対策を行う。現在の研究テーマは医療英語のニー
ズ分析、談話分析等。主な著書は、『TOEIC® TEST リスニングスピードマスター NEW
EDITION』（J リサーチ出版）、『新 TOEIC® TEST 1 分間マスター リスニング編・リーディン
グ編』（日本経済新聞出版社）、『TOEIC® LISTENING AND READING TEST 15 日で 500
点突彼！リスニング攻略・リーディング攻略』（三修社）、『TOEIC® テスト 究極アプローチ』（成
美堂）、『TOEFL ITP® テスト 完全制覇』（ジャパンタイムズ）など多数。

装幀・本文デザイン　　斉藤 啓（ブッダプロダクションズ）
制作協力　　　　　　　渾天堂株式会社、株式会社CPI Japan

極めろ！ 英検®準 1 級合格力 リーディング

2024 年 3 月 13 日　初版第 1 刷発行

著者	松本恵美子
発行者	藤嵜 政子
発行所	株式会社　スリーエーネットワーク
	〒 102-0083　東京都千代田区麹町 3 丁目 4 番
	トラスティ麹町ビル 2 F
	電話：03-5275-2722［営業］03-5275-2726［編集］
	https://www.3anet.co.jp/
印刷・製本	萩原印刷株式会社

©2024 Emiko Matsumoto　Printed in Japan
ISBN978-4-88319-934-1　C0082